To Mum,

Merry Christmas 2009

Happy Cooking! :)

Love

Fraser, KerryAnn, Taylor & Callum
xxx

COOK'S COLLECTION

Good Housekeeping
COOK'S COLLECTION

Good Housekeeping Institute
TRIED · TESTED · TRUSTED

COLLINS & BROWN

First published in Great Britain in 2008 by
Collins & Brown
10 Southcombe Street
London W14 0RA

An imprint of Anova Books Company Ltd

This edition published in 2009 for WHSmith

The Good Housekeeping website is
www.allaboutyou.com/goodhousekeeping

10 9 8 7 6 5 4 3 2 1

British Library Cataloguing-in-Publication Data:
A catalogue record for this book is available from the British Library.

ISBN 978-1-84340-555-9

Reproduction by Dot Gradations Ltd, UK
Printed by Times Offset, Malaysia

PICTURE CREDITS:

Neil Barclay pages 16, 23 top right, 82 bottom right, 99 bottom left, 113 bottom right, 252 top right, 265 bottom left.

Nicki Dowey pages 23 top left, 33, 46 top left, 46 top right, 55 top left, 55 top right, 55 bottom right, 64 top left, 64 top right, bottom left, 72, 99 top right, 106 top right, 113 top left, 120 top left, 120 top right, 120 bottom right, 127 bottom right, 134 top right, 134 bottom left, 134 bottom right, 141 top right, 141 top left, 141 bottom left, 161 bottom left, 168 top left, 175 bottom right, 194 bottom left, 194 top right, 194 bottom right, 207 top right, 207 bottom right, 223, 229, 235, 246 top right, 246 bottom left, 246 bottom right, 252 bottom left, 259 top left, 259 top right, 265 top left, 265 bottom right, 284 top left, 284 bottom left, 291 bottom left, 291 bottom right, 303 top right, 303 bottom left, 312 top left, 312 top right, 321 bottom left, 321 bottom right, 328 top right, 328 bottom right, 328 top left, 347 top right, 347 top left, 353 top right, 353 bottom left, 353 bottom right, 359 top right, 365 top right, 371 bottom left, 371 bottom right, 371 top right, 383 top left, 383 top right, 383 bottom right, 392 top right, 392 bottom left, 392 bottom right, 409 bottom left, 416 bottom left, top left and right, 424 top right, 438, 445 top right, bottom left and bottom right, 453, 460, 468, 505 bottom right, 512 top right, bottom left and bottom right.

Lucinda Symons 134 top left, 194 top left, 505 top left, bottom left and top right, 512 top left.

Craig Robertson pages 23 bottom left, 38, 46 bottom left, 46 bottom right, 55 bottom left, 64 bottom right, 82 bottom left, 82 top right, 99 bottom right, 106 top left, 113 bottom left, 113 top right, 120 bottom left, 127 top left, 127 top right, 141 bottom right, 154, 161 bottom right, 161 top left, 161 top right, 168 bottom left, 168 top right, 168 bottom right, 175 top left, 175 top right, 175 bottom left, 207 top left, 252 top left, 252 bottom right, 259 bottom left, 259 bottom right, 265 top right, 277 top right, 284 top right, 291 top left, 303 bottom right, 312 bottom right, 312 top right, 328 bottom left, 341, 347 bottom left, 347 bottom right, 353 top left, 359 bottom right, 359 top left, 365 top left, 365 bottom right, 365 bottom left, 371 top left, 392 top left, 409 top left, 409 top right, 416 bottom right, 487.

Will Heap pages 23 bottom right, 92, 106 bottom left, 207 bottom left, 383 bottom left.

Martin Brigdale pages 99 top left, 246 top left, 270, 277 top left, 277 bottom left, 277 bottom right, 284 bottom right, 291 top right, 303 top left, 312 top left, 359 bottom left, 409 bottom right, 424 top left, 424 bottom left, 424 bottom right, 445 top left.

Clive Streeter page 106 bottom right.

Contents

Introduction

A recipe book for every occasion – that's the phrase we coined in the *Good Housekeeping* offices when we started working on this book. Because, quite simply, it is just that. Food and the way we cook have changed dramatically over the past couple of decades. Catching up with friends, once the preserve of the weekend, can be done over a casual bowl of pasta midweek. A Saturday night dinner is still special, of course, but more often than not we call it supper. And where once the host would make everything herself, now a couple of timesaving ingredients make it easier to create a feast.

This book has everything you need, from quick snacks and simple salads to basic midweek suppers and easy bakes. Via your queries through the email, hotline and letters, we know time is precious for many of you, so we've included lots of recipes that you can whiz up easily. All of them have been triple-tested in the Good Housekeeping Institute, too, which means they'll work every time you make them. Plus there's nutritional information for calories, fat and carbohydrates for each dish and a whole section dedicated to vegetarian recipes.

Whichever recipe you decide to cook first out of the Cook's Collection, we hope it'll spur you on to cooking more!

Enjoy,

Emma

Emma Marsden
Good Housekeeping Cookery Editor

Basics

We're all busy, busy, but finding time to make a good stock will really pay off when you use it as the base for your soups and casseroles. You'll know exactly what's gone into it – no additives – and once it's on the heat the stock can be left to simmer away while you get on with life's other pleasures. The four main stocks are light, dark, fish and vegetable. Once they're made, freeze them in small quantities so you'll always have some available.

Making your own pastry, too, is very satisfying and fun, and some can be made in the food processor, if you don't like getting your hands dirty! Choux must be one of the easiest pastries to make – and just think of all the profiteroles you can produce. Shortcrust is a versatile pastry that can be made plain or with additional ingredients – check out the variations with the recipe, while Sweet Tart Pastry is a richer, sweet version of shortcrust.

There's nothing nicer than homemade – be it a simple chicken soup, a great apple pie, or a crisp salad dressed with your own salad dressing. Try out these recipes and taste the difference.

Fish Stock

900g (2lb) fish bones
  and trimmings,
  washed and dried
2 carrots, peeled and
  chopped
1 onion, peeled and
  chopped

2 celery sticks, sliced
bouquet garni (2 bay
  leaves, few thyme
  sprigs, small bunch of
  parsley)
6 white peppercorns
½tsp sea salt

1 Put the fish trimmings into a large pan. Add the
   vegetables, 900ml (1½ pints) cold water, the bouquet
   garni, peppercorns and salt. Bring slowly to the boil
   and skim the surface. Cover the pan, reduce the heat
   and simmer for about 30 minutes.
2 Strain the stock through a fine sieve into a bowl and
   check the seasoning. Cool quickly, cover and keep in
   the fridge for up to two days. Use the stock as required.

Makes 900ml (1½ pints)
Preparation: 10 minutes
Cooking time: 35 minutes
Per 100ml (3½fl oz): 5 cals; trace fat;
1g carbohydrate

Turkey Stock

turkey giblets
1 carrot, peeled and
  thickly sliced
1 onion, peeled and cut
  into wedges

1 celery stick, thickly
  sliced
8 black peppercorns
2 bay leaves

1 Put all the ingredients in a pan with 900ml (1½ pints)
   cold water. Cover and bring slowly to the boil, then
   reduce the heat and simmer for 2 hours, occasionally
   skimming any scum from the surface.
2 Strain the stock through a fine sieve into a bowl.
   Discard the giblets, vegetables and herbs. Cover the
   stock and chill for up to one day. Use the stock as
   required.

Makes 900ml (1½ pints)
Preparation: 5 minutes
Cooking time: about 2 hours
Per 100ml (3Vfl oz): 10 cals; trace fat;
2g carbohydrate

Chicken Stock

225g (8oz) onions,
  peeled and roughly
  chopped
150g (5oz) trimmed
  leeks, roughly
  chopped
225g (8oz) celery
  sticks, roughly
  chopped

1.6kg (3½lb) raw
  chicken bones
bouquet garni (2 bay
  leaves, few thyme
  sprigs, small bunch
  of parsley)
1tsp black
  peppercorns
½tsp sea salt

1 Put all the ingredients in a pan with 3 litres (5 pints)
   cold water. Cover the pan, bring slowly to the boil and
   skim the surface. Partially cover the pan, reduce the heat
   and simmer gently for 2 hours. Check the seasoning.
2 Strain the stock through a fine sieve into a bowl and cool
   quickly. Cover and keep in the fridge for up to three
   days. Remove the fat from the surface and use the
   stock as required.

Makes 1.2 litres (2 pints)
Preparation: 10 minutes
Cooking time: about 2 hours
Per 100ml (3½fl oz): 10 cals; 1g fat; 1g carbohydrate

Vegetable Stock

225g (8oz) onions,
  peeled and roughly
  chopped
225g (8oz) celery
  sticks, roughly
  chopped
225g (8oz) trimmed
  leeks, roughly
  chopped

225g (8oz) carrots,
  peeled and roughly
  chopped
2 bay leaves
few thyme sprigs
small bunch of parsley
10 black peppercorns
½tsp sea salt

1 Put all the ingredients into a large pan with 1.7 litres
   (3 pints) cold water. Cover the pan, bring slowly to the
   boil and skim the surface. Partially cover the pan,
   reduce the heat and simmer for 30 minutes. Check the
   seasoning.
2 Strain the stock through a fine sieve into a bowl and
   leave to cool. Cover and keep in the fridge for up to
   three days. Use the stock as required.

Makes 1.2 litres (2 pints)
Preparation: 10 minutes
Cooking time: 35 minutes
Per 100ml (3½fl oz): 5 cals; trace fat;
1g carbohydrate

450g (1lb) stewing
  meat, cut into pieces
450g (1lb) meat bones
  (according to the
  flavour required, use
  veal, beef, lamb or
  pork bones)
1 large onion, peeled
  and sliced

1 large carrot, peeled
  and sliced
2 celery sticks, sliced
bouquet garni (2 bay
  leaves, few thyme
  sprigs, small bunch of
  parsley)
1tsp black
  peppercorns
½tsp sea salt

1 To impart flavour and colour, first brown the meat and
   bones. Put them into a roasting tin and roast at 220°C
   (200°C fan oven) mark 7 for 30–40 minutes until well
   browned, turning occasionally.
2 Transfer the meat and bones to a large pan, add the
   remaining ingredients plus 2 litres (3½ pints) cold water.
   Cover the pan, bring slowly to the boil and skim the
   surface. Partially cover the pan, reduce the heat and
   simmer gently for 4–5 hours. Check the seasoning.

3 Strain the stock through a fine sieve into a bowl and cool
   quickly. Cover and keep in the fridge for up to three
   days. Remove the fat layer from the surface and use the
   stock as required.

Makes 900ml (1½ pints)
Preparation: 10 minutes
Cooking time: 4–5 hours
Per 100ml (3½fl oz): 10 cals; 1g fat;
1g carbohydrate

Basic Gravy

A rich gravy is traditionally served with roast meat and
poultry. If possible, make the gravy in the roasting tin while
the joint (or bird) is resting. This will incorporate the meat
juices that have escaped during roasting.
1 Carefully pour (or skim) off the fat from a corner of the
   roasting tin, leaving the sediment behind. Put the tin on
   the hob over a medium heat and pour in 300–450ml
   (½–¾ pint) vegetable water, or chicken, vegetable or
   meat stock as appropriate.
2 Stir thoroughly, scraping up the sediment, and boil
   steadily until the gravy is a rich brown colour. A little
   gravy browning can be added to intensify the flavour
   and colour.

Makes about 300ml (½ pint)
Preparation: 2 minutes
Cooking time: 2–3 minutes
Per 100ml (3½fl oz): 10 cals; 2g fat;
1g carbohydrate

Variations
Thick gravy: Sprinkle 1–2tbsp flour into the roasting
tin and cook, stirring, until browned, then gradually
stir in the liquid and cook, stirring for 2–3 minutes
until smooth and slightly thickened.
Rich wine gravy: Deglaze the roasting tin with about
150ml (¼ pint) red or white wine, or 90ml (3fl oz)
fortified wine such as sherry or Madeira, and allow to
bubble for a minute or two before adding the stock
or water. For a sweeter flavour, add 2tbsp redcurrant
jelly with the wine.

Shortcrust Pastry

225g (8oz) plain flour, plus extra to dust
pinch of salt

125g (4oz) butter, or half white vegetable fat and half butter, cut into pieces

1 Sift the flour and salt into a bowl. Add the fat and mix lightly, then, using your fingertips, rub the fat into the flour until the mixture resembles fine breadcrumbs.
2 Sprinkle 3–4tbsp cold water evenly over the surface and stir with a round-bladed knife until the mixture begins to stick together in large lumps. If the dough seems dry, add a little extra water. With one hand, collect the dough together to form a ball.
3 Knead lightly on a lightly floured surface for a few seconds to form a smooth, firm dough; do not over-work. Wrap the dough in clingfilm and leave to rest in the fridge for 30 minutes before rolling out.

Alternatively, to make the pastry in a food processor, put the flour and salt in the processor bowl with the butter. Whiz until the mixture resembles fine crumbs, then add the water. Process briefly, using the pulse button, until the mixture just comes together in a ball. Continue from step 3. Shortcrust pastry can be stored in the fridge for up to three days, or frozen.

Makes a '225g (8oz) quantity'
Preparation: 10 minutes, plus resting
Per 25g (1 oz): 110 cals; 6g fat; 12g carbohydrate

Variations

Wholemeal pastry: Replace half the white flour with wholemeal flour. A little extra water may be needed to mix the dough.
Nut pastry: Replace 50g (2oz) of the flour with finely chopped or ground walnuts, hazelnuts or almonds. Add to the rubbed-in mixture just before the cold water.
Cheese pastry: Stir in 3–4tbsp freshly grated Parmesan cheese or 75g (3oz) finely grated Cheddar cheese and a small pinch of mustard powder before adding the water.
Herb pastry: Stir in 3tbsp finely chopped herbs, such as parsley, sage, thyme or rosemary, before adding the water.
Olive pastry: Stir in 4tbsp finely chopped pitted black olives, at stage 2.
Poppy seed pastry: Add 15g (½oz) poppy seeds before adding the water.

Sweet Tart Pastry

225g (8oz) plain flour
pinch of salt
150g (5oz) butter, cubed

2tbsp golden caster sugar
1 egg yolk

1 Sift the flour and salt into a large bowl and rub in the butter using your fingertips until the mixture resembles breadcrumbs. Stir in the sugar. Alternatively, use a food processor to incorporate the butter into the flour, then add the sugar and pulse to mix. Tip into a bowl and continue.
2 Mix the egg yolk with 3tbsp cold water, then add to the dry ingredients and mix with a round-bladed knife to a dough.
3 Knead gently until just smooth. Wrap the pastry in clingfilm and leave to rest in the fridge for 30 minutes abefore rolling out. Use as required. Tart pastry can be stored in the fridge for up to three days, or frozen.

Makes a '225g (8oz) quantity'
Preparation: 10 minutes, plus resting
Per 25g (1 oz): 110 cals; 7g fat; 11g carbohydrate

Puff Pastry

**450g (1lb) strong plain
(bread) flour, plus
extra to dust
pinch of salt**

**450g (1lb) butter,
chilled
1tbsp lemon juice**

1 Sift the flour and salt together into a bowl. Cut off 50g (2oz) butter and flatten the remaining large block with a rolling pin to a slab, about 2cm (¾ inch) thick, and set aside.

2 Cut the 50g (2oz) butter into small pieces and rub into the flour, using your fingertips.

3 Using a round-bladed knife, stir in the lemon juice and enough chilled water to make a soft elastic dough you will need about 300ml (½ pint).

4 Turn out on to a lightly floured surface and quickly knead the dough until smooth. Cut a cross through half the depth, then open out to form a star.

5 Roll out, keeping the centre four times as thick as the flaps. Put the slab of butter in the centre of the dough. Fold the flaps over the dough, envelope-style.

6 Press gently with a rolling pin and roll out to a rectangle, measuring 40.5 x 20.5cm (16 x 8 inches).

7 Fold the bottom third up and the top third down, keeping the edges straight. Wrap in clingfilm and leave to rest in the fridge for 30 minutes.

8 Put the pastry on a lightly floured surface with the folded edges to the sides. Repeat the rolling, folding, resting and turning sequence five times.

9 Shape the puff pastry as required, then rest it in the fridge for about 30 minutes before baking.

Makes a '450g (1lb) quantity'
Preparation: 40 minutes, plus resting
Per 25g (1 oz): 100 cals; 8g fat; 7g carbohydrate

The Shortest-ever Walnut Pastry

**50g (2oz) walnuts
175g (6oz) plain flour,
sifted, plus extra
to dust**

**125g (4oz) chilled
unsalted butter, diced**

1 Put the walnuts and flour in a food processor and whiz to chop the nuts roughly. Add the butter and continue to process until the mixture resembles fine crumbs. Add 3tbsp cold water and blend to combine.

2 Tip the pastry out on to a floured surface and knead lightly. Shape into a round flat disc, wrap and chill for 1 hour.

3 Roll out the pastry on a lightly floured surface to a 30.5cm (12 inch) circle and use to line a 23 x 4cm (9 x 1½ inch) fluted tin, leaving the edges hanging over the rim of the tin. Prick the base all over, cover with clingfilm and chill for 20 minutes. Preheat the oven to 200°C (180°C fan oven) mark 6.

4 Line the pastry case with greaseproof paper and cover with baking beans. Put on a baking sheet and bake for 20 minutes. Remove the greaseproof paper and beans and continue to cook for a further 15 minutes. Take out of the oven and cool for 5 minutes, then trim the edge with a small sharp knife. Use as required.

Makes 1 x 23 x 4cm (9 x 1½inch) pastry case
Preparation: 15 minutes, plus chilling
Cooking time: 35 minutes, plus cooling
Per 25g (1 oz): 110 cals; 8g fat; 9g carbohydrate

Trouble-shooting: if your pastry shrinks

Shrinking is caused when the pastry is overstretched when rolling out or when making it in a processor. If you're doing the latter, once you've added the water you should pulse until the mixture just comes together – no longer – then take it out and knead lightly by hand.

Pastry needs chilling twice to relax it, for 20 minutes each time. First, pop it in the fridge just after you've made it (wrap it in clingfilm to stop it getting too firm, which makes rolling out easier), then chill it again when you've lined the tin.

Lightly dust the work surface with flour to prevent sticking – too much will dry out the pastry and lead to cracking when you're rolling it out.

Lift the pastry into the tin and press down gently. Leave the edges hanging loosely over the rim of the tin and bake.

Choux Pastry

65g (2½oz) plain flour　　**50g (2oz) butter**
pinch of salt　　**2 eggs, lightly beaten**

1　Sift the flour and salt on to a large sheet of greaseproof paper.
2　Pour 150ml (¼ pint) cold water into a medium pan, add the butter and melt over a low heat. Increase the heat and bring to a rolling boil.
3　Take off the heat, immediately tip in all the flour and beat vigorously, using a wooden spoon. Continue beating until the mixture is smooth and leaves the sides of the pan to form a ball; do not over-beat. Leave for 1–2 minutes to cool slightly.
4　Gradually add the eggs, beating well between each addition, adding just enough to give a smooth dropping consistency. The choux pastry should be smooth and shiny. Use as required. It can be either spooned or piped into shape, usually directly on to a dampened baking sheet.

Makes a '2–egg quantity'
Preparation: 10 minutes
Per 25g (1 oz): 50 cals; 4g fat; 3g carbohydrate

Suet Crust Pastry

300g (11oz) self-raising　　**150g (5oz) shredded**
**　flour**　　**　suet or vegetarian**
½tsp salt　　**　suet**

1　Sift the flour and salt into a bowl, add the shredded suet and stir to mix.
2　Using a round-bladed knife, mix in enough cold water to make a soft dough – you will need about 175ml (6fl oz). If the dough seems too dry, add a little extra water.
3　Knead very lightly until smooth. Use as required.

Makes a '300g (11oz) quantity'
Preparation: 10 minutes
Per 25g (1 oz): 90 cals; 5g fat; 10g carbohydrate

Herb pistou

¾tsp sea salt
6 garlic cloves, peeled and chopped
15g (½oz) chopped basil
12tbsp olive oil

1 Using a pestle and mortar or a strong bowl and the end of a rolling pin, or a mini processor, pound together the salt and garlic until smooth.
2 Add the basil and pound down to a paste then blend in the olive oil, a little at a time.

Serves 6
Preparation: 45 minutes
Per serving: 291 cals; 64g fat; 38g carbohydrate

Two-minute Dressing

2tbsp white wine vinegar
4tbsp olive oil
1½tsp mustard (Dijon or wholegrain)

1 Put all the ingredients into a screw-topped jar, screw the jar shut and shake to emulsify.

Makes 90ml (4fl oz)
Preparation: 2 minutes
Per 1tbsp serving: 66 cals; 7g fat; 0g carbohydrate

Five-minute Mayonnaise

2 large egg yolks
1tsp English mustard
salt and pepper
200ml (7fl oz) grapeseed or sunflower oil
100ml (3½fl oz) extra-virgin olive oil
1tsp white wine vinegar or lemon juice, plus extra to season

1 Put the egg yolks into a 850ml (1½ pint) bowl. Add the mustard and season with 1tsp salt and plenty of pepper, then mix thoroughly with a wooden spoon.
2 Combine the oils in a jug. Sit the bowl on a damp tea-towel to hold it steady. Add about ½tsp oil to the egg mixture and whisk in. Stop whisking as you add each ½tsp oil, then continue whisking until the mixture emulsifies. (The yolks thicken and the mixture starts to look like mayonnaise.) Turn the bowl occasionally to mix everything in. Keep adding the oil, 1tbsp at a time now, until you've added about half of it. If the mayonnaise starts to curdle (called 'splitting') don't worry – add about 1tbsp cold water and stir in with a spoon, then continue with the recipe. If this doesn't work, put another egg yolk in a clean bowl and gradually whisk in the curdled mixture, 1tbsp at a time.
3 Add the vinegar or lemon juice, which will thin the mixture a little. Now begin pouring in the remaining oil in a thin, steady stream, whisking all the time. When all the oil has been added the mayonnaise should be thick and wobbly.
4 Taste the mayonnaise for seasoning and, if necessary, stir in a little more salt and pepper, a splash of vinegar or a squeeze of lemon juice. Cover and keep chilled for up to four days.

Makes 300ml (½ pint)
Preparation: 15 minutes
Per 1tbsp serving: 110 cals; 12g fat; 0g carbohydrate

Brunch

Brunch can be a fabulous start to the day – especially if shared with friends and family. Everyone can muck in and help – no need for formality – and even if you've only got eggs and bread in the cupboard you can still rustle up some yummy food.

Kick off with a Spicy Tomato Cocktail while you decide what everyone wants – add some vodka to really get things going! Then, how about a pan-fry of Ham and Eggs with Hash Potatoes; Brussels Sprout Bubble and Squeak Cakes; or Simply Sausages – the sound of sausages sizzling in the pan will soon have people sitting at the table. Make big platefuls so that everyone can tuck in.

You can't beat eggs – boiled, poached, scrambled, fried or made into omelettes. Eat them with soldiers, buttery toast or good bread.

Then there's kedgeree, a real brunch favourite, tasty and filling. Try the Kedgeree with Lentils and Salmon, topped with caramelised onions and coriander sprigs.

And to follow? Take your pick from Orange Eggy Bread, indulgent pancakes drizzled with syrup, or naughty French toast.

Next, a delicious, soothing smoothie, to round off a relaxing start to the day ahead.

Scrambled Eggs with Smoked Salmon

6 large eggs
salt and pepper
25g (1oz) butter, plus
  extra to spread
100g (3½oz)
  mascarpone
125g pack smoked
  salmon, torn roughly
  into pieces

6 slices rye or
  sourdough bread
snipped chives, to
  garnish

1 Using a sharp knife, carefully crack and tap off the pointed end of each egg. Pour the egg yolks and whites into a bowl. Remove and discard the sac from the bottom of the shells, rinse out the shells, then turn them upside down and leave to dry.
2 Beat the eggs together and season well. Melt the butter in a non-stick pan over a low heat. Add the eggs and stir constantly until the mixture thickens. Add the mascarpone and season well. Cook for 1–2 minutes longer until the mixture becomes just firm, then fold in the smoked salmon.

3 Toast the bread, spread with the butter and cut into soldiers. Spoon the egg mixture back into the eggshells, garnish with chives and serve with the soldiers.

Serves 6
Peparation: 15 minutes
Cooking time: 5 minutes
Per serving: 300 cals; 20g fat; 15g carbohydrate

Frittata

50g (2oz) butter
2tbsp olive oil
2 large red onions,
  peeled and finely
  sliced
4tbsp chopped flat-

  leafed parsley
12 eggs, lightly beaten
salt and pepper
2tbsp freshly grated
  Parmesan cheese

1 Heat the butter and olive oil gently in a large frying pan. Add the onions and cook over a low heat until they're very soft and lightly caramelised.
2 Add the parsley, then pour in the eggs and season. Cook over a gentle heat, lifting the edges occasionally, until the eggs are nearly cooked through. Sprinkle with the Parmesan, then turn out, cut into wedges and serve with salad.

Serves 8
Peparation: 10 minutes
Cooking time: 30 minutes
Per serving: 410 cals; 45g fat; 0g carbohydrate

Creamy Baked Egg Starter

butter, to grease
4 sun-dried tomatoes
salt and pepper

4 eggs
4tbsp double cream

1 Preheat the oven to 180°C (160°C fan oven) mark 4. Grease four ramekins.
2 Put 1 tomato in each ramekin and season. Carefully break an egg on top of each, then drizzle 1tbsp cream over each egg.
3 Bake for 15–18 minutes – the eggs will continue to cook once they have been taken out of the oven.
4 Leave to stand for 2 minutes before serving.

Serves 4
Preparation: 5 minutes
Cooking time: 15–18 minutes
Per serving: 170 cals; 14g fat; 3g carbohydrate

See picture, page 23

Eggs Benedict

2tbsp white wine
  vinegar, plus extra to
  poach
9 black peppercorns,
  crushed
2 large or 3 medium
  egg yolks
250g (9oz) unsalted
  butter, cut into small
  pieces

2tsp lemon juice
salt and pepper
4 very fresh eggs
4 English muffins
4 slices ham or 150g
  (5oz) grilled bacon
  rashers
parsley, to garnish

1 Put 2tbsp vinegar in a small pan with 2tbsp water and
  the black peppercorns. Bring to the boil and simmer until
  the liquid is reduced by half.
2 Whiz the egg yolks in a food processor for 1 minute.
  Strain the reduced vinegar, adding it to the yolks while
  the machine is running.
3 Melt the butter in a small pan, and cook until it begins
  to brown around the edges. With the food processor
  running on full speed, add two-thirds of the melted
  butter. Add the lemon juice, then the remaining butter.
  Season and put to one side.

4 Take a wide, shallow pan of boiling water and add
  1tbsp vinegar to each 600ml (1 pint) water. Carefully
  break an egg into a saucer, make a whirlpool with a
  large spoon in the boiling water and lower the egg into
  the water. Reduce the heat and cook gently for
  3 minutes or until the white is just set and the yolk soft.
  Using a draining spoon, lift the egg out of the pan and
  put in a shallow dish of warm water. Repeat with the
  remaining eggs.
5 Meanwhile, split the muffins in half and toast. Warm
  the ham in the microwave for 1 minute on Medium
  (based on a 900W oven). Put the ham on the muffin
  halves, top each with an egg, some Hollandaise sauce
  and the other muffin half. Garnish with parsley and
  serve.

Serves 4
Preparation: 10 minutes
Cooking time: 15 minutes
Per serving: 800 cals; 64g fat; 30g carbohydrate

Kedgeree with Herb Butter

450g (1lb) smoked
  haddock or fresh
  salmon
150ml (¼ pint) full-fat
  milk
225g (8oz) basmati rice
75g (3oz) cooked
  cockles, well drained
1tsp coriander seeds,
  finely crushed
3 hard-boiled eggs,
  shelled and quartered

2tbsp double cream
3–4tbsp chopped
  chives
salt and pepper
50g (2oz) butter
1–2tsp lemon juice
2tbsp chopped
  tarragon
lemon or lime wedges
  and herbs, to garnish

1 Put the haddock in a shallow pan with the milk. Cover
  and simmer for 8 minutes or until cooked. Drain,
  reserving 2–3tbsp of the cooking liquor. Flake the fish,
  discarding the skin and bones.
2 Cook the rice in boiling salted water for 10 minutes or
  until just tender. Drain, rinse with boiling water and
  drain again.

3 Return the rice to the pan and add the haddock,
  reserved liquor, cockles, coriander seeds, eggs,
  cream and chives. Season lightly, then heat gently for
  2 minutes.
4 Meanwhile, melt the butter, stir in the lemon juice,
  chopped tarragon and seasoning and pour into a
  warmed jug.
5 Tip the kedgeree into a serving dish, garnish with the
  lemon or lime wedges and herbs and serve with the
  herb butter.

Serves 4
Preparation: 10 minutes
Cooking time: about 20 minutes
Per serving: 540 cals; 22g fat; 47g carbohydrate

Energy-boosting Brunch

2tbsp vegetable oil
1 small onion, peeled
  and chopped
1 garlic clove, peeled
  and crushed
1 small chilli, deseeded
  and finely chopped1
  red, green or yellow
  pepper, deseeded and
  chopped

400g can chopped
  tomatoes
salt and pepper
4 eggs
2 flour tortillas

1 Heat 1tbsp oil in a small pan, add the onion and cook gently for 10 minutes. Add the garlic, chilli and chopped pepper and cook for 10 minutes. Add the tomatoes, season and simmer for 10 minutes.

2 Heat the remaining oil in a non-stick pan for 1 minute. Crack 1 egg into a cup, then pour it into the hot fat. Straight away, do the same with the other egg. Cook for a few minutes until the eggs are just set, spooning over the fat from time to time.

4 Toast the tortillas in a dry frying pan over a high heat for 30 seconds on each side. Put on to two plates and top with the sauce, then the eggs and season well. Roll the tortillas up and tuck in the ends. Scrape the rest of the tomato sauce into a sealed container and chill for another use.

Serves 2
Preparation: 10 minutes
Cooking time: 40 minutes
Per serving: 510 cals; 30g fat; 39g carbohydrate

Pan-fried Mushroom and Feta Omelette

50g (2oz) butter
225g (8oz) large
  mushrooms, thinly
  sliced
3 garlic cloves, peeled
  and sliced
50g (2oz) sun-dried

tomatoes, chopped
4 large eggs, beaten
black pepper
100g (3½oz) feta
  cheese, crumbled
thyme sprigs, to
  garnish

1 Melt the butter in an 18cm (7 inch) non-stick omelette pan and fry the mushrooms with the garlic until they are a deep golden brown and beginning to go crisp around the edges. Add the sun-dried tomatoes and stir over the heat for 1–2 minutes. Preheat the grill.

2 Roughly spread the mushroom mixture over the base of the pan. Beat 2tbsp cold water into the eggs and season with pepper (both feta cheese and the tomatoes can be salty, so no extra salt should be needed). Pour the eggs over the mushrooms, gently swirling the pan to spread the eggs. Add the feta. Leave to set, undisturbed, over a low heat for 1–2 minutes or until the eggs are lightly cooked and the feta is just beginning to melt.

3 Sprinkle the omelette with pepper and scatter with thyme sprigs to garnish. Cut into wedges and serve immediately.

Serves 4
Preparation: 5 minutes
Cooking time: 15 minutes
Per serving: 270 cals; 23g fat; 3g carbohydrate

Brussels Sprout Bubble and Squeak Cakes

5tbsp vegetable oil or dripping
175g (6oz) onions, peeled and finely sliced
175g (6oz) cooked Brussels sprouts, roughly chopped
700g (1½lb) leftover mashed potatoes
salt and pepper
nutmeg to taste
Sweet Onion and Mustard Sauce (page 484), to serve
finely chopped chives, to garnish

1 Preheat the oven to 130°C (110°C fan oven) mark ½. Heat the oil or dripping in a non-stick frying pan, add the onions and cook for 10 minutes or until golden. Add the Brussels sprouts and fry for 5 minutes. Tip the sprouts and onions into the mashed potatoes and mix well, then season and add grated nutmeg to taste.

2 Using a 9cm (3½ inch) diameter plain cutter, shape the potato mixture into eight individual cakes. Fry the cakes in a hot, non-stick frying pan for 2–3 minutes on each side. Keep covered in a low oven while you make the Sweet Onion and Mustard Sauce.

3 Serve the bubble and squeak cakes with Sweet Onion and Mustard Sauce, garnished with chopped chives.

Makes 8
Preparation: 10 minutes
Cooking time: 25 minutes
Per serving: 110 cals; 9g fat; 7g carbohydrate

Kedgeree with Lentils and Salmon

50g (2oz) butter
700g (1½lb) onions, peeled and sliced
2tsp garam masala
1 garlic clove, peeled and crushed
75g (3oz) split green lentils, soaked in 300ml (½ pint) boiling water for 15 minutes, then drained
750ml (1¼ pints) vegetable stock
225g (8oz) basmati rice
1 green chilli, deseeded and finely chopped
salt and pepper
350g (12oz) salmon fillet
coriander sprigs, to garnish

1 Melt the butter in a large flameproof casserole. Add the onions and cook for 5 minutes or until soft. Remove one-third from the pan and put to one side. Increase the heat and cook the remaining onions for 10 minutes to caramelise. Remove and put to one side.

2 Return the first batch of onions to the pan, add the garam masala and garlic and cook, stirring, for 1 minute. Add the drained lentils and stock, cover and cook for 15 minutes. Add the rice and chilli, season, then bring to the boil, cover the pan, reduce the heat and simmer for 5 minutes.

3 Put the salmon fillet on top of the rice, cover and cook gently for 15 minutes or until the rice is cooked, the stock is absorbed and the salmon opaque.

4 Lift off the salmon and divide into flakes. Return the salmon to the pan and fork through the rice. Garnish with the reserved caramelised onions and the coriander sprigs and serve.

Serves 4
Preparation: 15 minutes, plus soaking
Cooking time: 50 minutes
Per serving: 540 cals; 21g fat; 62g carbohydrate

BLT-topped Bagels with Hollandaise Sauce

3 large bagels, cut in half horizontally
25g (1oz) butter, softened
12 smoked streaky bacon rashers, rind removed
2tsp olive oil

3 tomatoes, cut into thick slices
150ml (¼ pint) bought Hollandaise sauce
75g (3oz) mixed lettuce leaves
crushed black pepper, to garnish

1 Preheat the grill to high, then grill the halved bagels until golden. Spread generously with the butter. Cover the bagels with a piece of foil and keep them warm. Grill the bacon for 2–3 minutes or until crisp, then keep warm. Heat the olive oil in a small frying pan until very hot and fry the tomatoes for about 1 minute until lightly charred.

2 Put the Hollandaise sauce in a small pan and heat gently. To assemble, top the warm bagels with a few lettuce leaves, the tomatoes and bacon. Spoon the warm Hollandaise sauce over the bacon and garnish with the pepper. Serve at once.

Serves 6
Preparation: 15 minutes
Cooking time: 8 minutes
Per serving: 500 cals; 40g fat; 22g carbohydrate

Bacon Butty

12 bacon rashers
12 slices crusty white bread

tomato ketchup to taste

1 Heat a griddle pan and fry the bacon over a medium heat until crisp. Remove from the pan and keep warm.
2 Press one side of each bread slice on the griddle to soak up the juices. Put 2 bacon rashers on each of six slices, add ketchup, top with the remaining slices and serve.

Serves 6
Preparation: 5 minutes
Cooking time: 10 minutes
Per serving: 420 cals; 26g fat; 35g carbohydrate

Orange Eggy Bread

2 large eggs
150ml (¼pint) milk
finely grated zest and juice of 1 orange
8 slices raisin bread

butter, for frying
1tbsp caster sugar
orange slices, to serve

1 Lightly whisk the eggs with the milk and orange zest, then dip the bread into the mixture.
2 Heat the butter in a frying pan and fry the bread on both sides until golden. Sprinkle with the sugar and serve with orange slices.

Serves 4
Preparation: 5 minutes
Cooking time: 5 minutes
Per serving: 340 cals; 15g fat; 44g carbohydrate

Top left: Creamy Baked Egg Starter, page 18; top right: Croque Monsieur, page 30; bottom left: Golden Honey Fruits, page 32; bottom right Lemon and Blueberry Pancakes, page 34.

Hash Browns with Smoked Salmon and Scrambled Eggs

**1.4kg (3lb) unpeeled
  potatoes, cut into
  2.5cm (1 inch) chunks
salt and pepper
50g (2oz) butter
2tbsp olive oil
1 bunch spring onions,
  finely sliced on
  the diagonal
50g (2oz) shallots,
  peeled and chopped**

**10 large eggs, beaten
4tbsp soured cream
450g (1lb) smoked
  salmon, sliced
crushed black
  peppercorns and
  spring onion curls, to
  garnish**

1 To make the hash browns, put the potatoes in a pan of lightly salted, boiling water, bring back to the boil and cook for 3 minutes. Drain well and dry on kitchen paper. Heat 25g (1oz) butter and the olive oil in a large frying pan, add the potatoes and cook for 8 minutes, scraping the crispy bits from the bottom of the pan. Add the spring onions and seasoning and cook for 1–2 minutes or until the potatoes are golden and crisp. Cover with a lid or piece of foil and keep warm.

2 To make the scrambled eggs, heat the remaining butter in a large, non-stick, heavy-based frying pan. Add the shallots and cook for 3 minutes until softened. Put the eggs and soured cream in a bowl with a little seasoning and whisk lightly together. Add the egg mixture to the shallots and cook, stirring with a fork, for about 1 minute, bringing the set eggs in from the side of the pan to the centre. When the eggs are just starting to set, remove the pan from the heat – be careful not to overcook the eggs.

3 Spoon the scrambled eggs over the hash browns and put the smoked salmon on top. Garnish with the peppercorns and spring onion curls and serve.

Serves 6
Preparation: 20 minutes
Cooking time: 20 minutes
Per serving: 550 cals; 29g fat; 37g carbohydrate

Smoked Haddock and Bacon Bites

**350g (12oz) potatoes,
  peeled
salt and pepper
40g (1½oz) butter
450g (1lb) smoked
  haddock
4 rashers, about 125g
  (4oz), smoked streaky
  bacon, rind removed**

**2tbsp chopped chives
1 large egg, beaten
75g (3oz) fresh white
  breadcrumbs
oil, for frying
lemon slices and flat-
  leafed parsley,
  to garnish**

1 Put the potatoes in a pan of lightly salted water, cover, bring to the boil, then reduce the heat and simmer for 20 minutes or until soft. Drain, return to the pan and dry over a low heat for a few minutes, then mash them with the butter.

2 Meanwhile, preheat the grill. Put the haddock, skin side up, in a pan with just enough water to cover. Bring to the boil, then reduce the heat and simmer gently for 10 minutes or until just cooked. Remove the fish from the pan and when cool enough to handle skin and flake the flesh. Grill the bacon for 5 minutes or until crisp. Cool and crumble into small pieces.

3 Put the mashed potato, haddock, bacon and chives in a bowl and mix until well combined. Season with pepper. Shape into 20 golf ball-sized pieces. Dip each in the beaten egg, then roll them in breadcrumbs to coat.

4 Heat the oil to 190°C (375°F) or until a cube of bread sizzles when dropped in. Deep-fry the haddock bites until golden and crisp, then drain on kitchen paper. Garnish with the lemon and parsley and serve.

Serves 4
Preparation: 30 minutes
Cooking time: 35 minutes
Per serving: 510 cals; 30g fat; 24g carbohydrate

Ham and Eggs with Hash Potatoes

1.8kg (4lb) potatoes,
   peeled
salt and pepper
5tbsp olive oil
6 garlic cloves
2 rosemary sprigs or
   2tsp dried
6 slices ham off the
   bone, about 175g
   (6oz)

6 large eggs
6tbsp double cream
125g (4oz) hard cheese,
   such as Cheddar,
   grated
rosemary sprigs, to
   garnish

1 Preheat the oven to 200°C (180°C fan oven) mark 6. Cut the potatoes into small 2cm (¾ inch) cubes and put in a pan of lightly salted water. Bring to the boil and cook for 3 minutes. Drain well.

2 Put the olive oil in a large roasting tin and heat in the oven for 5 minutes. Add the potatoes and whole unpeeled garlic cloves to the hot oil, season well, then return to the oven for 30 minutes. Add the rosemary and return to the oven for a further 20–30 minutes, stirring occasionally.

3 Divide the potatoes among six individual gratin dishes, each about 12.5cm (5 inch) base diameter. When they are cool, arrange a slice of ham on top of each dish of potatoes and make a dip in the centre of each.

4 Crack the eggs carefully one by one on to the ham. Drizzle 1tbsp cream over each egg and season well. Sprinkle the grated cheese on top of the cream.

5 Bake for 20–25 minutes or until the egg white is just set and the yolk still soft. Garnish with rosemary sprigs and serve immediately with a green salad, if wished.

Serves 6
Preparation: 35 minutes, plus cooling
Cooking time: 1½ hours
Per serving: 610 cals; 34g fat; 52g carbohydrate

Simply Sausages

8 thick, good-quality
   pork sausages
olive oil, if necessary
2 red onions, peeled
   and finely chopped
2 large red peppers,
   deseeded and roughly
   chopped
150ml (¼ pint) light
   stock

1 large glass red wine,
   about 225ml (8fl oz)
410g can brown or
   green lentils, drained
   and rinsed
4tbsp chopped flat-
   leafed parsley

1 Snip the sausage skins to let the fat run, then brown the sausages slowly in a non-stick flameproof casserole for 4–5 minutes. If they begin to stick, add a little olive oil.

2 Add the onions to the pan and fry for about 7 minutes until soft. Stir in the red peppers and fry until they begin to soften.

3 Pour in the stock and red wine, then bring to the boil and let the mixture bubble for 2 minutes. Stir the lentils into the pan, then cover it tightly with a lid or a piece of foil, reduce the heat and simmer gently on the hob for about 15–20 minutes until most of the liquid has been absorbed and the peppers are quite soft. Stir in the chopped parsley, then serve at once.

Serves 4
Preparation: 15 minutes;
Cooking time: 40 minutes
Per serving: 440 cals; 24g fat; 32g carbohydrate

Spanish Omelette with Chorizo

225g (8oz) piece salami, chorizo or garlic sausage, roughly chopped
50g (2oz) stale baguette or garlic bread, roughly chopped
8 large eggs
2 spring onions, finely chopped
1 small bunch of chives, or any other fresh herbs you fancy, finely chopped
salt and pepper
1tbsp olive oil

1 Heat a large, 28cm (11 inch), frying pan and fry the salami or chorizo pieces over a gentle heat until the fat begins to run. Increase the heat and cook the meat until golden and crisp. Remove from the pan (leaving the fat in the pan) and set aside. Add the bread to the pan and fry until it's also golden and crisp. Remove the pan from the heat, mix the croûtons with the cooked salami and keep warm until needed.

2 Beat the eggs together with the spring onions and chives, then season well. Heat the olive oil in the pan used for the salami and bread. When very hot, add the egg mixture, allowing the liquid to spread across the base of the pan. Cook for 2 minutes, then, using a spatula, draw the cooked edges into the centre, tilting the pan so the runny mixture runs into the gaps.

3 When the omelette is almost set, reduce the heat and spoon the salami and croûton mixture evenly over the top. Cook for a further 30 seconds, then cut the omelette into four wedges. Serve with a soft, leafy salad and some crusty bread.

Serves 4
Preparation: 5 minutes
Cooking time: 15 minutes
Per serving: 520 cals; 42g fat; 7g carbohydrate

Bacon and Tuna Hash

450g (1lb) new potatoes, cut into small chunks
salt and pepper
25g (1oz) butter
125g (4oz) streaky bacon rashers or lardons, cut into 2.5cm (1 inch) strips
1 large onion, peeled and roughly chopped
125g (4oz) pitted green or black olives
200g can tuna in oil, drained and flaked
coriander sprigs, to garnish

1 Put the potatoes in a pan of lightly salted water, bring to the boil, then reduce the heat and simmer, partially covered, for 5–10 minutes or until beginning to soften. Drain and set aside.

2 Melt the butter in a non-stick frying pan, add the bacon and cook on a medium heat until beginning to brown, then add the onion. Cook for 5 minutes or until soft. Add the potatoes and olives, reduce the heat and cook for 10 minutes.

3 Using a spatula, turn the hash over and continue to cook for a further 10 minutes, turning every now and again. Add the tuna and cook for a further 4–5 minutes or until the potatoes are done to the centre and the tuna is hot. Season to taste. Garnish with coriander sprigs and serve.

Serves 4
Preparation: 10 minutes
Cooking time: 35 minutes
Per serving: 430 cals; 31g fat; 22g carbohydrate

Chorizo Hash

700g (1½lb) large floury potatoes, peeled and cut into large chunks
salt
175g (6oz) chorizo sausage, in one piece
1 large onion, peeled and finely chopped
4 eggs

1 Put the potatoes in a pan of lightly salted water, bring to the boil, then reduce the heat and simmer, partially covered, for 15–20 minutes until just tender. Drain well, then return to the pan and cover with a lid to keep warm and dry off any excess moisture.

2 While the potatoes are cooking, peel and discard the rind from the sausage and cut it into small dice. Fry the diced sausage in a large non-stick ovenproof pan over a high heat until it has turned a deep golden brown and is beginning to go crispy at the edges – about 15 minutes.

3 Remove the sausage from the pan with a slotted spoon and set aside. Add the onion and fry over a medium heat for a good 10 minutes until it turns golden brown (there should be enough oil from the sausage without having to add any extra oil).

4 Preheat the oven to 200°C (180°C fan oven) mark 6. Cut the potatoes into smaller dice. Return the sausage and potatoes to the pan and cook over a medium heat for 5 minutes, without stirring, until a golden crust forms on the bottom of the mixture. Break up the mixture, then cook again until another crust forms. Break up the mixture once more and leave to cook for a further 2–3 minutes.

5 Make four dips in the hash and crack an egg into each one. Bake for about 7 minutes or until the egg whites are set but the yolks are still soft. Season the eggs with salt and serve immediately.

Serves 4
Preparation: 10 minutes
Cooking time: 35–45 minutes
Per serving 340 cals; 16g fat; 32g carbohydrate

Sausage Hash Browns

700g (1½lb) medium potatoes, unpeeled
salt
50g (2oz) butter
1 small onion, peeled and chopped
450g (1lb) pork sausages
2 red onions, peeled and cut into rings
sunflower oil, to brush
450g (1lb) small vine-ripened tomatoes

1 Put the potatoes in a pan of lightly salted water, bring to the boil and par-boil for 10 minutes. Drain, then cut into 2.5cm (1 inch) cubes.

2 Heat the butter in a large heavy-based frying pan. Add the onion and fry for 1 minute. Add the potatoes and fry over a medium heat for 25 minutes or until crisp and brown, turning frequently. Meanwhile, preheat the grill to medium-high.

3 Grill the sausages for about 20 minutes, turning from time to time, until browned and cooked through to the centre. Halfway through cooking, brush the onion rings with oil and add to the grill pan with the tomatoes. Grill until softened and lightly caramelised.

4 Serve the sausages on top of the hash brown potatoes, with the onion rings and tomatoes.

Serves 4
Preparation: 15 minutes
Cooking time: 35 minutes
Per serving: 740 cals; 51g fat; 56g carbohydrate

Rösti Potatoes with Fried Eggs

900g (2lb) red potatoes,
scrubbed and left
whole

salt and pepper
40g (1½oz) butter
4 large eggs

1 Put the potatoes in a pan of well salted water, bring to the boil and par-boil for 5–8 minutes. Drain and leave to cool for 15 minutes.
2 Peel the potatoes and coarsely grate them lengthways to give long strands. Divide into eight portions and shape into mounds.
3 Melt half the butter in a large non-stick frying pan. Once it is bubbling and beginning to brown, put four of the potato mounds in the pan, spacing them well apart, and flatten them a little.
4 Preheat the oven to 150°C (130°C fan oven) mark 2. Fry the rosti slowly for about 6–7 minutes until golden brown, then turn them over and brown the other side for 6–7 minutes. Transfer the rösti to a warmed baking tray and keep warm in the oven while you fry the rest.

5 Just before serving, carefully break the eggs into the hot pan and fry for about 2 minutes until the white is set and the yolk is still soft. Season and serve at once, with the rösti.

Serves 4
Preparation: 20 minutes, plus cooling
Cooking time: 35–40 minutes
Per serving: 330 cals; 15g fat; 39g carbohydrate

Smoked Cod Rarebit

450ml (¾ pint) milk
1 bay leaf
2tbsp parsley
1 onion, peeled and
sliced
2 slices lemon
2 pieces undyed
smoked cod loin,
about 175g (6oz)
each, skinned
2 thick slices white
crusty bread

125g (4oz) mature
Cheddar cheese
1 small egg, beaten
4tbsp double cream
1tsp each Dijon
mustard and
Worcestershire sauce
25g (1oz) butter,
softened
black pepper

1 Preheat the grill to high. Heat the milk, bay leaf, parsley, onion and lemon slices together in a small deep-sided frying pan and add the fish. Poach for 6–8 minutes or until the fish is cooked through. Remove the fish from the pan with a fish slice and discard the milk.
2 Toast the bread on both sides until golden, then place in a dish.

3 Mix 75g (3oz) Cheddar with the egg, cream, mustard, Worcestershire sauce, butter and a pinch of pepper in a bowl. Put the fish on the toast, top with the cheese mixture and sprinkle over the remaining Cheddar.
4 Put on the lower shelf of the grill and cook for 5–6 minutes, until the cheese topping is bubbling, golden and set. Serve straight away.

Serves 2
Preparation: 15 minutes
Cooking time: 15 minutes
Per serving: 760 cals; 51g fat; 21g carbohydrate

Cheddar and Stilton Rarebits

1 small thin French
  stick
50g (2oz) butter, melted
75g (3oz) Stilton
  cheese
2 large egg yolks
25g (1oz) walnuts,
  roughly chopped
salt and pepper

75g (3oz) Cheddar
  cheese, coarsely
  grated
1tsp English mustard
  powder
a good pinch of mild
  chilli seasoning
oregano sprigs, to
  garnish

1 Preheat the oven to 200°C (180°C fan oven) mark 6. Slice the bread into rounds about 5mm–1cm (¼–½ inch) thick. Brush both sides with the melted butter and bake for 10–12 minutes. Transfer to a wire rack to cool.

2 Using a fork, mash the Stilton with 1 egg yolk and stir in the walnuts. Season and spread over half of the toasts, right to the edges. Mix the Cheddar with the remaining egg yolk, the mustard powder and chilli and spread on the remaining toasts.

3 Preheat the grill to high. Arrange the toasts on a grill pan and grill for a few minutes until bubbling and golden. Cool slightly, then serve warm, garnished with the oregano sprigs.

Makes about 6–8
Preparation: 15 minutes
Cooking time: 10–15 minutes, plus cooling
Per rarebit: 320–240 cals; 21–16g fat;
22–17g carbohydrate

Polenta with Mixed Mushrooms

50g (2oz) butter
1.1kg (2½lb) mixed
  mushrooms
1 red chilli, deseeded
  and finely chopped
3 garlic cloves, peeled
  and sliced
100g (3½oz) sun-dried
  tomatoes,
  roughly chopped

1tsp chopped thyme,
  plus thyme sprigs
  to garnish
salt and pepper
1kg pack ready-made
  polenta
3tbsp olive oil
truffle oil (optional)

1 Melt half the butter in a deep-sided frying pan or wok. Add half the mushrooms and cook over a high heat until all the liquid has evaporated, then put to one side. Repeat with the remaining butter and mushrooms. Fry the chilli and garlic in the pan for 2 minutes, then add to the mushrooms, along with the sun-dried tomatoes and thyme. Mix well and season.

2 Slice the polenta into 16 pieces, about 1cm (½ inch) thick. Heat the olive oil in a non-stick frying pan and fry the polenta in batches, for 3–4 minutes on each side, or until golden.

3 To serve, arrange two slices of polenta per person on a plate, top with the mushroom sauce and drizzle with a little truffle oil, if using. Garnish with thyme sprigs.

Serves 8
Preparation: 10 minutes
Cooking time: 20 minutes
Per serving: 240 cals; 11g fat; 29g carbohydrate

Mini Ham Croissants

oil
225g (8oz) ready-made
 puff pastry
flour, to dust
3tbsp Dijon mustard
100g (3½oz) sliced ham

1 large egg yolk,
 beaten
sesame seeds and
 mustard seeds, to
 sprinkle

1 Preheat the oven to 200°C (180°C fan oven) mark 6. Lightly oil one or two baking sheets. Roll out the pastry on a lightly floured surface until it measures 18 x 23cm (7 x 9 inches). Cut it lengthways to make two equal strips. Spread each strip with mustard and cut diagonally to make 10 triangles. Cut the ham into strips 10cm (4 inches) long and 5mm (¼ inch) wide. Put two strips of ham on the long edge of one triangle and roll it up from that edge. Repeat with each triangle.

2 Put the croissants on the baking sheets, curling the ends to form crescents. Tuck the point of each triangle underneath to stop the croissants unravelling as they bake. Brush the tops with beaten egg and sprinkle the sesame and mustard seeds over. Bake for 10–15 minutes or until crisp and golden. Serve warm. You can freeze the croissants, then heat them in a moderate oven for 5–6 minutes or until crisp.

Makes 20
Preparation: 30 minutes
Cooking time: 15 minutes
Per croissant: 60 cals; 4g fat; 4g carbohydrate

Croque Monsieur

a little softened butter,
 plus extra to fry
4 slices white bread
a little Dijon mustard

125g (4oz) Gruyère
 cheese
4 slices ham

1 Butter both sides of each slice of bread. Spread mustard on one side of two slices.
2 Divide the cheese and ham in half and make two sandwiches, with one mustard-spread side facing inwards on each.
3 Heat a griddle pan and fry the sandwiches over a high heat for 2–3 minutes on each side until the bread is golden and crisp and the cheese starts to melt.
4 Slice each sandwich in half and serve.

Serves 2
Preparation: 5 minutes
Cooking time: 6 minutes
Per serving: 720 cals; 49g fat; 39g carbohydrate

See picture, page 23

Toasted Cheese Sandwich

50g (2oz) mature
 Cheddar cheese,
 finely grated
2tbsp mayonnaise
pinch of English
 mustard powder

salt and pepper
2 slices white country-
 style bread
2tbsp good-quality
 chutney

1 Preheat the grill to high. Mix the cheese with the mayonnaise and mustard powder and season well.
2 Spread the mixture over one slice of bread and place under the grill for 1–2 minutes until the cheese is bubbling and golden.
3 Spread the chutney over the second slice of bread and sandwich together with the toasted cheese.
4 Grill the sandwich to toast on each side, then cut in half and serve.

Serves 1
Preparation: 5 minutes
Cooking time: 5 minutes
Per serving: 700 cals; 43g fat; 60g carbohydrate

Buttermilk Pancakes

125g (4oz) butter
175g (6oz) self-raising
  flour, sifted with 1tsp
  bicarbonate of soda
½tsp each ground
  cinnamon and freshly
  grated nutmeg
50g (2oz) golden caster
  sugar
1 large egg, beaten
284ml carton
  buttermilk

vegetable oil
700g (1½lb) rindless
  thin streaky bacon
  rashers
6 apples, cored and cut
  into eighths
4tbsp maple syrup,
  plus extra to pour
parsley, to garnish

1 Melt 50g (2oz) butter and leave to cool. Put the flour, cinnamon, nutmeg and sugar in a bowl.
2 Make a well in the centre of the flour and add the melted butter, egg and buttermilk. Mix the liquids together, then stir into the flour until thoroughly combined and smooth.
3 Preheat the oven to 140°C (120°C fan oven) mark 1. Preheat the grill to medium-high. Heat a non-stick frying pan, then brush with a little oil. Pour 1tbsp batter into the pan and cook until the underside is golden brown. Using a palette knife, flip the pancake over and briefly cook the other side. Remove the pancake from the pan and keep it warm in the oven between a folded clean cloth. Repeat with the remaining batter.
4 Grill the bacon until crisp. Drain on kitchen paper.
5 Heat half the remaining butter in a frying pan until foaming, then fry half the apples until golden. Remove the apples from the pan and keep warm. Repeat with the remaining butter and apples. Return the apples to the pan, add the 4tbsp maple syrup, bring to the boil and bubble for 1 minute.
6 Serve the pancakes with apples, bacon and extra maple syrup and garnish with parsley.

Serves 6
Preparation: 25 minutes
Cooking time: 30 minutes
Per serving: 820 cals; 56g fat; 53g carbohydrate

Orange Pancakes

175g (6oz) plain flour
pinch of salt
2tsp caster sugar
2 large eggs, plus 1
  large egg yolk
475ml (16fl oz) milk
150g (5oz) butter
grated zest of 2 small
  oranges, plus extra
  zest to decorate

75g (3oz) icing sugar
2tbsp Grand Marnier
  (optional)
475ml (16fl oz) fresh
  orange juice

1 Sift the flour, salt and caster sugar into a bowl. Beat the eggs and egg yolk together in a separate bowl. Make a well in the centre of the flour mixture and add the eggs. Using a whisk or wooden spoon, and starting in the centre, gradually mix the eggs with the flour, slowly adding the milk as you do. Beat until you have a batter covered with bubbles. Cover and leave to stand in a cold place for at least 30 minutes.
2 Just before cooking the pancakes, melt 50g (2oz) butter and stir into the batter (this improves the flavour and texture of the pancakes and means you don't have to grease the pan after cooking each pancake).
3 Meanwhile, make the orange sauce. Put the remaining butter, the orange zest, icing sugar, Grand Marnier, if using, and orange juice into a pan and cook over a low heat until the butter has melted and the sugar has dissolved.
4 Put a non-stick crêpe pan over a high heat and pour in a small ladleful of batter – enough to form a film on the base. When bubbles appear on the surface, loosen the edges with a palette knife, flip over and cook briefly on the other side. Fold the pancake and slide on to a plate, spoon some of the sauce on top, sprinkle with orange zest and serve. Repeat with the remaining batter.

Makes 14–16 pancakes
Preparation: 15 minutes, plus standing
Cooking time: 25 minutes
Per serving: 200 cals; 11g fat; 22g carbohydrate

French Toast

2 eggs
150ml (¼ pint) semi-
  skimmed milk
generous pinch of
  freshly grated nutmeg
  or cinnamon

4 slices white bread, or
  fruit bread, crusts
  removed and each
  slice cut into four
  fingers
50g (2oz) butter
vegetable oil
1tbsp golden caster
  sugar

1 Beat the eggs, milk and nutmeg or cinnamon together
   in a shallow dish.
2 Dip the pieces of bread into the mixture and coat well.
3 Heat half the butter with 1tbsp oil in a heavy-based
   frying pan. When the butter is foaming, fry the egg-
   coated bread pieces in batches, until golden on both
   sides, adding more butter and oil as needed. Sprinkle
   with sugar to serve.

Makes 16 fingers
Preparation: 5 minutes
Cooking time: 10 minutes
Per serving: 70 cals; 5g fat; 5g carbohydrate

Five-minute Do-it-yourself Pain au Chocolat

4 croissants
butter, to spread

100g bar good-quality
  plain dark chocolate
  (with minimum 50%
  cocoa solids), broken
  into pieces
icing sugar, to dust

1 Preheat the oven to 200°C (180°C fan oven) mark 6.
   Split open each croissant, spread with butter and put
   the chocolate inside.
2 Put them on a baking sheet, cover with foil and bake
   for 5 minutes or until the chocolate has melted, then
   dust with icing sugar and serve.

Serves 4
Preparation: 5 minutes
Cooking time: 5 minutes
Per croissant: 379 cals; 25g fat; 42g carbohydrate

Golden Honey Fruits

900g (2lb) selection of
  tropical fruit, such as
  pineapple, mango,
  papaya and banana
3tbsp runny honey

Greek-style yogurt, to
  serve
mixed spice, to
  sprinkle

1 Preheat the grill to high. Peel the fruit as necessary and
   cut into wedges.
2 Put the fruit on a foil-lined grill pan, drizzle with the
   honey and cook under the grill for 5–8 minutes, until
   caramelised.
3 Serve with the yogurt sprinkled with a little mixed spice.

Serves 4
Preparation: 5 minutes
Cooking time: 5–8 minutes
Per serving: 160 cals; trace fat; 40g carbohydrate

See picture, page 23

Strawberry and Melon Cup

300g (11oz) Ogen
  melon, quartered,
  peeled and deseeded
350g (12oz)
  strawberries, hulled
  and sliced

1.3 litres (2¼ pints)
  chilled lemonade
450ml (¾ pint) Pimms
ice cubes and sprigs of
  borage or mint,
  to serve

1 Put the melon in a food processor or blender and whiz
   until smooth, then sieve.
2 Pour the melon into a jug, add the strawberries and
   top up with the lemonade and Pimms. Add plenty of ice
   cubes and decorate with sprigs of borage or mint to
   serve.

Makes 1.7 litres (3 pints)
Preparation: 10 minutes
Per the whole jug: 590 cals; 0g fat;
253g carbohydrate

*Top left: Strawberry and Pineapple Smoothie, page 34; top right:
Prune, Apple and Cinnamon Smoothie, page 36; bottom left,
Strawberry Melon Cup, page 32; bottom right: Spicy Tomato
Cocktail, page 37.*

Lunch

You want something quick but tasty, filling but light. Soup always fits the bill and there's a soup to suit whatever the weather. Try a bowl of light and refreshing Herb and Lemon Soup for a lazy lunch in the sun, or, when there's a nip in the air, a warming Autumn Vegetable Soup, served with chewy wedges of Welsh rarebit.

Need something a bit more substantial, or perhaps you've got friends coming round? You can't go wrong with fish – light and healthy. Trout with Apple and Watercress Salad is delicious oven-baked fish served with a moreish mixture of baby new potatoes, apples, beetroot and watercress. Or there's Lime and Coriander Crab Cakes, served with a chilli mayo – irresistible. Make and chill them in advance, then all you have to do is whack them in hot oil for a few minutes and hey presto, lunch is served.

And don't forget the lunchtime classics – tortillas and frittatas. How versatile they are, inexpensive, satisfying and nourishing – and a great way to use up vegetables. The Pancetta Tortilla is a meal in itself, stuffed with tender slices of leeks and potatoes and spiced with tasty pancetta. Real feel-good food.

Miso Mushroom and Spinach Soup

1tbsp vegetable oil
1 medium onion, peeled, halved and finely sliced
120g pack shiitake mushrooms, finely sliced
225g bag baby spinach leaves
4 x 284ml cartons fresh fish stock
4tbsp mugi miso (fermented soya beans)

1 Heat the oil in a large pan and gently sauté the onion for 15 minutes.
2 Add the mushrooms and cook for 5 minutes, then stir in the spinach and stock. Heat for 3 minutes, then stir in the mugi miso – don't boil the soup as miso is a live culture.
3 Spoon into bowls and serve.

Serves 6
Preparation: 5 minutes
Cooking time: 25 minutes
Per serving: 60cals; 3g fat; 6g carbohydrate

See picture, page 46

Celery Soup

25g (1oz) butter
1tbsp olive oil
1 medium leek, sliced
6 celery sticks, finely sliced
1tbsp finely chopped sage
600ml (1 pint) hot chicken stock
300ml (½ pint) full-fat milk
salt and pepper

1 Melt the butter in a pan and add the olive oil. Fry the leek for 10–15 minutes until soft.
2 Add the celery and sage to the pan and cook for 5 minutes to soften. Add the hot stock and milk, season, cover the pan and bring to the boil. Reduce the heat and simmer for 10–15 minutes or until the celery is tender. Cool the soup slightly, then whiz in a liquidiser until smooth. Pour the soup into a clean pan, reheat gently and season to taste. Serve in warmed bowls.

Serves 4
Preparation: 5 minutes
Cooking time: 45 minutes
Per serving: 130 cals; 11g fat; 5g carbohydrate

Mixed Mushroom Soup

15g (½oz) dried porcini mushrooms
1tbsp oil, plus 50ml (2fl oz) to shallow-fry
1 small onion, peeled and chopped
450g (1lb) chestnut mushrooms, chopped
600ml (1 pint) hot vegetable stock
salt and pepper
2 slices white bread, crusts removed, cut into cubes
2 garlic cloves, peeled and finely sliced
chopped flat-leafed parsley, to garnish

1 Put the porcini into a bowl, pour over 75ml (3fl oz) boiling water and soak for 10 minutes. Strain the mushrooms, reserving the liquid, then roughly chop the porcini, keeping 1tbsp to use as a garnish.
2 Heat 1tbsp oil in a pan, add the onion and porcini and cook over a medium heat for 5 minutes. Add the chestnut mushrooms, increase the heat and brown lightly for 5 minutes.
3 Add the porcini liquid and hot stock, season well and bring to the boil. Reduce the heat and simmer for 20 minutes.

4 To make the croûtons, heat the 50ml (2fl oz) oil in a frying pan, add the bread and garlic and stir-fry for 2 minutes until golden. Drain on kitchen paper.
5 Cool the soup slightly, then whiz in a liquidiser until smooth. Pour the soup into a clean pan and reheat gently. Serve in warmed bowls, topped with the croûtons, reserved porcini and a sprinkling of chopped parsley.

Serves 4
Preparation: 15 minutes, plus soaking
Cooking time: 35 minutes
Per serving: 210 cals; 15g fat; 14g carbohydrate

Courgette and Leek Soup

1tbsp olive oil
1 onion, peeled and
 finely chopped
2 leeks, sliced
900g (2lb) courgettes,
 grated
1.3 litres (2¼ pints) hot
 vegetable or chicken
 stock

4 short rosemary
 sprigs
salt and pepper
1 small baguette
125g (4oz) Gruyère
 cheese, grated

1 Heat the olive oil in a large pan. Add the onion and leeks and cook for 5–10 minutes. Add the courgettes and cook, stirring, for a further 5 minutes.
2 Add the hot stock and 3 rosemary sprigs, then bring to the boil. Season, reduce the heat and simmer for 20 minutes.
3 Preheat the grill to medium-high. Slice the bread diagonally into eight and grill for 1–2 minutes on one side until golden. Turn the bread over, sprinkle with the cheese and season. Grill for a further 1–2 minutes. Keep the croûtes warm.
4 Cool the soup slightly. Remove the rosemary stalks and whiz the soup in a liquidiser until smooth. Pour the soup into a clean pan and reheat gently. Serve in warmed bowls with the croûtes and sprinkled with the remaining rosemary leaves.

Serves 8
Preparation: 15 minutes
Cooking time: 35–40 minutes
Per serving: 310 cals; 14g fat; 32g carbohydrate

Squash and Sweet Potato Soup

1 tbsp olive oil
1 large onion, peeled
 and finely chopped
1–2 red chillies,
 deseeded and
 chopped
2 tsp coriander seeds,
 crushed
1 butternut squash,
 about 750g (1lb 10oz),
 peeled, deseeded and
 roughly chopped

2 medium sweet
 potatoes, peeled and
 roughly chopped
2 tomatoes, skinned
 and diced
1.7 litres (3 pints) hot
 vegetable stock
salt and pepper

1 Heat the olive oil in a large pan, add the onion and fry for about 10 minutes until soft. Add the chillies and coriander seeds to the pan and cook for 1–2 minutes.
2 Add the squash, potatoes and tomatoes and cook for 5 minutes. Add the hot stock, then cover the pan and bring to the boil. Simmer gently for 15 minutes or until the vegetables are soft.
3 Whiz the soup in batches in a blender or food processor until smooth. Adjust the seasoning and reheat to serve.

Serves 8
Preparation: 15 minutes
Cooking time: 25 minutes
Per serving: 100 cals; 2g fat; 19g carbohydrate

Leek and Potato Soup

25g (1oz) butter
1 onion, peeled and
  finely chopped
1 garlic clove, peeled
  and crushed
550g (1¼lb) leeks,
  chopped

200g (7oz) floury
  potatoes
1.3 litres (2¼ pints) hot
  vegetable stock
salt and pepper

1 Melt the butter in a pan and cook the onion over a low heat for 10–15 minutes until soft.
2 Add the garlic and cook for 1 minute, then add the leeks and cook for 5–10 minutes until softened. Add the potatoes and toss together with the leeks.
3 Add the hot stock, bring to the boil, then reduce the heat and simmer for 20 minutes until the potatoes are tender.
4 Cool the soup a little, then whiz in a liquidiser until smooth. Pour the soup into a clean pan, reheat gently and season to taste. Serve in warmed bowls.

Serves 6
Preparation: 10 minutes
Cooking time: 50 minutes
Per serving: 90 cals; 4g fat; 11g carbohydrate

See picture, page 39

Herb and Lemon Soup

1.7 litres (3 pints)
  chicken stock
125g (4oz) dried orzo or
  other soup pasta
3 eggs
juice of 1 large lemon

2tbsp each finely
  chopped chives and
  chervil
salt and pepper
very fine lemon slices,
  to garnish

1 Bring the stock to the boil in a large pan. Add the pasta and cook for 5 minutes or according to the time stated on the pack.
2 Beat the eggs in a bowl until frothy, then add the lemon juice and 1tbsp cold water. Slowly stir in two ladles of the hot stock. Return the mixture to the pan, then warm through over a very low heat for 2–3 minutes. Don't boil the soup after adding the eggs – they will curdle.
3 Add the herbs and season. Serve in soup bowls, garnished with lemon slices.

Serves 6
Preparation: 10 minutes
Cooking time: 15–20 minutes
Per serving: 120 cals; 4g fat; 15g carbohydrate

See picture, page 46

Minestrone with Croûtes

1tbsp olive oil
1 onion, peeled and
  finely sliced
1 garlic clove, peeled
  and crushed
2 medium courgettes,
  finely diced
2 red peppers,
  deseeded and finely
  diced
1 small aubergine,
  finely diced
400g can chopped
  tomatoes

1.3 litres (2¼ pints) hot
  vegetable stock
50g (2oz) dried soup
  pasta
400g can cannellini
  beans, drained and
  rinsed
3tbsp roughly torn
  basil leaves, plus
  extra sprigs to
  garnish
4 slices French stick
125g (4oz) grated
  Cheddar cheese

1 Heat the olive oil in a large pan, add the onion and garlic and cook over a medium heat for 10 minutes until soft.

2 Add the courgettes, peppers and aubergine to the pan and cook for 5 minutes. Stir in the tomatoes, then add the hot stock and simmer, half-covered, for 30 minutes. Stir in the pasta and cannellini beans and simmer for 10 minutes until the pasta is cooked, then stir in the basil.
3 To make the croûtes, grill the French stick slices on one side until golden. Turn them over, sprinkle 25g (1oz) grated Cheddar over each and grill for 1–2 minutes.
4 Pour the soup into warmed bowls, top each with a croûte and serve.

Serves 4
Preparation 20 minutes
Cooking time: 1 hour
Per serving: 340 cals; 10g fat; 51g carbohydrate

Beetroot Soup

750g (1lb 10oz) raw
  beetroot
1tbsp olive oil
1 onion, peeled and
  finely chopped
275g (10oz) potatoes,
  peeled and roughly
  chopped
2 litres (3½ pints) hot
  vegetable stock

juice of 1 lemon
salt and pepper
125ml (4fl oz) soured
  cream
25g (1oz) mixed root
  vegetable crisps
  (optional)
2tbsp snipped chives

1 Peel the beetroot and cut into 1cm (½ inch) cubes.
   Heat the olive oil in a large pan, add the onion and cook
   for 5 minutes to soften. Add the beetroot and potatoes
   and cook for a further 5 minutes.
2 Add the hot stock and lemon juice and bring to the
   boil. Season, reduce the heat and simmer, half-
   covered, for 25 minutes. Cool slightly, then whiz in a
   blender or food processor until smooth.
3 Pour the soup into a clean pan and reheat gently.
   Divide the soup among warmed bowls. Swirl 1tbsp
   soured cream on each portion, scatter with a few
   vegetable crisps, if using, and sprinkle with snipped
   chives to serve.

Serves 0
Preparation: 15 minutes
Cooking time: 40–45 minutes
Per serving: 290 cals; 25g fat; 15g carbohydrate

See picture, page 46

Pumpkin and Butternut Squash Soup

900g (2lb) pumpkin,
  peeled
  and roughly diced
750g (1lb 10oz)
  butternut squash,
  peeled and roughly
  diced
125g (4oz) shallots,
  blanched in boiling
  water, drained, peeled
  and roughly chopped
1 fat garlic clove,
  peeled and chopped

1tsp coriander seeds,
  crushed
125g (4oz) butter,
  melted
salt and pepper
600ml (1 pint) each
  vegetable
  stock and full-fat milk
basil sprigs and soured
  cream, to garnish

1 Preheat the oven to 220°C (200°C fan oven) mark 7.
   Put the pumpkin, squash, shallots, garlic and coriander
   seeds in a large roasting tin and toss with the melted
   butter. Season the vegetables well and bake for about
   30 minutes until golden and just cooked through.
2 Meanwhile, in separate pans, heat the stock and milk.
3 Transfer the vegetables to a large pan, then pour the
   hot stock into the roasting tin and stir to loosen the
   remaining bits in the tin. Add this to the vegetables in
   the pan, then stir in the milk.
4 Put three-quarters of the soup into a food processor or
   blender and whiz until smooth. Mash the remaining
   soup mixture, then stir the two together and reheat
   gently. Pour into warmed bowls, garnish with basil and
   swirls of soured cream, then serve with small Yorkshire
   puddings or crusty bread.

Serves 4
Preparation: 20 minutes
Cooking time: 40 minutes
Per serving: 430 cals; 32g fat; 28g carbohydrate

Hot and Sour Turkey Soup

1tbsp vegetable oil
2 turkey breasts, about
  300g (11oz), cut into
  strips
5cm (2 inch) piece
  fresh root ginger,
  peeled and grated
4 spring onions, finely
  sliced
1–2tbsp Thai red curry
  paste

75g (3oz) long-grain
  wild rice
1.1 litres (2 pints) hot
  weak chicken or
  vegetable stock or
  boiling water
200g (7oz) mangetout,
  sliced
juice of 1 lime

1 Heat the oil in a deep pan. Add the turkey strips and cook over a medium heat for 5 minutes until browned.
2 Add the ginger and spring onions and cook for a further 2–3 minutes. Stir in the curry paste and cook for 1–2 minutes to warm the spices.
3 Add the rice and stir to coat in the curry paste. Pour the hot stock or water into the pan, stir once, then bring to the boil. Reduce the heat, cover the pan and leave to simmer for 20 minutes.

4 Add the mangetout and cook for 5 minutes or until the rice is cooked. Just before serving, squeeze in the lime juice and stir to mix. Ladle into bowls.

Serves 4
Preparation: 20 minutes
Cooking time: 30–35 minutes
Per serving: 210 cals; 6g fat; 18g carbohydrate

Summer Vegetable Soup with Herb Pistou

3tbsp sunflower oil
1 medium onion,
  peeled and finely
  chopped
225g (8oz) waxy
  potatoes, peeled and
  finely diced
175g (6oz) carrots,
  peeled and finely
  diced
1 medium turnip,
  peeled and finely
  diced
salt and pepper
4 bay leaves
6 large sage leaves

2 courgettes, about
  375g (13oz),
  finely diced
175g (6oz) French
  beans, trimmed
  and halved
125g (4oz) shelled
  small peas
225g (8oz) tomatoes,
  deseeded and finely
  diced
1 small head broccoli,
  broken into florets
Herb Pistou (see page
  15) or ready-made
  pesto, to serve

1 Heat the oil in a large pan, add the onion, potatoes, carrots and turnip and fry over a gentle heat for 10 minutes. Add 1.7 litres (3 pints) cold water, season well, bring to the boil and add the bay and sage leaves. Reduce the heat and simmer for 25 minutes.

2 Add the courgettes, French beans, peas and tomatoes to the pan. Return to the boil, then simmer for 10–15 minutes. Add the broccoli 5 minutes before the end of the cooking time.
3 Remove the bay and sage leaves and adjust the seasoning. Pour the soup into bowls, remove 12 French beans, add a spoonful of Herb Pistou or pesto and garnish with the reserved French beans.

Serves 4–6
Preparation: 45 minutes
Cooking time: 1 hour
Per serving: 200–130 cals; 11–7g fat ; 20–13g carbohydrate

Spicy Thai Soup

1tbsp vegetable oil
1 medium onion,
 peeled and finely
 sliced
1–1½tbsp tom yum
 soup paste
1.4 litres (2½ pints) hot
 fish or vegetable
 stock
450g (1lb) raw shelled
 prawns
2tbsp chopped
 coriander, plus sprigs
 to garnish
1 lime, quartered, to
 serve

1 Heat the oil in a deep pan, add the onion and cook
 over a medium heat for 10 minutes until softened and
 golden. Stir in the tom yum paste and cook, stirring, for
 2 minutes.
2 Pour in the hot stock, bring to the boil, then reduce the
 heat and simmer for 5 minutes.
3 Add the prawns and cook for a further 3–4 minutes
 until they're cooked through and have turned bright
 pink. Stir in the chopped coriander, then pour the soup
 into warmed bowls, garnish each with a coriander sprig
 and serve with a lime wedge to squeeze over.

Serves 4
Preparation: 10 minutes
Cooking time: 20–25 minutes
Per serving:150 cals; 4g fat; 4g carbohydrate

Autumn Vegetable Soup

50g (2oz) butter
1 medium onion,
 peeled and diced
450g (1lb) potatoes,
 peeled and diced
100g (3½oz) pack diced
 smoked bacon
1 garlic clove, peeled
 and chopped
100g (3½oz) white of
 leek, chopped
2 Cox's Orange Pippins
 apples, unpeeled,
 cored and chopped
2tsp dried thyme
1tsp dill seeds
 (optional)
salt and pepper
600ml (1 pint) good-
 quality dry cider
900ml (1½ pints) hot
 vegetable stock
125g (4oz) Savoy
 cabbage leaves,
 shredded

1 Melt the butter in a large pan, then add the onion,
 potatoes, bacon, garlic, leek, apple, thyme and dill,
 if using. Season, stir, then cover and cook gently for
 15 minutes.
2 Add the cider and bring to the boil. Reduce the heat and
 simmer for 5 minutes. Add the hot stock and simmer
 for about 15 minutes until the potatoes are soft.
3 Pour half the soup into a liquidiser and whiz until
 smooth, then add to the remaining soup. Reheat
 gently, add the shredded cabbage and simmer for a
 further 3 minutes. Ladle into warmed bowls and serve.

Serves 4
Preparation: 15 minutes
Cooking time: 45 minutes
Per serving: 380 cals; 21g fat; 34g carbohydrate

Roasted Tomato Soup with Cod and Pesto

800g (1¾lb) ripe
 tomatoes, halved
2 garlic cloves, peeled
 and chopped
1 small red onion,
 peeled and finely
 chopped
200ml (7fl oz) olive oil
salt and pepper

25g (1oz) each
 chopped basil and
 flat-leafed parsley
1tbsp lemon juice
450ml (¾ pint) hot
 vegetable stock
4 x 150g (5oz) thick cod
 steaks

1 Preheat the oven to 220°C (200°C fan oven) mark 7. Put the tomatoes, 1½ garlic cloves and the onion in a roasting tin, drizzle with 50ml (2fl oz) olive oil and season well. Cook in the oven for 25 minutes, stirring occasionally.

2 Meanwhile, make the pesto: whiz the herbs, the remaining garlic, the lemon juice and 100ml (3½fl oz) olive oil in a food processor to form a thick paste; season to taste.

3 Put the tomatoes in a food processor or blender and whiz briefly to form a thick, chunky purée. Pour into a pan with the hot stock, then stir together and gently heat through.

4 Season the fish. Heat the remaining olive oil in a large non-stick frying pan and fry the fish for about 2 minutes on each side. Ladle the hot soup into warmed bowls, then put a piece of fish in the middle of each. Drizzle with a generous spoonful of pesto and serve.

Serves 4
Preparation: 15 minutes
Cooking time: 35 minutes
Per serving: 498 cals; 0g fat; 0g carbohydrate

Hot Spicy Gazpacho

75g (3oz) ciabatta, cut
 into small cubes
4tbsp extra-virgin olive
 oil
large pinch each sea
 salt flakes and
 paprika
900g (2lb) very ripe
 cherry tomatoes
1 cucumber, peeled,
 halved lengthways
 and deseeded
1 garlic clove, peeled
 and chopped

1 red chilli, deseeded
 and finely chopped
2 spring onions, finely
 chopped
4tbsp extra-virgin olive
 oil
1tbsp red wine vinegar
1tbsp golden caster
 sugar
salt and pepper
extra paprika and a
 handful of wild rocket,
 to garnish

1 Preheat the oven to 190°C (170°C fan oven) mark 5. To make the croûtons, put the bread in a bowl, add the olive oil and sprinkle with sea salt flakes and paprika. Toss everything together, transfer to a baking tray and bake, turning occasionally, for 10 minutes or until golden brown.

2 To make the soup, put all the remaining ingredients, except the seasoning and garnishes, into a blender or food processor and whiz until smooth. Pour into a pan and heat gently until warm, then season to taste.

3 To serve, spoon the soup into warmed bowls, top each with a few croûtons, sprinkle over a little paprika and garnish with a rocket leaf.

Serves 4
Preparation: 20 minutes
Cooking time: 15 minutes
Per serving: 340 cals; 28g fat; 21g carbohydrate

Top left: Herb and Lemon Soup, page 42; top right: Beetroot Soup, page 43; bottom left: Roasted Tomato Soup with Cod and Pesto, page 47; bottom right: Miso Mushroom and Spinach Soup, page 40.

Smoked Cod and Sweetcorn Chowder

130g pack diced
pancetta
50g (2oz) butter
3 leeks, about 450g
(1lb), trimmed and
thinly sliced
25g (1oz) plain flour
568ml carton semi-
skimmed or full-fat
milk
700g (1½lb) undyed
smoked cod loin or
haddock, skinned and
cut into 2cm (¾ inch)
cubes

326g can sweetcorn in
water, drained
450g (1lb) small new
potatoes, sliced
142ml carton double
cream
½tsp paprika
salt and pepper
2tbsp chopped flat-
leafed parsley,
to garnish

1 Fry the pancetta in a large non-stick pan, until the fat runs out. Add the butter to the pan to melt, then add the leeks and cook until softened.
2 Stir in the flour and cook for a few seconds, then pour in the milk and 300ml (½ pint) water.
3 Add the fish to the pan with the sweetcorn and potatoes. Bring to the boil, then reduce the heat and simmer for 10–15 minutes until the potatoes are cooked.
4 Stir in the cream and paprika, season and cook for 2–3 minutes to warm through. Ladle into wide shallow bowls and sprinkle each with a little chopped parsley.

Serves 6
Preparation: 15 minutes
Cooking time: 40 minutes
Per serving: 530 cals; 30g fat; 36g carbohydrate

Spicy Thai Chicken Soup

1tbsp vegetable oil
1 small onion, peeled
and sliced
300g (11oz) stir-fry
chicken pieces
1–2tbsp red Thai curry
paste
600ml (1 pint) hot
chicken stock
400g can chopped
tomatoes

100g (3½oz) sugarsnap
peas, halved
150g (5oz) baby
sweetcorn, halved
4tbsp chopped
coriander
grated zest of ½ lime
1 lime, quartered, to
serve

1 Heat the oil in a large frying pan or wok. Add the onion and fry for 5 minutes until it begins to soften. Add the chicken and cook for a further 5 minutes until golden brown, then add the curry paste and fry for 1 minute to warm the spices through.
2 Pour in the hot stock and tomatoes, then simmer for 5 minutes. Add the sugarsnap peas and baby sweetcorn and cook for 1 minute until the chicken is cooked through. Pour the soup into warmed bowls, sprinkle with coriander and lime zest, and serve each bowl with a wedge of lime.

Serves 4
Preparation: 2–3 minutes
Cooking time: 17 minutes
Per serving: 180 cals; 8g fat; 8g carbohydrate

Coconut Broth and Chicken Noodles

1tbsp vegetable oil
2tbsp tom yum (or Thai red curry) soup paste
900ml (1½ pints) hot chicken stock
400ml can unsweetened coconut milk
200g (7oz) thread egg noodles

2 x large skinless boneless chicken breasts, cut into thin strips
350g (12oz) pack stir-fry vegetables
salt and pepper
coriander leaves, to garnish

1 Heat the oil in a large pan and fry the soup paste for about 10 seconds. Add the hot stock and coconut milk, bring to the boil, then reduce the heat and simmer for about 5 minutes.
2 Meanwhile, cook the noodles in plenty of boiling water for the time stated on the packet.
3 Add the chicken strips to the simmering soup and cook for 3 minutes. Add the stir-fry vegetables, mix well and season.
4 Divide the egg noodles among four large warmed bowls, pour the soup on top, then garnish with the coriander and serve with prawn crackers.

Serves 4
Preparation: 5 minutes
Cooking time: 15 minutes
Per serving: 440 cals; 19g fat; 42g carbohydrate

Chicken and Bean Soup

1tbsp olive oil
1 onion, peeled and finely chopped
4 celery sticks, chopped
1 red chilli, deseeded and roughly chopped
2 skinless boneless chicken breasts, cut into strips
1 litre (1¾ pints) hot chicken or vegetable stock

100g (3½oz) bulgur wheat
2 x 400g cans cannellini beans, drained and rinsed
400g can chopped tomatoes
25g (1oz) flat-leafed parsley, roughly chopped

1 Heat the olive oil in a large heavy-based pan. Add the onion, celery and chilli and cook over a low heat for 10 minutes until softened. Add the chicken and stir-fry for 3–4 minutes until golden.
2 Add the hot stock to the pan and bring to a simmer. Stir in the bulgur wheat and simmer for 15 minutes. Stir in the cannellini beans and tomatoes and return to a simmer. Sprinkle the chopped parsley over and ladle into warmed bowls.

Serves 4
Preparation: 10 minutes
Cooking time: 30 minutes
Per serving: 370 cals; 8g fat; 49g carbohydrate

Turkey, Ham and Spinach Broth

125g (4oz) green or
yellow split peas,
soaked overnight in
double their volume
of cold water
25g (1oz) butter
225g (8oz) onions,
peeled and chopped
1tbsp ground coriander
40g (1½oz) pearl barley
2 litres (3½ pints) ham
or turkey stock
1 each bay leaf, celery
stick and thyme sprig
225g (8oz) potatoes,
peeled and cut into
chunks

400g (14oz) carrots,
peeled and
cut into chunks
salt and pepper
150g (5oz) each cooked
turkey and ham, cut
into chunks
150g (5oz) baby
spinach leaves
coriander sprigs and
black pepper, to
garnish
50g (2oz) finely grated
Parmesan cheese, to
serve (optional)

1 Drain the split peas, put in a pan and cover with cold
   water. Bring to the boil, reduce the heat and simmer for
   10 minutes. Drain the peas and discard the liquid.

2 Meanwhile, melt the butter in a pan, add the onions
   and cook for 5 minutes or until soft but not coloured.
   Add the ground coriander and cook for 30 seconds.
3 Add the split peas, pearl barley and stock to the pan.
   Tie the bay leaf, celery and thyme sprig together and
   add to the pan. Bring to the boil, reduce the heat and
   simmer for 40 minutes or until the peas and barley are
   tender. Add the potatoes and cook for 5 minutes, then
   add the carrots and cook for 5–10 minutes. Season.
4 Add the turkey, ham and spinach to the pan and bring
   back to the boil, then reduce the heat and simmer for
   2–3 minutes. Pour into warmed bowls, garnish with
   coriander sprigs and pepper and serve with grated
   Parmesan, if using.

Serves 6
Preparation: 20 minutes, plus soaking
Cooking time: 1¼ hours
Per serving: 300 cals; 6g fat; 34g carbohydrate

Easy Pea Soup

1 small French stick,
thinly sliced
2tbsp basil oil, plus
extra to drizzle
454g bag frozen peas,
defrosted

600ml (1 pint)
vegetable stock
salt and pepper

1 Preheat the oven to 220°C (200°C fan oven) mark 7. To
   make the croûtons, put the bread on a baking sheet,
   drizzle with 2tbsp basil oil and bake for 10–15 minutes
   until golden.
2 Meanwhile, put the peas in a food processor, add the
   stock and season, then whiz for 2–3 minutes.
3 Pour the soup into a pan and bring to the boil, then
   reduce the heat and simmer for 10 minutes. Spoon
   into warmed bowls, add the croûtons, drizzle with oil
   and sprinkle with salt and pepper.

Serves 4
Preparation: 2 minutes, plus defrosting
Cooking time: 15 minutes
Per serving: 260 cals; 10g fat; 35g carbohydrate

Grilled Artichoke Salad

400g can artichoke
hearts, drained and
halved
salt and pepper

olive oil
3 little gem lettuces
Vinaigrette Dressing
(see opposite)

1 Preheat the grill. Season the artichoke hearts and
   brush with the olive oil, then grill until charred.
2 Toss the lettuces in the dressing with the artichokes
   and serve.

Serves 4
Preparation: 2 minutes
Cooking time: 5 minutes
Per serving without dressing: 40 cals; 4g fat;
2g carbohydrate

 See picture, page 55

Vinaigrette Dressing

200ml (7fl oz) extra-
  virgin olive oil
200ml (7fl oz)
  grapeseed oil
125ml (4fl oz) white
  wine vinegar

pinch each sugar and
  English
  mustard powder
2 garlic cloves, peeled
  and crushed
  (optional)

1 Put the oils, vinegar, sugar, mustard powder and garlic,
   if using, into a large screw-topped jar. Shake well,
   season to taste and store in a cool place.

Makes about 600ml (1 pint)
Preparation: 5 minutes
Per 1tsp: 27 cals; 3g fat; trace carbohydrate

Melon with Cucumber Salad and Bresaola

20 slices bresaola,
  about 200g (7oz)
3 Charentais melons,
  peeled and sliced
½ cucumber, deseeded
  and finely diced

2tbsp extra-virgin olive
  oil
salt and pepper
3 ciabatta loaves or
  country-style bread

1 Preheat the oven to 200°C (180°C fan oven) mark 6.
   Put the bresaola on two baking sheets and roast for
   10–15 minutes or until crisp.
2 Make the salad. Put the melon and cucumber in a large
   serving bowl, drizzle over the olive oil and season well.
   Divide between 10 plates and add the crisp bresaola.
   Serve with the bread.

Serves 10
Preparation: 10 minutes
Cooking time: 5 minutes
Per serving: 300 cals; 9g fat; 45g carbohydrate

Special Green Salad

1 head cos lettuce or
  Chinese leaves,
  trimmed, shredded
  and rinsed
200g bag continental
  salad leaves
1 cucumber, halved
  lengthways and sliced
3 ripe-and-ready
  avocados

25g (1oz) pine nuts,
  toasted
6tbsp olive or walnut
  oil
4tbsp cider vinegar
2tbsp maple syrup
1tsp English mustard
  powder
salt and pepper

1 Put the cos lettuce or Chinese leaves into the base of
   a glass bowl. Top with the salad leaves and cucumber.
2 Quarter the avocados. Peel, remove the stone and
   slice. Add to the salad with the pine nuts.
3 To make dressing, put the oil into a screw-topped jar
   with the vinegar, maple syrup and mustard. Season.
   Shake well. Drizzle over the salad just before serving.

Serves 12
Preparation: 15 minutes
Cooking time: 2–3 minutes
Per serving: 170 cals; 16g fat; 3g carbohydrate

Spring Onion and Potato Salad

900g (2lb) new
  potatoes
salt and pepper
4 large spring onions,
  finely sliced

4tbsp each Greek-style
  yogurt, mayonnaise
  and wholegrain
  mustard
squeeze of lemon juice

1 Put the potatoes in a pan of lightly salted water, bring
   to the boil, then reduce the heat and simmer, partially
   covered, for about 20 minutes until tender. Drain well,
   then tip into a bowl.
2 Add the remaining ingredients, toss everything
   together and serve.

Serves 6
Preparation: 5 minutes
Cooking time: 20 minutes
Per serving: 120 cals; 1g fat; 25g carbohydrate

Radicchio and Walnut Salad

1 small radicchio
1 oak leaf lettuce
6tbsp olive oil
1 small red chilli,
 deseeded and finely
 chopped

2tbsp red wine vinegar
2tsp Dijon mustard
salt and pepper
25g (1oz) walnut pieces
1 red onion, peeled and
 thinly sliced

1 About 2 hours before serving, separate the leaves from the lettuces and tear large ones in half. Put them in a sink of ice-cold water and swirl around, then dry in a salad spinner or in a colander lined with kitchen paper. Put the leaves on to a clean tea-towel, wrap loosely and put in the salad drawer of the fridge.
2 Preheat the grill to high. Heat 1tbsp olive oil in a pan and fry the chilli for 1–2 minutes. Remove the pan from the heat and stir in the remaining olive oil, the vinegar and the mustard. Cool, season and set aside.
3 Toast the walnuts under the grill for 1 minute then cool and chop.

4 Just before serving, put the salad leaves into a salad bowl. Add the walnuts, onion and dressing and toss well.

Serves 6
Preparation: 15 minutes
Cooking time: 5 minutes
Per serving: 230 cals; 23g fat; 5g carbohydrate

Asparagus, Spinach and Potato Salad

450g (1lb) small
 potatoes
125ml (4fl oz) extra-
 virgin olive oil
salt and pepper
2 shallots, blanched in
 boiling water, drained,
 peeled and finely
 chopped

4tbsp white wine
 vinegar
900g (2lb) asparagus,
 trimmed and woody
 stems removed
225g (8oz) young
 spinach leaves, any
 tough stalks removed

1 Preheat the oven to 220°C (200°C fan oven) mark 7. Put the potatoes in a roasting tin, drizzle with 1tbsp olive oil and season. Roast for 20–30 minutes or until just soft to the centre, then remove from the oven and cool.
2 Meanwhile, make the dressing. In a small bowl, whisk together some salt, pepper, the shallots, vinegar and the remaining oil. Slice the potatoes thickly, put into a large bowl, pour the dressing over and marinate for 10 minutes.

3 Cook the asparagus in boiling salted water for 3–4 minutes – the thick end of the stalks should be just tender with some bite. Drain carefully and put into a bowl of ice-cold water to retain the colour and stop the spears cooking further. Drain again, then add to the potatoes with the spinach. Toss together carefully and serve.

Serves 6
Preparation: 5 minutes
Cooking time: 20–30 minutes, plus marinating
Per serving: 270 cals; 20g fat; 16g carbohydrate

Grilled Corn and Sprouting Bean Salad

2 corn on the cob
2.5cm (1 inch) piece
  fresh root ginger,
  peeled and finely
  grated
finely grated zest and
  juice of 1 orange
4tsp soy sauce

salt and pepper
3tbsp olive oil
225g (8oz) beansprouts
2 little gem lettuces
mixed salad leaves,
  such as baby spinach
  and frisée lettuce

1 Preheat the grill to high. Grill the corn until golden brown on all sides. Cool, then carefully cut the kernels from the cob with a sharp knife.
2 Whisk together the ginger, orange zest, 3tbsp orange juice and the soy sauce and season, then whisk in the olive oil.
3 Toss the corn kernels and beansprouts with the ginger dressing and leave to marinate for 10 minutes.
4 Just before serving, toss the dressing mixture into the salad leaves.

Serves 6–8
Preparation: 30 minutes, plus marinating
Cooking time: 10 minutes
Per serving: 120–90 cals; 7–6g fat;
10–8g carbohydrate

Throw-it-all-together Salad

2–4 chargrilled chicken
  breasts, torn into
  strips
2 medium carrots,
  peeled into strips
½ cucumber, cut into
  ribbons
handful of coriander
  leaves, roughly
  chopped
½ head Chinese leaves,
  shredded

4 handfuls of
  watercress
4 spring onions,
  shredded
5tbsp peanut butter
2tbsp sweet chilli
  sauce
juice of 1 lime
salt and pepper

1 Put the chicken, carrot, cucumber, coriander leaves, Chinese leaves, watercress and spring onions into a large salad bowl.
2 To make the dressing, put the peanut butter, sweet chilli sauce and lime juice into a small bowl and mix well. Season to taste. Add 2–3tbsp cold water, 1tbsp at a time, if the dressing is too thick to pour.
3 Drizzle the dressing over the top of the salad, toss together and serve.

Serves 4
Preparation: 10 minutes
Per serving with 2 chicken breasts: 220 cals; 13g fat;
7g carbohydrate
Per serving with 4 chicken breasts: 300 cals; 16g fat;
7g carbohydrates

Warm Lentil and Poached Egg Salad

1tbsp olive oil
1 onion, peeled and finely chopped
1 carrot, peeled and finely chopped
1 celery stick, finely chopped
2 red peppers, deseeded and roughly chopped
200g (7oz) flat mushrooms, sliced

225g (8oz) lentils, rinsed and drained
600ml (1 pint) hot vegetable stock
4 eggs
100g (3½oz) spinach
2tbsp good-quality balsamic vinegar
pepper

1 Heat the olive oil in a large pan. Add the onion, carrot and celery and cook for 5 minutes. Add the red peppers and mushrooms, cover the pan and cook for a further 5 minutes. Stir in the lentils and hot stock. Bring to the boil, then reduce the heat, cover the pan and simmer for 25–30 minutes.

2 Meanwhile, bring a large pan of water to the boil. Carefully break an egg into a saucer, make a whirlpool with a large spoon in the boiling water and lower the egg into the water. Repeat with the remaining eggs. Cook gently for 3–4 minutes, then lift them out with a slotted spoon, drain on kitchen paper and keep warm.

3 A couple of minutes before the end of the lentil cooking time, add the spinach and cook until wilted. Stir in the vinegar. Spoon on to four plates or bowls and top each with a poached egg. Season with pepper and serve.

Serves 4
Preparation: 20 minutes
Cooking time: 35–40 minutes
Per serving: 340 cals; 12g fat; 36g carbohydrate

Oriental Duck Salad

225g (8oz) new potatoes
salt and pepper
1tsp Chinese five-spice powder
2 x 150g (5oz) duck breasts, skin removed

2tbsp plum sauce
150g (5oz) cherry tomatoes
1 small mango, peeled and sliced
75g (3oz) watercress
1tbsp rice vinegar

1 Put the potatoes in a pan of lightly salted water, bring to the boil, then reduce the heat and simmer, partially covered, for 15–20 minutes. Drain and set aside. Preheat the oven to 230°C (210°C fan oven) mark 8.

2 Rub the five-spice powder and some salt into the duck. Put the duck in a roasting tin, spoon over the plum sauce and cook in the oven for 10 minutes.

3 Halve the potatoes, add to the roasting tin and cook for 5 minutes. Add the tomatoes and cook for 5 minutes.

4 Remove the tin from the oven, put the duck on a board, cover and leave to rest for 5 minutes. Keep the potatoes and tomatoes warm.

5 Slice the duck and put in a salad bowl with any juices. Add the potatoes, mango, watercress and vinegar to the bowl, then season, toss and top with the roasted tomatoes.

Serves 2
Preparation: 15 minutes
Cooking time: 35 minutes
Per serving: 408 cals; 11g fat; 46g carbohydrate

Top left: Warm Lentil and Poached Egg Salad, page 54; top right: Trout with Apple and Watercress Salad, page 58; bottom left: Easy Pea Soup, page 50; bottom right: Chicken and Bulgur Wheat Salad, page 56.

Salmon Pâté

250g (9oz) smoked salmon
3tbsp half-fat fromage frais
1½tbsp creamed horseradish
salt and white pepper
6tbsp olive oil
1tbsp lemon juice
120g bag herb salad
6 slices white bread

1 Put the salmon in a blender and whiz to chop roughly. Add the fromage frais and horseradish and pulse briefly to combine. Put in a bowl, season and chill.
2 Pour the olive oil and lemon juice into a screw-topped jar, season well and shake together.
3 To shape the pâté, use two dessertspoons and scrape a spoonful of pâté from one to the other several times to form a smooth oval. Put one on each plate with a pile of salad and drizzle with the dressing; serve with melba toast.
4 To make the melba toast, preheat the grill. Toast the bread, remove the crusts and cut through the middle of each slice to make two thin squares. Scrape away and discard any doughy bits. Halve each square diagonally and put on a baking sheet untoasted side up. Grill until golden.

Serves 6
Preparation: 15 minutes
Per serving: 190 cals; 15g fat; 2g carbohydrate

Smoked Salmon Tortilla

450g (1lb) potatoes, peeled
salt and pepper
1tbsp olive oil
1 onion, peeled and finely sliced
200g (7oz) broccoli florets, blanched
75g (3oz) smoked salmon, cut into strips
4 large eggs, beaten
2tbsp chopped dill

1 Put the potatoes in a pan of lightly salted water, bring to the boil, then reduce the heat and simmer, partially covered, for 12 minutes until just tender. Drain and set aside to cool a little.
2 Meanwhile, heat the olive oil in a 20.5cm (8 inch) non-stick frying pan and fry the onion over a medium heat for 10 minutes until it is soft and golden.
3 Slice the potatoes into rounds and put into the pan, then add the broccoli and smoked salmon.
4 Preheat the grill to medium-high. Season the beaten eggs, stir in the dill and pour into the pan. Cook over a low heat for 8–10 minutes until set underneath. Run a palette knife around the rim every couple of minutes to prevent the tortilla sticking, and make sure it doesn't catch on the bottom.
5 Put the pan under the grill and cook for 3–4 minutes until the tortilla is completely set and turning golden. Serve with a crisp green salad.

Serves 4
Preparation: 10 minutes
Cooking time: 35 minutes
Per serving: 260 cals; 12g fat; 24g carbohydrate

Top left: Lime and Coriander Crabcakes with Chilli Mayo, page 60; top right: Grilled Polenta and Gorgonzola Salad, page 57; bottom left: Mixed Mushroom Frittata, page 66; bottom right: Egg and Bacon Tarts, page 63.

Frittata with Potatoes

4tbsp vegetable oil
1 onion, peeled and
finely sliced
700g (1½lb) potatoes,
peeled and sliced into
rounds

10 eggs
salt and pepper
3tbsp chopped flat-
leafed parsley

1 Heat 1tbsp oil in a large non-stick frying pan, add the onion and fry over a medium heat for 5–10 minutes until golden. Remove the onion and set aside. Fry the potatoes, a handful at a time, in the same pan, adding more oil as necessary. Fry each batch until golden on both sides, then set aside with the onions. When all the potatoes are cooked, put them back in the pan with the onions to form an even layer on the bottom of the pan.
2 Preheat the grill to medium-high. Put the eggs in a jug, season well and beat with a whisk or fork until combined. Pour into the pan and cook over a medium heat for 5 minutes until golden and firm underneath.

3 Sprinkle the parsley on top and put under the grill for 2–3 minutes until the top sets.
4 Divide the frittata into wedges and serve immediately.

Serves 4
Preparation: 20 minutes
Cooking time: 30 minutes
Per serving: 440 cals; 26g fat; 29g carbohydrate

Mixed Mushroom Frittata

1tbsp olive oil
300g (11oz) mixed
mushrooms, sliced
2tbsp chopped thyme
zest and juice of ½
lemon

6 eggs
50g (2oz) watercress,
chopped
salt and pepper

Serves 4
Preparation: 15 minutes
Cooking time: 15–20 minutes
Per serving: 180 cals; 14g fat; 0g carbohydrate

See picture, page 64

1 Heat the olive oil in a large deep frying pan over a medium heat. Add the mushrooms and thyme and stir-fry for 4–5 minutes until starting to soften and brown. Stir in the lemon zest and juice, then bubble for 1 minute. Reduce the heat.
2 Preheat the grill to medium-high. Break the eggs into a bowl and beat. Add the watercress, season and pour into the pan. Cook for 7–8 minutes until the sides and base are firm, but the centre is still a little soft.
3 Place under the grill and grill for 4–5 minutes until just set. Cut into quarters to serve.

Pancetta Tortilla

450g (1lb) potatoes,
  peeled
salt and pepper
1tbsp olive oil
1 onion, peeled and
  finely sliced

2 leeks, about 300g
  (11oz), cut into 5mm
  (¼ inch) rounds
65g pack diced
  pancetta
4 large eggs, beaten
2tbsp chopped parsley

1 Put the potatoes in a pan of lightly salted water, bring to the boil, then reduce the heat and simmer, partially covered, for 12 minutes until just tender. Drain and set aside to cool a little.
2 Meanwhile, heat the olive oil in a 20.5cm (8 inch) non-stick frying pan and fry the onion over a medium heat for 10 minutes until soft and golden. Add the leeks and pancetta and fry for 10 minutes until the leeks are softened. Remove half the mixture from the pan and set aside.
3 Slice the potatoes into rounds and put into the pan, spooning over the reserved leek and pancetta mixture as you do.

4 Preheat the grill to medium-high. Season the beaten eggs, stir in the parsley and pour into the pan. Cook over a low heat for 8–10 minutes until set underneath. Run a palette knife around the rim every couple of minutes to prevent the tortilla sticking, and make sure it doesn't catch on the bottom.
5 Put the pan under the grill and cook for 3–4 minutes until the tortilla is completely set and turning golden. Serve with a crisp green salad.

Serves 4
Preparation: 10 minutes
Cooking time: 35 minutes
Per serving: 300 cals; 16g fat; 25g carbohydrate

Courgette and Parmesan Frittata

40g (1½oz) butter
1 small onion, peeled
  and finely chopped
225g (8oz) courgettes,
  finely sliced
6 eggs

salt and pepper
25g (1oz) freshly grated
  Parmesan cheese,
  plus shavings to
  garnish

1 Melt 25g (1oz) butter in an 18cm (7 inch) non-stick frying pan and cook the onion for about 10 minutes until softened. Add the courgettes and fry gently for 5 minutes or until they begin to soften.
2 Meanwhile, beat the eggs in a bowl and season well. Preheat the grill.
3 Add the remaining butter to the pan and heat. Pour in the eggs and cook for 2–3 minutes or until golden underneath and cooked round the edges.

4 Sprinkle the Parmesan over the frittata and grill under a medium-high heat for 1–2 minutes or until just set. Scatter with Parmesan shavings, cut into quarters and serve with crusty bread.

Serves 4
Preparation: 10 minutes
Cooking time: 12 minutes
Per serving: 260 cals; 20g fat; 4g carbohydrate

Variation
Cherry tomato and rocket frittata: Replace the courgettes with 175g (6oz) vine-ripened cherry tomatoes, frying them for 1 minute only, until they begin to soften. Immediately after pouring in the eggs, scatter 25g (1oz) rocket leaves over the surface. Continue as above.

Courgette Tortilla

**450g (1lb) potatoes,
  peeled**
salt and pepper
1tbsp olive oil
**1 onion, peeled and
  finely sliced**
**1 large courgette,
  grated**

**100g (3½oz) thawed
  frozen peas**
50g (2oz) feta cheese
4 large eggs, beaten
1tbsp chopped mint

1 Put the potatoes in a pan of lightly salted water, bring to the boil, then reduce the heat and simmer, partially covered, for 12 minutes until just tender. Drain and set aside to cool a little.
2 Meanwhile, heat the olive oil in a 20.5cm (8 inch) non-stick frying pan and fry the onion over a medium heat for 10 minutes until soft and golden. Add the courgette to the pan and cook for 5 minutes.
3 Slice the potatoes into rounds and put into the pan, then add the peas and crumble in the feta cheese.
4 Preheat the grill to medium-high. Season the beaten eggs, add the chopped mint and pour into the pan. Cook over a low heat for 8–10 minutes until set underneath. Run a palette knife around the rim every couple of minutes to prevent the tortilla sticking, and make sure it doesn't catch on the bottom.
5 Put the pan under the grill and cook for 3–4 minutes until completely set and turning golden. Serve with a crisp green salad.

Serves 4
Preparation: 10 minutes
Cooking time: 35 minutes
Per serving: 280 cals; 14g fat; 25g carbohydrate

Cherry Tomato Tortilla

**450g (1lb) potatoes,
  peeled**
salt and pepper
1tbsp olive oil
**1 onion, peeled and
  finely sliced**
**250g (9oz) cherry
  tomatoes**

4 large eggs, beaten
**2tbsp basil leaves,
  roughly torn**
**40g (1½oz) freshly
  grated Parmesan
  cheese**

1 Put the potatoes in a pan of lightly salted water, bring to the boil, then reduce the heat and simmer, partially covered, for 12 minutes until just tender. Drain and set aside to cool a little.
2 Meanwhile, heat the olive oil in a 20.5cm (8 inch) non-stick frying pan and fry the onion over a medium heat for 10 minutes until soft and golden.
3 Slice the potatoes into rounds and put into the pan, then put the cherry tomatoes on top.
4 Preheat the grill to medium-high. Season the beaten eggs, add the torn basil leaves and pour into the pan. Cook over a low heat for 8–10 minutes until set underneath. Run a palette knife around the rim every couple of minutes to prevent the tortilla sticking, and make sure it doesn't catch on the bottom.
5 Sprinkle the Parmesan over the tortilla, then put the pan under the grill and cook for 3–4 minutes until completely set and turning golden. Garnish with sprigs of basil and serve with a crisp green salad.

Serves 4
Preparation: 10 minutes
Cooking time: 35 minutes
Per serving: 270 cals; 13g fat; 26g carbohydrate

Classic French Omelette

2–3 eggs
salt and pepper
1tbsp milk or water

25g (1oz) unsalted
butter

1 Whisk the eggs in a bowl just enough to break them down – over-beating spoils the texture of the omelette. Season and add the milk or water.

2 Heat the butter in an 18cm (7 inch) omelette pan or non-stick frying pan until it is foaming, but not brown.

3 Add the beaten eggs. Stir gently with a fork or wooden spatula, drawing the mixture from the sides to the centre as it sets and letting the liquid egg in the centre run to the sides. When set, stop stirring and cook for a further 30 seconds or until the omelette is golden brown underneath and still creamy on top; don't overcook.

4 If you are making a filled omelette (see below), add the filling at this point.

5 Tilt the pan away from you slightly and use a palette knife to fold over a third of the omelette to the centre, then fold over the opposite third. Slide the omelette out on to a warmed plate, letting it flip over so that the folded sides are underneath. Serve immediately, with a salad and warm bread.

Serves 1
Preparation: 5 minutes
Cooking time: about 2 minutes
Per serving: 300 cals; 28g fat; 0g carbohydrate

Omelette variations and fillings:
Herb: Add 1 tsp each finely chopped chervil, chives and tarragon, or 1tbsp chopped parsley, to the beaten egg mixture before cooking.
Tomato: Fry 2 skinned and chopped tomatoes in a little butter for 5 minutes or until soft and pulpy. Put in the centre of the omelette before folding.
Cheese: Grate 40g (1½oz) Gruyère or Cheddar cheese. Sprinkle half on the omelette before folding. Sprinkle the rest over the finished omelette.
Goat's cheese: Soften about 25g (1oz) mild goat's cheese and blend with a little crème fraîche. Season with salt and pepper and put in the centre of the omelette before folding.
Mushroom: Thickly slice 50g (2oz) mushrooms (preferably wild) and cook in butter until soft. Put in the centre of the omelette before folding.
Smoked salmon: Toss 25g (1oz) chopped smoked salmon with a little chopped dill and 1–2tbsp crème fraîche. Scatter over the omelette before folding.

Spanish Omelette

900g (2lb) potatoes, peeled and left whole
salt and pepper
4tbsp vegetable oil
1 onion, peeled and finely sliced
3tbsp chopped flat-leafed parsley
8 eggs
3 streaky bacon rashers

1 Put the potatoes in a pan of lightly salted water, bring to the boil, then reduce the heat and simmer, partially covered, for 15–20 minutes until just cooked. Drain and set aside to cool a little..

2 Meanwhile, heat 1tbsp oil in an 18cm (7 inch) non-stick frying pan and fry the onion for 5–10 minutes until softened, then remove and set aside.

3 Cut the potatoes into thick slices. Reheat the pan and add the sliced potatoes, onion and 2tbsp parsley in layers, adding more oil as necessary. Preheat the grill to high.

4 Beat the eggs, season well and add to the pan. Cook for 5–10 minutes until firm underneath. Meanwhile, grill the bacon until golden and crisp, then cut into pieces.

5 Grill the omelette in the pan for 2–3 minutes until just set. Scatter the bacon and remaining parsley over the top and cut into wedges. Serve with a green salad.

Serves 4
Preparation: 10–15 minutes
Cooking time: 30–45 minutes
Per serving: 530 cals; 32g fat; 38g carbohydrate

Mushroom Soufflé Omelette

50g (2oz) small chestnut mushrooms, sliced
3tbsp crème fraîche
2 eggs, separated
salt and pepper
15g (½oz) butter
5 chives, roughly chopped

1 Preheat the grill to medium-high. Heat a small non-stick frying pan for 30 seconds. Add the mushrooms and cook, stirring, for 3 minutes to brown slightly, then stir in the crème fraîche and turn off the heat.

2 Lightly beat the egg yolks in a bowl, add 2tbsp cold water and season.

3 Whisk the egg whites in a clean grease-free bowl until stiff but not dry, then gently fold into the egg yolks. Be careful not to overmix.

4 Heat an 18cm (7 inch) non-stick frying pan and melt the butter in it. Add the egg mixture, tilting the pan in all directions to cover the base. Cook over a medium heat for 3 minutes or until the underside is golden brown.

5 Gently reheat the mushrooms and add the chives. Put the pan under the grill for 1 minute, or until the surface of the omelette is just firm and puffy. Tip the mushroom mixture on top. Run a spatula around and underneath the omelette to loosen it, then carefully fold it and turn on to a plate.

Serves 1
Preparation: 5 minutes
Cooking time: 7 minutes
Per serving: 480 cals; 44g fat; 1g carbohydrate

Warm Goat's Cheese Salad

1tbsp each walnut oil and sunflower oil
1tsp balsamic or sherry vinegar
salt and pepper
4 slices goat's cheese log (with rind)
1 quantity Pesto Sauce (page 489), made with rocket instead of basil and 1tbsp chopped parsley

50g (2oz) rocket leaves
1 bunch of watercress, trimmed
40g (1½oz) walnut halves, toasted

1 To make the dressing, whisk the walnut and sunflower oils with the vinger in a bowl, seasoning to taste.
2 Preheat the grill. Lay the goat's cheese slices on a foil-lined baking sheet. Put under the grill, as close to the heat as possible, for 1–2 minutes until browned.
3 Put a slice of goat's cheese on each plate and top with a spoonful of rocket pesto. Toss the rocket and watercress leaves with the dressing and then arrange around the goat's cheese. Scatter the walnuts over the salad and serve immediately.

Serves 4
Preparation: 20 minutes
Cooking time: 1–2 minutes
Per serving: 520 cals; 46g fat; 2g carbohydrate

Variation
Use halved crottins de Chavignol (small hard goat's cheeses) instead of the log chèvre.

Pasta with Pesto, Potatoes and Beans

350g (12oz) dried pasta shapes, such as trofie
salt
175g (6oz) fine green beans, roughly chopped
175g (6oz) small salad potatoes, such as Anya, thickly sliced

2 x 125g tubs fresh pesto sauce or see Pesto Sauce, page 489)
freshly grated Parmesan cheese, to serve

1 Cook the pasta in a large pan of boiling salted water for 5 minutes.
2 Add the beans and potatoes to the pan and continue to boil for 7–8 minutes or until the potatoes are just tender.
3 Drain the pasta, beans and potatoes in a colander, then tip everything back into the pan and stir in the pesto sauce. Serve scattered with Parmesan.

Serves 4
Preparation: 5 minutes
Cooking time: 15 minutes
Per serving: 710 cals; 35g fat; 74g carbohydrate

Nibbles
and snacks

If you want something to nibble on with drinks before a meal, or something to munch on while watching a video, there are plenty here to choose from. Don't just open a packet of nuts – be adventurous and then enjoy the compliments.

Nothing could be easier than Parma Ham Bites – you can't go wrong. Just wrap the ham around stoned prunes and drizzle with luscious extra-virgin olive oil   they'll be gobbled up in a flash. Or jazz up mixed olives with chilli, garlic and herbs. Make loads – they'll keep for ages.

Feeling a bit more adventurous? Try Mini Yorkshires with Steak and Horseradish – sounds complicated, but it's easy, and your friends will be amazed.

If you need a quick snack during the day to boost your energy, something with bread usually fits the bill. Check out the toasts, wraps, pittas, crostini, ciabatta, foccaccia and rolls. Feeling hungry yet? These interesting breads will transform the humble sandwich into something to be proud of: Pork Pittas with Salsa; Goat's Cheese and Red Onion Crostini; Marinated Mushrooms in Crusty Rolls – food to enjoy alone or to share.

Roasted Almonds

Preheat the oven to 180°C (160°C fan oven) mark 4. Toss unblanched almonds, a little oil and sea salt in a roasting tin and cook in the oven for 10 minutes. Remove from the oven, cool and store.

Parmesan Crisps

Preheat the oven to 200°C (180°C fan oven) mark 6. Spoon freshly grated Parmesan cheese on to a greaseproof paper-lined baking sheet, season and flatten a little. Cook in the oven for 5 minutes, then remove from the oven and cool a little. Use a spatula to lift the crisps on to a serving dish.

See picture, page 82

Crunchy Breadsticks

Preheat the oven to 180°C (160°C fan oven) mark 4. Wrap pancetta rashers around breadsticks and cook in the oven for 5 minutes. Remove from the oven and serve.

Chicory Boats

Tear the leaves off a bulb of chicory. Top each leaf with a cube of Shropshire blue or Stilton cheese and a dot of fruity chutney.

Parma Ham Bites

Wrap half slices of Parma ham firmly around stoned prunes, then drizzle a little extra-virgin olive oil over the top of each.

Smoked Salmon Rolls

Mix crème fraîche with a little Dijon mustard, spread on strips of smoked salmon and roll up. Dot the rolls with black pepper.

Posh Cheese and Pineapple

Top cubes of hard cheese, such as Spanish Manchego, with pieces of chopped mango and secure each with a cocktail stick.

Guacamole Crisps

Dollop a little guacamole on to tortilla crisps. Cut a few roasted red peppers into slivers and put on top of the guacamole.

Chorizo Sticks

Wrap a slice of chorizo or salami around a cube of quince paste. Secure with a cocktail stick.

Peppadew Olives

230g jar stuffed green
  olives, drained
375g jar mild
  peppadew sweet
  peppers, drained

basil leaves, to garnish

1 Push a cocktail stick through each olive, then push the olives into the peppadew shells.
2 Just before serving, put a basil leaf into each pepper shell to garnish.

Serves 8
Preparation: 10 minutes
Per serving: 35 cals; 3g fat; 2g carbohydrate

Marinated Mixed Olives

340g jar large green
  olives, drained,
  reserving jar
340g jar Kalamata or
  other tasty black
  olives, drained,
  reserving jar
small pinch of dried
  oregano
1 thyme sprig
2 bay leaves
3 fat garlic cloves,
  peeled

1 bird's eye chilli,
  sliced almost in half
  but keeping the stalk
  intact
200ml (7fl oz) extra-
  virgin olive oil
100ml (3½fl oz) red
  wine vinegar
2tbsp whole black
  peppercorns

1 Put all the ingredients in a medium-sized plastic container. Cover with a lid and chill for at least one day, stirring occasionally.
2 Sterilise the olive jars. Spoon the mixture into the jars and seal.

Makes 2 x 340g jars
Preparation: 10 minutes, plus marinating
Per serving: 180 cals; 20g fat; 0g carbohydrate

Gravadlax on Rye Bread

4 slices rye bread
2 x 140g packs
  gravadlax with
  mustard and dill
  sauce (minimum
  4 large slices)

juice of 1 lemon
pepper
dill sprigs, to garnish

1 Spread the bread with the mustard and dill sauce (you may not need it all). Cut each slice lengthways into four strips, then widthways in half to make eight pieces.
2 Cut the gravadlax into strips and crumple a strip over each piece of rye bread. Cover with clingfilm. Just before serving, squeeze over a little lemon juice, season with pepper and garnish with a dill sprig.

Makes 32
Preparation: 15 minutes
Per canapé: 20 cals; trace fat; 2g carbohydrate

Spiced Mixed Nuts

400g (14oz) unsalted and unroasted nuts (a mixture of Brazil nuts, almonds and pecans)
½tsp each cayenne pepper, ground cinnamon and sea salt
generous pinch of pepper
2tbsp golden caster sugar
2tbsp olive oil

1 Preheat the oven to 190°C (170°C fan oven) mark 5. Put the nuts in a roasting tin and sprinkle over the cayenne pepper, cinnamon, sea salt, pepper and sugar. Drizzle over the olive oil, stir to mix, then spread out in a single layer.
2 Bake for 15–20 minutes until golden and crisp. Remove from the oven and cool in the tin, then store in an airtight container for up to two weeks.

Serves 8
Preparation: 5 minutes
Cooking time: 15–20 minutes
Per serving: 280 cals; 26g fat; 6g carbohydrate

Roasted Walnuts with Rosemary

200g (7oz) walnut halves
4tbsp extra-virgin olive oil
4 fat garlic cloves, peeled and halved
small handful of rosemary leaves
salt and pepper

1 Put the walnuts, olive oil, garlic and rosemary in a large bowl and mix gently to coat. Cover and leave for 1 hour.
2 Preheat the oven to 180°C (160°C fan oven) mark 4. Spread the mixture out on a foil-lined baking sheet and cook in the oven for about 15 minutes, stirring occasionally. Keep an eye on the nuts – they should be pale golden brown and smell toasted when ready.
3 As soon as the nuts come out of the oven, season them with salt – not too much – and pepper, then pick out and discard the garlic. Leave to cool, then put the nuts into an airtight container and chill until needed.

Makes 1 medium tin, enough for 6 servings
Preparation: 10 minutes, plus marinating
Cooking time: 20 minutes
Per serving: 250 cals; 26g fat; 2g carbohydrate

Hot Stilton Bites

250g (9oz) ready-rolled puff pastry
flour, to dust
125g (4oz) Stilton cheese, crumbled
25g (1oz) freshly grated Parmesan cheese
1tsp each cayenne pepper, poppy seeds and black mustard seeds

1 Preheat the oven to 220°C (200°C fan oven) mark 7 and put a baking sheet in to heat up. Roll out the pastry on a lightly floured surface to a thickness of 1cm (½inch) and cut into 5cm (2 inch) squares.
2 Scatter all the remaining ingredients over the pastry. Transfer the squares to the baking sheet and bake for 10 minutes or until golden.
3 Remove from the oven and leave to cool for a few minutes, then transfer to a serving plate.

Serves 6
Preparation: 15 minutes
Cooking time: 10 minutes
Per serving: 260 cals; 19g fat; 15g carbohydrate

Mini Yorkshires with Steak and Horseradish

1tbsp sunflower oil
300g (11oz) rump steak
2 x 120g packs mini
** Yorkshire puddings**
6tbsp crème fraîche
1tbsp horseradish
pepper
sprigs of watercress,
** to garnish**

1 Preheat the oven to 200°C (180°C fan oven) mark 6. Heat the oil in a frying pan, then sear the steak over a medium to high heat to brown on both sides. For rare, remove from the pan immediately and slice into 24 pieces; for medium rare, reduce the heat and cook for a further 3 minutes (5 minutes for well done) before slicing – these timings are a rough guide only.
2 Meanwhile, put the Yorkshires in a roasting tin and heat in the oven for 10 minutes.
3 Mix the crème fraîche with the horseradish. Arrange the steak on the Yorkshires. Top with horseradish cream. Season with pepper and garnish each pudding with a watercress sprig.

Makes 24
Preparation: 20 minutes
Cooking time: 10 minutes
Per canapé: 60 cals; 4g fat; 3g carbohydrate

Roquefort and Cranberry Chipolatas

400g pack ready-to-eat
** cocktail sausages**
75g (3oz) Roquefort
** cheese, sliced**
3tbsp cranberry sauce

1 Preheat the grill to medium-high. Cut the sausages lengthways to make a slit, then stuff each with a small slice of Roquefort and put on a baking sheet.
2 Cook the sausages under the grill for about 2 minutes or until the cheese starts to melt. Skewer each sausage on to a cocktail stick and top with a little cranberry sauce to serve.

Makes 40
Preparation: 15 minutes
Cooking time: 2 minutes
Per canapé: 40 cals; 3g fat; 2g carbohydrate

Top left: Parmesan Crisps, page 74; top right: Tomato Crostini with Feta Basil Dressing, page 88; bottom left: Artichoke and Goat's Cheese Toasts, page 85; bottom right: Chicken and Salsa Verde Crostini, page 89.

Anchovy Rolls

14 thin slices white
** bread**
125g (4oz) butter,
** softened**
2tbsp Dijon mustard
4tbsp finely grated
** Parmesan cheese**
50g can anchovies in
** olive oil, drained**
olive oil, to drizzle
black pepper

1 Preheat the oven to 200°C (180°C fan oven) mark 6. Remove the crusts and butter the bread. Spread each slice with mustard, then sprinkle with half the Parmesan and place 1 anchovy fillet on each side of each slice. Roll the bread up tightly and cut in half.
2 Pack the rolls on to a baking sheet, seam side down, drizzle with the olive oil and sprinkle with the remaining cheese and the pepper. Transfer to the oven and cook for 15–20 minutes until golden. Serve warm.

Makes 28
Preparation: 15 minutes
Cooking time: 15–20 minutes
Per roll: 80 cals; 5g fat; 7g carbohydrate

Sausage and Sage Rolls

**6 good-quality pork
   sausages
flour, to dust
375g pack ready-rolled
   shortcrust pastry**

**1 egg, beaten with a
   pinch of salt
24–48 sage leaves**

1 Slit the sausage skins and remove the meat. Put it into a bowl and mix well, using your hands.
2 Lightly dust a clean work surface and rolling pin with flour and open out the pastry. Roll slightly until it is about 1cm (½ inch) bigger. Cut in half lengthways to make two long strips, then position one strip so that the longest edge is nearest to you.
3 Dust your hands with flour. Take half the sausagemeat and roll it into a long sausage, then lay it down the middle of one pastry strip. Brush a little beaten egg along the long edge of the pastry furthest away from you. Take the near edge and roll over the sausagemeat to give a neat roll. Trim the long and short edges with a sharp knife, then cut the roll into 5cm (2 inch) pieces. Repeat with the rest of the pastry and sausagemeat.

4 Brush each roll with beaten egg, put one or two sage leaves on top, then brush again. Put on a baking sheet and chill for 15 minutes. Preheat the oven to 200°C (180°C fan oven) mark 6.
5 Bake the sausage rolls for 25 minutes until crispy and golden, then remove from the oven and use a palette knife to lift the rolls off the baking sheet and on to a wire rack to cool.

Makes 24
Preparation: 20 minutes, plus chilling
Cooking time: 25 minutes
Per roll: 120 cals; 9g fat; 8g carbohydrate

Finger Doughnuts

**75g (3oz) unsalted
   butter, chopped
5tbsp golden caster
   sugar, plus extra
   to sprinkle**

**125g (4oz) plain flour
pinch of salt
3 large eggs, beaten
sunflower oil, to
   deep-fry**

1 Put the butter, 1tbsp sugar and 250ml (8fl oz) water into a pan and melt the butter slowly.
2 Bring to the boil, then add the flour and salt. Using a wooden spoon, quickly beat the mixture together until it leaves the sides of the pan. Take off the heat and leave to cool slightly.
3 Add the eggs, a little at a time, and continue to beat the mixture to make a smooth, glossy dough.

4 Heat the oil in a deep-fat fryer to 190°C or until a cube of bread browns in 30 seconds. Spoon the dough into a piping bag fitted with a 2cm (¾ inch) star-shaped nozzle. Pipe 10cm (4 inch) lengths of dough straight into the oil and cook for 3–5 minutes until golden, turning the doughnuts halfway through to brown them evenly. Lift out and drain on kitchen paper. Sprinkle heavily with sugar. Serve with hot chocolate .

Serves 6, makes about 24
Preparation: 10–15 minutes
Cooking time: 15–20 minutes
Per serving: 260 cals; 20g fat; 18g carbohydrate

Cheese on Toast

2 slices white or brown
  bread
2tbsp mayonnaise
dash of Worcestershire
  sauce

125g (4oz) Cheddar or
  Red Leicester cheese,
  grated

1 Preheat the grill to high. Toast the bread on one side,
   then turn over
2 Spread the untoasted side of each slice with
   mayonnaise and sprinkle a dash of Worcestershire
   sauce onto each. Scatter over the grated cheese, then
   cook under a hot grill until golden and bubbling.

Serves 1
Preparation: 5 minutes
Cooking time: 5 minutes
Per serving: 910 cals; 67g fat; 40g carbohydrate

The Best Turkey Sandwich

4 slices walnut bread
2–4tbsp mayonnaise
2–4tbsp mango
  chutney
6 slices cooked cold
  turkey

2 little gem lettuces,
  sliced
salt and pepper

1 Spread two slices of bread with 1–2tbsp each of
   mayonnaise and the other two with 1–2tbsp each of
   mango chutney. Put 3 slices of turkey on top of the
   chutney, followed by 2–3 slices of lettuce. Season well,
   top with the other slice of bread and serve.

Serves 2
Preparation: 5 minutes
Per serving: 650 cals; 25g fat; 60g carbohydrate

Artichoke and Goat's Cheese Toasts

225g jar artichoke
  antipasto, drained
  and oil reserved
225g (8oz) firm goat's
  cheese, such as
  Crottin, rind removed
  and diced
1tbsp chopped thyme
grated zest of 1 lemon
1tbsp lemon juice
½tsp grainy mustard

salt and pepper
4 thick slices flavoured
  bread, such as olive
  or rosemary, toasted
70g pack cured
  Serrano or Parma
  ham
olive oil, to drizzle
thyme sprigs and
  crushed black pepper,
  to garnish

1 Halve the artichokes and put into a large bowl with the
   goat's cheese and thyme.
2 Whisk the lemon zest and juice with the mustard, 3tbsp
   reserved oil and seasoning, then stir into the artichokes.
3 Divide the mixture between the slices of toast and
   arrange the ham on top. Drizzle with olive oil, garnish
   with thyme sprigs and pepper and serve immediately.

Serves 4
Preparation: 15 minutes
Per serving: 410 cals; 25g fat; 23g carbohydrate

The Ultimate Toasted Sandwich

50g (2oz) mature
  Cheddar cheese,
  finely grated
2tbsp mayonnaise
pinch of English
  mustard powder
salt and pepper

2 slices white country-
  style bread
2tbsp chutney, such as
  redcurrant and red
  onion chutney

1 Preheat the grill to high. Mix the cheese with the
   mayonnaise and mustard and season well.
2 Spread the cheese mixture over one slice of bread and
   place under the grill for 1–2 minutes or until the cheese
   is bubbling and golden. Remove from the grill.
3 Spread the chutney over the second slice of bread and
   sandwich together with the toasted cheese.
4 Grill the sandwich on each side to brown, then cut in
   half and serve.

Serves 1
Preparation: 10 minutes
Cooking time: 5 minutes
Per serving: 700 cals; 43g fat; 60g carbohydrate

Tomato Crostini with Feta and Basil Dressing

1 small garlic clove, peeled and crushed
3tbsp chopped basil
25g (1oz) pine nuts
2tbsp extra-virgin olive oil
grated zest and juice of 1 lime
50g (2oz) feta cheese
salt and pepper
4 large tomatoes, preferably vine-ripened, thickly sliced

150g tub fresh tomato salsa
50g (2oz) pitted black olives, roughly chopped
4 thick slices country-style bread
basil leaves, to garnish

1 Put the garlic, basil, pine nuts, olive oil, lime zest and juice in a food processor and whiz to a smooth paste. Add the cheese and blend. Thin with 1tbsp water if necessary. Season.
2 Put the tomatoes, salsa and olives in a bowl and toss together. Divide the tomato mixture between the slices of bread and spoon the basil dressing over the top. Garnish with basil leaves and serve.

Serves 2–4
Preparation: 20 minutes
Per serving: 580–290 cals; 33–16g fat; 57–28g carbohydrat

See picture, page 82

Cannellini and Chorizo Crostini

70g pack chorizo sausages, thinly sliced
100g can cannellini beans, drained and rinsed
2tbsp chopped flat-leafed parsley

2tbsp olive oil
salt and pepper
8 crostini
2tbsp thick mayonnaise

1 Fry the chorizo in a non-stick frying pan until crisp. Remove and drain on kitchen paper.
2 Toss the beans with the parsley and olive oil and season well.
3 Spread each crostini with a little mayonnaise, top with the chorizo and beans and serve.

Makes 8 crostini
Preparation: 20 minutes
Cooking time: 5 minutes
Per crostini: 150 cals; 9g fat; 13g carbohydrate

Chicken and Salsa Verde Crostini

3tbsp each roughly
  chopped coriander,
  mint and basil
1 garlic clove, peeled
  and roughly chopped
2tbsp Dijon mustard
3 anchovy fillets
1tbsp capers
50ml (2fl oz) olive oil
juice of ½ lemon
1 loaf walnut bread, cut
  into 1cm (½ inch)
  slices
2tbsp olive oil

1tbsp sea salt flakes
175g (6oz) cooked
  chicken breast, cut
  into 15 slices
125g (4oz) sun-dried
  tomatoes in oil,
  drained and sliced
  into 15 pieces
50g (2oz) walnuts,
  lightly toasted and
  finely chopped, and
  flat-leafed parsley,
  to garnish

1 To make the salsa verde, put all the herbs, the garlic, mustard, anchovies, capers, olive oil and lemon juice in a food processor and whiz until smooth. Cover and chill.
2 Preheat the grill to high. To make the crostini, cut the bread slices into 2.5cm (1 inch) pieces. Place on a baking sheet, brush with olive oil and sprinkle with sea salt flakes. Place under the grill for 1 minute on each side or until lightly toasted.
3 To serve, place a slice of chicken on each crostini base, top with a spoonful of salsa verde and a slice of sun-dried tomato, then garnish with a sprinkling of walnuts and flat-leafed parsley.

Makes 15
Preparation: 20 minutes, plus chilling
Cooking time: 2 minutes
Per crostini: 170 cals; 10g fat; 15g carbohydrate

See picture, page 82

Dolcelatte and Prune Crostini

175g (6oz) dolcelatte or
  Gorgonzola cheese
75g (3oz) pitted ready-
  to-eat prunes or
  dates, roughly
  chopped
50g (2oz) walnuts,
  chopped

1tsp chopped
  rosemary
pepper
4–8 slices ciabatta
olive oil, to drizzle
rosemary sprigs and
  coarse sea salt,
  to garnish

1 Preheat the grill to high. Crumble the cheese and mix with the prunes or dates, walnuts, rosemary and pepper.
2 Lightly toast the ciabatta, drizzle with olive oil and spoon the prune mixture on top. Place under the grill until the cheese has melted. Garnish with rosemary sprigs and sea salt, then serve.

Serves 8
Preparation: 10 minutes
Cooking time: 5 minutes
Per serving: 450 cals; 27g fat; 38g carbohydrate

Tomato and Garlic Crostini

225g (8oz) cherry
  tomatoes, halved
2 garlic cloves, peeled
  and thickly sliced
1tbsp extra-virgin olive
  oil
pinch of sugar

salt and pepper
1tbsp good-quality
  pesto
8 crostini
crushed black pepper,
  to garnish

1 Preheat the grill to medium-high. Put the cherry tomatoes in a roasting tin, scatter over the garlic slices, drizzle with olive oil and grill for 2–3 minutes or until the tomatoes soften. Sprinkle with the sugar and season.
2 Spread the pesto on each crostini, top with the grilled tomatoes and garlic. Garnish with crushed black pepper and serve.

Makes 8 crostini
Preparation: 20 minutes
Cooking time: 3 minutes
Per crostini: 90 cals; 3g fat; 12g carbohydrate

Goat's Cheese and Red Onion Crostini

1 red onion, about 300g
  (11oz), peeled and
  finely sliced
2tbsp olive oil, plus
  extra to drizzle
75g (3oz) soft goat's
  cheese

8 crostini
black pepper
chopped thyme, to
  garnish

1 Preheat the grill to high. Put the onion on a baking sheet, drizzle with 2tbsp olive oil and grill for 5 minutes or until soft and just beginning to char.
2 Spread the goat's cheese on each crostini, then top with the onion and pepper. Drizzle with oil, garnish with thyme and serve.

Makes 8 crostini
Preparation: 20 minutes
Cooking time: 5 minutes
Per crostini: 130 cals; 7g fat; 14g carbohydrate

Marinated Mushrooms in Crusty Rolls

1tbsp chopped
 tarragon
2tbsp red wine vinegar
2tsp wholegrain
 mustard
1tbsp truffle oil
4tbsp grapeseed oil

salt and pepper
225g (8oz) very fresh
 button mushrooms,
 halved or quartered
4 crusty bread rolls
tarragon leaves, to
 garnish

1 For the marinade, put the tarragon, vinegar, mustard
 and the truffle and grapeseed oils in a small bowl, whisk
 together and season.
2 Pour the marinade over the mushrooms and marinate
 for at least 30 minutes.
3 Just before serving, hollow out the crusty rolls and
 spoon in the mushrooms, then garnish with tarragon
 leaves.

Serves 4

Preparation: 15 minutes, plus marinating
Per serving: 360 cals; 27g fat; 25g carbohydrate

Garlic Mushrooms on Ciabatta

3 garlic cloves, peeled
 and crushed
2tbsp chopped chives
grated zest of 1 lemon
juice of ½ lemon
125g (4oz) unsalted
 butter, melted

salt and pepper
6 field mushrooms,
 thinly sliced
6 slices ciabatta bread
chopped parsley, to
 garnish

1 Preheat the oven to 180°C (160°C fan oven) mark 4. Put
 the garlic, chives, lemon zest, lemon juice and melted
 butter in a bowl, mix to combine, then season.
2 Put the mushrooms in an ovenproof dish, pour the
 butter mixture over, cover with foil and cook in the oven
 for 40–45 minutes or until the mushrooms are tender.
3 Meanwhile, grill the ciabatta. Remove the mushrooms
 from the oven and pile on to the ciabatta. Garnish with
 parsley and serve with salad leaves.

Serves 6

Preparation: 5 minutes
Cooking time: 45 minutes
Per serving: 260 cals; 19g fat; 20g carbohydrate

Supper

Whether it's a tray for one in front of the telly, or a family meal for four, six or eight, supper is generally a time to unwind, relax and eat good food that you've enjoyed making.

A big steaming dish of Cheesy Shepherd's Pie is a real favourite – and it can be made a day or so ahead and reheated, like many stews and braises.

Hate washing up? Try the Foil-baked Haddock – succulent fish and vegetables in their own oven-baked parcel. Just add a big squeeze of lemon to the contents, turn out on to a plate and throw away the foil. Simple!

If you're a bit short of cash, tasty cuts of chicken, fish and meat are an ideal choice – like Sticky Chicken, using chicken thighs; Stuffed Pasta Shells with plump coarse sausages; or Mackerel with Hot Tomato Sauce.

Perhaps you've got a few friends coming round for supper – roasts are popular and can be left to their own devices while you all have a drink and chat. Try Cider Roast Pork cooked with red onions, apples and thyme, or Marinated Lamb with Tapenade Stuffing.

Good food and good company, what could be better?

Chicked Chicken with Potatoes and Roasted Tomatoes

3 large potatoes,
  peeled and sliced
3tbsp olive oil
4 chicken breasts, with
  skin

125g (4oz) cream
  cheese with herbs
salt and pepper
300g (11oz) cherry
  tomatoes on the vine

1 Preheat the oven to 220°C (200°C fan oven) mark 7. Line a roasting tin with baking parchment. Spread the potatoes in the tin, drizzle with 2tbsp olive oil, toss to coat, then roast for 20–25 minutes.

2 Using a sharp knife, ease the skin away from each chicken breast, leaving it attached along one side. Spread the cream cheese across each breast, then smooth the skin back over it. Brush the skin with the remaining oil and season.

3 Heat a non-stick frying pan over a medium heat until hot, then fry the chicken, skin side down, for 5 minutes until browned. Carefully turn the chicken over and fry for 5 minutes on the other side.

4 Reduce the oven temperature to 190°C (170°C fan oven) mark 5. Put the chicken on top of the potatoes, add the tomatoes and roast for 10–12 minutes until the chicken is cooked through, the potatoes are crisp and the tomatoes roasted.

Serves 4
Preparation: 10 minutes
Cooking time: 30–40 minutes
Per serving: 660 cals; 43g fat; 32g carbohydrate

See picture, page 106

Chicken with Fennel and Tarragon

1tbsp olive oil
4 chicken thighs
1 onion, peeled and
  finely chopped
1 fennel bulb, sliced
½ lemon

200ml (7fl oz) hot
  chicken stock
200ml carton crème
  fraîche
1 small bunch tarragon

1 Preheat the oven to 200°C (180°C fan oven) mark 6. Heat the olive oil in a large flameproof casserole. Add the chicken and fry for 5 minutes until brown, then remove from the pan and put to one side to keep warm.

2 Add the onion to the pan and fry for 5 minutes, then add the fennel and cook for 5–10 minutes until softened.

3 Squeeze the juice from the lemon and pour into the pan, then add the hot stock. Bring to a simmer and cook until the sauce is reduced by half.

4 Stir in the crème fraîche and return the chicken to the pan. Stir once to mix, then cover, transfer to the oven and cook for 25–30 minutes.

5 To serve, roughly chop the tarragon and stir it into the sauce.

Serves 4
Preparation: 10 minutes
Cooking time: 45–55 minutes
Per serving: 280 cals; 22g fat; 6g carbohyydrate

See picture, page 106

Top left: Chicken with Peanut Sauce, page 96; top right: Mediterranean Chicken, page 94; bottom left: Chicken Cacciatore, page 97; bottom right: Chicken with Spicy Couscous, page 96.

Marinated Lamb with Tapenade Stuffing

50g can anchovy fillets, drained and chopped
125g (4oz) pitted black olives
2 garlic cloves, peeled
1tbsp each chopped rosemary, thyme and flat-leafed parsley
4tbsp olive oil
salt and pepper
1.8kg (4lb) leg of lamb, boned, or 2.7kg (6lb) shoulder of lamb, boned

300ml (½ pint) robust red wine
2 sprigs each rosemary and thyme
2 bay leaves
1tsp redcurrant jelly
450ml (¾ pint) lamb stock

1 To make the tapenade, put the anchovies, olives, garlic and chopped herbs in a food processor and whiz until smooth. Gradually add 2tbsp olive oil, then season with pepper.

2 Stuff the bone cavity of the lamb with the mixture and sew up with thread or secure with cocktail sticks. Season again with pepper.

3 Make incisions all over the lamb and put in a large non-metallic bowl with the remaining oil, the wine, rosemary

and thyme sprigs and the bay leaves. Marinate for at least 6 hours or overnight.

4 Preheat the oven to 220°C (200°C fan oven) mark 7. Drain the lamb, reserving the marinade, then pat dry. Heat a large frying pan and quickly brown the lamb on all sides over a high heat. Place in a roasting tin and roast for 30 minutes, then reduce the heat to 200°C (180°C fan oven) mark 6 and cook for a further 45 minutes–1 hour, basting from time to time.

5 Remove the tin from the oven, transfer the lamb to a board and keep warm. Skim the fat from the tin and discard. Add the reserved marinating liquor, the redcurrant jelly and stock. Put on the hob, bring to the boil and bubble for 5–10 minutes. Adjust the seasoning and strain.

6 Carve the lamb in thick slices and serve with the pan juices, with ratatouille and sauté potatoes.

Serves 6
Preparation: 30 minutes, plus marinating
Cooking time: 1 hour 40 minutes
Per serving: 480 cals; 29g fat; 1g carbohydrate

Chargrilled Lamb with Lemon

about 700g (1½lb) diced leg of lamb (don't trim away all the fat)
2 medium onions, peeled and cut into thin wedges
2 garlic cloves, peeled and sliced
1tsp cumin seeds or ground cumin

4tbsp olive oil
salt and pepper
few sprigs of thyme, plus extra thyme leaves to garnish
1 lemon
170g tub hummus
150g tub Greek-style natural yogurt

1 Put the lamb in a bowl with the onions, garlic, cumin and olive oil. Toss everything together and set aside to marinate for at least 15 minutes, but ideally about 1 hour.

2 Preheat the grill to its highest setting. Spread the lamb mixture in an even layer over the bottom of the grill pan. Season generously and sprinkle with thyme. Roughly chop the lemon and squeeze the juice over the lamb, then add the lemon pieces to the pan.

3 Place the pan under the grill, about 5cm (2 inches) away from the heat. Turn the mixture over with a wooden spoon as it browns. After about 12–15 minutes the lamb should be nicely charred on the outside and just pink in the middle and the flesh in the lemon pieces will be soft and mellow.

4 Put the hummus into a small serving bowl, stir in 2tbsp of the pan juices and the yogurt and serve with the lamb.

Serves 4
Preparation: 10 minutes, plus marinating
Cooking time: 12–15 minutes
Per serving: 690 cals; 55g fat; 13g carbohydrate

Top left: Stuffed Chicken with Potatoes and Roasted Tomatoes, page 98; top right: Chicken with Fennel and Tarragon, page 98; bottom left: Chicken and Leek Pie, page 97; bottom right: Chicken in Pot, page 100.

Peppered Salmon with Herb Mayonnaise

50g (2oz) baby spinach leaves
25g (1oz) watercress
6tbsp chopped herbs such as parsley, dill or tarragon
1tbsp lemon juice
½ quantity of Five-minute Mayonnaise (page 15)
3tbsp coarsely ground black pepper
salt
4 x 175g (6oz) organic salmon fillets
2tbsp olive oil

1 Put the spinach and watercress in a medium pan and stir over a medium heat for 1–2 minutes until it is just starting to wilt. Tip into a colander and refresh briefly under cold water. Squeeze out the excess moisture.

2 Put the spinach, watercress, herbs, lemon juice and mayonnaise in a blender and whiz for 5 seconds. For a smoother sauce, whiz for another 10 seconds. Chill.

3 Put the pepper and a pinch of salt on a plate and press the salmon into it, skin side down.

4 Heat the olive oil in a large frying pan until hot and fry the salmon, skin side down, for 2–3 minutes. Flip the fish and cook for a further 3–4 minutes.

5 Serve each portion with 2tbsp herb mayonnaise and freshly cooked vegetables such as green beans and peas, plus cherry tomatoes.

Serves 4
Preparation: 15 minutes
Cooking time: 7–10 minutes
Per serving: 680 cals; 52g fat; 0g carbohydrate

Salmon with Roasted Vegetables and Pine Nuts

2 large leeks, cut into chunks
2 large courgettes, sliced
2 fennel bulbs, cut into chunks
125ml (4fl oz) hot vegetable stock
salt and pepper
zest of ½ lemon
4 x 100g (3½oz) salmon fillets
15g (½oz) pine nuts, toasted

1 Preheat the oven to 200°C (180°C fan oven) mark 6. Put the leeks in a roasting tin and add the courgettes and fennel. Pour over the hot stock, season well and roast for 30 minutes or until tender.

2 Meanwhile, sprinkle the lemon zest evenly over the salmon fillets and season to taste. Put on a baking sheet lined with greaseproof paper and cook in the oven with the vegetables for the last 20 minutes of the cooking time.

3 Remove the vegetables and salmon from the oven. Scatter the pine nuts over the roasted vegetables and mix well. Divide the vegetables among four plates and top each with a piece of salmon.

Serves 4
Preparation: 20 minutes
Cooking time: 30 minutes
Per serving: 250 cals; 15g fat; 6g carbohydrate

Top left: Grilled Chicken with Mango and Fennel Salsa, page 100; top right: Greek Lamb and Feta Layer, page 105; bottom left: Roast Spiced Leg of Lamb, page 105; bottom right: Chicken Rarebit, p103.

Roast Cod with Herb Crust

4tbsp each chopped parsley and coriander	**2 slices wholemeal bread, torn into rough chunks**
zest of 1 lemon	
2tbsp olive oil	**4 x 125g (4oz) cod fillets**
25g (1oz) ground almonds	

1 Preheat the oven to 200°C (180°C fan oven) mark 6. Put all the ingredients except the cod into a food processor and whiz to chop finely.
2 Put the cod into a baking dish. Spread the breadcrumb mixture on top of each piece of fish. Roast for 15 20 minutes, then serve with boiled new potatoes and green vegetables.

Serves 4
Preparation: 5 minutes
Cooking time: 15–20 minutes
Per serving: 230 cals; 11g fat; 9g carbohydrate

Cod with Sweet Potato Mash

3 large sweet potatoes, peeled and cut into cubes	**1tbsp chopped dill, plus 1tbsp extra for the sauce**
salt and pepper	**150g tub Greek-style yogurt**
2tbsp olive oil	
4 x 125g (4oz) Icelandic cod fillets	**1tbsp capers, drained and roughly chopped**
zest and juice of 1 lemon	**3tbsp cornichons, roughly chopped**

1 Preheat the oven to 200°C (180°C fan oven) mark 6. Put the potatoes in a pan of lightly salted water, bring to the boil, then reduce the heat and simmer, partially covered, for 15 minutes until tender. Drain well, return to the pan to dry off and mash. Stir in 1tbsp olive oil and season to taste. Keep warm.

2 Meanwhile, put the cod in a shallow ovenproof dish and drizzle with the remaining oil, the lemon zest and juice. Season, cover with foil and bake for 20–25 minutes until cooked through. Remove from the oven and sprinkle 1tbsp dill on top.
3 To make the tartare sauce, mix the yogurt, capers and cornichons with the remaining 1tbsp dill in a small bowl. Season and stir to mix. Serve the fish with the mash and a dollop of the sauce.

Serves 4
Preparation: 20 minutes
Cooking time: 20–25 minutes
Per serving: 310 cals; 8g fat; 34g carbohydrate

Top left: Foil Baked Haddock, page 115; top right: Braised Lamb Shanks, page 109; bottom left: Lamb with Butter Beans and Spinach, page 108; bottom right: Roasted Cod with Fennel, page 119.

Stuffed Pasta Shells

2tbsp olive oil
1 large onion, peeled
   and finely chopped
a few rosemary or
   oregano sprigs,
   chopped, plus extra
   to garnish (optional)
125g (4oz) small flat
   mushrooms, sliced, or
   1 small aubergine,
   diced
6 plump coarse
   sausages, skinned

175ml (6fl oz) red wine
300ml (½ pint) passata
4tbsp sun-dried tomato
   paste
pinch of sugar
250g (9oz) large dried
   pasta shells
142ml carton half-fat
   single cream
   (optional)

1 Heat the olive oil in a deep frying pan. Stir in the onion and rosemary or oregano and cook over a gentle heat for 10 minutes or until the onion is soft and golden.
2 Add the mushrooms or aubergine and cook over a medium heat until soft and beginning to brown at the edges. Tip the mixture into a bowl.
3 Crumble the sausagemeat into the hot pan and stir over a high heat with a wooden spoon, breaking the meat up as you do so, until browned all over.

4 Reduce the heat slightly and pour in the wine. Leave to bubble and reduce down by about half. Return the onion mixture to the pan and add the passata and sun-dried tomato paste. Bubble gently for another 10 minutes. Add a pinch of sugar if the sauce tastes a little sharp.
5 While the sauce is simmering, cook the pasta in a large pan of boiling salted water for 10 minutes or until just tender. Drain well and rinse with cold running water to cool. Meanwhile, preheat the oven to 180°C (160°C fan oven) mark 4.
6 Fill the pasta shells with the sauce and put in a shallow ovenproof dish. Drizzle over any extra sauce and the cream, if using, and bake for 30 minutes or until piping hot. Sprinkle with extra herbs, if using, and serve with a big bowl of salad.

Serves 6
Preparation: 15 minutes
Cooking time: about 1 hour
Per serving: 467 cals; 27g fat; 42g carbohydrate

Mozzarella Pasta

1tbsp olive oil
1 onion, peeled and
   finely chopped
1 garlic clove, peeled
   and crushed
1tbsp tomato purée
400g can chopped
   tomatoes in
   rich tomato juice
salt and pepper

125g (4oz) low-fat
   mozzarella cheese,
   roughly chopped
500g pack fresh penne
   pasta
2tbsp basil leaves,
   freshly torn, plus
   extra sprigs to
   garnish

1 Heat the olive oil in a pan, add the onion and garlic and cook over a medium heat for 10 minutes until soft. Add the tomato purée and cook for 1 minute.
2 Stir in the tomatoes, season well and simmer for 25 minutes. Stir in the mozzarella and cook for a further 5 minutes, stirring, until the cheese has melted.

3 Meanwhile, cook the pasta in boiling salted water for the time stated on the packet. Drain, reserving a little of the water and return to the pan. Add the basil leaves, then toss through the cooked penne, adding a little reserved pasta water if necessary, and garnish with extra basil sprigs to serve.

Serves 4
Preparation: 5 minutes
Cooking time: 40 minutes
Per serving: 560 cals; 11g fat; 100g carbohydrate

Top left: Cider Roast Pork, page 133; top right: Spicy sausages with Pasta, page 128; bottom left: Steak with Onions and Tagliatelle, page 128; bottom right: Stuffed Pasta Shells, page 126.

Italian Sausage Stew

25g (1oz) dried porcini
  mushrooms
300g (11oz) whole
  rustic Italian salami
  sausages, such as
  salami Milano
2tbsp olive oil
1 onion, peeled and
  sliced
2 garlic cloves, peeled
  and chopped
1 small chilli, chopped
1 tender rosemary
  stem, plus sprigs
  to garnish

400g can chopped
  tomatoes
200ml (7fl oz) red wine
salt and pepper
175g (6oz) instant
  polenta
50g (2oz) butter
50g (2oz) freshly grated
  Parmesan cheese,
  plus shavings to serve
  (optional)
75g (3oz) fontina
  cheese, cubed

1 Put the dried mushrooms into a small bowl, pour on
   100ml (3½fl oz) boiling water and leave to soak for
   20 minutes (or soften in the microwave on High for
   3½ minutes and leave to cool). Cut the salami into 1cm
   (½ inch) slices and put to one side.

2 Heat the olive oil in a pan, add [...]
   chilli and fry gently for 5 minutes. [...]
   the rosemary stem and add then [...]

3 Add the salami and fry for 2 min [...]
   until browned. Drain and chop [...]
   add them to the pan. Stir in the [...]
   season with pepper and sim [...]
   5 minutes.

4 Meanwhile, make the polenta. Put 750ml (1¼ pints)
   boiling water and 1tsp salt into a heavy-based pan.
   Return to the boil, sprinkle in the polenta, stirring, and
   cook according to the instructions on the packet. Add
   the butter, Parmesan and fontina and mix well.

5 Serve the sausage stew accompanied by the polenta,
   topped with Parmesan shavings, if you like, and
   garnished with rosemary sprigs.

Serves 4
Preparation: 10 minutes, plus soaking
Cooking time: 15 minutes
Per serving: 780 cals; 48g fat; 47g carbohydrate

See picture, page 134

Sausages with Mustard Mash and Red Onion Gravy

900g (2lb) floury
  potatoes, such as
  Maris Piper, peeled
  and cut into even
  chunks
25g (1oz) butter
1 red onion, peeled and
  sliced
2tbsp plain flour
450ml (¾ pint) hot beef
  stock

1tsp tomato purée
2tbsp chopped flat-
  leafed parsley
salt and pepper
2tbsp milk
2tbsp wholegrain
  mustard
1tsp vegetable oil
8 thick pork sausages

1 Put the potatoes in a pan of lightly salted water, bring
   to the boil, then reduce the heat and simmer, partially
   covered, for 15–20 minutes until tender.

2 Melt half the butter in a small pan and fry the onion
   over a medium heat for 10 minutes until soft and
   translucent. Stir in the flour and cook for 1 minute. Add
   the hot stock gradually, stirring the gravy until smooth.
   Stir in the tomato purée and simmer for 5 minutes until
   thickened. Stir in the parsley and season.

3 Drain the potatoes well and return to the hot pan to
   dry, then mash. Put the pan back on the hob over a
   low heat, push the potatoes to one side of the pan and
   add the milk and remaining butter to warm through.
   Beat the milk and butter into the potatoes, then
   season, stir in the mustard and keep warm.

4 Heat the oil in a frying pan and fry the sausages over a
   medium heat for 10–12 minutes, turning occasionally,
   until golden and cooked through. Serve with the mash,
   drizzled with the gravy.

Serves 4
Preparation: 15 minutes
Cooking time: 30–35 minutes
Per serving: 620 cals; 35g fat; 61g carbohydrate

*Top left: Braised Beef with mustard and Capers, page 139; Top
right: Fennel Pork with Cabbage and Apple, page 137; bottom left:
Italian Sausage Stew, page 135; bottom right: Spicy Pork and Bean
Stew, page 136.*

Beef with Beer and Mushrooms

700g (1½lb) braising
  steak, cut into large
  chunks about 5cm (2
  inches) across
2tsp plain flour
2tbsp oil
25g (1oz) butter
2 large onions, peeled
  and finely sliced
225g (8oz) carrots,
  peeled and cut into
  large sticks

200ml (7fl oz) Guinness
300ml (½ pint)
  vegetable stock
2tsp tomato purée
2tsp English mustard
2tsp light muscovado
  sugar
salt and pepper
225g (8oz) large field or
  portabellini
  mushrooms

1 Preheat the oven to 150°C (130°C fan oven) mark 2. Toss the meat in the flour. Heat the oil and butter in a large casserole over a medium heat and brown the meat a few pieces at a time, removing it with a slotted spoon. The flavour and colour of the finished casserole depend on the meat taking on a good deep colour now. Stir the onions into the pan and cook for about 10 minutes until golden brown and beginning to soften and caramelise.

2 Return all the meat to the pan, then add the carrots and stir in the Guinness, stock, tomato purée, mustard, sugar and plenty of seasoning. Bring to the boil, stir well, then cover tightly with foil or a lid, and simmer gently in the oven for 1½ hours.

3 Remove the pan from the oven, stir in the whole mushrooms and return to the oven for a further 45 minutes–1 hour until the meat is meltingly tender. Serve with plenty of buttery mashed potatoes.

Serves 4
Preparation: 15 minutes
Cooking time: 2¾–3 hours
Per serving: 420 cals; 20g fat; 19g carbohydrate

Chilli Steak and Corn on the Cob

50g (2oz) butter,
  softened
1 large red chilli,
  deseeded and
  finely chopped
1 garlic clove, peeled
  and crushed
25g (1oz) freshly grated
  Parmesan cheese

1tbsp finely chopped
  basil
4 corn on the cob, each
  cut into three
1tbsp olive oil
4 x 150g (5oz) sirloin
  steaks

1 Put the butter in a bowl and beat with a wooden spoon. Mix in the chilli, garlic, Parmesan and basil. Cover and chill to firm up.

2 Meanwhile, bring a large pan of water to the boil. Add the corn, cover to bring back up to the boil, then simmer half-covered for about 10 minutes or until tender. Drain well.

3 Heat a little olive oil in a large frying pan or griddle and cook the steaks on a high heat for 2–3 minutes on each side for medium-rare or 4–5 minutes for medium, 6–7 minutes for well done. Divide the corn and steaks among four warmed plates and top with the butter. Serve with a mixed green salad.

Serves 4
Preparation: 5 minutes
Cooking time: 15 minutes
Per serving: 390 cals; 23g fat; 10g carbohydrate

Top left: Italian Meatballs in Tomato Sauce, page 140; top right: Beef with Beer and Mushrooms, page 140; bottom left: Chilli Bolognese, page 142; bottom right: Chilli Steak with Corn on the Cob, page 140.

One pot

What better than to assemble all the ingredients you need for a great meal, cook it and then tuck in, knowing you've only got one pan to wash up? Casseroles, roasts, stews and braises are not only delicious, they can also have all kinds of amazing vegetables, beans and pasta added to make complete meals in just one pot, giving you time to finish off that good book, watch your favourite soap, or just relax.

There are classics such as Seafood Paella, with the wonderful colour, flavour and aroma of saffron. Make it in a lovely big paella or frying pan and take to the table so that everyone can dig in.

Then the slow-cooked dishes – Braised Oxtail, full of flavour, sticky and warming; Chicken in a Pot, cooked in wine with bacon, carrots, parsnips and celery; or Beef Casserole with Black Olives – chunks of beef simmered with bacon, mushrooms, onions and olives in a gravy enriched with brandy and red wine.

And the exotics: bring back memories of holidays in the sun with Caribbean Chicken – a hint of chilli, a dash of rum, some black-eyed beans, and lashings of cool beer to enjoy it with.

One pot – many flavours.

Pheasant Casserole with Cider and Apples

2 large oven-ready
  pheasants
salt and pepper
2tbsp plain flour, plus
  extra to dust
4 crisp eating apples,
  such as Granny
  Smiths
1tbsp lemon juice
50g (2oz) butter
4 rindless streaky
  bacon rashers, halved
2 onions, peeled and
  chopped
2 celery sticks,
  chopped

1tbsp dried juniper
  berries, lightly
  crushed
2.5cm (1 inch) piece
  fresh root ginger,
  peeled and finely
  chopped
300ml (½ pint)
  pheasant or chicken
  stock
750–900ml (1¼–1½
  pints) dry cider
150ml (¼ pint) double
  cream

1 Cut each pheasant into 4 portions, season and dust with flour. Quarter, core and cut the apples into wedges, then toss in the lemon juice.

2 Melt the butter in a large flameproof casserole and brown the pheasant portions, in batches, over a high heat until deep golden brown on all sides. Remove with a slotted spoon and put to one side.

3 Preheat the oven to 170°C (150°C fan oven) mark 3. Add the bacon to the casserole and fry for 2–3 minutes until golden. Add the onions, celery, apples, juniper and ginger and cook for 8–10 minutes. Stir in the flour and cook, stirring, for 2 minutes, then add the stock and cider and bring to the boil, stirring.

4 Return the pheasant to the casserole and bring to a simmer. Cover, transfer to the oven and cook for 45 minutes to 1 hour, or until the pheasant is tender (older pheasants will take a little longer).

5 Transfer the pheasant to a warmed dish and keep warm. Strain the sauce through a sieve and return to the casserole. Stir in the cream, bring to the boil and let bubble for 10 minutes or until syrupy. Return the pheasant to the sauce and check the seasoning before serving.

Serves 6–8
Preparation: 50 minutes
Cooking time: 1¾ hours
Per serving: 670–500 cals; 40–31g fat; 20–15g carbohydrate

Pot-roasted Pheasant with Red Cabbage

25g (1oz) butter
1tbsp oil
2 oven-ready young
  pheasants, halved
2 onions, peeled and
  sliced
450g (1lb) red cabbage,
  cored and finely
  shredded

1tsp cornflour
250ml (8fl oz) red wine
2tbsp redcurrant jelly
1tbsp balsamic vinegar
salt and pepper
4 rindless smoked
  streaky bacon
  rashers, halved

1 Preheat the oven to 200°C (180°C fan oven) mark 6. Melt the butter with the oil in a large flameproof casserole. Add the pheasant halves and brown on all sides, then remove and put to one side. Add the onions and cabbage to the casserole and fry for 5 minutes, stirring frequently, until softened.

2 Blend the cornflour with a little water. Add to the casserole with the wine, redcurrant jelly, vinegar and seasoning. Bring to the boil, stirring.

3 Arrange the pheasant halves, skin side up, on the cabbage. Lay the bacon on top. Cover the casserole and cook for 30 minutes or until tender (older pheasants will take an extra 10–20 minutes).

4 Serve the pheasant and cabbage with the cooking juices spooned over.

Serves 4
Preparation: 20 minutes
Cooking time: 40 minutes
Per serving: 570 cals; 31g fat; 15g carbohydrate

Top left: Pot-roasted Pheasant with Red Cabbage, page 160; top right: Peppered Winter Stew, page 162; bottom left: Chicken Casserole, page 156; bottom right, Caribbean Chicken, page 152.

Vegetarian

Cooking vegetarian food is a great chance to be creative and inventive. There are loads of lovely spices, herbs, pulses and grains just waiting for a chance to get together with luscious vegetables in tarts, pies, bakes and stews. Take some creamy, cheesy polenta, top with vivid broad beans, tender asparagus and baby carrots and sit back and wait for the compliments – that's Parmesan Polenta with Minted Summer Vegetables.

Or, for a real winter treat, roasted vegetables must be up there with the best. Winter Roasted Vegetable Tart gives you a chance to show off your pastry-making skills (or buy ready-made to save time) and then fill the tart with vegetables, mushrooms and chestnuts – great comfort food.

Then for anyone who sneers at nut roast, give them a slice of Nut and Cranberry Terrine, with its filling of walnuts, leeks, rice and dolcelatte cheese and the topping of cranberries in redcurrant jelly.

And who can resist risottos? Try the moreish Garlic and Parmesan Risotto, or the Risotto Galette with melted Taleggio – a risotto 'sandwich' oozing with melted cheese. Spectacular.

Creamed Celeriac and Fresh Parmesan Soup

2tbsp oil
175g (6oz) onions, peeled and roughly chopped
1 garlic clove, peeled and crushed
450g (1lb) each celeriac and potatoes, peeled and roughly chopped
1.1 litres (2 pints) vegetable stock
1 sachet bouquet garni

600ml (1 pint) full-fat milk
284ml carton double cream
1tbsp lemon juice
salt and pepper
8tbsp grated Parmesan cheese
Toasted Parmesan cheese, to garnish (see below)

1   Heat the oil in a large pan, then add the onions and garlic. Cook slowly for 4–5 minutes or until golden brown.
2   Add the celeriac, potatoes, stock and bouquet garni, bring to the boil, then reduce the heat and simmer for 20–25 minutes or until the celeriac and potatoes are tender.
3   Remove the pan from the heat, cool slightly and discard the bouquet garni. Blend the soup in a liquidiser in batches until smooth. Pour into a clean pan, add the milk, cream and lemon juice and season. Simmer for a further 10 minutes.
4   To serve, put 1tbsp grated Parmesan in the bottom of each serving bowl. Ladle in the soup, grind over some black pepper and garnish with the toasted Parmesan.

Serves 8
Preparation: 10 minutes
Cooking time: 35 minutes
Per serving: 385 cals; 29g fat; 18g carbohydrate

Toasted Parmesan

To make the toasted Parmesan, sprinkle 25g (1oz) finely grated Parmesan cheese on a baking sheet. Put under a hot grill until melted and golden. Cool, then crumble and store in an airtight container for up to one week.

Serves 8
Preparation: 25 minutes
Cooking time: 35 minutes
Per serving: 310 cals; 24g fat; 16g carbohydrate

Jerusalem Artichoke Soup

125g (4oz) butter
175g (6oz) onions, peeled and chopped
1 garlic clove, peeled and crushed
50g (2oz) celery, chopped
900g (2lb) Jerusalem artichokes, peeled and chopped

125g (4oz) carrots, peeled and chopped
300ml (½ pint) dry white wine
1 sachet bouquet garni
salt and pepper
142ml carton double cream

1   Melt the butter in a large pan, add the onions and garlic and cook for 2 minutes. Add the remaining vegetables and cook for 5 minutes.
2   Add the wine, bring to the boil and simmer until reduced by half. Add 1.1 litres (2 pints) water and the bouquet garni. Bring back to the boil, then reduce the heat and simmer until the vegetables are tender.
3   Cool slightly, remove the bouquet garni, then blend in a liquidiser until smooth.
4   Pour the soup into a clean pan and gently reheat, season and add half the cream. Spoon into bowls, drizzle with the remaining cream and serve.

Serves 6
Preparation: 10 minutes
Cooking time: 45 minutes
Per serving: 350 cals; 29g fat; 19g carbohydrate

Stuffed Acorn Squash

1 small acorn squash
salt and pepper
1 tbsp olive oil
2 tbsp frozen meatless
 stuffing mix, thawed

thyme sprigs, to
 garnish (optional)

1 Preheat the oven to 200°C (180°C fan oven) mark 6. Cut the stalk off the squash, then scoop out and discard the seeds.
2 Season the squash, drizzle with olive oil and spoon in the stuffing. Cover with foil, then roast for 1 hour or until tender. Remove from the oven, garnish with thyme, if using, and serve.

Serves 1
Preparation: 10 minutes
Cooking time: 1 hour
Per serving: 280 cals; 15g fat; 32g carbohydrate

Glamorgan Sausages

150g (5oz) Caerphilly
 cheese, grated
200g (7oz) fresh white
 breadcrumbs
3 spring onions, finely
 chopped
1 tbsp chopped flat-
 leafed parsley

leaves of 4 thyme
 sprigs
salt and pepper
3 large eggs,
 1 separated
vegetable oil

1 Preheat the oven to 140°C (120°C fan oven) mark 1. Mix the cheese with 150g (5oz) breadcrumbs, the spring onions and herbs in a large bowl. Season well.
2 Add the whole eggs plus the extra yolk and mix well to combine. Cover and chill for 5 minutes.
3 Lightly beat the egg white in a shallow bowl. Tip the rest of the breadcrumbs on to a large plate.
4 Take 2 tbsp of the mixture and shape into a small sausage, about 4cm (1½ inches) long. Roll first in the egg white, then in the breadcrumbs to coat. Repeat to make 12 sausages in total.

5 Heat 2 tsp oil in a large heavy-based pan until hot and fry the sausages in two batches for 6–8 minutes, turning until golden all over. Keep warm in the oven while cooking the rest. Serve with a chutney.

Serves 4
Preparation: 25 minutes
Cooking time: 15 minutes
Per serving: 380 cals; 24g fat; 25g carbohydrate

Couscous-stuffed Mushrooms

125g (4oz) couscous
20g pack fresh flat-leafed parsley, roughly chopped
280g jar mixed antipasti in oil, drained and oil put to one side
8 large flat Portabellini mushrooms

25g (1oz) butter
25g (1oz) plain flour
300ml (10fl oz) skimmed milk
75g (3oz) mature Cheddar cheese, grated, plus extra to sprinkle
green salad, to serve

1   Preheat the oven to 220°C (200°C fan oven) mark 7. Put the couscous in a bowl with 200ml (7fl oz) boiling water, the parsley, antipasti and 1tbsp of the reserved oil. Stir well.
2   Put the mushrooms on to a non-stick baking tray and spoon a little of the couscous mixture into the centre of each. Cook in the oven while you make the sauce.

3   Whisk together the butter, flour and milk in a small pan over a high heat until the mixture comes to the boil. Reduce the heat as soon as it starts to thicken and whisk constantly until smooth. Take the pan off the heat and stir in the cheese.
4   Spoon the sauce over the mushrooms and sprinkle with the remaining cheese. Put back into the oven for a further 7–10 minutes until golden. Serve with a green salad.

Serves 4
Preparation: 3 minutes
Cooking time: about 12 minutes
Per serving: 390 cals; 17g fat; 35g carbohydrate

See picture, page 194

Garlic Cheese Pizza

280g pack pizza base mix
2 x 150g packs garlic and herb cheese
12 whole sun-dried tomatoes, drained of oil and cut into rough pieces

40g (1½oz) pine nuts
12 fresh basil leaves
3tbsp olive oil
green salad, to serve

1   Put a pizza stone or large baking sheet in the oven and preheat to 220°C (200°C fan oven) mark 7.
2   Mix the pizza base dough according to the packet instructions. On a lightly floured worksurface, knead for a few minutes or until smooth. Roll out to a 33cm (13 inch) round. Transfer the dough to the preheated pizza stone or baking sheet. Pinch a lip around the edge.
3   Crumble the cheese over the dough and flatten with a palette knife, then sprinkle on the sun-dried tomatoes, pine nuts and basil leaves.

4   Drizzle with the oil and bake for 20–30 minutes until pale golden and cooked to the centre. Serve with a green salad.

Serves 4
Preparation: 20 minutes
Cooking time: 30 minutes
Per serving: 536 cals; 30g fat; 54g carbohydrate

See picture, page 194

Family-size Tomato, Basil and Mozzarella Sandwich

1 loaf of bread, such as cholla
4 ripe plum tomatoes
2tbsp extra-virgin olive oil
salt and pepper
1–2 fresh mozzarella, about 150g (5oz), drained, sliced and seasoned
12–15 basil leaves

1 Put the bread on a board. Make two deep parallel cuts along the length of the loaf, but don't go all the way through.
2 Cut the tops off 2 tomatoes and use a teaspoon to scoop the juice and seeds into a bowl. Add the olive oil and season well.
3 Slice the 2 hollow and the 2 whole tomatoes finely and season well.
4 Divide the tomato juice between the open sections in the bread, then do the same with the sliced tomatoes, followed by the mozzarella and basil. Slice the loaf horizontally to serve

Serves 4
Preparation: 10 minutes
Per serving: 360 cals; 17g fat; 37g carbohydrate

Deli Pizza

6tbsp tomato pizza sauce
2 pizzeria-style pizza bases
100g (3½oz) soft goat's cheese
1 red onion, peeled and finely sliced
100g (3½oz) sunblush tomatoes
100g (3½oz) olives
handful of basil, roughly torn

1 Put a large baking sheet on the top shelf of the oven and preheat to 220°C (200°C fan oven) mark 7.
2 Spread a thin layer of the tomato sauce over the pizza bases. Top with dollops of goat's cheese, then scatter over the onion, tomatoes and olives.
3 Bake on the preheated baking sheet for 15 minutes or until golden and crispy. Remove from the oven, scatter over the torn basil and serve immediately with a crisp green salad.

Serves 4
Preparation: 5 minutes
Cooking time: 15 minutes
Per serving: 370 cals; 10g fat; 57g carbohydrate

Parmesan Polenta with Minted Summer Vegetables

900ml (1½ pints) vegetable stock
125g (4oz) polenta
3tbsp double cream
125g (4oz) Parmesan cheese, finely grated
4tbsp chopped mint, plus mint sprigs to garnish
salt and pepper
50g (2oz) butter
50g (2oz) shallots, blanched in boiling water, drained, peeled and finely chopped
2 garlic cloves, peeled and thinly sliced
125g (4oz) fresh broad beans, skinned, or fresh peas, shelled
125g (4oz) asparagus tips or French beans, cut on the diagonal
125g (4oz) baby carrots
1tbsp golden caster sugar
2tsp grainy mustard
1tbsp white wine vinegar

1 To make the Parmesan polenta, bring 600ml (1 pint) stock to the boil in a large pan, then reduce to a simmer. Add the polenta in a slow, steady stream, stirring all the time for about 5 minutes until thick. Stir in the remaining stock and the cream, then cook for a further 10 minutes, stirring all the time, until the polenta resembles mashed potato. Add the Parmesan and 2tbsp mint, then season well. Remove from the heat and keep warm.
2 To make the minted vegetables, melt the butter in a large pan and add the shallots and garlic. Cook for 5 minutes, then add the vegetables, sugar and 50ml (2fl oz) water. Bring to the boil, cover and cook for about 5 minutes or until the vegetables are tender and the liquid becomes syrupy.
3 Toss the hot vegetables with the remaining mint, the mustard and vinegar and season well. Serve immediately with the polenta and garnish with mint sprigs.

Serves 4
Preparation: 10 minutes
Cooking time: 15 minutes
Per serving: 450 cals; 27g fat; 35g carbohydrate

Spicy Vegetable Stew

4tbsp sunflower oil
2.5cm (1 inch) piece
 fresh root ginger,
 peeled and grated
1tsp ground cinnamon
2tsp each ground
 coriander, ground
 cumin and ground
 turmeric
1kg (2¼lb) plum
 tomatoes, peeled,
 deseeded and flesh
 roughly chopped
2 bay leaves
8 cloves, crushed
750ml (1¼ pints)
 vegetable stock
175g (6oz) ground
 almonds

salt and pepper
350g (12oz) carrots,
 peeled and cut into
 2.5cm (1 inch) pieces
1 cauliflower, about
 1kg (2¼lb), broken
 into small florets
350g (12oz) green
 beans, topped and
 halved
350g (12oz) young
 courgettes, cut into
 5cm (2 inch) lengths
 and sliced into
 quarters
142ml carton double
 cream
coriander sprigs, to
 garnish

1 Heat the oil in a large casserole, add the ginger and all the spices and fry for 1–2 minutes or until the spices release their aroma.
2 Add the tomatoes and cook over a high heat until the tomatoes are soft and pulpy – about 10 minutes. Add the bay leaves, cloves, stock and ground almonds to the pan, then season well. Bring to the boil, add the carrots and cook for 5 minutes. Add the cauliflower and cook for 5–7 minutes.
3 Meanwhile, bring a large pan of cold water to the boil. Add the green beans, bring back to the boil, then add the courgettes. Bring back to the boil again, then drain thoroughly.
4 Add the beans, courgettes and cream to the pan. Bring to the boil, then reduce the heat and simmer for 5 minutes to heat through. Spoon into a warmed dish and garnish with coriander to serve.

Serves 10
Preparation: 40 minutes
Cooking time: 35 minutes
Per serving: 290 cals; 23g fat; 11g carbohydrate

Courgette Puff Pie

450g (1lb) courgettes,
 trimmed and sliced
3tbsp olive oil
375g pack ready-rolled
 puff pastry
flour, to dust
2 eggs
2tbsp crème fraîche
75g (3oz) Gruyère
 cheese, grated

2 garlic cloves, peeled
 and crushed
4tbsp chopped flat-
 leafed parsley
salt and pepper
50g (2oz) fresh white
 breadcrumbs

1 Preheat the oven to 200°C (180°C fan oven) mark 6. Put the courgettes on a large baking sheet and drizzle with the olive oil. Roast for 8 minutes, then transfer the courgettes to a sheet of greaseproof paper.
2 Roll out the pastry on a floured surface to a 30.5cm (12 inch) square. Lift on to the baking sheet.
3 Crack 1 egg into a bowl, add the crème fraîche and whisk lightly. Add 50g (2oz) of the cheese, along with the garlic and parsley. Season and mix until well combined.
4 Arrange the courgettes on top of the pastry, leaving a clear margin around the edge, and pour the egg and crème fraîche mixture over them. Scatter the breadcrumbs and remaining cheese over the filling.
5 Lift the pastry sides up and over the edge of the filling to create a thick pastry rim. Chill for 10 minutes. Beat the remaining egg and brush over the pastry. Bake for 30 minutes or until the pastry is crisp and golden brown.

Serves 4
Preparation: 25 minutes, plus resting
Cooking time: 40 minutes
Per serving: 650 cals; 47g fat; 43g carbohydrate

Top left: Couscous Stuffed Mushrooms, page 186; top right: Mixed Mushroom Cannelloni, page 189; bottom left: Garlic Cheese Pizza, page 186; bottom right: Winter Roasted Vegetable Tart, page 193.

Spinach-baked Eggs with Mushrooms

3tbsp olive oil
125g (4oz) closed-cup
  chestnut mushrooms,
  quartered
225g bag baby spinach
  leaves

salt and pepper
2 large eggs
4tbsp double cream

1 Preheat the oven to 200°C (180°C fan oven) mark 6. Heat the olive oil in a large frying pan, add the mushrooms and stir-fry for 30 seconds, then add the spinach and stir-fry until wilted. Season well and divide between two 600ml (1 pint) ovenproof dishes.
2 Carefully break an egg into the centre of each dish and spoon the double cream over the top. Season well.
3 Cook for about 12 minutes, or until the eggs are just set. (Remember that they will continue to cook a little once they're out of the oven.) Serve immediately.

Serves 2
Preparation time: 5 minutes
Cooking time: 13 minutes
Per serving: 440 cals; 42g fat; 35g carbohydrate

Soured Cream and Onion Tarts

700g (1½lb) tomatoes,
  halved
salt and pepper
1tbsp chopped thyme
  or ½tsp dried
2tbsp olive oil
200g (7oz) chilled
  butter
175g (6oz) plain flour,
  plus extra to dust

6–7tbsp soured cream
900g (2lb) onions,
  peeled and finely
  sliced
125g (4oz) Roquefort
  cheese
thyme sprigs, to
  garnish

1 Preheat the oven to 170°C (150°C fan oven) mark 3. Put the tomatoes on a baking sheet, season, sprinkle with the thyme, drizzle with the olive oil and cook, uncovered, in the oven for 40 minutes until slightly shrivelled.
2 Meanwhile, cut 150g (5oz) butter into small dice and put in a food processor with the flour. Pulse until the butter is roughly cut up through the flour (you should still be able to see pieces of butter), then add the soured cream and pulse again for 2–3 seconds until the dough is just mixed.

3 Turn the dough out on to a lightly floured surface, cut into six and roll each piece thinly into a 12.5cm (5 inch) round. Put on two baking sheets, cover and chill for 30 minutes.
4 Melt the remaining butter in a pan, add the onions and cook slowly for about 15 minutes until very soft. Increase the heat and fry the onions for 3–4 minutes or until well browned and caramelised. Take off the heat and cool.
5 Spoon the onions into the centre of the pastry circles, leaving a 1cm (½ inch) edge. Crumble the cheese on top and add the tomatoes. Season, then roughly fold up the pastry edge.
6 Increase the oven temperature to 200°C (180°C fan oven) mark 6, and cook the tarts for 30 minutes until golden. Garnish with thyme sprigs and serve immediately.

Serves 6
Preparation: 20 minutes, plus chilling
Cooking time: about 1 hour
Per serving: 570 cals; 42g fat; 39g carbohydrate

Roasted Vegetable and Rocket Tartlets

375g pack ready-rolled
  puff pastry
plain flour, to dust
1 egg, beaten
2tbsp coarse sea salt
300g (11oz) vegetable
  antipasti in olive oil
  (mixed roasted
  peppers, artichokes,
  onions)

a little olive oil, if
  needed
2tbsp balsamic vinegar
salt and pepper
190g tub red pepper
  hummus
50g bag wild rocket

1 Preheat the oven to 220°C (200°C fan oven) mark 7. Unroll the puff pastry on a lightly floured surface and cut it into six equal-sized squares.
2 Put the pastry squares on a large baking sheet and prick each one all over with a fork. Brush all over with beaten egg and sprinkle the edges with sea salt. Bake for 5–7 minutes or until the pastry is golden brown and cooked through.
3 To make the dressing, pour off 1tbsp olive oil from the antipasti (you may need to add a little extra olive oil) into a bowl. Add the vinegar, season well, then put to one side.
4 To serve, divide the hummus among the pastry bases, spreading it over each. Put a tartlet on each plate and spoon over the antipasti – there's no need to be neat.
5 Whisk the dressing again. Add the rocket and toss to coat, then pile a small handful of leaves on top of each tartlet. Serve immediately.

Serves 6
Preparation: 10 minutes
Cooking time: 5–7 minutes
Per serving: 340 cals; 23g fat; 27g carbohydrate

See picture, page 207

Tomato and Butter Bean Stew

2tbsp olive oil
1 onion, peeled and
  finely sliced
2 garlic cloves, peeled
  and finely chopped
2 large leeks, sliced
2 x 400g cans cherry
  tomatoes

2 x 400g cans butter
  beans, drained and
  rinsed
150ml (¼ pint) hot
  vegetable stock
salt and pepper
1–2tbsp balsamic
  vinegar

1 Preheat the oven to 180°C (160°C fan oven) mark 4. Heat the olive oil in a flameproof casserole on the hob over a medium heat. Add the onion and garlic and cook for 10 minutes until golden and softened. Add the leeks and cook, covered, for 5 minutes. Add the tomatoes, beans and hot stock and season well. Bring to the boil, then cover and cook in the oven for 35–40 minutes until the sauce has thickened. Remove from the oven, stir in the vinegar and spoon into warmed bowls.

Serves 4
Preparation: 10 minutes
Cooking time: 50–55 minutes
Per serving: 280 cals; 8g fat; 39g carbohydrate

Mixed Vegetable Tempura

1.8 litres (3¼ pints)
vegetable oil
150g pack tempura mix
330ml bottle Japanese
lager (or a substitute
lager)
40g (1½oz) sesame
seeds
1tsp salt
150g (5oz) sweet
potato, peeled and
cut into fine
matchsticks

1 onion, peeled and cut
into wedges
150g (5oz) baby leeks,
cut into 5cm (2 inch)
pieces
1 red pepper, deseeded
and cut into
12 wedges
200g (7oz) fine green
beans, trimmed
Thai sweet chilli
dipping sauce, to
serve

1 Preheat the oven to 110°C (90°C fan oven) mark ¼.
Heat the oil in a deep-fat fryer on the chip setting or until
190°C. Put the tempura mix into a bowl and gradually
whisk in the lager to make a smooth batter. Add the
sesame seeds and salt.

2 Drop six pieces of vegetable into the tempura batter to
coat, then, using a draining spoon, lower into the hot
oil. Cook for 3 minutes until golden and puffy, drain on
kitchen paper, then keep warm in the oven. Repeat
with the remaining vegetables. Serve with a bowl of
chilli dipping sauce.

Serves 6
Preparation: 10 minutes
Cooking time: 15 minutes
Per serving: 240 cals; 9g fat; 33g carbohydrate

Cheap and Cheerful Vegetable Curry

3tbsp vegetable oil
1 onion, peeled and
finely sliced
2 garlic cloves, peeled
and crushed
2tbsp Balti curry paste
2 medium potatoes,
about 225g (8oz),
peeled and cut into
small cubes
1 small cauliflower, cut
into large florets,
smaller leaves
roughly torn and
reserved

2 medium carrots,
about 175g (6oz),
peeled and cut into
small cubes
1 vegetable stock cube
400g can chopped
tomatoes (optional)
salt and pepper
75g (3oz) frozen peas
(optional)

1 Heat the oil in a large heavy-based pan and add the
onion. Fry over a medium heat for 10–15 minutes until
golden. Add the garlic, cook for 30 seconds, then add
the curry paste and cook for 1 minute, stirring regularly.

2 Add the potatoes and cauliflower florets and fry, stirring
to coat in the oil, for 2 minutes. Add the carrots and cook
for 1 minute. Pour 600ml (1 pint) boiling water into a jug
and crumble in the stock cube. Add the stock to the
vegetables with the tomatoes, if using. Season well.

3 Cover and simmer for 10 minutes until the vegetables
are almost tender. Add the peas, if using, and cook for
2 minutes. Add the cauliflower leaves and cook for 30
seconds. Serve with bread, rice or on its own.

Serves 4
Preparation: 20 minutes
Cooking time: 35 minutes
Per serving: 230 cals; 12g fat; 24g carbohydrate

*Top left: Roasted Vegetable and Rocket Tartlets, page 197; top
right: Mixed Vegetable Tempura, page 206; bottom left: Smoked
Sesame Tofu, page 203; bottom right: Roasted Vegetable Salad
with Mustard Mayonnaise, page 213.*

No cook

Sometimes you just can't be bothered to cook. It's too hot, you're tired, short of time, or just want something light.

Crunchy, refreshing salads are the obvious answer, whether fruit-, fish-, meat- or cheese-based; with vegetables; or just green leaves – such as Crisp Green Salad with Blue Cheese Dressing, pairing crisp salad leaves with a Roquefort dressing and croûtons.

Fennel is great either cooked or raw – in Fennel Salad its lovely aniseed flavour works brilliantly with just a simple walnut oil and mustard dressing. Peppery watercress is another healthy salad choice – low in calories and rich in vitamins. Combined with pears and blue cheese it makes a salad bursting with flavour.

For something more substantial, grains, pulses and beans go really well with onions, herbs and a good dressing and are very quick to put together. Try a robust Bean, Celery and Chorizo Salad, or a Chickpea Salad with Lemon and Parsley. Dare to be different? Japanese Crab Salad looks fantastic and has a taste to match, while Thai Prawn Salad combines tiger prawns with chilli, ginger and sesame oil.

Fast food

You're hungry, you want food – and you want it now. Well, here are some solutions.

Stir-fries: yes, there's a bit of chopping involved, but buy a ready-prepared pack of vegetables and you're halfway there. The key to success is heat – whack up the heat under your wok or pan and keep the ingredients moving. Stir-fries can be as simple or as substantial as you feel like making them, from Chicken Stir-fry with Noodles – just eight ingredients, to Turkey and Broccoli Stir-fry, where beansprouts, mushrooms, spring onions and ginger are added to the main ingredients for a tasty quick meal.

Then there's nothing more satisfying than a plate of steaming hot pasta. Serve with a rich tomato sauce, such as Quick Tomato Sauce with Bacon, or indulge yourself with a bowl of penne and Smoked Salmon, Dill and Cream sauce. For something cheesy, try Walnut and Creamy Blue Cheese Tagliatelle – very moreish!

Or how about a Warm Spicy Chorizo Sausage and Chickpea Salad – warm salads are delicious. Try Chèvre en Croute; Egg and Pepper Pizza; or Flash-in-the-Pan Pork – pork escalopes, new potatoes and runner beans cooked in a creamy mustard and tarragon sauce and ready in 15 minutes.

Prawn and Pak Choi Stir-fry

2tsp sesame oil
1tbsp vegetable oil
1 medium onion,
   peeled and finely
   chopped
2 garlic cloves, peeled
   and finely chopped
2.5cm (1 inch) piece
   fresh root ginger,
   peeled and grated
1 small red chilli,
   deseeded
   and finely chopped
450g (1lb) peeled raw
   king
   prawns, deveined
200g (7oz) pak choi,
   roughly chopped
1–2tbsp teriyaki sauce

1 Heat both oils in a wok or large frying pan over a high heat. Add the onion, garlic, ginger and chilli and stir-fry for 3–4 minutes.
2 Add the prawns and cook for 2–3 minutes, stirring constantly, until they're cooked through and pink. Add the pak choi and teriyaki sauce, stir-fry for a further 2 minutes, then serve.

Serves 4
Preparation: 10 minutes
Cooking time: 7–9 minutes
Per serving: 170 cals; 7g fat; 6g carbohydrate

Stir-fry with Tofu

200g pack fresh tofu,
   cubed
4tbsp sweet chilli
   sauce
2tbsp light soy sauce
1tbsp sesame seeds
2tbsp toasted sesame
   oil
2 x 300g packs stir-fry
   vegetables

1 Put the tofu in a shallow container, pour over 1tbsp each sweet chilli sauce and light soy sauce, cover and marinate for 10 minutes.
2 Meanwhile, dry-fry the sesame seeds in a hot wok until golden. Remove and put to one side.
3 Add 1tbsp oil to the wok, add the marinated tofu and stir-fry for 5 minutes until golden. Remove and put to one side.
4 Heat the remaining oil in the wok, add the vegetables and stir-fry for 3–4 minutes. Stir in the cooked tofu.
5 Pour the remaining sweet chilli sauce and soy sauce over, then toss together and cook for 1 minute to heat through. Sprinkle with the sesame seeds and serve.

Serves 4
Preparation: 5 minutes, plus marinating
Cooking time: 12 minutes
Per serving: 170 cals; 11g fat; 10g carbohydrate

See picture, page 246

Stir-fried Prawns with Cabbage and Mangetout

225g (8oz) pak choi or
   Chinese
   mustard cabbage
2tbsp vegetable oil
2 garlic cloves, peeled
   and thinly sliced
1 lemon grass stalk,
   cut in half and bruised
2 kaffir lime leaves,
   torn into small pieces
1 small red onion,
   peeled and thinly
   sliced
1 hot red chilli,
   deseeded and thinly
   sliced
4cm (1½ inch) piece
   fresh root ginger,
   peeled and cut into
   long thin shreds
1tbsp coriander seeds,
   lightly crushed
450g (1lb) large peeled
   raw prawns, deveined
175g (6oz) mangetout,
   halved diagonally
2tbsp Thai fish sauce
   (*nam pla*)
juice of 1 lime, or to
   taste
fried sliced red chilli,
   deseeded, to garnish

1 Trim the pak choi or cabbage, discarding any damaged or discoloured leaves. Tear the leaves into manageable-sized pieces.

2 Heat the oil in a wok or large frying pan. Add the garlic, lemon grass, lime leaves, onion, chilli, ginger and coriander seeds and stir-fry for 2 minutes. Add the prawns, mangetout and pak choi or cabbage and stir-fry until the vegetables are cooked but still crisp and the prawns are pink and opaque, about 2–3 minutes.
3 Add the fish sauce and lime juice and heat through for 1 minute. Discard the lemon grass. Garnish with sliced red chilli and serve immediately while the vegetables are crisp.

Serves 4
Preparation: 30 minutes
Cooking time: 6 minutes
Per serving: 200 cals; 8g fat; 9g carbohydrate

See picture, page 246

Sweet Chilli Prawn Stir-Fry

1tbsp sesame oil
175g (6oz) peeled raw
  tiger prawns,
  deveined
220g pack green
  vegetable stir-fry,
  containing Swiss
  chard, courgettes,
  broccoli, green beans

60ml pack sweet chilli
  and ginger sauce

1 Heat the oil in a large wok, add the prawns and stir-fry
   for 2 minutes.
2 Add the courgettes, broccoli and green beans from
   the vegetable pack and stir-fry for 2–3 minutes.
3 Add the Swiss chard and the chilli and ginger sauce and
   cook for 1–2 minutes to heat through, then serve
   immediately.

Serves 2
Preparation: 2 minutes
Cooking time: 7 minutes
Per serving: 170 cals; 8g fat; 4g carbohydrate

Turkey and Broccoli Stir-fry

2tbsp vegetable or
  sunflower oil
500g (1lb 2oz) turkey
  fillet, cut in strips
2 garlic cloves, peeled
  and crushed
2.5cm (1 inch) piece
  fresh root ginger,
  peeled and grated
1 broccoli head,
  chopped into florets

8 spring onions, finely
  chopped
125g (4oz) button
  mushrooms, halved
100g (3½oz)
  beansprouts
3tbsp oyster sauce
1tbsp light soy sauce
125ml (4fl oz) hot
  chicken stock
juice of ½ lemon

1 Heat 1tbsp oil in a large non-stick frying pan or wok
   and stir-fry the turkey strips over a medium-high heat
   for 4–5 minutes until golden and cooked through.
   Remove from the pan and put to one side.
2 Heat the remaining oil in the same pan over a medium
   heat, then cook the garlic and ginger for 30 seconds,
   stirring all the time so they don't burn. Add the broccoli,
   spring onions and mushrooms, increase the heat and
   cook for 2–3 minutes until the vegetables start to
   brown but are still crisp.

3 Return the turkey to the pan and add the beansprouts,
   sauces, hot stock and lemon juice. Cook for 1–2
   minutes, tossing well to heat everything through, then
   serve.

Serves 4
Preparation: 15 minutes
Cooking time: 7–11 minutes
Per serving: 240 cals; 9g fat; 5g carbohydrate

See picture, page 246

Pork and Noodle Stir-fry

1tbsp sesame oil
5cm (2 inch) piece
  fresh root ginger,
  peeled and grated
2tbsp soy sauce
1tbsp fish sauce
½ red chilli, finely
  chopped
450g (1lb) stir-fry pork
  strips
2 red peppers, halved,
  deseeded and roughly
  chopped

250g (9oz) baby
  sweetcorn, halved
  lengthways
200g (7oz) sugarsnap
  peas, halved
300g (11oz)
  beansprouts
250g pack rice noodles

1 Put the oil into a large bowl. Add the ginger, soy sauce, fish sauce, chilli and pork strips. Mix well and leave to marinate for 10 minutes.
2 Heat a large wok until hot. Lift the pork out of the marinade with a slotted spoon, add to the pan and stir-fry over a high heat for 5 minutes. Add the red peppers, sweetcorn, sugarsnap peas, beansprouts and remaining marinade and stir-fry for a further 2–3 minutes until the pork is cooked.
3 Meanwhile, cook the noodles in a large pan of boiling water for the time stated on the pack. Drain the noodles, tip into the wok and toss together, then serve immediately.

Serves 4
Preparation: 10 minutes, plus marinating
Cooking time: 7–8 minutes
Per serving: 500 cals; 12g fat; 62g carbohydrate

See picture, page 246

Turkey and Sesame Stir-fry with Noodles

300g pack stir-fry
  turkey strips
3tbsp teriyaki marinade
3tbsp runny honey
500g pack egg noodles

1tbsp sesame oil, plus
  extra for the noodles
2tbsp sesame seeds
300g pack stir-fry
  vegetables

1 Put the turkey strips in a large glass bowl with the teriyaki marinade and honey and stir to coat. Cover and leave for 5 minutes to allow the flavours to soak in.
2 Cook the noodles in a large pan of boiling water according to the time stated on the packet. Drain well, then toss in a little oil.
3 Meanwhile, toast the sesame seeds in a dry wok over a medium heat, stirring until they turn golden. Tip on to a plate.
4 Heat 1tbsp oil in the same wok and add the turkey, reserving the marinade. Stir-fry on a very high heat for 2–3 minutes until cooked through and beginning to brown.
5 Add a drop more oil, if needed, then add the vegetables and leftover marinade. Continue to cook over a high heat, stirring, until the vegetables have started to soften and the sauce is warmed through.
6 Scatter with the sesame seeds and serve immediately with the drained egg noodles.

Serves 4
Preparation: 5 minutes
Cooking time: 10 minutes
Per serving: 660 cals; 15g fat; 100g carbohydrate

Chicken Stir-fry with Noodles

250g pack thick egg
  noodles
2tbsp vegetable oil
2 garlic cloves, peeled
  and crushed
4 skinless boneless
  chicken breasts, each
  sliced into 10 pieces
3 medium carrots, cut
  into thin strips, about
  5cm (2 inches) long

1 bunch of spring
  onions, sliced
200g (7oz) mangetout,
  ends trimmed
155g jar sweet chilli
  and lemon grass
  sauce

1 Cook the noodles in plenty of boiling water for the time
  stated on the packet.
2 Meanwhile, heat the oil in a wok or frying pan, then
  add the garlic and stir-fry for 1–2 minutes. Add the
  chicken pieces and stir-fry for 5 minutes, then add the
  carrot strips and stir-fry for a further 5 minutes. Add
  the spring onions, mangetout and sauce to the wok
  and stir-fry for 5 minutes.

3 Drain the cooked noodles well and add to the wok.
  Toss everything together and serve.

Serves 4   Preparation: 20 minutes
Cooking time: 20 minutes
Per serving: 540 cals; 14g fat; 70g carbohydrate

Stir-fried Pork with Chinese Greens

350g (12oz) stir-fry
  pork strips
4tbsp rice wine or dry
  sherry
2tbsp soy sauce
3tbsp stir-fry oil

450g (1lb) Chinese
  greens
2 x 300g packs stir-fry
  vegetables
about 1tbsp Chinese
  five-spice paste

1 Toss the pork with the rice wine or sherry, the soy
  sauce and 1tbsp oil (if you have time, leave the pork to
  marinate for 1 hour at this stage). Shred the Chinese
  greens and, together with the stir-fry vegetables, rinse
  in cold water.
2 Using a slotted spoon, lift the pork from the marinade;
  reserve the marinade. Heat a wok or large deep frying
  pan until very hot. Add 1tbsp oil to the wok, add half
  the pork – cook it in batches to ensure it fries and seals
  quickly – and stir-fry for about 1 minute or until
  beginning to brown at the edges. Put to one side and
  stir-fry the remaining pork.

3 Wipe out the wok, add the remaining oil and heat. Add
  the five-spice paste and all the vegetables and fry for
  a further 3–4 minutes. Return the pork and reserved
  marinade to the wok, bring to the boil and bubble for
  1–2 minutes. Serve immediately.

Serves 6
Preparation: 5 minutes
Cooking time: 10 minutes
Per serving: 200 cals; 11g fat; 7g carbohydrate

Sweet Chilli Beef Stir-fry

1tsp chilli oil

1tbsp each soy sauce
and runny honey

1 garlic clove, peeled
and crushed

1 large red chilli,
halved, deseeded and
chopped

400g (14oz) lean beef,
cut into strips

1tsp sunflower oil

1 broccoli head,
shredded

200g (7oz) mangetout,
halved

1 red pepper, halved,
deseeded and cut into
strips

1 Put the chilli oil in a medium-sized shallow bowl. Add the soy sauce, honey, garlic and chilli and stir well. Add the beef strips and toss in the marinade.

2 Heat the sunflower oil in a wok over a high heat until very hot. Cook the beef strips in two batches, then remove them from the pan and put to one side. Wipe the pan with kitchen paper to remove any residue.

3 Add the broccoli, mangetout, red pepper and 2tbsp water to the pan. Stir-fry for 5–6 minutes until starting to soften. Return the beef to the pan to heat through, then serve.

Serves 4
Preparation: 10 minutes
Cooking time: 10–11 minutes
Per serving: 200 cals; 7g fat; 8g carbohydrate

Fast food

Top left: Stir-fry with Tofu, page 242; top right: Pork and Noodle Stir-fry, page 244; bottom left: Turkey and Broccoli Stir-fry, page 243; bottom right: Stir-fried Prawns with Cabbage and Mangetout, page 242.

Quick Sauces for Pasta

How much pasta do I need?

Allow 75g (3oz) dried pasta shapes or noodles or 125g (4oz) fresh or filled pasta shapes per person. Cook the pasta until al dente – the pasta should have a slight bite. Follow the timings on the packet and start testing 1 minute before the recommended time. The pasta will continue to cook a little after draining.

Quick Tomato Sauce

1tbsp vegetable oil
1 small onion, peeled and finely chopped
1 garlic clove, peeled and chopped

400g can chopped tomatoes, can reserved
salt and pepper

1 Heat the oil in a medium pan for 30 seconds, then add the onion and cook over a very gentle heat for 15 minutes, stirring regularly until the onion is softened and translucent, but not browned. Add the garlic and continue to cook gently for 1 minute.
2 Add the tomatoes and stir well. Fill the empty tomato can up to about halfway with cold water and give it a swirl to catch any tomato juice, then add to the pan. Season the tomato sauce generously, then increase the heat to medium and leave the sauce to simmer for about 15 minutes until slightly thickened.

Serves 4
Preparation: 10 minutes
Cooking time: 35 minutes
Per serving: 60 cals; 3g fat; 6g carbohydrate

Variations on Quick Tomato Sauce

Quick Tomato Sauce with Bacon: Chop 2 rindless streaky bacon rashers and add to the pan with the onion at step 1. Cook for 10–15 minutes until the bacon is browned. Add the tomatoes and complete the recipe.
Serves 4
Preparation: 10 minutes
Cooking time: 35 minutes
Per serving: 110 cals; 8g fat; 6g carbohydrate

Quick Tomato Sauce with Red Pepper and Olives: Add 1 deseeded and sliced red pepper to the pan with the onion at step 1. At the end of step 2, when the tomato sauce has finished simmering, add 6 pitted, chopped olives and cook for 1–2 minutes to heat through.
Serves 4
Preparation: 15 minutes
Cooking time: 37 minutes
Per serving: 70 cals; 4g fat; 8g carbohydrate

Quick Tomato Sauce with Tuna: Drain an 80g can of tuna in oil or brine (you can use some of the oil to cook the onion in step 1). At the end of step 2, when the tomato sauce has thickened and finished simmering, stir in the tuna and cook for 2–3 minutes to warm through. Toss with the pasta.
Serves 4
Preparation: 10 minutes
Cooking time: 38 minutes
Per serving: 80 cals; 4g fat; 6g carbohydrate

Tomato, Prawn and Garlic Sauce

350g (12oz) cooked
  peeled prawns
4tbsp sun-dried tomato
  paste
1tbsp olive oil
15g (½oz) butter
3 garlic cloves, peeled
  and sliced

4 large tomatoes,
  about 400g (14oz),
  chopped
125ml (4fl oz) white
  wine
20g pack flat-leafed
  parsley,
  roughly chopped

1 Put the prawns in a bowl with the tomato paste and stir well.
2 Heat the olive oil and butter in a frying pan and gently cook the garlic until golden. Add the tomatoes and wine. Leave the sauce to bubble for about 5 minutes, then stir in the prawns and parsley. Stir through drained, cooked tagliatelle.

Serves 4
Preparation: 10 minutes
Cooking time: 10 minutes
Per serving (sauce only): 190 cals; 8g fat; 5g carbohydrate

Lemon and Parmesan Sauce

salt and pepper
125g (4oz) frozen petit
  pois
zest and juice of
  ½ lemon

75g (3oz) fr
  Parmesan

1 Cook conchiglioni pasta in a large pan of boiling salted water for the time stated on the packet. Add the petit pois to the pasta water for the last 5 minutes of the cooking time.
2 Drain the pasta and peas, put back in the pan and add the lemon zest and juice and Parmesan. Season with plenty of pepper, toss and serve immediately.

Serves 4
Preparation: 5 minutes
Cooking time: 12 minutes
Per serving (sauce only): 100 cals; 6g fat; 3g carbohydrate

Cherry Tomato Vinaigrette

1tbsp olive oil
2 x 250g packs cherry
  tomatoes
salt and pepper

1tbsp balsamic vinegar
pinch of sugar
20g pack basil, roughly
  chopped

1 Heat the olive oil in a large frying pan and add the tomatoes. Season generously and leave to simmer gently for 5 minutes.
2 Add the vinegar, a pinch of sugar and the basil and cook for 1–2 minutes, then stir through drained, cooked penne.

Serves 4
Preparation: 5 minutes
Cooking time: 7 minutes
Per serving (sauce only): 60 cals; 4g fat; 5g carbohydrate

Wine and Mushroom Sauce

1tbsp olive oil
1 onion, peeled and
  finely chopped
300g (11oz)
  mushrooms, sliced
125ml (4fl oz) white
  wine

500ml carton low-fat
  crème fraîche
2tbsp chopped
  tarragon

1 Put the olive oil in a large pan and fry the onion for 7–10 minutes until soft. Add the mushrooms and cook for 3–4 minutes.
2 Pour in the wine and bubble for 1 minute, then stir in the crème fraîche. Heat until bubbling, then stir in the tarragon and stir through drained, cooked pappardelle.

Serves 4
Preparation: 5 minutes
Cooking time: 12–16 minutes
Per serving (sauce only): 310 cals; 22g fat; 10g carbohydrate

rgette and Anchovy Sauce

50g can anchovies
1 garlic clove, peeled and crushed

pinch of dried chilli
400ml (14fl oz) passata
2 courgettes, diced

1 Gently heat the oil from the anchovies in a frying pan. Add the garlic and chilli and cook for 1 minute.
2 Add the passata, courgettes and anchovies. Bring to the boil, then reduce the heat and simmer for about 10 minutes, stirring well, until the anchovies have melted. Stir through drained, cooked penne.

Serves 4
Preparation: 5 minutes
Cooking time: 15 minutes
Per serving (sauce only): 60 cals; 3g fat; 4g carbohydrate

Smoked Salmon, Dill and Cream Sauce

200ml carton half-fat crème fraîche
140g pack smoked salmon, roughly chopped

20g pack dill, finely chopped
salt and pepper
lemon wedges, to serve

1 Put the crème fraîche into a large bowl and add the smoked salmon and dill. Season well and mix, then gently stir through drained, cooked penne and serve immediately with lemon wedges to squeeze over.

Serves 4
Preparation: 5 minutes
Per serving (sauce only): 140 cals; 9g fat; 2g carbohydrate

Tuna, Capers, Chilli and Olive Sauce

2tbsp olive oil
2 garlic cloves, peeled and sliced
1 red chilli, deseeded and chopped
2 x 200g cans tuna, drained

50g (2oz) pitted black olives, chopped
2tbsp capers
juice of ½ lemon
salt and pepper
4tbsp chopped flat-leafed parsley

1 Heat the olive oil in a pan. Add the garlic and chilli and cook gently for 2 minutes, then add the tuna, olives, capers and lemon juice.
2 Season and heat through, then stir into drained, cooked linguine and scatter with the parsley.

Serves 4
Preparation: 5 minutes
Cooking time: 5 minutes
Per serving (sauce only): 150 cals; 8g fat; trace carbohydrate

Salmon and Broccoli Sauce

225g (8oz) salmon fillets
2tsp sesame oil
200g (7oz) cooked peeled king prawns
150g (5oz) mangetout
150g (5oz) purple sprouting broccoli, shredded

2tbsp teriyaki marinade
small handful of roughly chopped coriander

1 Preheat the grill to medium-high. Put the salmon on a baking sheet and grill for 4 minutes on each side.
2 Heat the oil in a wok and stir-fry the prawns, mangetout and broccoli for 3–4 minutes or until just tender.
3 Flake the salmon into the wok and add the teriyaki marinade. Warm through, stir into cooked pappardelle and serve scattered with coriander, if you like.

Serves 4
Preparation: 5 minutes
Cooking time: 10 minutes
Per serving (sauce only): 230 cals; 13g fat; 3g carbohydrate

Quick and Easy Carbonara

150g (5oz) smoked
  bacon rashers,
  chopped
1tbsp olive oil
2 large egg yolks
142ml carton double
  cream

50g (2oz) freshly grated
  Parmesan cheese
chopped flat-leafed
  parsley

1 Fry the bacon in the olive oil for 4–5 minutes. Add to drained, cooked pasta, such as tagliatelle and keep hot.
2 Put the egg yolks in a bowl, add the cream and whisk together. Add to the pasta with the Parmesan and some parsley and toss well.

Serves 4
Preparation: 5 minutes
Cooking time: 5 minutes
Per serving (sauce only): 440 cals; 42g fat;
1g carbohydrate

See picture, page 252

Simple Salmon Pasta

500g pack dried
  linguine pasta
salt and pepper
a little olive oil
1 fat garlic clove,
  peeled and crushed

200ml carton ha
  crème fraîche
225g (8oz) hot-smoked
  salmon, flaked
200g (7oz) peas
two handfuls of basil,
  roughly torn

1 Cook the pasta in a large pan of boiling salted water for the time stated on the packet, then drain, reserving a couple of tablespoons of the cooking water.
2 Meanwhile, heat the olive oil in a large pan, add the garlic and fry gently until golden. Add the crème fraîche, the flaked salmon and peas and stir in. Cook for 1–2 minutes until warmed through, then add the reserved water from the pasta – this stops the pasta absorbing too much of the crème fraîche.
3 Toss the pasta into the sauce, season well and serve garnished with the torn basil.

Serves 4
Preparation: 2 minutes
Cooking time: 8 minutes
Per serving: 680 cals; 19g fat; 100g carbohydrate

See picture, page 252

Spaghetti with Lemon and Nut Butter

50g (2oz) butter
75g (3oz) toasted
  hazelnuts, roughly
  chopped
6 garlic cloves, peeled
  and thinly sliced
grated zest and juice of
  2 lemons
450g (1lb) fresh
  spaghetti or 225g
  (8oz) dried

salt and pepper
4tbsp each chopped
  basil and flat-leafed
  parsley
2tbsp single cream
  (optional)

1 Melt the butter in a medium-sized pan until it turns a pale golden brown. Add the hazelnuts and garlic and fry for about 30 seconds. Add the lemon zest and put to one side.

2 Cook the pasta in a large pan of boiling salted water for the time stated on the packet. Drain well, add to the butter mixture and stir over a low heat for 2–3 minutes. Stir in the herbs, 4tbsp lemon juice and the cream, if using. Season generously and serve immediately.

Serves 4
Preparation: 10 minutes
Cooking time: 15 minutes
Per serving (fresh pasta): 500 cals; 23g fat;
60g carbohydrate
Per serving (dried pasta): 370 cals; 19g fat;
44g carbohydrate

Sugarsnaps and Prosciutto Pasta Sauce

50g (2oz) pine nuts
150g (5oz) sugarsnap
  peas
125g (4oz) spinach

70g pack prosciutto,
  roughly torn
black pepper

1 Dry-fry the pine nuts in a frying pan until golden brown,
  then put to one side.
2 Cook conchiglioni pasta and add the sugarsnap peas
  to the water 4 minutes before the end of the cooking
  time.
3 Just before draining, add the spinach, then drain
  everything thoroughly and return to the pan. Add the
  pine nuts and prosciutto, season well with pepper and
  toss to mix.

Serves 4
Preparation: 5 minutes
Cooking time: 7 minutes
Per serving (sauce only): 150 cals; 11g fat;
3g carbohydrate

Pasta with Creamy Pesto Sauce

450g (1lb) fresh
  tagliatelle pasta
salt and pepper
5tbsp freshly grated
  Parmesan cheese
25g (1oz) pine nuts,
  toasted
200ml carton low-fat
  fromage frais

2 garlic cloves, peeled
40g (1½oz) torn basil
  leaves
40g (1½oz) roughly
  chopped flat-leafed
  parsley

1 Cook the pasta in a large pan of boiling salted water for
  the time stated on the packet, then drain.
2 Meanwhile, put the Parmesan, pine nuts, fromage frais
  and garlic into a food processor and whiz to a thick
  paste. Scrape into a bowl and season generously. Add
  the herbs and whiz for 2–3 seconds.
3 Stir the pesto sauce into the drained pasta, check the
  seasoning and serve.

Serves 4
Preparation: 8 minutes
Cooking time: 5 minutes
Per serving: 450 cals; 13g fat; 62g carbohydrate

Clam Spaghetti

450g (1lb) dried
  spaghetti or linguine
  pasta
salt and pepper
150ml (¼ pint) olive oil
3 garlic cloves, peeled
  and crushed
150ml (¼ pint) dry
  white wine

2 x 400g cans chopped
  tomatoes
squeeze of lemon juice
1.1kg (2½lb) clams,
  cleaned
chives, parsley and
  lemon wedges,
  to garnish

1 Cook the pasta in a pan of boiling salted water for the
  time stated on the packet. Drain and return to the pan
  with a little of the cooking liquid.
2 Meanwhile, heat the olive oil in a large heavy-based
  pan. Add the garlic and cook for 30 seconds. Add the
  wine and leave to bubble for 1 minute, then add the
  tomatoes and bubble for a further 2 minutes. Add the
  lemon juice and season.

3 Add the clams to the tomato sauce, cover and simmer
  for 1 minute or until the clams have opened up. Discard
  any clams that do not open. Toss the cooked pasta
  with the sauce and add a good grinding of black
  pepper. Garnish with chives, parsley and lemon
  wedges and serve.

Serves 4
Preparation: 10 minutes
Cooking time: 15 minutes
Per serving: 800 cals; 36g fat; 90g carbohydrate

*Top left: Roast Tomato Pasta, page 255; top right: Simple Salmon
Pasta, page 251; bottom left: Quick and Easy Carbonara, page 251;
bottom left: Pesto Cod and Beans; page 261.*

Courgette and Lemon Spaghetti

**350g (12oz) dried
spaghetti
salt and pepper
4tbsp olive oil
1–2 garlic cloves,
peeled and sliced
1 rosemary sprig
700g (1½lb) courgettes,
pared into ribbons**

**grated zest and juice of
1 large lemon
5tbsp double cream
50g (2oz) pine nuts,
toasted
zest of 1 lemon and
crushed black pepper,
to garnish**

1 Cook the pasta in a large pan of boiling salted water for the time stated on the packet, then drain.
2 Meanwhile, heat the olive oil in a large frying pan, add the garlic and rosemary and cook for 1–2 minutes. Remove from the heat and leave the oil to infuse for 5 minutes. Strain and reserve the oil and garlic, then discard the rosemary sprig.
3 Pour half the oil back into the pan, add half the courgettes and cook over a high heat for 1–2 minutes or until golden, then put to one side. Repeat with the remaining oil and courgettes. Wipe out the pan. Return the courgettes to the pan with the reserved garlic, the lemon zest, juice and cream and bring to the boil, then bubble for 1–2 minutes or until the sauce has thickened slightly. Season well.
4 Add the spaghetti to the courgette mixture, toss well together and heat through. Divide between bowls, sprinkle the pine nuts over and garnish with the lemon zest and black pepper to serve.

Serves 4
Preparation: 25 minutes
Cooking time: 20 minutes
Per serving: 620 cals; 33g fat; 69g carbohydrate

Pasta with Broccoli and Thyme

**500g pack dried
rigatoni pasta
salt and pepper
900g (2lb) tenderstem
broccoli, ends
trimmed, or 2 broccoli
heads, chopped into
florets and stalks
peeled and sliced**

**150ml (¼ pint) hot
vegetable stock
2 garlic cloves, peeled
and crushed
2tbsp olive oil
250g tub mascarpone
2tbsp chopped thyme
100g (3½oz) pecorino
cheese, grated**

1 Cook the pasta in a large pan of boiling salted water for the time stated on the packet. Drain well, reserving about a ladleful of the cooking water.
2 Meanwhile, make the sauce: put the broccoli in a pan with the hot stock. Bring to the boil, then cover the pan, reduce the heat and simmer for 3–4 minutes until tender – the stock should have evaporated.
3 Add the garlic and olive oil to the pan and cook for 1–2 minutes to soften the garlic. Add the mascarpone, thyme and pecorino and carefully mix.
4 Return the pasta to the pan, then add the broccoli sauce. Toss everything together, adding a little of the reserved cooking water if necessary, then season to taste and divide among four warmed pasta bowls and serve.

Serves 4
Preparation: 15 minutes
Cooking time: 15 minutes
Per serving: 950 cals; 48g fat; 100g carbohydrate

Spaghetti with Chilli and Garlic

400g (14oz) dried
  spaghetti
salt and pepper
5tbsp extra-virgin olive
  oil
1 red chilli, deseeded
  and finely chopped
1–2 garlic cloves,
  peeled and sliced

50g (2oz) Parmesan
  cheese, grated, plus
  extra to serve
handful of flat-leafed
  parsley, roughly
  chopped

1 Cook the pasta in plenty of boiling salted water for the
  time stated on the packet.
2 When the pasta is nearly cooked, heat the olive oil in
  a small pan, add the chilli and garlic and cook for
  1 minute.
3 Drain the pasta well, put back in the pan, then add the
  chilli and garlic oil, Parmesan and parsley. Season well
  and toss everything together. Spoon into bowls and
  serve with plenty of extra Parmesan grated over.

Serves 4
Preparation: 5 minutes
Cooking time: 10–12 minutes
Per serving: 550 cals; 22g fat; 74g carbohydrate

Walnut and Creamy Blue Cheese Tagliatelle

400g (14oz) dried
  tagliatelle pasta
salt and pepper
1tsp olive oil
1 garlic clove, peeled
  and crushed
25g (1oz) walnut
  pieces, toasted

100g (3½oz)
  Gorgonzola cheese,
  chopped into cubes
142ml carton single
  cream
50g (2oz) rocket

1 Cook the pasta in a large pan of boiling salted water for
  the time stated on the packet.
2 When the pasta is nearly cooked, heat the olive oil in a
  small pan, add the garlic and walnuts. Cook for 1 minute
  – the garlic should be just golden. Add the Gorgonzola
  and cream. Season with a little salt and plenty of pepper.
3 Drain the pasta well and return to the pan with a couple
  of spoonfuls of cooking water. Add the creamy sauce
  and the rocket, toss well and serve immediately.

Serves 4
Preparation: 5 minutes
Cooking time: 10–12 minutes
Per serving: 550 cals; 26g fat; 60g carbohydrate

Roast Tomato Pasta

400g (14oz) dried
  rigatoni pasta
salt and pepper
700g (1½lb) cherry
  tomatoes
few glugs of olive oil

50g (2oz) pine nuts
large handful of basil
  leaves, freshly torn
plenty of freshly grated
  Parmesan cheese, to
  serve

1 Preheat the oven to 240°C (220°C fan oven) mark 9.
  Cook the pasta in a large pan of boiling salted water for
  the time stated on the packet
2 Meanwhile, cut half the tomatoes in two and arrange
  them in a large roasting tin, cut side up. Add the
  remaining tomatoes, drizzle them with olive oil and
  season. Put the pine nuts on a separate roasting tray
  and roast both for 15 minutes until the tomatoes are
  softened and lightly caramelised.

3 Drain the pasta well and add to the roasting tin when
  the tomatoes are done. Scatter over the pine nuts and
  basil, then stir thoroughly so the pasta gets coated in
  all the juices. Taste and season again, if necessary,
  then stir in an extra glug or two of oil if the pasta needs
  it. Serve sprinkled with a generous amount of
  Parmesan.

Serves 4
Preparation: 5 minutes
Cooking time: 15 minutes
Per serving: 560 cals; 19g fat; 80g carbohydrate

See picture, page 252

Smoky Bacon and Tomato

	20g pack flat-leafed parsley, very roughly chopped
chopped	125g (4oz) full-flavoured melting cheese such as dolcelatte, Gorgonzola, Taleggio or Camembert, cut into rough chunks
450g (1lb) vine-ripened tomatoes, roughly chopped	

1   Cook the pasta in plenty of boiling salted water for the time stated on the packet.
2   Meanwhile, stir-fry the bacon in a non-stick frying pan over a high heat until the fat begins to run and the bacon turns golden. Remove with a slotted spoon.
3   Add the tomatoes to the bacon fat in the pan and continue to stir over the heat until they just begin to soften and break up at the edges.
4   Drain the pasta well, then toss with the bacon, tomatoes and chopped parsley. Season with plenty of pepper.
5   Stir the chopped cheese into the pasta just before serving so it begins to melt in the heat of the pan.

Serves 4
Preparation: 10 minutes
Cooking time: 15 minutes
Per serving: 670 cals; 34g fat; 68g carbohydrate

Pasta with Leeks, Pancetta and Mushrooms

450g (1lb) dried conchiglie pasta	225g (8oz) chestnut mushrooms, sliced
salt and pepper	1 garlic clove, peeled and crushed
50g (2oz) butter	
125g (4oz) pancetta, diced	150g pack soft herb cream cheese
2 medium leeks, thickly sliced	

1   Cook the pasta in a large pan of boiling salted water for the time stated on the packet, then drain.
2   Meanwhile, melt the butter in a pan and add the pancetta, leeks, mushrooms and garlic. Cook over a medium heat for 5–10 minutes until the leeks are tender. Reduce the heat, add the herb cheese and season well. Add the pasta to the sauce, toss and serve.

Serves 4
Preparation: 5 minutes
Cooking time: 15–20 minutes
Per serving: 790 cals; 43g fat; 85g carbohydrate

Penne with Leeks and Salami

**400g (14oz) dried
  penne pasta
salt and pepper
150g (5oz) salami, cut
  into cubes
2 medium leeks, sliced
1 garlic clove, peeled
  and crushed**

**1tbsp olive oil
100ml (3½fl oz) crème
  fraîche
handful of flat-leafed
  parsley, chopped
freshly grated
  Parmesan cheese, to
  serve**

1 Cook the pasta in a large pan of boiling salted water for the time stated on the packet.
2 Meanwhile, heat a non-stick pan over a medium heat and fry the salami for 2–3 minutes. There's no need for oil at this point – the heat will release the fat from the meat. Add the leeks and garlic to the pan with the olive oil and toss to coat. Reduce the heat to low, cover the pan and cook for 10 minutes or until the leeks are soft and translucent.

3 Add the crème fraîche to the pan and season well. Continue to cook on the lowest heat until the sauce is warmed through.
4 Drain the pasta, reserving a little of the cooking water. Tip the pasta back into the pan with the sauce, the parsley and a splash of the reserved water. Toss well to coat. Serve with plenty of grated Parmesan.

Serves 4
Preparation: 5 minutes
Cooking time: 15 minutes
Per serving: 720 cals; 36g fat; 78g carbohydrate

Spicy Mushroom Pasta

**1tbsp olive oil
1 onion, peeled and
  finely chopped
1 garlic clove, peeled
  and crushed
250g (9oz) chestnut
  mushrooms, sliced
65g pack pancetta,
  diced
1 red chilli, sliced**

**1tbsp tomato purée
400g can chopped
  tomatoes
  in rich tomato juice
salt and pepper
500g pack dried penne
  pasta
2tbsp basil leaves,
  freshly torn**

1 Heat the olive oil in a pan, add the onion, garlic, mushrooms, pancetta and chilli and cook over a medium heat for about 10 minutes until soft. Add the tomato purée and cook for 1 minute. Stir in the tomatoes, season well and simmer for 25 minutes.

2 Cook the pasta in boiling salted water for the time stated on the packet. Drain, reserving a little of the water and return the pasta to the pan. Add the basil leaves to the tomato sauce, then toss through the cooked penne, adding a little reserved pasta water if necessary, and serve.

Serves 4
Preparation: 10 minutes
Cooking time: 35 minutes
Per serving: 570 cals; 12g fat; 100g carbohydrate

Speedy Macaroni Cheese

225g (8oz) short-cut
  macaroni
salt and pepper
50g (2oz) butter or
  margarine
50g (2oz) plain flour
900ml (1½ pints) milk
½ tsp grated nutmeg
  or mustard powder

225g (8oz) mature
  Cheddar cheese,
  grated
3 tbsp fresh white or
  wholemeal bread-
  crumbs

1 Cook the macaroni in a large pan of boiling salted water until *al dente*.
2 Meanwhile, melt the butter in a pan, stir in the flour and cook, stirring, for 1 minute. Remove from the heat and gradually stir in the milk. Bring to the boil and cook, stirring, until the sauce thickens. Remove from the heat. Season with salt and pepper, and add the nutmeg or mustard.

3 Drain the macaroni and add to the sauce, together with three quarters of the cheese. Mix well, then turn into an ovenproof dish.
4 Preheat the grill to high. Sprinkle the breadcrumbs and remaining cheese over the macaroni. Put under the grill for 2–3 minutes until golden brown on top and bubbling. Serve immediately.

Serves 4–6
Preparation: 10 minutes
Cooking time: 15 minutes
Per serving: 680–460 cals; 34–23g fat; 67–45g carbohydrate

Asparagus and Cheese Pasta

225g (8oz) wide-ribbon
  dried pasta, such as
  pappardelle
salt and pepper
350g (12oz) asparagus
  or French beans
175g (6oz) leeks, cut
  into fine shreds
284ml carton single
  cream

75g (3oz) mature
  Cheddar cheese,
  grated
25g (1oz) freshly grated
  Parmesan cheese
125g (4oz) thinly sliced
  cooked smoked ham,
  roughly chopped

1 Cook the pasta in a large pan of boiling salted water until just tender, then drain.
2 Meanwhile, cook the asparagus or French beans in boiling salted water for 7–10 minutes or until just tender. Add the leeks to the pan for the last 30 seconds, then drain the vegetables well and keep warm while you make the sauce.

3 Put the cream into a small pan with half each of the Cheddar and Parmesan. Heat until just beginning to boil, stirring now and then to prevent it from boiling over.
4 Add the hot vegetables to the pasta and toss with the smoked ham and remaining cheese. Season with plenty of pepper (you won't need to add salt as the ham and cheese already make the dish quite salty).
5 Serve immediately on hot plates and hand the cream sauce around separately.

Serves 4
Preparation: 15 minutes
Cooking time: 15 minutes
Per serving: 480 cals; 26g fat; 35g carbohydrate

Top left: Warm Chicken Liver Salad, page 263; top right: Asparagus and Quail's Egg Salad, page 262; bottom left: Flash-in-the-Pan Pork page 260; bottom right: Bacon and Egg Salad, page 262.

...pasta

...h peeled
...d brown-
...rooms,

25g (1oz) butter
275g (10oz) peppered
  salami, cut into strips

125g (4oz) soft cheese
  with garlic and herbs
142ml carton single
  cream
4tbsp milk
freshly grated
  Parmesan cheese, to
  serve (optional)

1 Cook the pasta in boiling salted water for the time stated on the packet.
2 Meanwhile, fry the shallots in the butter until golden. Add the mushrooms and fry for about 5 minutes or until beginning to soften. Add the salami and fry, stirring, for 1–2 minutes. Reduce the heat and stir in the soft cheese, cream and milk. Simmer, stirring, for about 2 minutes until piping hot.

3 Drain the pasta, put back in the pan and stir in the sauce. Serve immediately with a little Parmesan sprinkled over, if you like.

Serves 4
Preparation: 15 minutes
Cooking time: 15 minutes
Per serving: 870 cals; 53g fat; 74g carbohydrate

Flash-in-the-pan Pork

700g (1½lb) new
  potatoes, scrubbed
salt
175g (6oz) runner
  beans, sliced
a little sunflower or
  olive oil
4 pork escalopes
150ml (¼ pint) each hot
  chicken stock
  and cider

2tbsp wholegrain
  mustard
150g tub Greek-style
  yogurt
leaves of 4 tarragon
  stems
squeeze of lemon juice

3 Just before serving, reduce the heat and add the yogurt, tarragon leaves and lemon juice to taste. Put the pork back into the pan to coat with sauce and warm through. Serve with the potatoes and beans.

Serves 4
Preparation: 5 minutes
Cooking time: 15 minutes
Per serving: 430 cals; 17g fat; 31g carbohydrate

See picture, page 259

1 Cook the potatoes in a large pan of boiling salted water for 10 minutes. Add the beans and cook for 5 minutes or until tender. Drain and keep warm.
2 Meanwhile, heat the oil in a large non-stick frying pan and cook the pork over a medium heat for 3 minutes on each side until browned. Remove from the pan and keep warm. Add the hot stock, cider and mustard and increase the heat to reduce the liquid by half.

Pesto Cod and Beans

4 small Icelandic cod
  fillets
4tbsp red pesto
good glug of olive oil
2 x 410g cans butter
  beans, drained and
  rinsed

2 garlic cloves, peeled
  and crushed
225g (8oz) spinach
squeeze of lemon juice

1 Preheat the grill to medium. Spread each cod fillet evenly with 1tbsp red pesto and grill them for 10–15 minutes until the flesh is opaque and just cooked.
2 Meanwhile, heat the olive oil in a pan and add the beans and garlic. Cook for 10 minutes, stirring occasionally and mashing the beans lightly as you do.
3 A couple or so minutes before serving, add the spinach to the pan and allow it to wilt. Spoon the butter bean mash on to warmed plates and top with the cod and any juices from the tin. Squeeze a little lemon juice over each piece of fish and serve.

Serves 4
Preparation: 5 minutes,
Cooking time: 15 minutes
Per serving: 410 cals; 13g fat; 26g carbohydrate

See picture, page 246

Smoked Trout Sandwich in Seconds

125g pack smoked
  trout, flaked
3tbsp Greek-style
  yogurt

salt and pepper
2 slices of Swedish-
  style rye bread
100g bag bistro salad

1 Put the smoked trout in a bowl, then mix in the yogurt. Season and spoon on to each slice of rye bread. Top with the salad and serve.

Serves 1–2
Preparation: 5 minutes
Per serving: 210 cals; 6g fat; 20g carbohydrate

Sardines with Herbs

900g (2lb) sardines (at
  least 12), gutted
125ml (4fl oz) olive oil
3tbsp lemon juice, plus
  2tsp grated lemon zest

4tbsp chopped mixed
  herbs, such as
  parsley, chervil and
  thyme
salt and pepper

1 Preheat the grill to medium-high. Rinse the sardines and pat dry with kitchen paper.
2 Pour the olive oil into a bowl and mix in the lemon juice, lemon zest, herbs and seasoning.
3 Lay the sardines on a grill rack, drizzle the herb dressing over them and grill for 5–7 minutes each side, basting frequently with the dressing. Serve hot or cold, accompanied by plenty of crusty bread.

Serves 4
Preparation: 10 minutes
Cooking time: 10 minutes
Per serving: 340 cals; 25g fat; 0g carbohydrate

Spicy Noodle Salad

250g (9oz) cooked rice
  noodles
175g (6oz) each
  blanched broccoli and
  mangetout
2tsp sesame oil

2tbsp plum sauce
4tbsp dark soy sauce
sliced spring onions
  and chopped red
  chillies, to serve

1 Mix the noodles with the broccoli and mangetout, then toss with the oil, plum and soy sauces.
2 Sprinkle with the spring onions and chillies and serve.

Serves 4
Preparation: 5 minutes
Cooking time: 15 minutes
Per serving: 110 cals; 3g fat; 16g carbohydrate

Bacon and Egg Salad

4 eggs
250g (9oz) rindless
  smoked bacon
  rashers
150g (5oz) cherry
  tomatoes
2 slices of thick-cut
  bread

3tbsp mayonnaise
½ lemon
25g (1oz) freshly grated
  Parmesan cheese
black pepper
2 little gem lettuces

1 Heat a pan of water until simmering, add the eggs and boil for 6 minutes. Cool completely under cold water, then peel and put to one side.

2 Meanwhile, heat a griddle pan, then fry the bacon for 5 minutes until crisp. Remove from the pan, chop into large pieces and leave to cool.

3 Add the tomatoes and bread to the pan and fry in the bacon juices for 2–3 minutes until the bread is crisp and the tomatoes are starting to char. Remove from the heat, chop the bread into bite-sized croûtons and put to one side.

4 To make the dressing, put the mayonnaise into a bowl, squeeze in the lemon juice, add the Parmesan and mix. Season with pepper.

5 Separate the lettuce leaves and put into a large serving bowl. Cut the eggs in half and add to the bowl with the bacon, tomatoes and croûtons. Drizzle over the dressing, toss lightly and serve.

Serves 4
Preparation: 10 minutes
Cooking time: about 10 minutes
Per serving: 360 cals; 23g fat; 14g carbohydrate

See picture, page 259

Mixed Leaves with Avocado and Cherry Tomatoes

1tbsp cider or white
  wine vinegar
1tsp golden caster
  sugar
4tbsp walnut oil
salt and pepper

1 ripe avocado, peeled
  and flesh diced
150g (5oz) cherry
  tomatoes
about 200g (7oz) mixed
  salad leaves

1 Whisk together the vinegar, sugar and oil in a large bowl and season.

2 Toss the avocado in the dressing with the tomatoes and salad leaves. Serve at once.

Serves 6
Preparation: 10 minutes
Per serving: 150 cals; 14g fat; 3g carbohydrate

Asparagus and Quail's Egg Salad

24 quail's eggs
24 asparagus spears,
  trimmed
salt and pepper
juice of ½ lemon
5tbsp olive oil

4 large spring onions,
  finely sliced
100g bag watercress,
  roughly chopped
few dill and tarragon
  sprigs

1 Add the quail's eggs to a pan of boiling water and cook for 2 minutes, then drain and plunge into cold water. Cook the asparagus in boiling salted water for 2 minutes or until just tender. Drain, plunge into cold water and leave to cool.

2 Whisk together the lemon juice, olive oil and seasoning. Stir in the spring onions and put to one side.

3 Peel the quail's eggs and cut in half. Put into a large bowl with the asparagus, watercress, dill and tarragon. Pour over the dressing and lightly toss all the ingredients together. Season and serve.

Serves 8
Preparation: 30 minutes
Cooking time: 2 minutes
Per serving: 180 cals; 14g fat; 3g carbohydrate

See picture, page 259

Hot Tomato Salad

700g (1½lb) mixed cherry tomatoes (red and yellow, if possible), halved
2 garlic cloves, peeled and sliced
2tbsp capers, drained and rinsed
1tsp golden caster sugar

salt and pepper
125ml (4fl oz) extra-virgin olive oil
1 ready-to-bake olive ciabatta loaf
2tbsp chopped basil
balsamic or red wine vinegar, to taste
basil sprigs, to garnish

1   Preheat the oven to 200°C (180°C fan oven) mark 6. Put the tomatoes, garlic, capers and sugar into a small roasting tin and stir to mix. Season well and pour on the olive oil.
2   Transfer to the oven and cook for 10–12 minutes or until the tomatoes are hot and beginning to soften. Pop the bread in the oven to bake alongside.
3   Remove the tomatoes from the oven and stir in the basil with a few drops of vinegar to taste. Slice the hot bread and spoon over the warm tomatoes and juices. Garnish with basil sprigs and serve.

Serves 6
Preparation: 5 minutes
Cooking time: 10–12 minutes
Per serving: 310 cals; 20g fat; 27g carbohydrate

Warm Chicken Liver Salad

1–2tbsp balsamic vinegar
1tsp Dijon mustard
5tbsp olive oil
salt and pepper
2 x 225g tubs chicken livers
200g (7oz) streaky

bacon rashers, de-rinded and cut into small pieces (lardons)
½ curly endive, about 175g (6oz)
100g (3½oz) rocket
1 bunch of spring onions, sliced

1   Unless you have very good, aged balsamic vinegar, put the vinegar in a small pan and reduce it by half. This will give the dressing a nice mellow flavour. To make the dressing, put the vinegar, mustard and 4tbsp olive oil in a small bowl and season. Whisk together and put to one side.
2   Drain the chicken livers, then trim them and cut into pieces.
3   Fry the lardons in a non-stick frying pan, until beginning to brown, stirring from time to time. Add the remaining oil and the chicken livers and stir-fry over a high heat for 2–3 minutes or until just pink in the centre. Season to taste.
4   Toss the endive, rocket and spring onions with the dressing in a large bowl. Quickly combine the warm livers and bacon and serve at once.

Serves 4
Preparation: 20 minutes
Cooking time: 8–10 minutes
Per serving: 520 cals; 43g fat; 2g carbohydrate

See picture, page 259

Warm Spicy Chorizo Sausage and Chickpea Salad

5tbsp olive oil
200g (7oz) chorizo or
    spicy sausage, thinly
    sliced
225g (8oz) red onion,
    peeled and chopped
1 large red pepper,
    deseeded and roughly
    chopped
3 garlic cloves, peeled
    and finely chopped

1tsp cumin seeds
2 x 400g cans
    chickpeas, drained
    and rinsed
2tbsp chopped
    coriander
juice of 1 lemon
salt and pepper

1   Heat 1tbsp olive oil in a non-stick frying pan and cook the chorizo or spicy sausage over a medium heat for 1–2 minutes or until lightly browned. Remove the chorizo with a slotted spoon and put to one side. Fry the onion in the chorizo oil for 10 minutes or until browned.

2   Add the red pepper, garlic, cumin and chickpeas to the onion and cook for a further 5 minutes, stirring frequently to prevent sticking. Remove the pan from the heat and add the chorizo.

3   Add the coriander, lemon juice and remaining olive oil. Season well and serve immediately.

Serves 4
Preparation: 15 minutes
Cooking time: 17 minutes
Per serving: 470 cals; 32g fat; 29g carbohydrate

Hummus with Rocket and Mint Salad

400g can chickpeas,
    drained and rinsed
juice of 1 lemon
4tbsp tahini
1 garlic clove, peeled
    and crushed
175ml (6fl oz) extra-
    virgin olive oil
salt and pepper
3tbsp sherry vinegar

3 x 50g bags wild
    rocket
12 small mint leaves
12 peppadew sweet
    piquant peppers
    (mild)
6tbsp sliced jalapeño
    chillies
4 sesame seed
    flatbreads

1   To make the hummus, put the chickpeas, lemon juice, tahini, garlic and 75ml (3fl oz) olive oil in a food processor. Season generously, then whiz to a paste. Spoon the hummus into a non-metallic bowl, then cover and chill overnight.

2   To make the dressing, put the remaining olive oil, the sherry vinegar and a pinch of salt in a screw-topped jar. Tighten the lid and shake well to mix. Chill overnight.

3   To serve, divide the hummus between six small (150ml/¼ pint) pots. Put on to six plates. Put the rocket and mint leaves in a bowl, then drizzle the dressing over. Divide the salad, peppers, jalapeño chillies and sesame seed flatbreads among the six plates. Note: once the salad is dressed, you need to serve within 20 minutes.

Serves 6
Preparation: 15 minutes
Cooking time: 5 minutes
Per serving: 470 cals; 31g fat; 39g carbohydrate

Top left: Hummus with Rocket and Mint Salad, page 264, top right: Egg and Pepper Pizza, page 266; bottom left: Warm Spicy Chorizo Sausage and Chickpea Salad, page 265; bottom right: Lamb Steaks with Mixed Bean Salad, page 266.

Lamb Steaks with Mixed Bean Salad

150g (5oz) sunblush
tomatoes in oil
1 garlic clove, peeled
and crushed
few rosemary sprigs
salt and pepper
4 x 175g (6oz) leg of
lamb steaks

½ small red onion,
peeled and finely
sliced
2 x 400g cans mixed
beans, drained and
rinsed
large handful of rocket

1 Preheat the grill to high. Drain the sunblush tomatoes, reserving the oil. Put the garlic in a large shallow dish with 1tbsp oil from the tomatoes. Snip the rosemary leaves into small pieces and add half to the dish. Season, then add the lamb and toss to coat.
2 Grill the lamb for 3–4 minutes on each side until cooked but still just pink. Roughly chop the tomatoes. Put into a pan with the onion, beans, remaining rosemary, rocket and 1tbsp oil from the tomatoes. Warm until the rocket starts to wilt. Serve the lamb with the salad.

Serves 4
Preparation: 5 minutes
Cooking time: about 10 minutes
Per serving: 370 cals; 16g fat; 15g carbohydrate

See picture, page 265

Egg and Pepper Pizza

150g (5oz) red and
yellow marinated
peppers in oil
8tbsp passata

4 small pizza bases
4 eggs
125g (4oz) watercress

1 Preheat the oven to 220°C (200°C fan oven) mark 7. Preheat two large baking sheets, big enough to fit two pizzas each.
2 Drain the peppers, reserving the oil, and chop them into thin strips. Spoon 2tbsp passata over each pizza base and scatter strips of pepper round the edges. Make a dip in the passata in the middle of each pizza and break an egg into it. Carefully slide the pizzas on to the preheated baking sheet. Transfer to the oven and cook for 12 minutes until the egg is thoroughly cooked.
3 Top the pizzas with the watercress, drizzle over a little of the reserved oil from the peppers and serve.

Serves 4
Preparation: 5 minutes
Cooking time: 12 minutes
Per serving: 330 cals; 12g fat; 40g carbohydrate

See picture, page 265

Pan-fried Mushrooms and Feta Omelette

50g (2oz) butter
225g (8oz) large
mushrooms, thinly
sliced
3 garlic cloves, peeled
and sliced
50g (2oz) sun-dried
tomatoes, roughly
chopped

4 large eggs, beaten
black pepper
100g (3½oz) feta
cheese, crumbled
thyme sprigs, to
garnish

1 Melt the butter in an 18cm (7 inch) diameter non-stick omelette pan and fry the mushrooms with the garlic until they're a deep golden brown and beginning to go crisp around the edges. Add the sun-dried tomatoes and stir over the heat for 1–2 minutes. Meanwhile, preheat the grill to high.
2 Roughly spread the mushroom mixture over the base of the pan. Beat 2tbsp cold water into the eggs and season with pepper (both feta cheese and sun-dried tomatoes can be salty so no extra salt should be needed to season the omelette). Pour over the mushrooms, gently swirling the pan to spread the eggs. Leave to set undisturbed on a low heat for 1–2 minutes, then sprinkle the feta over.
3 Put the pan under the grill for about 1–2 minutes or until the eggs are lightly cooked and the feta cheese is just beginning to melt.
4 Sprinkle the omelette with black pepper and scatter with thyme sprigs to garnish. Cut into wedges and serve immediately.

Serves 4
Preparation: 5 minutes
Cooking time: 15 minutes
Per serving: 280 cals; 22g fat; 5g carbohydrate

15-minute Couscous

225g (8oz) couscous
75g (3oz) dates,
  roughly chopped
large pinch of saffron
  strands
40g (1½oz) butter
salt and pepper
25g (1oz) flaked
  almonds

1 Put the couscous, dates, saffron and 25g (1oz) butter in a bowl. Add 300ml (½ pint) boiling water, season and stir to mix. Cover and leave to soak for 10 minutes or until all the water is absorbed and the couscous is soft.
2 To make each portion, line a 300ml (½ pint) bowl with clingfilm, spoon in a quarter of the couscous and press down firmly. Invert a dinner plate on to the couscous and turn out, discarding the clingfilm. Repeat with the rest of the couscous.
3 Fry the almonds in the remaining butter until golden and scatter over each portion of couscous. Serve on its own or as an accompaniment.

Serves 4
Preparation: 5 minutes, plus soaking
Per serving: 350 cals; 12g fat; 55g carbohydrate

Posh Mushrooms on Toast

4 large flat
  mushrooms, such as
  portabello
4tbsp mascarpone
salt and pepper
8 slices of Parma ham
4 slices of good firm
  bread, such as
  sourdough
rocket or other salad

1 Preheat the oven to 230°C (210°C fan oven) mark 8. Trim the mushroom stalks and put the mushrooms, stalk side up, on a roasting tray and spoon 1tbsp mascarpone on top of each. Season well, then put 2 slices of ham on top of each, arranging them so that the whole mushroom is covered. Cook in the oven for 10 minutes.
2 Meanwhile, toast the bread. Top each slice of toast with a mushroom and serve with a handful of rocket.

Serves 4
Preparation: 5 minutes
Cooking time: 10 minutes
Per serving: 250 cals; 12g fat; 24g carbohydrate

Chèvre en Croute

½ short baguette
1–2tbsp hazelnut oil
1 small garlic clove,
  peeled and crushed
125g (4oz) chèvre log,
  about 2.5cm (1 inch)
  in diameter, cut into
  six slices
paprika
6 thyme sprigs

1 Preheat the oven to 180°C (160°C fan oven) mark 4. Cut six 1cm (½ inch) thick slices from the baguette. Mix the oil with the garlic and brush both sides of the bread. Put on a baking sheet. Bake for about 5 minutes.
2 Remove from the oven. Put a slice of chèvre on each baguette slice. Top with paprika and a thyme sprig.
3 Return the croûtes to the oven for a further 7 minutes, or until the cheese is soft and spongy. Serve warm with a mixed leaf salad.

Serves 6
Preparation: 5 minutes
Cooking time: 12 minutes
Per serving: 110 cals; 7g fat; 8g carbohydrate

Cheese Bites

butter, to grease
225g (8oz) puff pastry
50g (2oz) olives, pitted and halved or quartered
125g (4oz) firm buttery cheese, such as Jarlsberg or Emmental, or a soft cheese such as mozzarella, cut into small dice
50g (2oz) sun-dried tomatoes in oil, drained and roughly chopped
50g (2oz) capers, roughly chopped
50g can anchovy fillets, roughly chopped
50g (2oz) pesto sauce
salt and pepper

1 Preheat the oven to 200°C (180°C fan oven) mark 6. Lightly grease a baking sheet. Roll out the pastry to 3mm (⅛ inch), then, using a 5cm (2 inch) round cutter, stamp out 24 circles. Put them on the baking sheet.
2 Arrange some olives, cheese, sun-dried tomatoes, capers and anchovies on each pastry circle. Spoon over a little pesto sauce and season.
3 Transfer to the oven and cook for 10–15 minutes, until well risen and crisp. Serve immediately.

Makes about 24
Preparation: 5 minutes
Cooking time: 10–15 minutes
Per bite: 80 cals; 6g fat; 4g carbohydrate

Easy Wrap

1tsp each salt and pepper
1 avocado
2 cooked chicken breasts, cut into bite-sized pieces
1 carrot, peeled and grated
small handful of rocket
juice of ½ lemon
3tbsp mayonnaise
4 soft tortillas

1 Mix the salt with the pepper in a large bowl. Peel and chop the avocado. Add the chicken, carrot, avocado and rocket and mix well.
2 In a separate bowl, mix the lemon juice with the mayonnaise, then spread over the tortillas. Divide the chicken mixture among the tortillas, roll up and serve in napkins.

Serves 4
Preparation: 10 minutes
Cooking time: about 10 minutes
Per serving: 360 cals; 23g fat; 14g carbohydrate

Smoked Haddock Rarebit

**4 x 150g (5oz) skinned
  smoked haddock
  fillets
salt and pepper
1 large ciabatta**

**200g (7oz) spinach
300g carton cheese
  sauce
2 large tomatoes,
  sliced**

1 Preheat the grill. Season the haddock and put into a shallow ovenproof dish. Grill for 6–8 minutes until opaque and cooked through.
2 Slice the ciabatta in half lengthways, then halve again horizontally. Grill on both sides until golden.
3 Put the spinach in a pan, cover and cook for 1–2 minutes until starting to wilt. Season and tip into a bowl. Add the cheese sauce to the pan and bring to the boil, then reduce the heat and simmer for 1–2 minutes until hot.
4 Top each piece of ciabatta with a piece of fish, then add the spinach and tomato slices. Pour over the cheese sauce and grill for 2–3 minutes to heat through. Season well with pepper and serve.

Serves 4
Preparation: 5 minutes
Cooking time: 10–15 minutes
Per serving: 500 cals; 16g fat; 43g carbohydrate

Better than a takeaway

Sometimes nothing but a curry will do. And once the idea's in your head, it really gets the tastebuds going.

You might fancy an Indian – Prawn Madras served with Coconut Chutney, or a Thai Green Chicken Curry served with Thai Rice. Or perhaps noodles are more your thing. The Yellow Bean Noodles with Tiger Prawns are ready in no time, while the Chinese Speedy Beef Noodles are spiced up with chilli.

Curry doesn't necessarily mean hot – it can be aromatic and spicy, such as the Salmon Laksa Curry, where succulent salmon is simmered in laksa stock, its heat tempered by soothing coconut milk. The noodles are then stirred into the broth, making this a complete meal in one.

Classic Saag Aloo; Chicken Satay Skewers; Crispy Duck with Hot and Sweet Dip; Thai Crab Balls with Sweet Chilli Sauce; Fried Yellow Bean Pork with Cashews – so many to choose from, and to go with it, all you need to do is rustle up some Easy Basmati Pilaf, Special Prawn Fried Rice, or Split Pea Roti, then sit back and enjoy.

So get out the chopsticks or put on some bangra, get cooking and prove that these are definitely 'better than a takeaway'.

Yellow Bean Noodles with Tiger Prawns

250g pack medium egg noodles
1tbsp stir-fry oil or sesame oil
1 garlic clove, peeled and sliced
1tsp peeled and freshly grated root ginger
1 bunch of spring onions, each cut into four

250g pack frozen peeled raw tiger prawns, thawed
200g pack pak choi, leaves removed and white base cut into thick slices
160g jar Chinese yellow bean stir-fry sauce

1 Put the noodles in a bowl, pour over 2 litres (3½ pints) boiling water and leave to soak for 4 minutes. Drain.
2 Heat the oil in a wok, add the garlic and ginger and stir-fry for 30 seconds. Add the spring onions and prawns and cook for 2 minutes.
3 Add the chopped white part of the pak choi and the yellow bean sauce. Pour boiling water to fill the sauce jar and pour this into the wok.

4 Add the noodles to the pan and cook for 1 minute, tossing every now and then to heat everything through. Finally, stir in the green pak choi leaves and serve.

Serves 4–6
Preparation: 10 minutes
Cooking time: 5 minutes, plus standing
Per serving: 340 cals; 6g fat; 51g carbohydrate

See picture, page 277

Thai-style Tiger Prawns with Pak Choi

3tbsp Thai red curry paste
200ml (7fl oz) coconut milk
juice of 1 lime
24 raw tiger prawns, peeled, with tail on and deveined
8 kaffir lime leaves
4 long lemon grass stalks, outer layer removed

2 x 200g packs pak choi, cut in half lengthways
1tbsp light soy sauce
salt and pepper
2tbsp sweet chilli sauce

1 Put the curry paste in a bowl and add the coconut milk, half the lime juice and the prawns. Stir to coat, then cover and chill for 15 minutes. Preheat the grill.
2 Carefully skewer six prawns and two lime leaves on to each lemon grass stalk. Cook under the grill for 5 minutes or until the prawns are pink and cooked through.

3 Meanwhile, put the pak choi in a steamer over a pan of boiling water, cover and cook for 3–4 minutes.
4 Toss the pak choi in the soy sauce and remaining lime juice and season. Serve with the prawn skewers, drizzled with sweet chilli sauce.

Serves 4–6
Preparation: 10 minutes, plus marinating
Cooking time: 5 minutes
Per serving: 168 cals; 8g fat; 8 carbohydrate

Thai Noodles with Prawns

1–2tbsp Thai red curry paste

175g (6oz) medium egg noodles, preferably wholewheat

2 small red onions, peeled and chopped

1 lemon grass stalk, sliced

1 Thai red chilli, deseeded and finely chopped

300ml (½ pint) half-fat coconut milk, or use half a can of full-fat coconut milk and make up the difference with water or stock

400g (14oz) peeled raw tiger prawns, deveined

salt and pepper

4tbsp chopped coriander, plus extra leaves to garnish

1 Put 2 litres (3½ pints) water into a large pan and bring to the boil. Add the curry paste, noodles, onions, lemon grass, chilli and coconut milk. Bring to the boil, then add the prawns and coriander, reduce the heat and simmer for 2–3 minutes or until the prawns turn pink.

2 Season and serve in large bowls sprinkled with coriander leaves.

Serves 4
Preparation: 10 minutes
Cooking time: 5 minutes
Per serving: 340 cals; 11g fat; 38g carbohydrate

See picture, page 291

Sesame Chilli Prawns

40 ready-cooked tiger prawns, about 450g (1lb), peeled, with tail on

5tbsp sweet chilli sauce

75g (3oz) toasted sesame seeds

1 Hold each prawn by the tail and dip into the chilli sauce, then into the sesame seeds.

2 Put on a tray lined with clingfilm, cover loosely and chill until required.

Makes 40
Preparation: 40 minutes
Per prawn: 20 cals; 1g fat; Tr carbohydrate

Thai Green Shellfish Curry

1tbsp vegetable oil
1 pack fresh Thai herbs
(containing 1 lemon
grass, 2 Thai chillies,
coriander leaves,
2 lime leaves), all
chopped
1–2tbsp Thai green
curry paste
400ml can coconut
milk

450ml (¾ pint)
vegetable stock
salt and pepper
375g (13oz) queen
scallops with corals
250g (9oz) raw tiger
prawns, peeled, with
tails on and deveined
coriander leaves, to
garnish

1 Heat the oil in a wok and fry the Thai herbs for
30 seconds. Add the curry paste and fry for 1 minute.
2 Add the coconut milk and stock and bring to the boil,
then reduce the heat and simmer for 5–10 minutes
until reduced a little. Season well.

3 Add the scallops and prawns and bring to the boil,
then reduce the heat and simmer gently for
2–3 minutes or until cooked. Spoon into bowls of Thai
jasmine rice and garnish with coriander.

Serves 6
Preparation: 5 minutes
Cooking time: 15 minutes
Per serving: 230 cals; 14g fat; 2g carbohydrate

See picture, page 277

Thai Red Seafood Curry

1tbsp oil
3tbsp Thai red curry
paste
450g (1lb) monkfish
tail, filleted and sliced
into rounds, about
350g (12oz) filleted
weight
350g (12oz) peeled
large raw prawns,
deveined
400ml can half-fat
coconut milk, or use

half a can of full-fat
coconut milk and
make up the
difference with water
or stock
200ml (7fl oz) fish stock
juice of 1 lime
1–2tbsp Thai fish sauce
125g (4oz) mangetout,
sliced lengthways
3tbsp torn coriander
salt and pepper

1 Heat the oil in a large non-stick sauté pan or wok. Add
the curry paste and cook, stirring, for 1–2 minutes.
2 Add the monkfish and prawns and stir well to coat in
the curry paste. Add the coconut milk, stock, lime juice
and fish sauce. Stir all the ingredients together and
bring just to the boil.

3 Add the mangetout, reduce the heat and simmer for
5 minutes or until both mangetout and fish are tender.
Stir in the coriander and season to taste. Serve with plain
boiled rice.

Serves 4
Preparation: 15 minutes
Cooking time: 8–10 minutes
Per serving: 350 cals; 19g fat; 5g carbohydrate

See picture, page 277

Better than a takeaway

Thai Crab Balls with Sweet Chilli Sauce

2tsp sesame oil
1 large red chilli, deseeded and finely chopped
2.5cm (1 inch) piece fresh root ginger, peeled and finely grated, plus 2tbsp finely chopped fresh root ginger
2 garlic cloves, peeled and crushed
8tbsp light muscovado sugar
3tsp Thai fish sauce
2tbsp light soy sauce
juice of 2 limes
1tbsp sunflower oil, plus extra for deep-frying

4 spring onions, finely chopped
1 lemon grass stalk, outer leaves discarded and remainder finely chopped
350g (12oz) fresh or frozen crab meat
2tbsp chopped coriander
75g (3oz) white breadcrumbs
3 eggs
black pepper
50g (2oz) plain flour
coriander sprigs and shredded red chilli, to garnish

1 To make the chilli sauce, put the sesame oil in a pan and heat gently. Add ½tsp chopped chilli, the 2tbsp chopped ginger and 1 garlic clove and cook for 1–2 minutes until softened. Add the sugar, 2tsp fish sauce and the soy sauce, then bring to the boil, reduce the heat and simmer for 2 minutes. Remove from the heat and stir in 8tbsp water and the lime juice. Pour into a serving bowl, cover and put to one side.

2 To make the crab balls, heat the sunflower oil in a small pan and add the spring onions, remaining garlic, the grated ginger, remaining chilli and the lemon grass. Cook gently for 2–3 minutes or until soft. Transfer to a bowl and cool, then stir in the crab meat, coriander, remaining fish sauce, 6tbsp breadcrumbs and 1 egg. Mix and season with pepper only. Shape tablespoonfuls of the mixture into 18 balls, put on a baking sheet and chill for 20 minutes.

3 Beat the remaining eggs. Coat each ball lightly with flour, roll in the beaten eggs, then in the remaining breadcrumbs. Heat the sunflower oil in a large pan and deep-fry the crab balls in batches for 3–4 minutes or until golden. Drain on kitchen paper and keep warm while frying the remaining balls. Garnish with coriander and shredded red chilli and serve with the sweet chilli sauce.

Makes 18 balls
Preparation: 30 minutes, plus chilling
Cooking time: 20 minutes
Per ball with sauce: 120 cals; 6g fat; 12g carbohydrate

Prawn Madras with Coconut Chutney

1 small and 2 medium onions, peeled
2.5cm (1 inch) piece fresh root ginger, peeled and finely chopped
2 garlic cloves, peeled and crushed
juice of ½ lemon
1tbsp each cumin seeds and coriander seeds
1tsp cayenne pepper
2tsp each ground turmeric and garam masala
salt
3tbsp groundnut oil

1tbsp black mustard seeds
125g (4oz) desiccated coconut
1 red chilli, deseeded and diced
1 green chilli, deseeded and finely chopped
600ml (1 pint) vegetable stock
450g (1lb) raw king prawns, peeled and deveined
2 bay leaves
coriander leaves, to garnish

1 To make the madras paste, finely chop 1 small onion and put into a food processor with the ginger, garlic, lemon juice, cumin and corianders seeds, cayenne pepper, turmeric and garam masala, 1tsp salt and 2tbsp water and whiz until smooth. Divide the paste into three equal portions, freeze two parts in separate bags to use within 3 months (see below) and put the rest into a large bowl.

2 To make the coconut chutney, grate 1 onion. Heat 1tbsp oil in a pan and add the mustard seeds. Cover the pan with a lid and cook over a medium heat until the seeds pop – you'll hear them jumping against the lid. Add the grated onion, coconut and red chilli and cook for 3–4 minutes to toast the coconut. Take off the heat and put to one side.

3 To make the curry, finely slice the remaining onion. Heat the remaining oil in a pan, add the sliced onion and fry for 10 minutes until soft and golden. Add the madras paste and green chilli and cook for 5 minutes. Add the stock and bring to the boil.

4 Reduce to a simmer and add the prawns and bay leaves. Cook for 3–5 minutes or until the prawns turn pink and are cooked. Garnish with coriander and serve with the coconut chutney and basmati rice.

Serves 4
Preparation: 10 minutes
Cooking time: 25 minutes
Per serving: 430 cals; 31g fat; 13g carbohydrate

To use the frozen paste: Put the paste in a microwave and cook on Defrost for 1 minute 20 seconds (based on 900W oven), or thaw at cool room temperature for 1 hour.

Thai Fishcakes with Chilli Mayo

1 bunch of spring
  onions
2.5cm (1 inch) piece
  fresh root ginger,
  peeled and roughly
  chopped
1 lemon grass stalk,
  roughly chopped
20g pack coriander
½ red chilli, deseeded
1tsp Thai fish sauce
  (optional)
½ quantity Five-minute
  Mayonnaise (page 15)
75g (3oz) fresh white

breadcrumbs
225g (8oz) each
  haddock and cooked
  peeled prawns
oil, for frying
2tbsp Thai sweet chilli
  sauce
20g pack basil, roughly
  chopped
1 fat garlic clove,
  crushed (optional)
2 limes, halved
120g bag baby leaf
  spinach

1 Put the spring onions, ginger, lemon grass, coriander, chilli and fish sauce, if using, in a food processor and whiz to a rough paste. Add 3tbsp mayonnaise, the breadcrumbs, fish and prawns and whiz for 5 seconds.
2 With wet hands, shape into eight patties, each about 5cm (2 inches) in diameter.

3 Heat a drizzle of oil in a non-stick frying pan. Fry the patties for 3–4 minutes on each side until crisp and golden.
4 Mix the chilli sauce, basil and garlic, if using, into the remaining mayonnaise. Serve with the fishcakes, lime and spinach leaves.

Serves 4
Preparation: 25 minutes
Cooking time: 8–10 minutes
Per serving: 470 cals; 29g fat; 11g carbohydrate

Prawn and Vegetable Pilau

250g (9oz) long-grain
  rice
1 broccoli head, broken
  into florets
150g (5oz) baby
  sweetcorn, halved
200g (7oz) sugarsnap
  peas
1 red pepper, halved,
  deseeded and cut into
  thin strips

400g (14oz) cooked
  peeled king prawns
1tbsp sesame oil
5cm (2 inch) piece
  fresh root ginger,
  peeled and grated
juice of 1 lime
1–2tbsp soy sauce

1 Put the rice in a very large, wide pan. Add 600ml (1 pint) boiling water. Cover and bring to the boil, then reduce the heat to low and cook the rice for the time stated on the packet.
2 About 10 minutes before the end of the rice cooking time, add the broccoli, sweetcorn, sugarsnaps and red pepper. Stir well, then cover and cook until the vegetables and rice are just tender.

3 Meanwhile, put the prawns into a bowl and add the sesame oil, ginger, lime juice and soy sauce. Stir the prawns and dressing into the cooked vegetables and rice and toss well.

Serves 4
Preparation: 10 minutes
Cooking time: 15–20 minutes
Per serving: 390 cals; 5g fat; 57g carbohydrate

See picture, page 284

Top left: Yellow Bean Noodles with Tiger Prawns, page 272; top right: Easy Thai Red Chicken Curry, page 278; bottom left: Thai Green Shellfish Curry, page 274; bottom right: Thai Red Seafood Curry, page 274.

Salmon Laksa Curry

1tbsp olive oil
1 onion, peeled and
    finely sliced
3tbsp laksa paste
200ml (7fl oz) coconut
    milk
900ml (1½ pints) hot
    vegetable stock
200g (7oz) baby
    sweetcorn, halved
    lengthways
salt and pepper
600g (1lb 6oz) piece
    skinless salmon fillet,
    cut into 1cm (½ inch)
    slices

225g pack baby
    spinach leaves
250g pack medium rice
    noodles
2 spring onions, sliced
    diagonally
2tbsp chopped
    coriander
1 lime, cut into four
    wedges

1   Heat the olive oil in a large pan, add the onion and fry over a medium heat for 10 minutes, stirring, until golden. Add the laksa paste and cook for 2 minutes. Add the coconut milk, hot stock and baby sweetcorn and season. Bring to the boil, then reduce the heat and simmer for 5 minutes.

2   Add the salmon and spinach and immerse them in the liquid. Cook for 4 minutes until the fish is opaque to the centre.

3   Meanwhile, put the noodles in a large bowl, pour boiling water over and soak for 30 seconds. Drain, then stir into the curry. Pour into bowls, garnish with the spring onions, coriander and lime and serve.

Serves 4
Preparation: 15 minutes
Cooking time: 22 minutes
Per serving: 680 cals; 33g fat; 58g carbohydrate

See picture, page 284

Salmon and Coconut Curry

1tbsp olive oil
1 red onion, peeled and
    sliced
2tbsp tikka masala
    curry paste
4 x 100g (3½oz) salmon
    steaks

400ml can coconut
    milk
juice of 1 lime
handful of coriander,
    roughly chopped

1   Heat the olive oil in a pan. Add the onion and cook over medium heat for 10 minutes until golden and softened.

2   Add the curry paste to the pan and cook for 1 minute to warm the spices. Add the fish and cook for 2 minutes, turning it once to coat it in the spices.

3   Pour in the coconut milk and bring to the boil, then reduce the heat and simmer for 5 minutes or until the fish is cooked through. Squeeze over the lime juice, sprinkle with coriander and serve with boiled rice or naan bread to soak up the creamy sauce.

Serves 4
Preparation: 2 minutes
Cooking time: 18 minutes
Per serving: 400 cals; 33g fat; 6g carbohydrate

Easy Thai Red Chicken Curry

1tbsp vegetable oil
3tbsp Thai red curry
    paste
4 skinless boneless
    chicken breasts,
    about 600g (1lb 6oz),
    sliced
400ml can coconut
    milk

300ml (½ pint) hot
    chicken or
    vegetable stock
juice of 1 lime
200g pack mixed baby
    sweetcorn and
    mangetout
2tbsp chopped
    coriander

1   Heat the oil in a wok or large pan. Add the curry paste and cook for 2 minutes. Add the chicken breasts and fry gently until browned.

2   Add the coconut milk, hot stock, lime juice and baby corn to the pan and bring to the boil. Add the mangetout, reduce the heat and simmer for 4–5 minutes until the chicken is cooked. Add the coriander and serve immediately with plain rice noodles.

Serves 4
Preparation: 5 minutes
Cooking time: 20 minutes
Per serving: 410 cals; 28g fat; 5g carbohydrate

See picture, page 277

Thai Green Chicken Curry

1tsp olive oil
1 small onion, peeled and finely sliced
1cm (½ inch) piece fresh root ginger, peeled and diced
½ small red chilli, deseeded and finely chopped
2 skinless boneless chicken breasts, about 250g (9oz), sliced

1tbsp Thai green curry paste
200ml (7fl oz) each coconut milk and hot vegetable stock
50g (2oz) Thai jasmine rice
1 pak choi, sliced into three pieces
125g (4oz) broccoli, cut into florets
125g (4oz) mangetout

1 Heat the olive oil in a pan and fry the onion until soft. Add the ginger, chilli and chicken and stir-fry for 5 minutes.
2 Add the curry paste, coconut milk and hot stock and bring to the boil, then reduce the heat and simmer for 15 minutes or until the chicken is cooked.
3 Meanwhile, put the rice in a pan, stir in 125ml (4fl oz) cold water and bring to the boil. Cover the pan, reduce the heat and simmer for about 8 minutes. Turn off the heat, cover with a tea-towel and replace the lid to absorb the steam.
4 Add the pak choi, broccoli and mangetout to the curry, then cover and cook for about 5 minutes.
5 Fluff up the rice with a fork and serve with the curry.

Serves 2
Preparation: 15 minutes
Cooking time: 25 minutes
Per serving: 475 cals; 8g fat; 34g carbohydrate

Coconut Thai Chicken

1tbsp Thai red curry paste
4tbsp coconut milk

salt and pepper
2 chicken breasts, with skin on

1 Put the curry paste and coconut milk in a bowl, season and mix well. Place the chicken breasts in the marinade, cover and leave for at least 30 minutes. Heat the grill to high.
2 Drain the chicken, reserving the marinade and grill the chicken, skin side down, for 5 minutes. Turn the chicken, brush with marinade and cook for 5 minutes or until golden and cooked through. (Insert a skewer into the thickest part of the chicken: if the juices run clear, it's done.) To crisp the skin, move the chicken closer to the heat.
3 Just before serving, spoon the reserved marinade over and return the chicken to the grill for 1 minute. Slice the chicken and serve.

Serves 2
Preparation: 5 minutes, plus marinating
Cooking time: 10 minutes
Per serving: 320 cals; 22 fat; 1g carbohydrate

10-minute Thai Curry

1tbsp vegetable oil
4 skinless boneless chicken breasts, about 600g (1¼lb), thinly sliced
400ml can Gang Musman red curry

200ml (7fl oz) coconut milk
150g (5oz) sugarsnap peas

1 Heat the oil in a large pan and fry the chicken over a medium-high heat for 5 minutes until golden.
2 Add the red curry, coconut milk and sugarsnap peas. Heat for 5 minutes or until the meat is cooked and the sauce is heated through, then serve with jasmine rice.

Serves 4
Preparation: 5 minutes
Cooking time: 12 minutes
Per serving: 240 cals; 16g fat; 10g carbohydrate

Chicken Glazed in Hoisin Sauce

450g (1lb) skinless
  boneless chicken
  breasts
½tsp salt
pinch of white pepper
8tsp medium-dry
  sherry
1tsp cornflour
1 egg white, lightly
  beaten
2tsp sesame oil
2tbsp vegetable oil
5 garlic cloves, peeled
  and roughly chopped

5 spring onions,
  roughly chopped
227g can sliced
  bamboo shoots,
  drained
227g can whole water
  chestnuts, drained
juice of 1 orange
244g jar hoisin sauce
50g (2oz) cashew nuts
1tbsp sesame seeds

1 Cut the chicken into 2cm (¾ inch) pieces. Put in a bowl with the salt, pepper and 2tsp sherry. Sprinkle with the cornflour and stir in the egg white. Leave for 15–20 minutes; stir in the sesame oil.
2 Heat 1tbsp vegetable oil in a wok. Add the chicken and cook for 2 minutes, then transfer to a plate.
3 Add the remaining oil to the wok and, when hot, add the garlic, spring onions, bamboo shoots and water chestnuts and stir-fry for 2 minutes. Pour the remaining sherry around the side of the wok and when the sizzling has stopped, return the chicken to the wok with the orange juice and hoisin sauce. Heat through gently, then stir in the cashew nuts and sesame seeds. Transfer to a warmed dish and serve immediately.

Serves 4
Preparation: 5 minutes, plus standing
Cooking time: 10 minutes
Per serving: 470 cals; 23g fat; 35g carbohydrate

Chicken Satay Skewers

1tbsp each coriander
  seeds and cumin
  seeds
2tsp ground turmeric
4 garlic cloves, peeled
  and roughly chopped
zest and juice of 1
  lemon
2 bird's eye chillies,
  deseeded and finely
  chopped
3tbsp vegetable oil
1tsp salt
4 boneless, skinless
  chicken breasts,
  about 600g (1¼lb)

200g (7oz) salted
  peanuts
1tbsp molasses sugar
½ lemon grass stalk,
  chopped
2tbsp dark soy sauce
juice of ½ lime
200ml pack coconut
  cream
½ cucumber, thinly
  sliced, to serve

1 Soak 24 x 15cm (6 inch) bamboo skewers in water. Put the coriander and cumin seeds and the turmeric in a dry frying pan and heat for 30 seconds. Tip into a processor and add the garlic, lemon zest and juice, chillies, 1tbsp oil and the salt. Whiz for 1–2 minutes to a paste.
2 Put the paste in a large shallow dish. Cut the chicken into finger-length strips, add to the dish and toss everything together. Cover and chill for at least 20 minutes or up to 12 hours.
3 To make the sauce, put the peanuts, sugar, lemon grass, soy sauce, lime juice and coconut cream in a processor and add 2tbsp water. Whiz to make a thick, chunky sauce and spoon into a dish.
4 Preheat the grill to high. Thread the chicken on to the skewers, drizzle with the remaining oil and grill for 4–5 minutes on each side or until the juices run clear. Serve with the sauce and the cucumber.

Serves 4
Preparation: 30 minutes, plus chilling
Cooking time: 40 minutes
Per serving: 610 cals; 47g fat; 9g carbohydrate

See picture, page 284

Tandoori Chicken with Cucumber Raita

24 garlic cloves, about 125g (4oz), peeled and crushed

5cm (2 inch) piece fresh root ginger, peeled and chopped

3tbsp each coriander seeds, cumin seeds, ground fenugreek and paprika

3 red chillies, deseeded and chopped

3tsp English mustard

2tbsp tomato purée

1tsp salt

4tbsp groundnut oil, plus extra to oil

3 x 150ml cartons natural yogurt

juice of ½ lemon

4 skinless boneless chicken breasts, about 600g (1¼lb), cut into finger-width pieces

½ cucumber

salt and pepper

mint sprigs, to garnish

1   To make the tandoori paste, put the garlic, ginger, coriander and cumin seeds, fenugreek, paprika, chillies, mustard, tomato purée and salt into a mini processor with 8tbsp water and whiz to a paste. Divide the paste into three equal portions, freeze two parts in separate bags to use within 3 months (see right) and put the rest into a large bowl.

2   To make the tandoori chicken, add half the oil, 2 cartons yogurt and the lemon juice to the paste. Add the chicken to it and stir well to coat. Cover the bowl, chill and marinate the chicken for at least 4 hours.

3   Preheat the oven to 220°C (200°C fan oven) mark 7. Oil a roasting tin. Put the chicken in it, drizzle the remaining oil over it and roast the chicken for 20 minutes or until cooked through.

4   Meanwhile, prepare the raita. Whisk the remaining carton of yogurt. With a vegetable peeler, scrape the cucumber into very thin strips. Put the strips in a bowl and pour the whisked yogurt over them. Season, then chill. Garnish the cucumber raita with mint sprigs and serve it with the chicken.

To use the frozen paste: Put the paste in a microwave and cook on Defrost for 1 minute 20 seconds (based on 900W oven), or thaw at cool room temperature for 1 hour.

Serves 4
Preparation: 45 minutes, plus marinating
Cooking time: 20 minutes
Per serving: 360 cals; 20g fat; 10g carbohydrate

Chicken Tikka Masala

2tbsp oil

1 onion, peeled and finely sliced

2 garlic cloves, peeled and crushed

6 skinless boneless chicken thighs, cut into strips

2tbsp tikka masala curry paste

200g can chopped tomatoes

450ml (¾ pint) hot vegetable stock

225g (8oz) baby spinach leaves

1   Heat the oil in a large pan, add the onion and fry over a medium heat for 5–7 minutes until golden. Add the garlic and chicken and stir-fry for about 5 minutes until golden.

2   Stir in the curry paste, then add the tomatoes and hot stock. Bring to the boil, then reduce the heat, cover the pan and simmer over a low heat for 15 minutes or until the chicken is cooked through.

3   Add the spinach to the curry, stir and cook until the leaves have just wilted. Serve with plain boiled rice, mango chutney and poppadoms.

Serves 4
Preparation: 15 minutes
Cooking time: 25 minutes
Per serving: 270 cals; 14g fat; 10g carbohydrate

Chicken Curry

1tbsp oil
4 chicken legs, skinned
1 onion, peeled and
  finely chopped
2tbsp mild or medium
  curry paste
2 leeks, sliced
200g can chopped
  tomatoes

1 small cauliflower,
  broken into florets
250g (9oz) small new
  potatoes
600ml (1 pint) hot
  chicken stock
150g (5oz) each
  spinach and frozen
  peas

1 Heat the oil in a large non-stick casserole dish and brown the chicken all over. After 5 minutes, add the onion to the pan and cook for 5–10 minutes until golden.
2 Add the curry paste and cook for 1 minute, then add the leeks, tomatoes, cauliflower, potatoes and hot stock. Bring to the boil, then reduce the heat, cover the pan and simmer for 20–30 minutes until the chicken is cooked and the potatoes are tender.

3 Add the spinach and peas and cook for 5 minutes until heated through. Serve with rice.

Serves 4
Preparation: 20–25 minutes
Cooking time: about 50 minutes
Per serving: 270 cals; 10g fat; 22g carbohydrate

Chicken Tikka with Coconut Dressing

125ml (4fl oz) crème
  fraîche
5tbsp coconut milk
4 pitta bread
200g bag mixed salad
  leaves
2 x 210g packs cooked
  chicken tikka
  fillets, sliced

2 spring onions, finely
  sliced
2tbsp mango chutney
15g (½oz) flaked
  almonds
25g (1oz) raisins

1 Mix the crème fraîche and coconut milk in a bowl and put to one side.
2 Split each pitta bread to form a pocket, then fill each pocket with a generous handful of salad leaves. Put the chicken tikka on top of the salad, sprinkle the spring onions over, add the mango chutney, drizzle with the crème fraîche mixture, then top with a sprinkling of flaked almonds and raisins. Serve.

Serves 4
Preparation: 10 minutes
Per serving: 560 cals; 23g fat; 54g carbohydrate

Quick Chicken Pilau

50g (2oz) butter
2 medium onions,
  peeled and finely
  sliced
600g tub cooked pilau
  rice

300g pack spicy fried
  chicken pieces
4tbsp chopped
  coriander

1 Melt the butter in a large non-stick frying pan or wok and cook the onions over a gentle heat for 15 minutes or until golden and caramelised.
2 Add the rice to the pan, stir to coat in the butter, then add the chicken pieces. Cook for 5 minutes to heat through, then stir in the coriander and serve.

Serves 4
Preparation: 5 minutes
Cooking time: 20 minutes
Per serving: 450 cals; 16g fat; 54g carbohydrate

Thai Red Turkey Curry

3tbsp vegetable oil
450g (1lb) onions, peeled and finely chopped
200g (7oz) French beans, trimmed
125g (4oz) baby sweetcorn, cut on the diagonal
2 red peppers, halved, deseeded and cut into thick strips
1tbsp Thai red curry paste, or to taste
1 red chilli, deseeded and finely chopped
1 lemon grass stalk, trimmed and very finely chopped
4 kaffir lime leaves, bruised
2tbsp peeled and finely chopped fresh root ginger
1 garlic clove, peeled and crushed
400ml can coconut milk
600ml (1 pint) chicken or turkey stock
450g (1lb) cooked turkey, cut into strips
150g (5oz) beansprouts
fresh coriander sprigs and lime zest, to garnish

1 Heat the oil in a large frying pan or wok, add the onions and cook for 4–5 minutes or until soft. Add the French beans, baby sweetcorn and red peppers to the pan and stir-fry for 3–4 minutes. Add the curry paste, chilli, lemon grass, lime leaves, ginger and garlic and cook for 2 minutes, stirring. Remove from the pan and put to one side.

2 Add the coconut milk and stock to the pan, bring to the boil and bubble vigorously for 5–10 minutes or until reduced by a quarter. Return the vegetables to the pan with the turkey and beansprouts. Bring back to the boil and cook for 1–2 minutes, then serve immediately, garnished with coriander sprigs and lime zest.

Serves 6
Preparation: 35 minutes
Cooking time: 25 minutes
Per serving: 300 cals; 16g fat; 11g carbohydrate

Oriental Crisp Duck Breast with Citrus Sauce

3 small whole ducks, each about 2.3kg (5lb), with legs removed
sea salt and black pepper
3 bunches of thyme
3 small oranges, cut into quarters, plus pared zest and juice of 4 oranges
125g (4oz) golden caster sugar
2tsp coriander seeds, roasted and crushed
3tbsp lemon juice
300ml (½ pint) balsamic vinegar or 150ml (¼ pint) each balsamic vinegar and stock
fresh rosemary sprigs, watercress and orange julienne strips, to garnish

1 Put the ducks on racks and pour boiling water over them until the skin becomes taut. Leave in a cool place for 4 hours and, once cold, store uncovered in the fridge overnight.

2 Preheat the oven to 200°C (180°C fan oven) mark 6. Season the ducks inside and out and insert a bunch of thyme and 4 orange quarters into each cavity. Put the ducks on racks over roasting tins and roast for 1–1½ hours or until the juices run clear when the thickest part of the duck is pierced. If necessary, transpose the roasting tins halfway through cooking time.

3 Meanwhile, make the sauce. Put the orange zest and juice and the sugar in a pan, bring to the boil, then reduce the heat and simmer for 5 minutes. Remove the zest. Add the coriander seeds and bubble for 4–5 minutes or until well reduced and a pale golden brown. Immediately add the lemon juice and vinegar, season, then bring to the boil and bubble until syrupy – about 10 minutes.

4 Transfer the ducks to a board. Cut the breasts from the carcass, garnish with rosemary, watercress and orange julienne strips and serve with the citrus sauce.

Serves 6
Preparation: 30 minutes, plus standing
Cooking time: 1½ hours
Per serving: 390 cals; 17g fat; 29g carbohydrate

Crispy Duck Pancakes

2.3kg (5lb) fresh oven-ready duckling
2 bay leaves
1tsp salt
10 black peppercorns
75g (3oz) butter
350g (12oz) onions, peeled and finely sliced
2 garlic cloves, peeled and finely sliced
2 red chillies, deseeded and finely sliced
2.5cm (1 inch) piece fresh root ginger, peeled and chopped
2 red peppers

175g (6oz) cucumber, deseeded
4 spring onions
125ml (4fl oz) hoisin sauce
3tsp teriyaki sauce
6tbsp chopped coriander
18 sheets filo pastry, about 225g (8oz)
1 egg, beaten
oil, for deep-frying
deep-fried spring onions and red chillies, to garnish
sweet chilli sauce, to serve

1 Put the duck, bay leaves, salt and peppercorns in a large pan with cold water to cover. Bring to the boil, reduce the heat, cover the pan and simmer for 2 hours. Drain off the resulting stock and cool. Strip the meat from the duck, discarding the skin and bones. Cut the flesh into long strips.

2 Heat 25g (1oz) butter in a medium-sized pan and cook the onions, garlic, chillies and ginger over a low heat for 30 minutes or until soft and golden, then cool slightly. Preheat the grill to high.

3 Cook the red peppers under the hot grill for about 10–15 minutes or until the skin is well blackened. Put to one side to cool, then skin, discard the seeds and slice into strips. Cut the cucumber and spring onions into 5cm (2 inch) fine matchsticks.

4 Mix the duck meat with the cooked onion mixture, the hoisin and teriyaki sauces and the coriander.

5 Melt the remaining butter in a small pan. Lay a sheet of filo pastry on a work surface and brush lightly with melted butter; repeat with two more sheets of filo pastry. Cut the filo into squares measuring about 15 x 15cm (6 x 6 inches). Complete the same process with the remaining filo pastry. Cover the pastry with a damp tea towel or clingfilm as you work to prevent it drying out.

6 Lay a few red pepper strips diagonally across the centre of each filo square, top with a little duck mixture, then with spring onions and cucumber. Lightly brush two opposite corners of pastry with beaten egg, then roll up into a cigar shape. Put to one side and continue until all the filling mixture and filo pastry are used up.

7 Heat the oil in a deep-fat fryer or large pan to 160°C or until a cube of bread begins to sizzle. Deep-fry each parcel for 3–4 minutes or until golden. Serve the pancakes immediately, allowing two per person, garnished with deep-fried spring onions and red chillies and accompanied by a small bowl of sweet chilli sauce for dipping.

Serves 6
Preparation: 30 minutes
Cooking time: 2¼ hours
Per serving: 640 cals; 34g fat; 37g carbohydrate

Top left: Chicken Satay Skewers, page 280; top right: Prawn and Vegetable Pilau, page 276; bottom left: Salmon Laksa Curry, page 278; bottom right: Chow Mein, page 287.

Crispy Duck with Hot and Sweet Dip

8 small duck legs
2 pieces star anise
4 fat garlic cloves,
  peeled and sliced
1 dried red chilli
grated zest and juice of
  1 orange

1tbsp fresh tamarind or
  lemon juice
fried garlic slivers,
  fried chilli pieces and
  star anise, to garnish
Hot and Sweet Dip (see
  below), to serve

1 Prick the duck legs all over with a skewer or fork. Put them in a large pan, cover with cold water and bring to the boil, then reduce the heat and simmer for 45 minutes.
2 Meanwhile, put the star anise, garlic, chilli, orange zest and juice and tamarind or lemon juice in a blender and whiz to a paste. Preheat the grill.

3 Drain the duck legs and put them, skin side down, on a foil-lined grill pan. Brush half the spice paste over the duck, grill for 5 minutes, then turn skin side up and brush the remaining paste over. Grill for a further 5–7 minutes or until the duck skin is well charred and crisp. Garnish with the fried garlic slivers, fried chilli pieces and star anise and serve with Hot and Sweet Dip.

Serves 4
Preparation: 10 minutes
Cooking time: 55 minutes
Per serving: 420 cals; 36g fat; trace carbohydrate

Hot and Sweet Dip

200ml (7fl oz) white
  wine vinegar
150g (5oz) golden
  caster sugar
75g (3oz) each
  cucumber, spring
  onion and mango, cut
  into fine shreds

1 dried red chilli or
  ¼tsp deseeded and
  shredded red chilli

1 Boil the vinegar and sugar together in a pan for 2 minutes, then stir in the cucumber, spring onion, mango and chilli. Put the mixture to one side and leave to cool. Allow the dip to come to room temperature before serving.

Serves 4
Preparation: 5 minutes
Cooking time: 2 minutes
Per serving: 170 cals; trace fat; 43g carbohydrate

Chinese Spare Ribs

10tbsp hoisin sauce
3tbsp tomato ketchup
1 garlic clove, peeled
  and crushed
salt and pepper

2 x 10-bone baby rack
  of pork ribs (available
  from butchers), cut in
  half to make 4 x
  5-bone racks

1 Put the hoisin sauce, ketchup and garlic in a large shallow dish. Season and stir until combined.
2 Add the pork ribs and toss to coat, spooning over the marinade to cover completely. You can either cook the ribs immediately or, if you have time, cover and chill them for 2 hours or overnight.
3 Preheat a grill until medium-high. Alternatively, preheat the barbecue – it's ready to use when the coals glow and are covered with light ash. Lift the ribs from the marinating dish and grill or barbecue for 10–12 minutes on each side. Alternatively, roast in a preheated oven at 200°C (180°C fan oven) mark 6 for 45 minutes.

Serves 4
Preparation: 10 minutes, plus marinating (optional)
Cooking time: 20–45 minutes
Per serving: 330 cals; 20g fat; 7g carbohydrate

Chow Mein

250g (9oz) dried
  medium egg noodles
1tbsp toasted sesame
  oil
2 skinless boneless
  chicken breasts, cut
  into thin strips
bunch of spring onions,
  thinly sliced on the
  diagonal
150g (5oz) mangetout,
  thickly sliced on the
  diagonal

125g (4oz) beansprouts
100g (3½oz) cooked
  ham, finely shredded
120g sachet chow mein
  sauce
salt and pepper
light soy sauce, to
  serve

1 Cook the noodles in boiling water for the time stated
  on the packet. Drain, rinse thoroughly under cold water
  and put to one side.
2 Meanwhile, heat a wok or large frying pan until hot,
  then add the oil. Add the chicken and stir-fry over a
  high heat for 3–4 minutes until browned all over. Add
  the sliced spring onions and mangetout, stir-fry for
  2 minutes, then stir in the beansprouts and ham and
  cook for 2 minutes.

3 Add the drained noodles, then pour over the chow
  mein sauce and toss together to coat evenly. Stir-fry for
  2 minutes or until piping hot. Season to taste and serve
  with light soy sauce to drizzle over.

Serves 4
Preparation: 10 minutes
Cooking time: 10 minutes
Per serving: 380 cals; 9g fat; 46g carbohydrate

See picture, page 284

Indonesian Pork Satay

3tbsp chilli soy sauce
1tbsp molasses sugar
1 garlic clove, peeled
  and grated
salt and pepper
500g (1lb 2oz) pork
  fillet, cut into finger-
  length strips
250g (9oz) crunchy
  peanut butter

100ml (3½ fl oz) half-fat
  coconut milk, or
  use half a can of full-
  fat coconut milk
  and make up the
  difference with water
  or stock
1tbsp chilli soy sauce
1tbsp vegetable oil

1 Soak 16 x 15cm (6 inch) bamboo skewers in cold
  water for 30 minutes. Meanwhile, put the soy sauce,
  sugar and garlic into a shallow dish, season and mix to
  dissolve the sugar. Add the pork, coat evenly, then
  cover and chill for at least 30 minutes or up to 12 hours.
2 To make the sauce: put the peanut butter into a bowl
  and gradually stir in 6tbsp hot water. Slowly add the
  coconut milk, stir until thinned, then add the soy sauce.
  Season, cover and chill for up to one day.

3 Thread the pork on to the skewers. Cook in batches on
  a hot, oiled griddle for 3–4 minutes on each side. Serve
  with the satay sauce, jasmine rice and cucumber
  batons.

Serves 4
Preparation: 15 minutes, plus marinating
Cooking time: 12–16 minutes
Per serving: 620cals; 48g fat; 8g carbohydrate

Garlic and Soy Ribs with Sweet Potatoes

450g (1lb) rack of pork
  ribs, cut in half
½ lemon
1tbsp chicken
  seasoning
4tbsp soy sauce
3tbsp malt vinegar
3tbsp light muscovado
  sugar
2 garlic cloves, peeled
  and crushed
½tsp peeled and
  freshly grated root
  ginger

1tsp Chipotle Tabasco
  (if you have only the
  regular variety, just
  add a couple of drops)
125ml (4fl oz) beef
  stock, cooled
4 sweet potatoes,
  scrubbed
olive oil and sea salt
  (optional)
4tbsp Greek-style
  yogurt
2 spring onions,
  roughly chopped

1 Put the pork ribs into a shallow dish. Rub the lemon over the meat, squeezing out the juice as you go, then sprinkle over the chicken seasoning, soy sauce, vinegar, sugar, garlic, ginger and Tabasco. Turn the ribs to coat evenly in the marinade. If you have time, cover and chill to marinate for at least 2 hours.

2 Preheat the oven to 200°C (180°C fan oven) mark 6. Put the ribs and marinade into a roasting tin and pour over the beef stock. Roast for 50–55 minutes, turning the ribs during cooking to coat in the sauce.

3 Meanwhile, drizzle the sweet potatoes with a little olive oil and sprinkle the skins with sea salt, if using, then wrap in foil and bake for 50–55 minutes until they are just tender.

4 To serve, transfer the ribs to a board and cut between each rib to separate. Slash the top of each potato and squeeze the sides to push up the sweet flesh. Top each potato with a dollop of yogurt, sprinkle over the spring onions and serve with the ribs.

Serves 4
Preparation: 15 minutes
Cooking time: 55 minutes
Per serving: 440 cals; 17g fat; 49g carbohydrate

Fried Yellow Bean Pork with Cashews

6 cardamom pods, split
2.5cm (1 inch) piece
  fresh root ginger,
  peeled and finely
  chopped
1tbsp five-spice
  powder
450g (1lb) pork
  tenderloin, thinly
  sliced
2tbsp oil
225g (8oz) small oyster
  mushrooms

125g (4oz) leek or
  spring onions, sliced
3 garlic cloves, peeled
  and sliced
2tbsp yellow bean
  sauce
pared zest and juice of
  1 small orange
50g (2oz) toasted
  cashew nuts

1 Rub the cardamom, ginger and five-spice powder into the pork and put to one side.

2 Heat half the oil in a wok or frying pan and fry the mushrooms quickly for about 1 minute. Remove the mushrooms with a slotted spoon before they begin to wilt. Add the remaining oil and, when hot, stir the pork, leek and garlic into the pan and stir-fry over a high heat for 5 minutes.

3 Return the mushrooms to the pan with the yellow bean sauce, orange zest and juice and the cashew nuts and cook, stirring over a high heat, until all the ingredients are coated in sauce and heated through. Serve immediately.

Serves 4
Preparation: 10 minutes
Cooking time: 10 minutes
Per serving: 320 cals; 21g fat; 7g carbohydrate

Lamb Korma with Red Onion Cachumber

3tbsp ground cinnamon
36 green cardamoms
30 cloves
18 bay leaves
1tbsp fennel seeds
salt and pepper
150ml carton natural yogurt
700g (1½lb) boneless lamb, cut into 2.5cm (1 inch) pieces
1tbsp golden caster sugar
3tbsp groundnut oil
1tsp ground turmeric
2tsp ground coriander
1 small onion, peeled and finely chopped
4 garlic cloves, peeled and crushed
1cm (½ inch) piece fresh root ginger, peeled and finely chopped
1 red onion, peeled and finely sliced
1 tomato, deseeded and diced
1tbsp chopped mint, plus sprigs to garnish
juice of ½ lime
50g (2oz) ground almonds
142ml carton double cream
large pinch of saffron

1 For the korma paste, put the cinnamon, cardamoms, cloves, bay leaves, fennel seeds and 1tsp salt into a mini processor and whiz to a powder. Tip the powder into a bowl and add 4tbsp water, stirring well to make a paste. Divide into three equal portions, then freeze two portions in separate bags to use within 3 months (see right) and put the remainder into a large bowl.
2 To make the curry, add the yogurt, lamb and sugar to the paste in the bowl and mix well. Cover the bowl, chill and marinate the lamb for at least 4 hours, preferably overnight.
3 Preheat the oven to 190°C (170°C fan oven) mark 5. Heat the oil in a flameproof casserole, add the turmeric and coriander and fry for 30 seconds. Add the chopped onion and stir-fry over a high heat for 10 minutes until softened and golden. Add the garlic and ginger and cook for 1–2 minutes, then add the lamb, cover the casserole and cook in the oven for 20 minutes.
4 Meanwhile, make the red onion cachumber. Put the sliced onion, tomato, mint and lime juice in a small bowl and toss them together, then season well with salt and chill until needed.
5 Take the casserole out of the c
oven temperature to 170°C (15
Add the ground almonds, crea
(3½fl oz) water. Season well wit
stir together. Cover the casserole
cook for 1½ hours or until tend
6 Serve the lamb korma, garnish
deep, warmed bowls, with the red onion cachumber in a separate dish, and some naan bread to wipe the bowl clean.

To use the frozen paste: Put the paste in a microwave and cook on Defrost for 1 minute 20 seconds (based on a 900W oven), or thaw at cool room temperature for 1–1½ hours.

Serves 4
Preparation: 20 minutes, plus marinating
Cooking time: 2 hours
Per serving: 660 cals; 49g fat; 15g carbohydrate

Lamb Curry with Pumpkin and Coconut

1tbsp oil, preferably
  stir-fry oil
550g (1¼lb) diced leg
  of lamb
225g (8oz) red onion,
  peeled and chopped
125g (4oz) block
  creamed coconut
2tsp Thai red curry
  paste
2.5cm (1 inch) piece
  fresh root ginger,
  peeled and chopped

salt
225g (8oz) pumpkin,
  peeled and cut into
  thin wedges
4tbsp mango chutney
basil leaves and fried
  red onion rings, to
  garnish

1 Heat the oil in a large pan and fry the lamb over a high heat until deep golden brown. Reduce the heat, add the onion and continue to fry, stirring, until the onion is soft and golden. Take a good 10 minutes to do this as it brings out the natural sweetness of the onions and adds to both the flavour and colour of the finished dish.

2 Meanwhile, pour 600ml (1 pint) boiling water over the creamed coconut and leave to dissolve.

3 Add the curry paste and ginger to the lamb and fry for 1–2 minutes. Stir in the coconut liquid and bring to the boil. Season with salt, then cover the pan, reduce the heat and simmer on a very low heat for 30 minutes.

4 Stir the pumpkin and chutney into the lamb, cover again and cook for 30 minutes or until the lamb and pumpkin are tender. Garnish with basil leaves and onion rings, then serve with basmati rice.

Serves 4
Preparation: 10 minutes
Cooking time: 1 hour 20 minutes
Per serving: 530 cals; 38g fat; 17g carbohydrate

Curried Lamb with Lentils

500g (1lb 2oz) stewing
  lamb on the bone, cut
  into eight (ask your
  butcher to do this)
1tbsp ground cumin
1tsp ground turmeric
2 garlic cloves, peeled
  and crushed
1 red chilli, deseeded
  and chopped
2.5cm (1 inch) piece
  fresh root ginger,
  peeled and grated

1tsp salt
2tbsp sunflower oil
1 onion, peeled and
  chopped
400g can chopped
  tomatoes
2tbsp vinegar
175g (6oz) red lentils,
  rinsed
traditional
  Mediterranean wraps
chopped coriander
  leaves, to serve

1 Put the lamb into a shallow sealable container, add the spices, garlic, chilli, ginger and salt. Stir well to mix, then cover and chill for 30 minutes or more.

2 Heat the oil in a large flameproof casserole. Add the onion and cook over a gentle heat for 5 minutes. Add the lamb and cook for 10 minutes, turning regularly, until the meat is evenly browned.

3 Add the tomatoes, vinegar, 450ml (¾ pint) boiling water and the lentils and bring to the boil. Reduce the heat, cover the casserole and simmer for 1 hour. Remove the lid and cook uncovered for 30 minutes, stirring occasionally, until the sauce is thick and the lamb is tender.

4 Remove the wraps from their plastic packaging and roll up together, then wrap in greaseproof paper or baking parchment, twisting the ends to secure. Microwave on High for 1½ minutes (based on a 900W oven) until warmed through. Spread the lamb curry on to the wraps, sprinkle with coriander and roll up individually to serve.

Serves 4
Preparation: 15 minutes
Cooking time: 1 hour 50 minutes
Per serving (not including wraps): 340 cals; 18g fat; 14g carbohydrate

Top left: Speedy Beef Noodes, page 292; top right: Thai Beef Curry, page 293; bottom left: Thai Noodles with Prawns, page 273; bottom right: Thai Vegetable Curry, page 295.

Vegetable Curry

3tbsp vegetable oil
1 onion, peeled and
  finely sliced
4 garlic cloves, peeled
  and crushed
2.5cm (1 inch) piece
  fresh root ginger,
  peeled and grated
3tbsp medium curry
  powder
6 curry leaves
150g (5oz) potatoes,
  peeled and cut into
  1cm (½ inch) cubes
125g (4oz) aubergine,
  cut into 2cm (¾ inch)
  long, 5mm (¼ inch)
  wide sticks

150g (5oz) carrots,
  peeled and cut into
  5mm (¼ inch) dice
900ml (1½ pints) hot
  vegetable stock
pinch of powdered
  saffron
salt and pepper
150g (5oz) green beans
75g (3oz) frozen peas
3tbsp chopped
  coriander leaves

1 Heat the oil in a large heavy-based pan. Add the onion
   and fry over a low heat for 5–10 minutes until softened
   and golden. Add the garlic, ginger, curry powder and
   curry leaves and fry for 1 minute. Add the potatoes
   and aubergine and fry, stirring, for 2 minutes. Add the
   carrots, hot stock, saffron, 1tsp salt and plenty of
   pepper. Cover and cook for 10 minutes until the
   vegetables are almost tender.
2 Add the beans and peas to the pan and cook for
   4 minutes. Scatter with coriander and serve.

Serves 4
Preparation: 20 minutes
Cooking time: 30 minutes
Per serving: 190 cals; 11g fat; 19g carbohydrate

Aubergine and Coconut Curry

5–6tbsp olive oil
1 medium aubergine,
  cut into chunks a bit
  bigger than bite-sized
1 medium onion,
  peeled and chopped
thumb-sized piece
  fresh root ginger,
  peeled
2tbsp garam masala or
  mild curry paste
400g can chickpeas,
  drained and rinsed
1 large sweet potato,
  peeled and cut into
  bite-sized chunks

400g can chopped
  tomatoes
400ml can coconut
  milk
salt and pepper
small bunch of
  coriander, roughly
  torn
about 125g (4oz)
  spinach leaves,
150g tub Greek-style
  natural yogurt
  (optional)

1 Heat about 4tbsp olive oil in a large non-stick pan and
   fry the aubergine until golden brown and beginning to
   soften. Transfer to a plate with a draining spoon, then
   add another 1–2tbsp olive oil to the pan and fry the
   onion over a medium heat for at least 10 minutes until
   soft and deep golden.
2 Coarsely grate the ginger into the onion, stir for
   2 minutes, then add the garam masala or curry paste.
   Reduce the heat and cook for 1–2 minutes. Add the
   aubergine, chickpeas, sweet potato, tomatoes and
   coconut milk, bring to the boil, then reduce the heat and
   simmer gently until the sweet potato is just tender –
   about 10–12 minutes. Taste and add seasoning. To
   serve, add the coriander and spinach leaves – they'll
   wilt in the heat of the pan. If you want to, top with
   generous spoonfuls of yogurt.

Serves 4
Preparation: 15 minutes
Cooking time: 30–35 minutes
Per serving: 570 cals; 43g fat; 34g carbohydrate

10

Better than a takeaway

Thai Vegetable Curry

2tbsp vegetable oil
1 large onion, peeled
   and finely chopped
4tsp Thai green curry
   paste
600ml (1 pint)
   vegetable stock
200g (7oz) washed new
   potatoes, cut in half
225g (8oz) easy-cook
   long-grain rice
200g (7oz) courgettes,
   cut on the diagonal

200g (7oz) carrots,
   peeled and cut on
   the diagonal
150g (5oz) broccoli,
   divided into florets
125g (4oz) tomatoes,
   cut in quarters
150g (5oz) frozen
   spinach, thawed
300ml (½ pint) coconut
   milk
coriander sprigs, to
   garnish (optional)

1 Heat the oil in a large frying pan. Add the onion and green curry paste, then cook for 4–5 minutes. Add the stock and potatoes, bring to the boil, then reduce the heat, cover the pan and cook for 20 minutes or until the potatoes are just tender.

2 Meanwhile, cook the rice for the time stated on the packet. Add the courgettes, carrots and broccoli to the curry. Cook for 3–4 minutes or until the vegetables are tender. At the last minute, add the tomatoes, spinach and coconut milk and heat through thoroughly. Serve the curry on a bed of rice and garnish with coriander sprigs.

Serves 4
Preparation: 15 minutes
Cooking time: 35 minutes
Per serving: 480 cals; 19g fat; 69g carbohydrate

See picture, page 291

Saffron Rice

500g (1lb 2oz) basmati
   rice
900ml (1½ pints) stock
   made with 1½ chicken
   stock cubes
5tbsp sunflower or
   light vegetable oil

salt
½tsp saffron
75g (3oz) blanched
   almonds and
   pistachio nuts,
   coarsely chopped, to
   garnish (optional)

1 Put the rice into a bowl and cover with warm water, then drain well through a sieve.

2 Put the stock, oil and a good pinch of salt into a pan, then cover and bring to the boil. Add the saffron and the rice.

3 Cover the pan and bring the stock back to the boil, then stir, reduce the heat to low and cook, covered, gently for 20 minutes until little holes appear all over the surface of the cooked rice and the grains are tender.

4 Fluff up the rice with a fork and transfer it to a warmed serving dish. Sprinkle the chopped almonds and pistachios on top, if using, and serve.

Serves 8
Preparation: 5–10 minutes
Cooking time: 25 minutes
Per serving: 350 cals; 13g fat; 50g carbohydrate

Basic Pilau Rice

50g (2oz) butter
225g (8oz) long-grain
  white rice
750ml (1¼ pints) hot
  chicken stock

salt and pepper
generous knob of
  butter, to serve

1 Melt the butter in a pan, add the rice and fry gently for
   3–4 minutes until translucent.
2 Slowly pour in the hot stock, season, stir and cover
   with a tight-fitting lid. Leave, undisturbed, over a very
   low heat for about 15 minutes until the water has been
   absorbed and the rice is just tender.
3 Remove the lid and cover the surface of the rice with
   a clean cloth. Replace the lid and leave to stand in a
   warm place for about 15 minutes to dry the rice before
   serving.
4 Fork through and add a knob of butter to serve.

Serves 4
Preparation: 5 minutes
Cooking time: 20 minutes, plus standing
Per serving: 320 cals; 13g fat; 45g carbohydrate

Thai Rice

500g (1lb 2oz) Thai rice
salt

handful of mint leaves

1 Cook the rice and mint in boiling salted water for 10–12
   minutes or until tender. Drain well and serve.

Serves 6
Cooking time: 10–12 minutes
Per serving: 300 cals; Tr fat; 67g carbohydrate

Thai Vegetable Curry

2tbsp vegetable oil
1 large onion, peeled and finely chopped
4tsp Thai green curry paste
600ml (1 pint) vegetable stock
200g (7oz) washed new potatoes, cut in half
225g (8oz) easy-cook long-grain rice
200g (7oz) courgettes, cut on the diagonal
200g (7oz) carrots, peeled and cut on the diagonal
150g (5oz) broccoli, divided into florets
125g (4oz) tomatoes, cut in quarters
150g (5oz) frozen spinach, thawed
300ml (½ pint) coconut milk
coriander sprigs, to garnish (optional)

1 Heat the oil in a large frying pan. Add the onion and green curry paste, then cook for 4–5 minutes. Add the stock and potatoes, bring to the boil, then reduce the heat, cover the pan and cook for 20 minutes or until the potatoes are just tender.

2 Meanwhile, cook the rice for the time stated on the packet. Add the courgettes, carrots and broccoli to the curry. Cook for 3–4 minutes or until the vegetables are tender. At the last minute, add the tomatoes, spinach and coconut milk and heat through thoroughly. Serve the curry on a bed of rice and garnish with coriander sprigs.

Serves 4
Preparation: 15 minutes
Cooking time: 35 minutes
Per serving: 480 cals; 19g fat; 69g carbohydrate

See picture, page 291

Saffron Rice

500g (1lb 2oz) basmati rice
900ml (1½ pints) stock made with 1½ chicken stock cubes
5tbsp sunflower or light vegetable oil
salt
½tsp saffron
75g (3oz) blanched almonds and pistachio nuts, coarsely chopped, to garnish (optional)

1 Put the rice into a bowl and cover with warm water, then drain well through a sieve.

2 Put the stock, oil and a good pinch of salt into a pan, then cover and bring to the boil. Add the saffron and the rice.

3 Cover the pan and bring the stock back to the boil, then stir, reduce the heat to low and cook, covered, gently for 20 minutes until little holes appear all over the surface of the cooked rice and the grains are tender.

4 Fluff up the rice with a fork and transfer it to a warmed serving dish. Sprinkle the chopped almonds and pistachios on top, if using, and serve.

Serves 8
Preparation: 5–10 minutes
Cooking time: 25 minutes
Per serving: 350 cals; 13g fat; 50g carbohydrate

Basic Pilau Rice

50g (2oz) butter
225g (8oz) long-grain
  white rice
750ml (1¼ pints) hot
  chicken stock

salt and pepper
generous knob of
  butter, to serve

1 Melt the butter in a pan, add the rice and fry gently for 3–4 minutes until translucent.
2 Slowly pour in the hot stock, season, stir and cover with a tight-fitting lid. Leave, undisturbed, over a very low heat for about 15 minutes until the water has been absorbed and the rice is just tender.
3 Remove the lid and cover the surface of the rice with a clean cloth. Replace the lid and leave to stand in a warm place for about 15 minutes to dry the rice before serving.
4 Fork through and add a knob of butter to serve.

Serves 4
Preparation: 5 minutes
Cooking time: 20 minutes, plus standing
Per serving: 320 cals; 13g fat; 45g carbohydrate

Thai Rice

500g (1lb 2oz) Thai rice
salt

handful of mint leaves

1 Cook the rice and mint in boiling salted water for 10–12 minutes or until tender. Drain well and serve.

Serves 6
Cooking time: 10–12 minutes
Per serving: 300 cals; Tr fat; 67g carbohydrate

Curried Vegetable Rice

1tbsp vegetable oil
1 small onion, peeled
  and chopped
½tsp Balti curry paste
1 large carrot, peeled
  and grated

150ml (¼ pint) rice
1 vegetable or chicken
  stock cube, crumbled
salt and pepper
handful of broccoli or
  cauliflower florets

1 Heat the oil in a large pan and fry the onion for 15 minutes until tender.
2 Add the curry paste and cook for 2–3 minutes.
3 Add the carrot and rice, then immediately add 300ml (½ pint) boiling water, the stock cube and plenty of seasoning. Cover the pan and bring to the boil, then reduce the heat and simmer for 10 minutes.
4 Add the broccoli or cauliflower florets and cook for 5 minutes, then serve.

Serves 2
Preparation: 5 minutes
Cooking time: 35 minutes
Per serving: 390 cals; 8g fat; 70g carbohydrate

Variation
Thai curried vegetable rice: Use 1–2tbsp of Thai curry paste instead of the regular Indian variety and substitute a 400g can of coconut milk in place of the tomatoes.

Special Prawn Fried Rice

1tbsp sesame oil
6tbsp nasi goreng
  paste
250g (9oz) cooked king
  prawns
200g (7oz) green
  cabbage, shredded
2 x 250g packs
  microwave rice

2tbsp soy sauce
1tbsp sunflower oil
2 eggs, beaten
2 spring onions, finely
  sliced
1 lime, quartered

1 Heat the sesame oil in a wok and fry the nasi goreng paste for 1–2 minutes. Add the prawns and cabbage and fry for 2–3 minutes. Next, add the rice and soy sauce and cook for 5 minutes, stirring occasionally.
2 To make the omelette, heat the sunflower oil in a non-stick frying pan (about 25.5cm/10 inches in diameter) and add the eggs. Swirl around to cover the base in a thin layer and cook for 2–3 minutes until set.
3 Roll up the omelette and cut into slivers. Serve the rice scattered with the egg and spring onions, with the lime quarters to squeeze over.

Serves 4
Preparation: 5 minutes
Cooking time: 8–10 minutes
Per serving: 380 cals; 15g fat; 43g carbohydrate

Vegetables

With their fresh clean taste and inherent goodness, vegetables really are the jewels in the kitchen. Steamed, baked, roasted, stir-fried, braised – cook them however you want, they're so versatile. And there are so many to choose from.

Big bowlfuls of creamy mash are just right for soaking up the last warm lashings of gravy on your plate. And we're not talking just mashed potatoes – try Parsnip Mash with Crisp Bacon, or Vegetable and Mustard Mash. But potatoes are great comfort food: pile a dish high with crispy Potato Croquettes with Bacon and Cheese, or crunchy Potato Frites and see how long you can resist them.

Perhaps it's time to try out something different. What about Braised Chicory in White Wine; Stir-fried Kale; Roasted Fennel with Oranges and Dill Mash; or Gratin of Chard? New and enticing smells will be wafting round your kitchen in no time.

Then there's cabbage – red, white or green, cooked with the sweetness of onions and cranberries, the pungency of garlic, or the earthiness of caraway. Simple, tasty and good for you. Vegetables don't have to be just an accompaniment – eat and enjoy them on their own.

Brussels Sprouts with Shallots and Pancetta

200g (7oz) diced pancetta
salt and pepper
900g (2lb) Brussels sprouts, peeled
200g (7oz) shallots, blanched in boiling water, drained and peeled
2tsp golden caster sugar
4tbsp red wine vinegar
150ml (¼ pint) red wine
1tsp juniper berries
1tbsp chopped thyme

1 Heat a large frying pan and dry-fry the pancetta for 5 minutes until golden. Remove with a slotted spoon and put to one side.
2 Bring a pan of salted water to the boil, add the sprouts and cook for 5 minutes. Drain the sprouts, plunge them into cold water for 10 minutes, then drain and put to one side.
3 Fry the shallots in the pancetta pan for 5 minutes. Add the sugar and cook for 5 minutes until caramelised. Add the vinegar, wine, juniper berries and thyme, cover and simmer for 10 minutes until almost tender. Uncover the pan, bring to the boil and reduce the liquid until syrupy.
4 Add the pancetta and sprouts to the pan and cook for 3–4 minutes until heated through, then season.

Serves 8
Preparation: 15 minutes
Cooking time: 40 minutes
Per serving: 210 cals; 17g fat; 8g carbohydrate

Brussels Sprouts with Chestnuts and Shallots

salt and pepper
900g (2lb) small Brussels sprouts, trimmed
1tbsp olive oil
8 shallots, blanched in boiling water and drained
200g pack peeled cooked chestnuts
15g (½oz) butter
pinch of freshly grated nutmeg

1 Bring a pan of salted water to the boil, add the Brussels sprouts and blanch for 2 minutes. Drain the sprouts and refresh with cold water.
2 Heat the olive oil in a wok or sauté pan. Peel and finely chop the shallots, add to the pan and stir-fry for 5 minutes until almost tender. Add the sprouts to the pan with the chestnuts and stir-fry for about 4 minutes to heat through. Add the butter and nutmeg, season and serve.

Serves 8
Preparation: 15 minutes
Cooking time: 10 minutes
Per serving: 140 cals; 5g fat; 18g carbohydrate

Herby Buttered Brussels Sprouts

salt and pepper
900g (2lb) Brussels sprouts, trimmed
125g (4oz) unsalted butter
4tbsp red wine vinegar
4tbsp each chopped chives and tarragon

1 Bring a pan of salted water to the boil, add the Brussels sprouts and cook for 5 minutes or until nearly tender. Drain the sprouts, plunge into cold water for 5 minutes, then drain again thoroughly and put to one side.
2 To make the beurre noisette sauce, melt the butter in a small pan and cook until brown. Add the vinegar and cook for 2 minutes. Stir in the herbs.
3 Heat a large frying pan and stir-fry the sprouts for 2–3 minutes, then season. Pour the beurre noisette sauce over, making sure the sprouts are evenly coated in butter and are thoroughly heated through.

Serves 8   Preparation: 10 minutes, plus standing
Cooking time: 8–10 minutes
Per serving: 160 cals; 14g fat; 4g carbohydrate

Creamy Brussels Sprouts

600ml (1 pint) milk
1 thick slice each onion
 and celery
6 peppercorns
1 small bay leaf
1.1kg (2½lb) Brussels
 sprouts, lightly
 trimmed
salt and pepper

40g (1½oz) butter
40g (1½oz) plain flour
½ whole nutmeg,
 grated, about 1tsp
4tbsp single cream
oregano sprigs, flat-
 leafed parsley and
 freshly grated
 nutmeg, to garnish

1 Put the milk in a pan with the onion, celery, peppercorns and bay leaf. Bring to the boil, remove from the heat and leave to infuse for 20–30 minutes.
2 Meanwhile, cook the sprouts in a pan of boiling salted water for 10–15 minutes until just tender. Drain and then plunge them into a bowl of icy cold water. Drain again and dry well.

3 Strain and reserve the milk. Melt the butter in a heavy-based pan. Take the pan off the heat, add the flour and stir until smooth. Stir in the milk and mix until smooth. Return to the heat and bring to the boil, stirring. Reduce the heat and simmer for 1–2 minutes, then add the nutmeg and season. Float the cream on top.
4 Pulse the sprouts briefly in a food processor until roughly chopped. Combine with the sauce, put in a pan over a low heat and stir until hot. Garnish with the oregano, parsley and nutmeg and serve.

Serves 8–10
Preparation: 15 minutes
Cooking time: 25 minutes, plus infusing
Per serving: 170–140 cals; 10–8g fat;
13–10g carbohydrate

Crisp Parsnip Cakes

700g (1½lb) parsnips,
 peeled and diced
salt and pepper
25g (1oz) unsalted
 butter
3tbsp plain flour, plus
 extra to dust

several pinches of
 ground mace
1 large egg, beaten
100g (3½oz) fresh
 white breadcrumbs
1tbsp oil

1 Cook the parsnips in boiling salted water for about 10 minutes until tender. Drain well and return to the pan. Add the butter and 1tbsp flour. Mash well, adding the mace and seasoning to taste. Leave to cool for 10 minutes.
2 Put the remaining flour on a plate. Pour the beaten egg into a shallow bowl. Scatter the breadcrumbs on to another plate. With lightly floured hands, divide the parsnip mash into six and roll into balls. Flatten slightly to form cakes.

3 Take one parsnip cake and dust with a little flour, then dip in the beaten egg and then roll it in the bread-crumbs to coat, shaking off any excess. Repeat with the remaining cakes. Chill for 15 minutes (or overnight if preparing ahead).
4 To cook, heat the oil in a large non-stick frying pan. Add the parsnip cakes and fry for 15 minutes, turning halfway through, until crisp and golden all over.

Serves 6
Preparation: 10 minutes, plus chilling
Cooking time: 25 minutes
Per serving: 190 cals; 8g fat; 26g carbohydrate

Crushed Roast Parsnip and Apple

900g (2lb) even-sized
  parsnips, peeled and
  cut into large chunks
700g (1½lb) old
  potatoes, peeled and
  cut into large chunks
2 crisp, tart eating
  apples, peeled, cored
  and chopped

salt and pepper
3tbsp oil
50g (2oz) butter
2tbsp chopped chives

1 Preheat the oven to 220°C (200°C fan oven) mark 7.
   Cook the parsnips, potatoes and apples together in
   boiling salted water for 3 minutes, then drain well.
2 Heat the oil in a small roasting tin and add the parsnip
   mixture. Stir to coat in the oil. Roast for 45 minutes or
   until very tender.
3 Roughly crush the mixture with the butter. Sprinkle with
   chives, season and serve.

Serves 6
Preparation: 25 minutes
Cooking time: 50 minutes
Per serving: 310 cals; 15g fat; 41g carbohydrate

Parmesan and Mustard Parsnips

700g (1½lb) small
  parsnips, peeled
  and halved
salt and pepper
50g (2oz) butter
2tbsp olive oil

100g (3½oz) freshly
  grated Parmesan
  cheese
5tbsp English mustard
  powder

1 Cook the parsnips in boiling salted water for 5 minutes,
   then drain well and keep warm.
2 Preheat the oven to 200°C (180°C fan oven) mark 6.
   Put the butter and olive oil in a roasting tin and heat in
   the oven for 5 minutes.
3 Mix the Parmesan with the mustard powder and
   season well. Coat the warm parsnips in the mixture,
   pressing the coating on well.
4 Put into the preheated roasting tin and cook in the
   oven for 30–40 minutes or until golden.

Serves 8
Preparation: 20 minutes
Cooking time: 40–45 minutes
Per serving: 190 cals; 13g fat; 11g carbohydrate

Sage-roasted Parsnips, Apples and Prunes

6–8tbsp olive oil
1.8kg (4lb) parsnips,
  peeled, quartered and
  cored
6 apples, peeled, cored
  and quartered
salt and pepper

16 ready-to-eat prunes
50g (2oz) butter
1–2tbsp freshly
  chopped sage leaves
1–2tbsp clear honey
  (optional)

1 Heat 3–4tbsp olive oil in a large flameproof roasting
   tin, add the parsnips in batches and fry over a medium
   heat until a rich golden brown all over. Remove from the
   tin and set aside. Add 3–4tbsp oil to the same tin. Fry
   the apples until golden brown. Remove from the tin
   and set aside.
2 Preheat the oven to 200°C (180°C fan oven) mark 6.
   Put the parsnips back in the tin, season with salt and
   pepper and roast for 15 minutes.
3 Add the apples and continue roasting for 10 minutes.
   Put the prunes in the tin and roast for a further 5
   minutes. At the end of this time, test the apples. If
   they're still firm, roast everything for a further 5–10
   minutes until the apples are soft and fluffy.
4 Put the tin on the hob over a very low heat. Add the
   butter and sage, drizzle with honey if you like, and
   spoon into a hot serving dish.

Serves 8
Preparation: 20 minutes
Cooking time: 45–55 minutes
Per serving: 313 cals; 16g fat; 40g carbohydrate

*Top left: Stir-fried Vegetables with Oyster Sauce, page 305; top right:
Creamy Baked Potatoes with Mustard Seeds, page 308; bottom left:
Baked Anchovy Potatoes and Parsnips, page 309; bottom right: Sage
Roasted Parsnips with Apples and Prunes, page 302.*

Crisp Bacon

1–2tbsp single cream
4 streaky bacon
** rashers**

...s in boiling salted water for ...nder. Meanwhile, preheat the grill. ...well, return to the pan and roughly mash with the butter. Beat in the cream and season with pepper.

2 Grill the bacon until crisp, then crumble and stir through the mash just before serving.

Serves 4
Preparation: 5 minutes
Cooking time: 15 minutes
Per serving: 290 cals; 17g fat; 27g carbohydrate

Roasted Parsnips with Leeks, Apple and Bacon

2 parsnips, peeled and   **50g (2oz) butter, diced**
** cut into six**   **4 rindless streaky**
** lengthways**   ** bacon rashers**
175g pack baby leeks,
** cut in half crossways**
2 medium red apples,
** unpeeled and cored,**
** each cut into six**
** wedges**

1 Preheat the oven to 220°C (200°C fan oven) mark 7. Put the parsnips, leeks and apples in a single layer in a roasting tin and dot the butter over them.
2 Lay the bacon on top of the vegetables, put in the oven and roast for about 25 minutes or until the parsnips are soft and the bacon is crisp.

Serves 2
Preparation: 10 minutes
Cooking time: 30 minutes
Per serving: 500 cals; 41g fat; 23g carbohydrate

Roast Parsnips with Honey Glaze

2tbsp oil   **salt and pepper**
700g (1½lb) each   **4tbsp runny honey**
** parsnips and sweet**
** potatoes, peeled and**
** cut into large chunks**

1 Preheat the oven to 200°C (180°C fan oven) mark 6. Heat the oil in a roasting tin on the hob. Add the parsnips and sweet potatoes and shake the tin to coat them with oil, then season. Roast for 45 minutes, turning the parsnips from time to time.
2 Remove from the oven and mix in the honey, then return to the oven and roast for a further 10–15 minutes or until the vegetables are glazed, sticky and a deep golden brown. Season and turn out into a serving dish. (Don't leave the vegetables in the tin as they may stick to the bottom.)

Serves 8–10
Preparation: 10 minutes
Cooking time: 1 hour
Per serving: 150–120 cals; 3–2g fat; 32–25g carbohydrate

Stir-fried Kale

1tbsp sesame oil   **450g (1lb) curly kale,**
1 garlic clove, peeled   ** finely sliced**
** and crushed**   **2tbsp soy sauce**
1tbsp sesame seeds

1 Heat the oil in a non-stick wok. Add the garlic and sesame seeds and cook for 30 seconds until golden. Add the cury kale and stir-fry for 5 minutes.
2 Add the soy sauce, bring to the boil, bubble to reduce slightly. Transfer to a dish and serve.

Serves 4
Preparation: 5 minutes
Cooking time: 6–7 minutes
Per serving: 90 cals; 7g fat; 2g carbohydrate

Creamy Kale

450g (1lb) curly kale
25g (1oz) unsalted
  butter
5tbsp double cream
¼tsp freshly grated
  nutmeg
salt and pepper

1 Remove and discard the tough central stem from each
   kale leaf, then wash thoroughly and drain. Put the kale
   into a large pan with a drizzle of water and simmer,
   covered, for 5 minutes until bright green and almost
   cooked. Drain off any liquid.
2 Return the kale to the pan. Add the butter and cream
   and heat through, stirring, for 2 minutes. Add the
   grated nutmeg, season generously and serve.

Serves 6
Preparation: 10 minutes
Cooking time: 7 minutes
Per serving: 100 cals; 10g fat; 1g carbohydrate

Curly Kale With Crispy Bacon

1.1kg (2½lb) curly kale,
  tough or discoloured
  outer leaves discarded,
  or 1.1–1.4kg (2½–3lb)
  Savoy cabbage,
  quartered, cored and
  coarsely shredded
salt and pepper
25g (1oz) butter
6 dry cure, rindless
  streaky bacon
  rashers, cut into
  strips

1 Blanch the curly kale for 20 seconds in boiling salted
   water or blanch the cabbage for 1–2 minutes. Drain
   and immediately plunge into cold water to stop further
   cooking. Drain again and tip out on to kitchen paper to
   dry. Put to one side.
2 Melt the butter in a wok or large frying pan. Add the
   bacon and fry gently for 3–4 minutes or until turning
   golden brown. Toss in the curly kale or cabbage and
   stir-fry for 3–4 minutes until coated with butter and
   heated through. Season well and serve.

Serves 6
Preparation: 5 minutes, plus cooling and draining
Cooking time: 5 minutes
Per serving: 190 cals; 16g fat; 3g carbohydrate

Stir-fried Vegetables with Oys

100ml (3½fl oz)
  vegetable stock
2tbsp oyster sauce
1tbsp light soy sauce
2tsp runny honey
1tsp cornflour
oil, for deep-frying
175g (6oz) tofu,
  drained, dried and cut
  into large cubes
2 garlic cloves, peeled
  and thinly sliced
1 green pepper,
  deseeded and sliced
225g (8oz) broccoli, cut
  into small florets,
  stalk sliced
125g (4oz) yard-l
  beans or French
  beans, trimmed and
  cut into short lengths
50g (2oz) beansprouts,
  washed and dried
50g can straw
  mushrooms, drained
125g (4oz) canned
  water chestnuts,
  drained
2tbsp chopped
  coriander, to garnish

1 To make the sauce, blend the stock, oyster and soy
   sauces, honey and cornflour together until smooth and
   put to one side.
2 Heat a 10cm (4 inch) depth of oil in a deep pan until a
   cube of bread dropped into the oil browns in 30
   seconds. Add the tofu and deep-fry for 1–2 minutes until
   golden. Drain and put to one side.
3 Heat 2tbsp oil, add the garlic and fry for 1 minute
   then remove and discard. Add the green pepper,
   broccoli and beans and stir-fry for 3 minutes. Add
   the beansprouts, mushrooms and water chestnuts
   and stir-fry for 1 minute.
4 Add the tofu and sauce to the vegetables and simmer,
   covered, for 3–4 minutes. Garnish with the coriander
   and serve.

Serves 4   Preparation: 30 minutes
Cooking time: 12–15 minutes
Per serving: 300 cals; 15g fat; 21g carbohydrate

See picture, page 303

ut ¼ Savoy cabbage,
shredded
100ml (3½fl oz) semi-
skimmed milk

a pan of lightly salted water, bring
...uce the heat and simmer, partially
covered, for 15–20 minutes or until the potatoes are
tender.
2 Meanwhile, melt the butter in a large frying pan. Add the
cabbage and stir-fry for 3 minutes.
3 Drain the potatoes well, then tip back into the pan and
put over a medium heat for 1 minute to drive off excess
moisture. Turn into a colander and cover to keep warm.
4 Pour the milk into the potato pan and bring to the boil,
then take off the heat. Add the potatoes and mash well
until smooth.

5 Add the cabbage and any butter from the pan to
the mash and mix well. Season to taste and serve
immediately.

Serves 4
Preparation: 10 minutes
Cooking time: 20 minutes
Per serving: 310 cals; 12g fat; 45g carbohydrate

Layered Potato and Tomato Gratin

**2 medium waxy
potatoes, such as
Desirée, peeled and
cut into 5cm (¼ inch)
slices
450ml (¾ pint)
vegetable stock
oil**

**350g (12oz) tomatoes,
sliced
1 garlic clove, peeled
and crushed
1tsp dried thyme
salt and pepper
2tbsp grated low-fat
Cheddar cheese**

1 Put the potatoes into a pan and cover with the stock.
Bring to the boil, reduce the heat and simmer until just
tender, then drain and reserve.
2 Preheat the oven to 200°C (180°C fan oven) mark 6.
Lightly oil an ovenproof dish. Layer the potatoes with
the tomatoes in the dish, sprinkling each layer with the
garlic, thyme and seasoning. Sprinkle with the
Cheddar.
3 Bake for 40–45 minutes, then serve.

Serves 2
Preparation: 5 minutes
Cooking time: about 1 hour
Per serving: 230 cals; 3g fat; 44g carbohydrate

Mustard Mash

**1.25kg (2¾lb) old
potatoes, peeled
and chopped
salt and pepper
100ml (3½fl oz) warm
milk**

**100ml (3½fl oz) olive
oil, plus extra to
drizzle
2tbsp Dijon mustard**

1 Put the potatoes in a pan of lightly salted water, bring
to the boil, then reduce the heat and simmer for 15–20
minutes until tender. Drain the potatoes well and return
to the hot pan to dry off any excess moisture, then
mash.
2 Put the pan back over a low heat, push the potatoes
to one side of the pan and add the milk to warm
through. Add the olive oil and mustard, season well
and mash into the potatoes. Serve drizzled with
olive oil.

Serves 6
Preparation: 5 minutes
Cooking time: 12 minutes
Per serving: 290 cals; 17g fat; 32g carbohydrate

Creamed Cumin and Turmeric Potatoes

575g (1¼lb) potatoes,
  peeled and roughly
  chopped
¼tsp salt, plus extra
  for boiling water
½tsp each ground
  turmeric and red chilli
  powder
2tbsp vegetable oil
1tsp cumin seeds
200g (7oz) Greek-style
  yogurt
100ml (3½fl oz) milk

1 Put the potatoes in a pan of lightly salted water, bring to the boil, then reduce the heat and simmer for about 10–15 minutes until tender. Drain and immediately mix with the turmeric and chilli powder.
2 Heat the oil in a heavy-based pan, add the cumin seeds and cook for 1 minute until they turn nut brown. Add the potatoes and cook for 10 minutes until lightly golden.
3 Add the yogurt, milk and ¼tsp salt, reduce the heat, cover the pan and cook for 5 minutes. Serve immediately.

Serves 4
Preparation: 10 minutes
Cooking time: about 25 minutes
Per serving: 240 cals; 13g fat; 26g carbohydrate

Potato Gratin

450ml (¾ pint) milk
150ml (¼ pint) double
  cream
2 bay leaves, bruised
2 strips of lemon zest,
  bruised
pinch of saffron
  strands
900g (2lb) even-sized,
  small waxy potatoes
1 small onion, peeled
  and grated
2 garlic cloves, peeled
  and finely chopped
25g (1oz) butter, diced
salt and pepper

1 Put the milk, cream, bay leaves and lemon zest into a pan. Bring slowly to the boil, then remove from the heat, add the saffron and put to one side to infuse for 10 minutes. Preheat the oven to 200°C (180°C fan oven) mark 6.
2 In the meantime, peel the potatoes, then cut into even, thin slices, preferably using a mandolin or food processor fitted with a fine slicing blade.
3 Arrange a layer of potato slices over the base of a 1.5 litre (2¼–2½ pint) gratin dish. Scatter over some of the onion, garlic and butter and season generously. Repeat the layers, finishing with potatoes and a few pieces of butter.
4 Strain the infused cream over the potatoes, pressing the herbs and lemon to extract as much flavour as possible. Cover the dish with foil, put on a baking sheet and bake for 1 hour.
5 Remove the foil and bake for 15–20 minutes until the potatoes are softened and golden brown on top.

Serves 4–6
Preparation: 15–20 minutes
Cooking time: 1¼ hours
Per serving: 450–300 cals; 25–17g fat;
49–33g carbohydrate

Creamy Baked Potatoes with Mustard Seeds

6 baking potatoes,
  about 1.4kg (3lb)
2tbsp sunflower oil
1tbsp coarse sea salt
4–5 plump garlic
  cloves, unpeeled
50g (2oz) butter

6tbsp crème fraîche
2tbsp mustard seeds,
  toasted and
  lightly crushed
salt and pepper
oregano sprigs, to
  garnish

Serves 6
Preparation: 15–20 minutes
Cooking time: 1¼ hours
Per serving: 450 cals; 19g fat; 69g carbohydrate

See picture, page 303

1 Preheat the oven to 200°C (180°C fan oven) mark 6. Prick the potato skins, rub with the oil and sprinkle with the salt. Put on a baking tray and bake for 40 minutes. Add the garlic and cook for 20 minutes.
2 Remove the tray from the oven. Slice the tops off the potatoes, scoop the flesh into a warm bowl, squeeze the garlic out of the skin and add to the potato with the butter, crème fraîche and mustard seeds. Mash and season. Spoon the mixture into the hollowed skins and put back on the tray.
3 Return to the oven and bake for 15 minutes or until golden brown. Garnish with oregano sprigs and serve.

Saffron Mash

900g (2lb) potatoes,
  peeled
salt
pinch of saffron
  strands

50g (2oz) butter
coarse sea salt, to
  sprinkle

1 Put the potatoes in a pan of lightly salted water, bring to the boil, then reduce the heat and simmer for 20–30 minutes until tender. Meanwhile, soak the saffron strands in 2tbsp boiling water.
2 Drain the potatoes well and return to the hot pan to dry off any excess moisture.
3 Mash the potatoes with the butter and beat in the saffron with its soaking liquid. Sprinkle with coarse sea salt and serve.

Serves 4–6
Preparation: 5 minutes
Cooking time: about 20–30 minutes
Per serving: 250–170 cals; 11–7g fat;
37–24g carbohydrate

Mini Baked Potatoes with Caraway Seeds

18 small potatoes,
  scrubbed
2tbsp olive oil

1tbsp each caraway
  seeds and sea salt
black pepper

1 Preheat the oven to 220°C (200°C fan oven) mark 7. Toss the potatoes in the olive oil and sprinkle over the caraway seeds and sea salt. Season with pepper.
2 Roast the potatoes for 35–45 minutes or until golden and cooked through. Serve with crispy bacon and soured cream.

Serves 6
Preparation: 5 minutes
Cooking time: 35–45 minutes
Per serving: 170 cals; 5g fat; 29g carbohydrate

Baked Anchovy Potatoes and Parsnips

3tbsp olive oil
450ml (¾pint) hot
  vegetable or chicken
  stock
1tbsp Dijon mustard
450g (1lb) each
  potatoes and
  parsnips, peeled and
  cut into bite-sized
  chunks
pepper
1 small onion, peeled
  and finely sliced

1 garlic clove, peeled
  and crushed
50g (2oz) canned
  anchovies in oil,
  drained and chopped
small handful of flat-
  leafed parsley,
  chopped
roast chicken or grilled
  lamb and spinach, to
  serve

1 Preheat the oven to 190°C (170°C fan oven) mark 5. Grease a 2 litre (3½ pint) ovenproof dish with 1tbsp olive oil.
2 Pour the stock into a pan, add the mustard and bring to the boil. Add the potatoes and parsnips, return to the boil then remove from the heat. Season with pepper.
3 Heat 2tbsp olive oil in a frying pan, add the onion and cook gently for 10 minutes until softened. Add the garlic to the onion and cook for 1–2 minutes, then remove from the heat and add the anchovies.
4 Put half the potatoes, parsnips and stock into the ovenproof dish, spoon over the onion and anchovy mixture over it, then cover with the remaining potatoes, parsnips and stock.
5 Cook, uncovered, in the oven for 1 hour or until tender and golden. Sprinkle the parsley over just before serving. Serve with roast chicken or grilled lamb and freshly cooked spinach.

Serves 6
Preparation: 5 minutes
Cooking time: 20 minutes
Per serving: 187 cals; 8g fat; 26g carbohydrate

See picture, page 303

Vegetables

Crispy Better-than-baked Potatoes

4 sweet potatoes, each
  about 175g (6oz)
200g pack cream
  cheese
4tbsp finely chopped
  chives

salt and pepper
55g pack smoked
  crispy bacon

1 Preheat the oven to 220°C (200°C fan oven) mark 7. Put the potatoes in a roasting tin and bake for 50–60 minutes or until soft.
2 Meanwhile, mix the cream cheese and chives and season.
3 Remove the tin from the oven, cut the potatoes in half, spoon in the cream cheese and chives and top with the crispy bacon.

Serves 4
Preparation: 5 minutes
Cooking time: 50–60 minutes
Per serving: 430 cals; 29g fat; 37g carbohydrate

Crushed Potatoes with Feta and Olives

700g (1½lb) new
  potatoes, unpeeled
salt and pepper
75ml (3fl oz) olive oil
75g (3oz) pitted black
  olives, shredded

2tbsp chopped flat-
  leafed parsley
200g (7oz) feta cheese,
  crumbled

1 Put the potatoes in a pan of lightly salted water, bring to the boil, then reduce the heat and simmer for 15 minutes or until tender. Drain, put back in the pan and crush roughly.
2 Add the olive oil, olives, parsley and feta cheese. Season and toss together – don't over-mix or the potatoes will become glutinous. Serve.

Serves 4
Preparation: 20 minutes
Cooking time: 15 minutes
Per serving: 410 cals; 29g fat; 29g carbohydrate

Potato and Onion Pan-fry

500g (1lb 2oz) potatoes, peeled and thickly sliced
salt and pepper
2–3tbsp olive oil
1 onion, peeled and cut into 8 wedges
1tbsp chopped flat-leafed parsley

1 Put the potatoes in a pan of lightly salted water and boil for 2–3 minutes. Meanwhile, heat the olive oil in a pan and fry the onion for 5 minutes. Drain the potatoes and add to the pan.
2 Cook for 5–10 minutes until golden and crisp, then season well and toss through the parsley to serve.

Serves 4
Preparation: 5 minutes
Cooking time: 10–15 minutes
Per serving: 170 cals; 8g fat; 23g carbohydrate

Potato Wedges with Dill Cream

2tbsp chopped dill
142ml carton soured cream
700g (1½lb) Desirée potatoes, scrubbed and cut into wedges
2tbsp olive oil
salt

1 Preheat the oven to 200°C (180°C fan oven) mark 6. Stir the dill into the soured cream. Put the potatoes in a roasting tin, drizzle with the olive oil and sprinkle with salt.
2 Roast for 40–50 minutes, then remove from the oven and serve with the dill cream.

Serves 4
Preparation: 5 minutes
Cooking time: 40–50 minutes
Per serving: 250 cals; 12g fat; 31g carbohydrate

Potato Croquettes with Bacon and Cheese

1kg (2¼lb) floury potatoes, such as King Edward, peeled and cut into large chunks
salt and pepper
125g (4oz) streaky bacon rashers, de-rinded and cut into narrow strips
125g (4oz) Lancashire cheese, crumbled, or Cheddar cheese, coarsely grated
50g (2oz) butter
2tbsp chopped flat-leafed parsley
2 large eggs, separated
125g (4oz) fine fresh breadcrumbs
vegetable oil, for frying
sea salt and marjoram sprigs, to garnish

1 Put the potatoes in a pan of lightly salted water, bring to the boil, then reduce the heat and simmer for 15–20 minutes until tender. Drain and return the potatoes to the pan. Meanwhile, fry the bacon in a non-stick frying pan until brown and crisp.
2 Mash the potatoes over a low heat to dry them out. Mix the potato, bacon, cheese, butter and parsley thoroughly and season well. Leave to cool.
3 Once the mixture is cold, add the egg yolks. Shape into 20 golf ball-sized portions. Lightly whisk the egg whites in a clean grease-free bowl. Dip the potato balls in the egg white, then in the breadcrumbs, making sure the coating covers the potato balls evenly. Arrange on a flat dish and chill, uncovered, until ready to fry.
4 Heat the oil in a deep frying pan until very hot. Carefully lower the potato balls into the oil in batches and cook for 2–3 minutes or until crisp and a chestnut brown colour. Drain on kitchen paper. Garnish with sea salt and marjoram sprigs and serve.

Makes 20
Preparation: 30 minutes
Cooking time: 35 minutes, plus cooling
per croquette: 140 cals; 9g fat; 11g carbohydrate

Top left: Grilled Sweet Potatoes with Feta, page 314; top right: Roasted Rosemary Potatoes, page 310; bottom left: Mustard Roast Potatoes and Parsnips, page 311; bottom right: Roasted Parma Potatoes, page 310.

Paprika Potato Wedges

700g (1½lb) potatoes, peeled and cut into chunky wedges

**salt and pepper
3tbsp oil
1tsp ground paprika**

1 Preheat the oven to 200°C (180°C fan oven) mark 6. Cook the potatoes in boiling salted water for 3 minutes, then drain, put into a roasting tin and toss in the oil, plenty of seasoning and the paprika.
2 Roast for 35–40 minutes, turning occasionally to brown evenly.

Serves 4
Preparation: 5 minutes
Cooking time: 40–45 minutes
Per serving: 220 cals; 10g fat; 30g carbohydrate

Potato Frites

700g (1½lb) baking potatoes, peeled and cut into long, very thin sticks

**oil, for frying
sea salt flakes and black pepper**

1 Dry the potatoes thoroughly in a clean tea-towel. Heat 1cm (½ inch) oil in a deep frying pan and fry the potatoes in batches for 3–4 minutes or until golden brown and very crisp.
2 Drain on kitchen paper, season with sea salt flakes and pepper and keep warm. Continue to fry the potato sticks in batches until all the potatoes are used up. Serve immediately.

Serves 4
Preparation: 15 minutes
Cooking time: 15 minutes
Per serving: 280 cals; 6g fat; 52g carbohydrate

Grilled Sweet Potatoes with Feta

**1 large sweet potato, weighing about 500g (1lb 2oz)
4tbsp olive oil, plus extra to brush
salt and pepper
200g (7oz) feta cheese
2tsp dried herbes de**

**Provence
50g (2oz) pitted black olives, chopped
1 garlic clove, peeled and crushed
flat-leafed parsley sprigs, to garnish**

1 Preheat the barbecue or griddle. Peel the sweet potato and cut lengthways into eight wedges. Put them in a pan of boiling water, bring back to the boil, simmer for 3 minutes, then drain and refresh in cold water. Drain, dry well on kitchen paper, then brush lightly with olive oil. Season with salt and pepper, then barbecue or grill for 10–15 minutes until well browned and cooked through.
2 Meanwhile, mash the cheese, herbs, olives, garlic and 4tbsp olive oil together. Serve the sweet potato with the feta cheese mixture, garnished with flat-leafed parsley.

Serves 4
Preparation: 15 minutes
Cooking time: 15–20 minutes
Per serving: 324 cals; 23g fat; 21g carbohydrate

Sweet Potato Mash

2 medium potatoes, about 400g (14oz), such as King Edward, peeled and cut into chunks

**900g (2lb) sweet potatoes, peeled and cut into chunks
salt and pepper
50g (2oz) butter**

1 Put all the potatoes in a large pan of lightly salted water. Bring to the boil, then reduce the heat and simmer, half covered, for 15–20 minutes until tender.
2 Drain well, add the butter and season generously. Mash until smooth, then serve.

Serves 6
Preparation: 10 minutes
Cooking time: 20 minutes
Per serving: 240 cals; 7g fat; 42g carbohydrate

Rösti Potatoes

4 medium potatoes,
such as Desirée,
about 1kg (2¼lb) in
total, scrubbed
salt and pepper

50g (2oz) butter,
melted, plus extra to
grease
4 slices Emmental
cheese

1 Put the potatoes in a large pan of cold salted water, cover and bring to the boil. Cook for 5–8 minutes, then drain, transfer to a bowl and leave to cool for 10 minutes.
2 Preheat the oven to 220°C (200°C fan oven) mark 7. Grease two large baking trays. Peel the potatoes, then grate coarsely into long strands by rubbing each one lengthways along a coarse grater. Divide into four.
3 Shape each portion into a mound and put well apart on the baking trays. Drizzle the melted butter over each mound, season generously and cook in the oven for about 30 minutes until golden.

4 Put a slice of cheese on each rösti and return to the oven for 10 minutes or until golden and bubbling. Serve immediately.

Serves 4
Preparation: 20 minutes, plus cooling
Cooking time: 40 minutes
Per serving: 380 cals; 18g fat; 43g carbohydrate

Celeriac Dauphinoise

700g (1½lb) potatoes,
peeled and
thinly sliced
450g (1lb) celeriac,
peeled and thinly
sliced
2 bay leaves
600ml (1 pint) milk

25g (1oz) diced butter,
plus extra to grease
salt and pepper
2 garlic cloves, peeled
and crushed
284ml carton double
cream

1 Put the potatoes and celeriac in a large pan with the bay leaves and milk. Bring just to the boil, then reduce the heat and cook for 5–8 minutes until tender. Drain, then discard the milk and bay leaves.
2 Preheat the oven to 180°C (160°C fan oven) mark 4. Grease a 1.4 litre (2½ pint) gratin dish with a little butter. Season the potatoes and celeriac well, then arrange in layers in the dish. Add the garlic and cream and dot with the diced butter.

3 Cover with foil and bake for 1 hour. Remove the foil and bake for another 15–20 minutes until golden, then serve.

Serves 6
Preparation: 20 minutes
Cooking time: 1 hour 25 minutes
Per serving: 380 cals; 28g fat; 26g carbohydrate

Braised Celery with Pancetta and Cheese

**1 head of celery, about
450g (1lb)
trimmed weight
125g (4oz) smoked
pancetta or rindless
streaky bacon
rashers, diced
25g (1oz) butter
1 large onion, peeled
and chopped**

**2 garlic cloves, peeled
and crushed
150ml (¼ pint) single
cream
salt and pepper
125g (4oz) Gruyère
cheese, grated**

1 Separate the celery sticks and cut each into 5cm (2 inch) lengths, on the diagonal.
2 Preheat a large sauté pan suitable for use under the grill. Add the pancetta or bacon and stir-fry over a high heat until it releases its fat and browns. Remove with a slotted spoon and put to one side.
3 Melt the butter in the pan, add the onion and garlic and fry gently for 10 minutes until softened. Add the celery and cook for 5 minutes.
4 Preheat the grill to its highest setting. Return the pancetta to the pan, add the cream and bring to the boil. Cover the pan, reduce the heat and simmer for 5 minutes; season to taste.
5 Scatter the cheese over the celery and put under the grill for 1–2 minutes until golden. Serve at once.

Serves: 4–6
Preparation: 10 minutes
Cooking time: 25 minutes
Per serving: 410–270 cals; 36–24g fat; 6–4g carbohydrate

Creamed Spinach

**900g (2lb) spinach
leaves, stalks
removed**

**4tbsp crème fraîche
salt and pepper**

1 Cook the spinach with just the water clinging to the leaves after washing in a covered pan for 3–4 minutes or until just wilted.
2 Stir in the crème fraîche and season to taste. Serve at once.

Serves 6
Preparation: 15 minutes
Cooking time: 5 minutes
Per serving: 80 cals; 5g fat; 3g carbohydrate

Spinach with Tomatoes

**50g (2oz) butter
2 garlic cloves, peeled
and crushed
450g (1lb) baby plum
tomatoes, halved**

**250g bag baby spinach
leaves
salt and pepper
freshly grated nutmeg,
to serve**

1 Melt 25g (1oz) butter in a pan and cook the garlic until just soft.
2 Add the tomatoes and cook for 4–5 minutes.
3 Put the spinach leaves and a little water in a clean pan, cover and cook for 2–3 minutes. Drain well, chop roughly and stir into the tomatoes.
4 Add the remaining butter and gently heat through. Season well, stir in a large pinch of nutmeg and serve.

Serves 6
Preparation: 10 minutes
Cooking time: 10 minutes
Per serving: 90 cals; 7g fat; 3g carbohydrate

See picture, page 321

Beetroot and Dill Salad

900g (2lb) beetroot	juice of 1 lemon
salt and pepper	2tbsp chopped dill
4tbsp olive oil	

1 Trim the stalks from the beetroot and discard, then rinse well. Put in a pan of cold salted water. Cover and bring to the boil, then reduce the heat and simmer, half-covered, for 20–25 minutes or until tender. Drain well, then slip the skins off the beetroot.
2 Halve each beetroot and put in a bowl. Add the olive oil, lemon juice and dill and season well. Toss together and serve.

Serves 6
Preparation: 5 minutes
Cooking time: 30–35 minutes
Per serving: 130 cals; 9g fat; 12g carbohydrate

Minted Peas with Cucumber

450g (1lb) shelled fresh or frozen peas	3tbsp vermouth, such as Noilly Prat
50g (2oz) butter	2tbsp chopped mint
1 bunch of spring onions, sliced	salt and pepper
175g (6oz) cucumber, halved lengthways, deseeded and thickly sliced	½tsp golden caster sugar
142ml carton crème fraîche	mint sprigs, to garnish

1 Bring a pan of water to the boil, add the peas and simmer for 5 minutes or until tender and just cooked through. Drain, return to the pan and keep warm.

Minted Peas with Spring Onions and Courgettes

450g (1lb) shelled fresh peas	200ml carton crème fraîche
225g (8oz) French beans	1tsp sugar (optional)
25g (1oz) butter	3tbsp roughly chopped mint leaves
1 bunch of spring onions, thickly sliced	salt and pepper
225g (8oz) courgettes, cut lengthways into wedges	

1 Cook the peas and French beans in a pan of boiling water for 5 minutes or until tender, then drain.
2 Heat the butter in a frying pan and sauté the spring onions and courgette wedges for 3 minutes. Add the crème fraîche, bring to a simmer and leave to bubble for 2 minutes. Stir in the peas, French beans, sugar, if using, and mint. Season to taste and serve at once.

Serves 6
Preparation: 15 minutes
Cooking time: 10 minutes
Per serving: 240 cals; 8g fat; 13g carbohydrate

2 Heat the butter in a frying pan. Add the spring onions and cucumber and sauté for 3 minutes. Add the crème fraîche and vermouth and bring to the boil, then bubble for 2–3 minutes. Add the peas and mint, season generously and add the sugar. Serve garnished with mint sprigs.

Serves 4–6
Preparation: 5 minutes
Cooking time: 10 minutes
Per serving: 330–220 cals; 26–17g fat; 16–11g carbohydraate

Red Cabbage with Ginger

2tbsp white wine
  vinegar
2.5cm (1 inch) piece
  fresh root
  ginger, peeled
1.4kg (3lb) red
  cabbage, outer leaves
  discarded, cored and
  finely shredded

salt
olive oil, to drizzle
thyme sprigs, to
  garnish

1 Add the vinegar and ginger to a large pan of water and
   bring to the boil. Add the cabbage, season with salt
   and cook for 5–10 minutes.
2 Drain and discard the ginger. Serve drizzled with olive
   oil and garnished with thyme sprigs.

Serves 6
Preparation: 5 minutes
Cooking time: 5–10 minutes
Per serving: 50 cals; 3g fat; 5g carbohydrate

Buttered Cabbage with Caraway Seeds

450g (1lb) finely
  shredded cabbage
½tsp caraway seeds

50g (2oz) butter
juice of ½ lemon

1 Cook the cabbage in boiling salted water until just
   tender. Drain well.
2 Meanwhile, fry the caraway seeds in a dry pan until
   toasted. Take the pan off the heat, add the butter and
   leave to melt in the heat of the pan.
3 Toss the butter through the cabbage and serve with a
   squeeze of lemon juice.

Serves 4
Preparation: 5 minutes
Cooking time: about 10 minutes
Per serving: 120 cals; 11g fat; 4g carbohydrate

Savoy Cabbage Parcels

3tbsp olive oil
125g (4oz) onion,
  peeled and finely
  chopped
1 garlic clove, peeled
  and crushed
125g (4oz) each
  aubergine and
  courgette, diced

½ red and ½ yellow
  pepper, diced
6 young Savoy
  cabbage leaves

1 To make the ratatouille stuffing, heat the olive oil in a
   frying pan, add the onion and cook until soft. Add the
   garlic and aubergine and cook for 2–3 minutes, stirring
   from time to time. Add the courgettes and diced
   peppers and continue to cook for 2–3 minutes or until
   the vegetables are soft. Put to one side.

2 Preheat the oven to 180°C (160°C fan oven) mark 4.
   Plunge the cabbage leaves into boiling water for 1–2
   minutes, drain, plunge into cold water and drain again.
   Dry on kitchen paper. Place a spoonful of the ratatouille
   in each cabbage leaf and shape into a parcel. Place in
   an ovenproof dish, cover and heat through in the oven
   for 7–10 minutes.

Serves 6
Preparation: 10 minutes
Cooking time: about 28 minutes
Per serving: 80 cals; 7g fat; 4g carbohydrate

*Top left: Stir-fried Green Vegetables, page 325; top right: Roasted
Root Vegetables, page 323; bottom left: Spinach with Tomatoes, page
316; bottom right: Asparagus with Lemon Dressing, page 323.*

Roast Vegetables with Tabbouleh

2 red peppers, deseeded and cut into 2cm (¾ inch) chunks
4 courgettes, about 450g (1lb), cut into 2cm (¾ inch) chunks
1 aubergine, about 350g (12oz), cut into 2cm (¾ inch) chunks
2 red onions, about 350g (12oz), peeled and cut into 2cm (¾ inch) chunks
6 garlic cloves, unpeeled
3tbsp olive oil
salt and pepper
375g pack bulgur wheat
½ cucumber, diced
6tbsp each roughly chopped mint and flat-leafed parsley
zest and juice of 2 lemons
6tbsp extra-virgin olive oil
2tsp harissa paste

1 Preheat the oven to 200ºC (180ºC fan oven) mark 6. Put the peppers, courgettes, aubergine, onions and garlic in a roasting tin, add the olive oil, toss well and season. Roast for 1 hour or until tender and starting to char.

2 Meanwhile, put the bulgur wheat in a bowl, add 1.1 litres (2 pints) boiling water and soak for 30 minutes.

3 Drain the bulgur in a sieve, then tip into a clean tea-towel. Wrap up tight and squeeze over the sink to extract the water. Tip into a large glass serving bowl, season and stir in the cucumber, mint and parsley.

4 Take the roasting tin out of the oven, remove the garlic from the tin and put to one side. Spoon the remaining roasted vegetables on top of the bulgur.

5 To make the dressing, squeeze the purée from the garlic cloves into a food processor, then add the lemon zest and juice, the extra-virgin olive oil and harissa. Season, then whiz for 1–2 minutes. Drizzle the dressing over the vegetables, toss everything together and serve.

Serves 6
Preparation: 30 minutes
Cooking time: 1 hour
Per serving: 430 cals; 19g fat; 57g carbohydrate

Vegetable and Mustard Mash

1.4kg (3lb) floury potatoes, such as Maris Piper, peeled and cut into large chunks
900g (2lb) parsnips or celeriac, peeled and cut into large chunks
salt and pepper
50g (2oz) butter
4tbsp snipped chives or chopped flat-leafed parsley
200g tub crème fraîche
3tbsp Dijon mustard

1 Put the potatoes and parsnips or celeriac in a pan of lightly salted water, bring to the boil, then reduce the heat and simmer for 20–25 minutes or until tender.

2 Meanwhile, melt the butter in a small pan, bring to the boil, take off the heat and skim off the white surface with a slotted spoon. Carefully pour the butter into a jug, discarding the milky substance at the bottom. Add the herbs and season well.

3 Drain the vegetables. Return them to the pan and put over a low heat for 1–2 minutes to dry, then crush with a potato masher. Beat in the crème fraîche and mustard and season well. Using two dessertspoons, shape the mash into ovals, spoon into a warm serving dish and drizzle with the herb butter.

Serves 10
Preparation: 30 minutes
Cooking time: 30 minutes
Per serving: 240 cals; 13g fat; 29g carbohydrate

Ratatouille

4tbsp olive oil
2 onions, peeled and
  thinly sliced
1 large garlic clove,
  peeled and crushed
350g (12oz) small
  aubergine, thinly
  sliced
450g (1lb) small
  courgettes, thinly
  sliced
450g (1lb) tomatoes,
  skinned, deseeded
  and roughly chopped

1 green and 1 red
  pepper, each
  deseeded and sliced
1tbsp chopped basil
2tsp chopped thyme
2tbsp chopped flat-
  leafed parsley
2tbsp sun-dried tomato
  paste
salt and pepper

1 Heat the olive oil in a large pan, add the onions and
   garlic and fry gently for 10 minutes or until softened
   and golden.
2 Add the aubergine, courgettes, tomatoes, sliced
   peppers, herbs, tomato paste and seasoning. Fry,
   stirring, for 2–3 minutes.
3 Cover the pan tightly and simmer for 30 minutes or
   until all the vegetables are just tender. If necessary,
   uncover towards the end of the cooking time to
   evaporate some of the liquid.
4 Taste and adjust the seasoning. Serve the ratatouille hot
   or cold.

Serves 4–6
Preparation: 20 minutes
Cooking time: about 45 minutes
Per serving: 220–150 cals; 15–10g fat;
18–12g carbohydrate

Stir-fried Green Vegetables

2tbsp oil
225g (8oz) courgettes,
  thinly sliced
175g (6oz) mangetout,
  trimmed

25g (1oz) butter
175g (6oz) frozen peas,
  thawed
salt and pepper

1 Heat the oil in a large frying pan or wok, add the
   courgettes and cook for 1–2 minutes. Add the
   mangetout and cook for 1 minute. Add the butter and
   peas and cook for 1 minute. Season and serve.

Serves 6
Preparation: 5 minutes
Cooking time: 3–4 minutes
Per serving: 110 cals; 8g fat; 5g carbohydrate

See picture, page 321

700g (1½lb) large Maris Piper potatoes, peeled and cut lengthways into 1cm (½ inch) wide x 7.5cm (3 inch) long chips
300g (11oz) large carrots, peeled and cut lengthways into 1cm (½ inch) wide x 7.5cm (3 inch) long chips

3 large parsnips, about 700g (1½lb) in total, peeled and cut lengthways into 1cm (½ inch) wide x 7.5cm (3 inch) long chips
4tbsp olive oil
2tsp all-purpose seasoning
½tsp sea salt

1 Preheat the oven to 220°C (200°C fan oven) mark 7. Put the vegetables in a bowl and toss with the olive oil, all-purpose seasoning and the salt, then transfer to two roasting tins.
2 Bake for 50–55 minutes or until the vegetables are tender and golden. Toss frequently and swap the tins over occasionally, so that the vegetables cook evenly.
3 Drain the vegetables on kitchen paper and serve warm with tomato ketchup.

Serves 6
Preparation: 30 minutes
Cooking time: 55 minutes
Per serving: 200 cals; 6g fat; 32g carbohydrate

Sweet Roasted Fennel

700g (1½lb) fennel bulbs, about 3 bulbs, quartered
3tbsp olive oil
50g (2oz) butter, melted

1 lemon, halved
1tsp golden caster sugar
salt and pepper
2 large thyme sprigs

1 Preheat the oven to 200°C (180°C fan oven) mark 6. Put the fennel in a large roasting tin and drizzle with the olive oil and melted butter, then squeeze the lemon juice over. Add the lemon halves to the tin. Sprinkle with the sugar and season generously. Add the thyme and cover with a damp piece of non-stick baking parchment.
2 Transfer to the oven and cook for 30 minutes, then remove the baking parchment and cook for 20–30 minutes or until lightly charred or tender.

Serves 4–6
Preparation: 10 minutes
Cooking time: 1 hour
Per serving: 210–140 cals; 20–14g fat; 4–3g carbohydrate

See picture, page 330

Florentine Fennel with White Wine

3tbsp olive oil
750g (1lb 10oz) fennel,
  sliced
150ml (¼ pint) white
  wine
salt and pepper

1 Heat the olive oil in a deep, lidded frying pan. Add the fennel and wine, then season generously.
2 Cover with a tight-fitting lid and bring to the boil, then reduce the heat and simmer gently for 30 minutes or until the fennel is very tender and the liquid is reduced.

Serves 6
Preparation: 5 minutes
Cooking time: 35 minutes
Per serving: 90 cals; 7g fat; 2g carbohydrate

Roasted Fennel with Oranges and Dill Mash

2 fennel bulbs, cut into
  wedges
2 red onions, peeled
  and cut into wedges
2tbsp olive oil
salt and pepper
1.1kg (2½lb) floury
  potatoes, such as
  King Edward, peeled
  and cut into chunks
50g (2oz) butter
2 oranges, peeled and
  segmented
50g (2oz) walnut
  halves, roughly
  chopped
juice of 1 orange
4tbsp chopped dill

1 Preheat the oven to 220°C (200°C fan oven) mark 7. Put the fennel in a large roasting tin, add the onions and half the olive oil and season well. Roast for 45 minutes or until soft.
2 Meanwhile, put the potatoes in a large pan of lightly salted water, bring to the boil, then reduce the heat and simmer gently for 15–20 minutes or until tender. Drain well, then return to the hot pan to dry off any moisture. Add the butter, season and mash until smooth. Keep warm.
3 Add the orange segments and walnuts to the vegetables in the roasting tin and cook for a further 5 minutes.
4 Mix the orange juice with the remaining oil and season well to taste. Fold the dill through the mash, then spoon on to four warm plates and top with the roasted vegetables. Drizzle over the orange juice and olive oil dressing and serve immediately.

Serves 4
Preparation: 30 minutes
Cooking time: 50 minutes
Per serving: 370 cals; 18g fat; 49g carbohydrate

Roasted Pepper, Fennel and Cherry Tomatoes

125g (4oz) butter, softened at room temperature
1tbsp rosemary leaves, stripped from the stem and chopped
2tbsp chopped mint
salt and pepper
olive oil, to brush

3 red peppers, cut into quarters, with the stalks still attached and deseeded
9 baby fennel, halved
6 sprigs of cherry tomatoes on the vine

1 Put the butter in a bowl and beat in the rosemary and mint, then season. Put the butter on to a piece of greaseproof paper and shape into a log. Wrap up and chill in the fridge.
2 Preheat the oven to 200°C (180°C fan oven) mark 6. Oil one large roasting tin and one smaller tin. Put the red peppers in the large tin and the fennel in the smaller tin. Brush the vegetables with olive oil and season. Divide the chilled butter among the pepper quarters, then roast the peppers and fennel for 20 minutes.
3 Put the tomatoes in the roasting tin with the peppers and put back in the oven to roast for 20 minutes. Serve with any buttery juices drizzled over.

Serves 6
Preparation: 15 minutes
Cooking time: 40 minutes
Per serving: 190 cals; 17g fat; 6g carbohydrate

Leeks with Red Wine

3–4tbsp olive oil
450g (1lb) small leeks (white part only), all of similar size

salt
1 wine glass of red wine
2tbsp good meat stock

1 Heat the olive oil in a large frying pan. Put the leeks in the pan and as soon as they have taken colour on one side, turn them over. Season with very little salt.
2 Pour over the wine (watch out for spluttering), let it bubble, then add the stock – or water if no stock is available. Cover the pan and cook at a moderate heat for 7–10 minutes, turning the leeks over once during the process. They are done when a skewer pierces the root end quite easily.
3 Transfer the leeks to a shallow oval dish. Cook the sauce for a minute or two until slightly reduced, then pour it over the leeks. Serve hot or cold.

Serves 4–6
Preparation: 10 minutes
Cooking time: 15 minutes
Per serving: 130–90 cals; 10–7g fat; 4–2g carbohydrate

Leek and Broccoli Bake

2tbsp olive oil
1 large red onion,
   peeled and cut into
   wedges
1 aubergine, chopped
2 leeks, cut into
   chunks
1 broccoli head, cut
   into florets and stalks
   chopped

3 large flat
   mushrooms, chopped
3 rosemary sprigs,
   chopped
2 x 400g cans cherry
   tomatoes
salt and pepper
50g (2oz) freshly grated
   Parmesan cheese

1 Preheat the oven to 200°C (180°C fan) mark 6. Heat the olive oil in a large flameproof dish. Add the onion, aubergine and leeks and cook on the hob for 10–12 minutes until golden and softened.
2 Add the remaining vegetables, half the rosemary, the tomatoes and 300ml (½ pint) boiling water. Season. Stir well, then cover and bake for 30 minutes

3 Meanwhile, put the Parmesan in a bowl. Add the remaining rosemary and season with pepper. When the vegetables are cooked, remove from the oven, uncover and sprinkle the Parmesan mixture over. Return to the oven and cook, uncovered, for 5–10 minutes until the topping is golden.

Serves 4
Preparation: 20 minutes
Cooking time: 45–55 minutes
Per serving: 220 cals; 12g fat; 15g carbohydrate

See picture, page 330

Buttery Runner Beans

450g (1lb) runner
   beans, de-stringed
   and sliced thickly on
   the diagonal
1 shallot, blanched in
   boiling water, drained,
   peeled and finely

chopped
knob of butter
salt and pepper

1 Cook the beans in boiling water for 3 minutes until tender.
2 Drain well, then add the shallot and butter and season well. Toss together and serve.

Serves 4
Preparation: 5 minutes
Cooking time: 3 minutes
Per serving: 50 cals; 2g fat; 6g carbohydrate

French Beans with Black Mustard Seeds

1tbsp olive oil
1 garlic clove, peeled
  and crushed
1tbsp black mustard
  seeds

450g (1lb) French
  beans
salt

1 Heat the olive oil in a large frying pan or wok for 30 seconds. Add the garlic and mustard seeds and cook for 30 seconds.
2 Add the beans to the pan and stir-fry for 5–7 minutes until just tender, yet still bright green. Season with salt and serve.

Serves 6
Preparation: 5 minutes
Cooking time: 5–7 minutes
Per serving: 40 cals; 3g fat; 2g carbohydrate

Pumpkin with Chickpeas

**900g (2lb) pumpkin or
  squash, such as
  butternut, crown
  prince or kabocha,
  peeled, deseeded and
  chopped into roughly
  2cm (¾ inch) cubes
1 garlic clove, peeled
  and crushed
2tbsp olive oil
salt and pepper
2 x 400g cans
  chickpeas, drained**

**½ red onion, peeled
  and thinly sliced
1 large bunch of
  coriander, roughly
  chopped
steamed spinach, to
  serve
1 large garlic clove,
  peeled and crushed
3tbsp tahini paste
juice of 1 lemon**

1 Preheat the oven to 220°C (200°C fan oven) mark 7. Toss the squash or pumpkin in the garlic and oil and season. Put in a roasting tin and roast for 25 minutes or until soft.

2 Meanwhile, put the chickpeas in a pan with 150ml (¼ pint) water over a medium heat, to warm through.
3 To make the tahini sauce, put the garlic in a bowl, add a pinch of salt, then whisk in the tahini paste. Add the lemon juice and 4–5tbsp cold water – enough to make a consistency somewhere between single and double cream – and season.
4 Drain the chickpeas, put in a large bowl, then add the pumpkin, onion and coriander. Pour on the tahini sauce and toss carefully. Adjust the seasoning and serve while warm, with spinach.

Serves 6
Preparation: 15 minutes
Cooking time: 25–30 minutes
Per serving: 228 cals; 12g fat; 22g carbohydrate

Top left: Pumpkin and Chickpeas, page 331; top right: Spicy Squash Quarters, page 323; bottom left: Sweet Roasted Fennel, page 326; bottom right: Leek and Broccoli Bake, page 329.

Butter-baked Pumpkin

900g (2lb) pumpkin,
 peeled, deseeded and
 cut into large chunks
2tbsp olive oil

25g (1oz) butter
salt and pepper
chopped flat-leafed
 parsley, to garnish

1 Preheat the oven to 220°C (200°C fan oven) mark 7. Put the pumpkin in a single layer in a roasting tin with 50ml (2fl oz) hot water, drizzle with the olive oil and dot with the butter. Season well and bake for about 30 minutes or until tender and golden, turning occasionally. The liquid will have evaporated by the time the pumpkin is cooked.
2 Remove the tin from the oven, sprinkle with the parsley and serve.

Serves 4
Preparation: 5 minutes
Cooking time: about 30 minutes
Per serving: 130 cals; 12g fat; 5g carbohydrate

Mushrooms with Cherry Tomatoes

3tbsp olive oil, plus
 extra to grease
6 portabello or large
 flat mushrooms
2 garlic cloves, peeled
 and finely sliced

6 sprigs of cherry
 tomatoes on the vine,
 each sprig weighing
 about 125g (4oz)
salt and pepper

1 Preheat the oven to 200°C (180°C fan oven) mark 6. Lightly oil a large roasting tin. Put the mushrooms into the tin, scatter over the garlic, arrange a sprig of cherry tomatoes – still on the vine – on top of each mushroom, easing to fit, then drizzle with the olive oil.
2 Season well, cover with foil and bake for 15 minutes. Remove the foil and continue to roast, uncovered, for a further 15 minutes.

Serves 6
Preparation: 5 minutes
Cooking time: 30 minutes
Per serving: 120 cals; 8g fat; 8g carbohydrate

Turkish Tomatoes

36 cherry tomatoes on
 the vine, picked from
 the stem
3tbsp extra-virgin olive
 oil

1tsp sea salt
½tsp dried chilli flakes
juice of 1 small lemon
3tbsp chopped dill

1 Heat a frying pan and, when moderately hot, add the tomatoes, 1tbsp olive oil and the salt. Cook, shaking the pan, until the tomatoes begin to colour and the skins of around six of them have burst.
2 Add the chilli flakes and lemon juice to the pan and shake for a few seconds. Add the remaining oil, count to 20, then take off the heat.
3 Tip the tomatoes into a bowl and cool for 10 minutes, then stir in the dill, cover with clingfilm and put to one side so that the flavours can mature.

Serves 6
Preparation: 5 minutes, plus infusing
Cooking time: 5 minutes
Per serving: 70 cals; 7g fat; 2g carbohydrate

Grilled Cherry Tomatoes

450g (1lb) cherry
  tomatoes
1tbsp each olive oil and
  balsamic vinegar

salt and pepper
pinch of sugar

1 Preheat the grill to its highest setting. Put the tomatoes
  in the grill tray and drizzle with the olive oil and vinegar.
  Season and add a pinch of sugar.
2 Grill for 4–5 minutes or until the skins just begin to turn
  brown and burst. Serve or keep warm until required.

Serves 8–10
Preparation: 2 minutes
Cooking time: 4–5 minutes
Per serving: 30–20 cals; 2–1g fat;
2–2g carbohydrate

Grilled Peppers with Pine Nuts

2 yellow peppers,
  halved and deseeded
olive oil, to brush
1tsp crushed coriander
  seeds
2tbsp mixed pine nuts
  and flaked almonds

salt and pepper
oregano sprigs, to
  garnish
soured cream, to serve

1 Preheat the grill to high. Brush the yellow peppers with
  a little olive oil and sprinkle with the coriander seeds.
  Put in a grill pan and grill for 5–10 minutes until charred
  and tender, adding the pine nuts and flaked almonds
  for the last 2 minutes of the cooking time.
2 Transfer the peppers to a serving dish and season.
  Garnish with oregano sprigs and serve with
  soured cream.

Serves 4
Preparation: 5 minutes
Cooking time: about 5–10 minutes
Per serving (without cream): 80 cals; 7g fat;
3g carbohydrate

Mixed Pepper Salad

700g (1½lb) red and
  yellow peppers,
  halved and deseeded
4tbsp olive oil
1 garlic clove, peeled
  and finely chopped

50g (2oz) pitted black
  olives
basil leaves
salt and pepper

1 Preheat the oven to 200°C (180°C fan oven) mark 6.
  Put the peppers in a roasting tin, drizzle with 2tbsp oil
  and cook for 45 minutes. Remove from the oven, skin
  the peppers and cut into thick slices.
2 Mix the garlic with the pepper slices, the remaining oil,
  the olives and basil. Season and serve.

Serves 6
Preparation: 5 minutes
Cooking time: 45 minutes
Per serving: 120 cals; 10g fat; 7g carbohydrate

Lemon and Orange Carrots

**900g (2lb) carrots,
  peeled and cut into
  long batons**
**150ml (¼ pint) orange
  juice**
juice of 2 lemons
**150ml (¼ pint) dry
  white wine**
50g (2oz) butter
**3tbsp light muscovado
  sugar**
**4tbsp coriander,
  roughly chopped**

1 Put the carrots, orange and lemon juice, wine, butter and sugar in a pan. Cover and bring to the boil.
2 Remove the lid and cook until almost all the liquid has evaporated – this should take about 10 minutes.
3 Serve sprinkled with the coriander.

Serves 8
Preparation: 5 minutes
Cooking time: 10–15 minutes
Per serving: 120 cals; 5g fat; 16g carbohydrate

Baby Carrots and Fennel

**450g (1lb) each baby
  carrots and fennel**
salt

1 Cook the carrots and fennel in boiling salted water for 4–5 minutes or until just tender.
2 Drain well and serve.

Serves 4
Preparation: 2 minutes
Cooking time: 4–5 minutes
Per serving: 50 cals; 1g fat; 9g carbohydrate

Chilli Red Onions with Goat's Cheese

**75g (3oz) unsalted
  butter, softened**
**2 medium red chillies,
  deseeded and finely
  diced**
1tsp crushed chillies
salt and pepper
**6 small red onions,
  peeled**
**3 x 100g Somerset
  goat's cheese**
**balsamic vinegar, to
  serve**

1 Preheat the oven to 200°C (180°C fan oven) mark 6. Put the butter in a small bowl, beat in the diced and crushed chillies and season well.
2 Cut the root off one of the onions and sit it on its base, then make several deep cuts in the top to create a star shape, slicing about two-thirds of the way down the onion. Do the same with the other five onions, then divide the chilli butter equally among them, pushing it down into the cuts. Put the onions in a small roasting tin, cover with foil and bake for 40–45 minutes or until they are soft.
3 About 5 minutes before the onions are ready, slice each goat's cheese in two, leaving the rind intact, then put on a baking sheet and bake for 2–3 minutes. Put the onion on top of the goat's cheese and serve drizzled with balsamic vinegar.

Serves 6
Preparation: 10 minutes
Cooking time: 40–45 minutes
Per serving: 230 cals; 18g fat; 10g carbohydrate

Gratin of Chard

600ml (1 pint) milk
½ onion, peeled
1 bay leaf
6 peppercorns
50g (2oz) butter, plus extra to grease
1kg (2¼lb) chard, green leaves separated from white stalks
salt and pepper
40g (1½oz) plain flour
pinch of freshly grated nutmeg
¼tsp French mustard
125g (4oz) freshly grated Parmesan cheese
142ml carton double cream

1 Pour the milk into a pan, add the onion, bay leaf and peppercorns, bring to the boil and remove from the heat. Cover and put to one side for 20 minutes to infuse.

2 Preheat the oven to 200°C (180°C fan oven) mark 6. Grease a 1.7 litre (3 pint) ovenproof dish. Tear the chard leaves into shreds, trim the ends of the stalks and slice. Cook the stalks in a pan of boiling salted water for about 4 minutes until just tender. Add the leaves to the pan for the last 30 seconds. Drain, then plunge into a bowl of icy cold water.

3 Melt the butter in a pan and stir in the flour. Cook for 30 seconds, then add the strained milk, discarding the onion, bay leaf and peppercorns. Bring the sauce to boil, stirring, then reduce the heat and simmer until creamy. Stir in a pinch of nutmeg, the mustard, 50g (2oz) Parmesan and the cream and season well.

4 Drain the chard well and mix with the sauce. Pour the mixture into the prepared dish. Sprinkle with the remaining Parmesan and bake for 25–30 minutes or until golden brown and bubbling.

Serves 6
Preparation: 10 minutes
Cooking time: 35–40 minutes, plus infusing
Per serving: 380 cals; 29 fat; 15g carbohydrate

Glazed Shallots with Balsamic Vinegar

1kg (2¼lb) medium-sized shallots, blanched in boiling water, drained and peeled, root left intact
50g (2oz) butter
1tbsp golden caster sugar
salt and pepper
2tbsp balsamic vinegar

1 Put the shallots in a pan of cold water, bring to the boil and cook for 5 minutes or until just soft; drain.

2 Heat the butter in a wide heavy-based pan. Add the shallots, sugar and seasoning. Cook over a medium heat, stirring occasionally, for 15–20 minutes or until shallots are brown, shiny and cooked to the centre. Add the vinegar, bring to the boil and bubble until the liquid has evaporated.

Serves 8–10
Preparation: 20 minutes
Cooking time: 15–20 minutes
Per serving: 100–80 cals; 5–4g fat; 12–9g carbohydrate

Cold desserts

You've had a great meal so far and now you're anticipating the dessert. What do you fancy – meringues, fools, ice cream, trifles, jellies, fruit? Something thick and creamy, or delicate and aromatic? A solid chunk of cheesecake, or a sublime slice of panna cotta?

If ice cream is what you're after, then there are so many to choose from: Apricot and Ginger; Cinnamon and Nutmeg; Ginger, Rum and Raisin, to mention just three, plus Banana and Chocolate Ice Cream Pie and Italian Ice Cream Cake.

What about fruit? Take your pick from Nectarines and Apricots with Pistachios; Marinated Strawberries; or Spiced Caramelised Clementines, for starters.

Perhaps jellies are more your thing. Sparkling Fruit Jellies capture grapes and raspberries in their depths; Port and Orange jellies are what it says on the label; while, for something a bit posher, Champagne and Ginger Jelly with Ginger Cream is an exciting combination.

Finally, an old favourite: trifle – layers of alcohol-soaked sponge, cream, custard and fruit. Make it as simple as a Crème Anglaise Trifle, or as seductive as a Tropical Fruit Trifle and Coconut Trifle. The perfect way the spoil yourself.

Amaretti with Lemon Mascarpone

**juice from ¼ lemon,
plus the rind pared
from ¼ lemon, white
skin removed, and
sliced finely into
longstrips, or lemon
zest (optional)**

**1tbsp golden caster
sugar, plus a little
extra to sprinkle
50g (2oz) mascarpone
13 single Amaretti
biscuits**

1 Put the lemon juice in a small pan. Add the sugar and dissolve over a low heat. Add the finely sliced lemon rind and cook for 1–2 minutes – it will curl up. Lift out, using a slotted spoon and put on to a sheet of baking parchment, reserving the syrup. Sprinkle the lemon rind with sugar to coat.
2 Beat the mascarpone in a bowl to soften, then stir in the sugar syrup.
3 Crush one of the Amaretti biscuits and put to one side, ready to dust.

4 Put a blob of mascarpone on to each remaining Amaretti biscuit, then top with a couple of strips of the crystallised lemon peel, or the lemon zest, if using. Sprinkle over the crushed Amaretti crumbs.

Makes 12
Preparation: 15 minutes
Cooking time: 5 minutes
Per serving: 20 cals; 1g fat; 2g carbohydrate

See picture, page 341

Apricot Fool

**410g can apricots,
drained
200g (7oz) Greek-style
yogurt**

**25g golden caster
sugar, to taste**

1 Put the apricots in a food processor and blend until smooth.
2 Stir the purée into the yogurt and sweeten to taste. Chill for 2 hours before serving.

Serves 4–6
Preparation: 5 minutes, plus chilling
Per serving: 160–100 cals; 5–3g fat;
27–18g carbohydrate

Oh-so-fruity Fool

**500g carton summer
fruit compôte**

**500g carton fresh
custard sauce**

1 Divide half the compôte among six serving glasses and add a thin layer of custard sauce. Repeat the process to use up all the compôte and sauce.
2 Stir each fool once to swirl the custard and compôte together, then serve.

Serves 6
Preparation: 5 minutes
Per serving: 154 cals; 4g fat; 27g carbohydrate

See picture, page 341

Passion Fruit and Lime Cream Pots

12 ripe passion fruit
568ml carton double
   cream
50g (2oz) golden caster
   sugar

zest and juice of 1 lime
biscuits to serve, such
   as biscuit curls or
   cigarettes russes

1 Rest a sieve over a large bowl. Halve the passion fruit and scrape the juice and seeds into the sieve. Stir the seeds with a spoon to extract all the juice, then discard the seeds.

2 Pour the cream into a heavy-based pan and add all but 1tbsp sugar. Heat gently until the sugar has dissolved, then bring to the boil and cook for 5–8 minutes, stirring continuously with a wooden spoon, making sure it doesn't catch on the bottom, until it has reduced a little.

3 Pour the mixture into a large jug, add the lime zest, 2tsp lime juice and a quarter of the passion fruit juice – it will thicken immediately, so stir it well to stop it going lumpy.

4 Pour the mixture into six 200ml (7fl oz) serving glasses. Leave to cool a little, then chill in the fridge for 1 hour for a soft set or overnight for a firm set.

5 Pour the remaining passion fruit and lime juice into a pan, add the remaining 1tbsp sugar and bring to the boil. Cook for 3 minutes until syrupy. Leave to cool.

6 About 20–30 minutes before serving, remove the creams from the fridge. When ready, pour a little passion fruit syrup on top of each set cream and serve with the biscuits.

Serves 6
Preparation: 15 minutes, plus chilling
Cooking time: 8–11 minutes
Per serving: 470 cals; 45g fat; 13g carbohydrate

Atholl Brose

125g (4oz) raspberries,
   plus extra to decorate
pinch of ground
   cinnamon
1tsp lemon juice
25g (1oz) golden caster
   sugar

300ml (½ pint) double
   cream
3tbsp thin honey
25–50ml (1–2fl oz)
   whisky, to taste
50g (2oz) coarse
   oatmeal, toasted

1 Put the raspberries, cinnamon, lemon juice, sugar and 2tbsp water into a small pan and heat gently for 1–2 minutes until the raspberries just soften. Remove from the heat and leave to cool.

2 Whip the cream in a bowl with the honey until it just begins to hold its shape, then beat in the whisky. Fold in the oatmeal.

3 Divide the raspberries among serving glasses and spoon the oatmeal cream on top. Chill in the fridge for 30 minutes.

4 Decorate each serving with a few raspberries and serve with crisp dessert biscuits, if you like.

Serves 4
Preparation: 10 minutes, plus chilling
Cooking time: 2 minutes
Per serving: 470 cals; 37g fat; 28g carbohydrate

Iced Plum Creams

450g (1lb) dark-skinned
  plums, halved with
  stones intact
200ml (7fl oz) sloe gin
75g (3oz) golden caster
  sugar

2 large eggs
150g (5oz) mascarpone
light sunflower oil, to
  grease
redcurrants, to
  decorate

1 Put the plums in a pan with the sloe gin and 40g (1½oz)
   sugar, cover with a tight-fitting lid and bring to the boil.
   Reduce the heat and simmer until the plums are tender
   – about 20 minutes. Cool and drain, reserving the juice.
   Remove the stones from the cooled plums and whiz the
   plums in a food processor until smooth, then put to
   one side.
2 Separate the eggs, reserve one white (discard the
   other). Whisk the yolks with the remaining sugar and the
   reserved plum juice for 2–3 minutes or until pale
   and lightly thickened. Whisk the plum purée and
   mascarpone together, then carefully fold in the egg
   yolk mixture. Whisk the reserved egg white in a clean
   grease-free bowl until stiff peaks form and carefully fold
   into the mixture.
3 Divide the plum mixture between six or eight 150ml
   (¼ pint) lightly oiled dariole moulds or ramekins. Cover
   and put in the freezer for 4 hours.
4 To serve, invert the creams on to plates and unmould.
   (You can eat the creams straight away, but it's better to
   give them 5–10 minutes in the fridge before serving.)
   Decorate with redcurrants and serve.

Makes 6–8 servings
Preparation: 40 minutes, plus freezing
Cooking time: 20 minutes
Per serving: 310–230 cals; 14–11g fat;
30–23g carbohydrate

Passion Fruit and Mango Brûlée

1 large ripe mango,
  peeled
2 passion fruit, halved
500ml carton reduced-
  fat crème fraîche

200g (7oz) mascarpone
2tbsp light muscovado
  sugar

1 Preheat the grill to high. Slice the mango flesh away
   from either side of the stone, then cut into cubes. Put
   into the base of four ramekin dishes.
2 Scoop out the passion fruit juice and seeds into a bowl
   and add the crème fraîche and mascarpone. Beat
   together with a wooden spoon to form a thick creamy
   mixture.
3 Spoon this mixture over the mango in the ramekins,
   then sprinkle the sugar over the top.
4 Put under the grill and cook until the sugar melts and
   forms a dark caramel. Cool slightly before serving.

Serves 4
Preparation: 6 minutes
Cooking time: 4 minutes
Per serving: 500 cals; 42g fat; 22g carbohydrate

*Top left: Baked Raspberry Creams, page 345; top right: Cherry
Crush, page 349; bottom left: Oh-so-Fruity Fool, page 338; bottom
right: Amaretti with Lemon Mascarpone, page 338.*

Tropical Fruit Salad

4 passion fruit, halved
100g (3½oz) golden
caster sugar
50ml (2fl oz) white rum
or Malibu
grated zest and juice of
1 lime
125g (4oz) cranberries

1 small pineapple,
peeled, halved and
cored
1 papaya, peeled and
halved
1 large ripe mango,
peeled
1 large banana

1 Scoop out the pulp from the passion fruit into a sieve set over a small pan and press with the back of a wooden spoon to extract the juice. Discard the seeds.
2 Add the sugar, rum, lime zest and juice to the passion fruit juice in the pan and heat gently to make a syrup. Add the cranberries and cook over a medium heat for 5 minutes. Leave to cool.
3 Slice the pineapple lengthways. Scoop out and discard the papaya seeds and slice lengthways. Slice the mango flesh away from either side of the stone, then slice lengthways. Slice the banana on the diagonal.
4 Put the pineapple, papaya, mango and banana into a large bowl, then add the cranberries and syrup. Leave to stand at room temperature for at least 30 minutes before serving to let the flavours develop.

Serves 8
Preparation: 20 minutes, plus standing
Cooking time: 7 minutes
Per serving: 120 cals; trace fat; 28g carbohydrate

Ginger and Mint Fruit Salad

70cl bottle ginger wine
225g (8oz) golden
caster sugar
25g (1oz) piece fresh
root ginger, peeled
3 large mangoes,
peeled and roughly
chopped
3 large papaya, peeled
and roughly chopped

2 Charentais melons,
peeled and roughly
chopped
450g (1lb) seedless red
grapes, removed from
stalks
2 mint sprigs, plus
extra to decorate

1 Put the wine, sugar and ginger in a pan with 600ml (1 pint) cold water and heat gently until the sugar has dissolved. Increase the heat and bring to the boil, then reduce the heat and simmer gently for 20–30 minutes. Leave to cool.
2 Put all the fruit in a large serving bowl and strain the cooled syrup over. Chill for at least 2 hours, preferably overnight.
3 To serve, chop the mint leaves and add to the fruit salad. Decorate with mint sprigs.

Serves 12
Preparation: 50 minutes, plus cooling and chilling
Cooking time: 30 minutes
Per serving: 205 cals; 0g fat; 42g carbohydrate

Top left: Watermelon with Feta Cheese and Honey, page 349; top right: Exotic Fruit Salad, page 348; bottom left: Quick Lemon Mousse, page 345; bottom right: Marinated Strawberries, page 349.

Champagne and Ginger Jelly with Ginger Cream

**8 gelatine leaves,
about 25g (1oz)
175g (6oz) golden
caster sugar
pared zest of 2
unwaxed lemons (use
a vegetable peeler to
remove zest in
long strips)**

**75cl bottle champagne
or sparkling wine
6–8tbsp ginger wine
284ml carton double
cream
7 balls stem ginger in
syrup, drained,
plus 2tsp of the syrup**

1   Pour 600ml (1 pint) cold water into a bowl. Break up the gelatine, add to the bowl and soak for 5 minutes.
2   Put the sugar in a pan and add the lemon zest and 400ml (14fl oz) cold water. Heat gently to dissolve the sugar, then simmer for 2–3 minutes. Remove from the heat and cool a little, then remove the lemon zest.
3   Lift the soaked gelatine out of the water and add it to the pan. Stir until melted.
4   Stir in the champagne and ginger wine. Ladle the jelly into 10 wine glasses and chill until set.
5   Meanwhile, make the ginger cream. Whip the cream in a bowl until soft peaks form. Chop 3 stem ginger balls and fold into the cream with the ginger syrup. Spoon into a serving dish and chill.
6   Just before serving, cut the remaining stem ginger balls into slivers and sprinkle on to the jellies. Serve with the ginger cream.

Serves 10
Preparation: 15 minutes
Cooking time: 20 minutes
Per serving: 150 cals; 0g fat; 20g carbohydrate

Sloe Gin Jelly

**350g (12oz) small black
seedless grapes or
strawberries
300ml (½ pint) sloe gin**

**125g (4oz) kumquats
2tsp powdered gelatine
75g (3oz) granulated
sugar**

1   Lightly prick the grapes with a cocktail stick and put in a bowl. Reserve 4tbsp sloe gin and pour the remainder over the grapes; cover and refrigerate for at least 2 hours or overnight.
2   Slice the kumquats. Put the reserved 4tbsp sloe gin in a bowl, sprinkle the gelatine over and leave to soak for 5 minutes.
3   Put 600ml (1 pint) water in a saucepan, add the sugar and cook over a low heat until the sugar has dissolved. Bring to the boil and bubble until the liquid has reduced by half, then leave to cool for 1 minute. Add the soaked gelatine, then stir until melted.
4   Add the macerated grapes and their liquid to the syrup with the kumquats and stir until well mixed. Place in a bowl and refrigerate until the jelly begins to set – about 1 hour.
5   Spoon the jelly into six or eight champagne flutes, then cover and refrigerate for 1 hour or until set. Take the glasses of sloe gin jelly out of the fridge about 30–45 minutes before serving to allow the jelly to soften slightly.

Serves 6–8
Preparation: 30 minutes, plus marinating and chilling
Cooking time: 15 minutes
Per serving: 220–160 cals; trace fat;
36–27g carbohydrate

Top left: Easy Vanilla Ice Cream, page 360; top right: Cinnamon and Nutmeg Ice Cream, page 358; bottom left: Spicy Ginger Ice Cream, page 361; bottom right: Almond Toffee Ice Cream, page 355.

Apricot and Almond Roulade

butter, to grease
25g (1oz) flaked
  almonds
5 large eggs, separated
150g (5oz) golden
  caster sugar, plus
  extra to dust
1tsp vanilla extract

125g (4oz) white
  almond paste, grated
3tbsp plain white flour
3tbsp Amaretto liqueur
6 ripe apricots
300ml (½ pint) crème
  fraîche

1 Preheat the oven to 180°C (160°C fan oven) mark 4. Grease a 33 x 23cm (13 x 9 inch) Swiss-roll tin with butter and line with greased non-stick baking parchment. Scatter the flaked almonds evenly over the parchment.
2 Whisk the egg yolks with 125g (4oz) sugar until pale and fluffy. Stir in the vanilla extract and grated almond paste. Sift the flour over the mixture then, using a metal spoon, fold in lightly.
3 Whisk the egg whites in another bowl until they are stiff but not dry. Gradually whisk in the remaining caster sugar. Using a large metal spoon, fold a quarter of the egg whites into the almond mixture to loosen it, then carefully fold in the remainder.
4 Turn the mixture into the prepared tin, gently easing it into the corners. Bake for about 20 minutes or until well risen and just firm to the touch. Remove from the oven, cover with a sheet of non-stick baking parchment and a damp tea-towel and leave until cool.
5 Remove the tea-towel and invert the roulade (and the paper) on to a sugar-dusted piece of baking parchment. Peel off the lining paper very slowly and carefully. Drizzle the roulade with the amaretto liqueur.
6 For the filling, halve and stone the apricots, then cut them into small pieces. Spread the roulade evenly with the crème fraîche and scatter the apricots over the top.
7 Starting from one of the narrow ends, carefully roll up the roulade, using the baking parchment to help. Transfer the roulade to a serving plate and dust with sugar to serve.

Serves 8
Preparation: 20 minutes, plus standing
Cooking time: 20 minutes
Per serving: 420 cals; 25g fat; 39g carbohydrate

Cinnamon and Nutmeg Ice Cream

½tsp each ground
  cinnamon and freshly
  grated nutmeg
50g (2oz) golden caster
  sugar

142ml carton double
  cream
250g tub mascarpone
400g carton fresh
  custard

1 Put the cinnamon, nutmeg, sugar and cream in a small pan, bring slowly to the boil, then put to one side to cool.
2 Put the mascarpone in a large bowl and beat until smooth. Stir in the custard and the cooled spiced cream. Pour the mixture into a shallow freezer container and freeze for 2–3 hours.
3 Beat to break up the ice crystals and freeze for a further 2–3 hours before using. The ice cream will keep in the freezer for up to one month.

Serves 8
Preparation: 10 minutes, plus freezing
Cooking time: 5 minutes
Per serving: 290 cals; 24g fat; 17g carbohydrate

See picture, page 353

Cognac and Crème Fraîche Ice Cream

500ml carton full-fat
  crème fraîche
175g (6oz) golden icing
  sugar, sifted

4tbsp special reserve
  Cognac

1 Whisk the crème fraîche, sugar and Cognac together – it will become thin, but continue whisking until it thickens slightly.
2 Pour into a 450g (1lb) loaf tin lined with clingfilm, cover and freeze for up to one month.

Serves 8
Preparation: 5 minutes, plus freezing
Per serving: 340 cals; 25g fat; 25g carbohydrate

Top left: Pistachio and Date Ice Cream, page 362; top right: Cognac and Créme Fraiche Ice Cream, page 358; bottom left: Chocolate Ice Cream, page 363; bottom right: Banana and Chocolate Ice Cream Pie, page 366.

Caramelised Orange Trifle

125g (4oz) light
  muscovado sugar
2 x 135g packs orange
  jelly, broken into
  cubes
100ml (3½fl oz) brandy
10 oranges
150g pack ratafia
  biscuits
4tbsp sweet sherry
500g carton fresh
  custard

2 x 250g tubs
  mascarpone
284ml carton double
  cream
¼tsp vanilla extract
flavourless oil, such as
  safflower
125g (4oz) granulated
  sugar

1 Put the muscovado sugar in a large heavy-based pan, add 100ml (3½fl oz) water and dissolve the sugar over a low heat. Increase the heat and cook for about 5 minutes until syrupy and thick.
2 Remove the pan from the heat and add 450ml (¾ pint) boiling water (stand back as it will splutter). Add the jelly and stir until dissolved, then add the brandy and put to one side.
3 Cut the peel off each orange, removing all pith. Slice the flesh into rounds, reserving any juice. Add the juice – about 125ml (4fl oz) – to the jelly and leave to cool.
4 Tip the ratafias into a 3.5 litre (6¼ pint) bowl and drizzle with sherry. Put the orange rounds on top, then pour the jelly over. Chill for 4 hours until set.
5 Pour the custard on top and smooth over. Put the mascarpone, cream and vanilla extract in a bowl and combine with an electric hand mixer. Spoon three-quarters of the mixture on to the custard and smooth the surface. Put the remainder in a piping bag and pipe ten swirls around the edge. Chill.
6 Line a large baking sheet with baking parchment and grease it with oil. Half-fill the sink with cold water. Put the granulated sugar in a heavy-based pan and heat gently until it has dissolved. Increase the heat and cook the sugar to a golden caramel. Immediately plunge the base of the pan into the sink. Take the pan out of the sink and rest it next to the parchment. Dip a fork into the caramel to pick up the syrup, then hold it high over the parchment and flick backwards and forwards over the paper – as the sugar cools it will form very thin threads and build up a golden nest of spun sugar. Leave on the parchment until ready to serve, then lift on to the trifle.

Serves 16
Preparation: 45 minutes, plus setting
Cooking time: 5 minutes
Per serving: 440 cals; 25g fat; 49g carbohydrate

Tropical Fruit and Coconut Trifle

1 small pineapple,
  roughly chopped
2 bananas, thickly
  sliced
2 x 400g cans mango
  slices in syrup,
  drained, syrup
  reserved
2 passion fruit, halved
175g (6oz) plain
  sponge, such as
  Madeira cake, roughly
  chopped

3tbsp dark rum
  (optional)
200ml (7fl oz) coconut
  cream
500g carton fresh
  custard
500g carton Greek-
  style yogurt
600ml (1 pint) double
  cream
6tbsp dark muscovado
  sugar

1 Put the pineapple pieces in a large trifle bowl, add the banana and mango slices and spoon over the passion fruit pulp. Top with the chopped sponge. Pour over the rum, if using, and 6tbsp of the reserved mango syrup.
2 Mix together the coconut cream and custard and pour the mixture over the sponge.
3 Put the yogurt and double cream in a bowl and whisk until thick. Spoon or pipe the mixture over the custard, then sprinkle with the sugar. Cover and chill for at least 1 hour before serving.

Serves 16
Preparation: 30 minutes, plus chilling
Per serving: 404 cals, 29g fat; 33g carbohydrate

Cold desserts

Top left: Chilled Vanilla Risotto, page 373; top right: Tropical Fruit and Coconut Trifle, page 371; bottom left: Carmelised Orange Trifle, page 370, bottom right: Iced Raspberry Soufflés, page 373.

Hot puddings

Warm, comforting and homely is how we think of hot puds. Eating a Date and Walnut Pudding with Chocolate Sauce is almost as good as having a cuddle – wedges of sticky sponge pudding anointed with hot chocolate fudge sauce. Heaven.

But they don't all need to be guaranteed to have you snoozing in front of the fire. That golden oldie Baked Egg Custard will take you right back to the nursery and remind you just how good a simple pudding can be.

For something a bit sexier, Hot Orange Soufflé is simple and impressive. Just get it to the table as soon as it's cooked and you've cracked it. Home-made pies and tarts served with lashings of hot custard are dead easy, but terrific to eat – Rustic Blackberry and Apple Pie; Rhubarb and Orange Crumble Tart; Plum and Cardamom Pie; and Maple Pecan Pie: all great favourites.

As are pancakes and fritters – Mango Pancakes are filled with fresh mango and passion fruit and bathed in a pineapple juice and Malibu sauce for an irresistible hot pud.

So forget the diet, and indulge yourself!

Baked Apricots with Almonds

12 apricots, halved and stoned	25g (1oz) unsalted butter
6tbsp golden caster sugar	25g (1oz) flaked almonds
2tbsp Amaretto liqueur	

1 Preheat the oven to 200°C (180°C fan oven) mark 6. Put the apricot halves, cut side up, in an ovenproof dish. Sprinkle with the sugar, drizzle with the liqueur, then dot each apricot half with a little butter. Scatter over the flaked almonds.
2 Bake for 20–25 minutes until the apricots are soft and the juices are syrupy. Serve warm, with crème fraîche.

Serves 6
Preparation: 10 minutes
Cooking time: 20–25 minutes
Per serving: 160 cals; 6g fat; 26g carbohydrate

Ginger-glazed Pineapple

2 medium-sized ripe pineapples, cut into four lengthways, with the stalk on	2tsp ground ginger, plus extra to dust
2tbsp light muscovado sugar	yogurt, to serve 1tsp runny honey (optional)

1 Remove the fibrous core from each pineapple quarter and cut along the skin to loosen the flesh, reserving the skin 'shells'. Cut the flesh into pieces and put back in the pineapple 'shell'. Wrap the green leaves of the stalk in foil so that they don't burn while grilling. Mix the sugar with the ground ginger.
2 Preheat the grill. Sprinkle each pineapple quarter with the sugar mixture, put on foil-lined baking sheets and cook under the grill for 10 minutes or until golden and caramelised.
3 Mix the yogurt with the honey, if using. Serve the pineapple with the yogurt and dust with ginger.

Serves 8
Preparation: 30 minutes
Cooking time: 10 minutes
Per serving: 100 cals; 0g fat; 27g carbohydrate

See picture, page 383

Pineapple Fritters

1 large ripe pineapple, peeled and cored, plus extra pineapple slices to decorate	50g (2oz) plain flour pinch of salt finely grated zest of ½ lemon
450g (1lb) papaya, peeled, deseeded and sliced	1 egg, separated 1tsp sunflower oil oil, for deep-frying
1½tbsp golden caster sugar	lemon zest, to decorate

1 Slice the pineapple into 1cm (½ inch) thick rings. Cut each ring into three or four pieces and dry on kitchen paper.
2 To make the sauce, put the papaya in a blender or food processor and whiz until smooth. Stir in the sugar, pour into a bowl and put to one side.
3 To make the batter, sift the flour and salt into a bowl. Stir in the lemon zest and make a well in the centre. Put the egg yolk and 4tbsp water in the well and gradually incorporate the flour mixture, adding enough extra water to produce the consistency of single cream.
4 Whisk the egg white in a clean grease-free bowl until stiff peaks form, then fold into the batter with the sunflower oil.
5 Heat the oil in a deep-fat fryer to 190°C or until a cube of day-old bread dropped into the oil browns in 30 seconds. Spear six pieces of pineapple on to a skewer and dip them in the batter to coat. Lower the pieces into the hot oil and fry for 3–4 minutes until puffed, golden and crisp. Remove the pineapple pieces with a slotted spoon, drain on kitchen paper and keep them warm while you cook the remaining pineapple in the same way.
6 Decorate with pineapple slices and lemon zest and serve at once with the papaya sauce.

Serves 4–6
Preparation: 30 minutes
Cooking time: 10 minutes
Per serving: 340–230 cals; 15–10g fat; 50–33g carbohydrate

Fruit Kebabs with Spiced Pear Dip

150g (5oz) ready-to-eat
    dried pears, soaked in
    hot water for about 30
    minutes
juice of 1 orange
1tsp peeled and finely
    chopped fresh
    root ginger
½tsp vanilla extract
50ml (2fl oz) very low-
    fat natural yogurt
½tsp ground
    cinnamon, plus extra
    to dust
1tsp dark runny honey,

plus 1tbsp
25g (1oz) hazelnuts,
    toasted and
    roughly chopped
3 large fresh figs, each
    cut into quarters
1 large ripe mango,
    skin and stone
    removed, flesh cut
    into cubes
1 baby pineapple or 2
    thick slices, skin
    removed and flesh cut
    into cubes

1   To make the dip, drain the pears and put in a food
    processor or blender with the orange juice, ginger,
    vanilla extract, yogurt, cinnamon and 50ml (2fl oz)
    water and whiz until smooth. Spoon the dip into a bowl.
    Drizzle with 1tsp honey, sprinkle with the hazelnuts and
    dust with a little cinnamon. Cover and put to one side
    in a cool place until ready to serve. Meanwhile, soak six
    20.5cm (8 inch) wooden kebab skewers in water for 30
    minutes to stop them burning when cooking.
2   Preheat the grill to its highest setting. To make the
    kebabs, thread alternate pieces of fruit on to each
    skewer, using at least two pieces of each type of fruit
    per skewer. Place the skewers on a foil-covered tray and
    cover the ends of the skewers with strips of foil to
    prevent them burning. Drizzle with 1tbsp honey and
    grill for about 4 minutes on each side, close to the heat,
    until lightly charred. Serve warm or at room
    temperature with the dip.

Makes 6 kebabs
Preparation: 20 minutes, plus soaking
Cooking time: 8 minutes
Per kebab, including dip: 90 cals; 2g fat;
17g carbohydrate

See picture, page 383

Sticky Maple Syrup Pineapple

1 large pineapple,
    peeled and cut
    lengthways into
    quarters

200ml (7fl oz) maple
    syrup

1   Remove the fibrous core from each pineapple quarter.
    Slice each quarter lengthways into four to make sixteen
    wedges.
2   Pour the maple syrup into a large non-stick frying pan
    and heat for 2 minutes. Add the pineapple and fry for
    3 minutes, turning once, until warmed through.
3   Arrange the pineapple on serving plates, drizzle the
    maple syrup over and around it and serve.

Serves 4
Preparation: 10 minutes
Cooking time: 5 minutes
Per serving: 230 cals; 0g fat; 57g carbohydrate

Hot Orange Soufflé

65g (2½oz) unsalted
  butter
2tbsp dried
  breadcrumbs
40g (1½oz) plain flour
grated zest and juice of
  2 small (or 1 large)
  oranges and 1 lemon

200ml (7fl oz) full-fat
  milk
125g (4oz) golden
  caster sugar
3tbsp Grand Marnier
4 large eggs, separated
icing sugar, to dust

1 Preheat the oven to 190°C (170°C fan oven) mark 5. Melt 15g (½oz) butter and use to grease a 1.4 litre (2½ pint) soufflé dish. Coat the dish with the breadcrumbs and put to one side.

2 Melt the remaining butter in a pan, add the flour, orange and lemon zest and cook for 30 seconds. Take the pan off the heat and gradually beat in the milk until smooth. Cook, stirring, over a low heat until the sauce is thickened and smooth. Continue to cook for a further 2 minutes.

3 Remove from the heat and stir in the sugar, orange and lemon juices and Grand Marnier, then beat in the egg yolks.

4 Whisk the egg whites in a clean grease-free bowl until stiff peaks form, then, using a large metal spoon, carefully fold into the sauce until evenly incorporated. Spoon into the soufflé dish and run a knife around the outside of the mixture.

5 Immediately bake for 25–30 minutes until the soufflé is risen and golden. Remove from the oven, dust with icing sugar and serve at once.

Serves 6
Preparation: 20 minutes
Cooking time: 25–30 minutes
Per serving: 310 cals; 14g fat; 38g carbohydrate

Roast Apples with Butterscotch Sauce

125g (4oz) sultanas
6tbsp brandy
6 large Bramley
  cooking apples, cored
4tbsp light muscovado
  sugar, plus 125g (4oz)
2tbsp apple juice
125g (4oz) butter

2tbsp each golden
  syrup and black
  treacle
284ml carton double
  cream
125g (4oz) chopped
  and toasted hazelnuts
ricotta cheese, to serve

1 Preheat the oven to 220°C (200°C fan oven) mark 7. Soak the sultanas in 2tbsp brandy for 10 minutes, then stuff each apple with equal amounts.

2 Put the apples in a roasting tin, sprinkle over 4tbsp sugar and the apple juice. Bake for 15–20 minutes or until soft.

3 Meanwhile, make the sauce. Melt the butter, remaining sugar, the golden syrup and treacle in a heavy-based pan, stirring constantly. When the sugar has dissolved and the mixture is bubbling, stir in the remaining brandy and the cream. Bring back to the boil and set aside.

4 Remove the apples from the oven and serve with the sauce, hazelnuts and a dollop of ricotta cheese.

Serves 6
Preparation: 5 minutes, plus soaking
Cooking time: 15–20 minutes
Per serving (without ricotta): 780 cals; 47g fat; 85g carbohydrate

Barbecued Figs with Honey and Marsala

12 large ripe figs
melted butter, to brush
1 cinnamon stick,
  roughly broken

6tbsp runny Greek-
  style honey
6tbsp Marsala
crème fraîche, to serve

1 Make a small slit in each fig, three-quarters of the way through. Take two sheets of foil large enough to hold the figs in one layer. With the shiny side uppermost, lay one piece on top of the other and brush the top piece all over with the melted butter.

2 Stand the figs in the middle of the foil and scatter over the broken cinnamon stick. Bring the sides of the foil together loosely, leaving a gap at the top, and pour in the honey and Marsala. Scrunch the edges of the foil together so that the figs are loosely enclosed.

3 Put the foil parcel on the barbecue and cook over medium hot coals for about 10–15 minutes, depending on how ripe the figs are, until very tender.

4 Just before serving, open up the foil slightly at the top and barbecue for a further 2–3 minutes to allow the juices to reduce and become syrupy.

5 Serve the figs immediately with a large dollop of crème fraîche and the syrupy juices spooned over.

Serves 6
Preparation: 10 minutes
Cooking time: 13–18 minutes
Per serving: 140 cals; 3g fat; 24g carbohydrate

See picture, page 383

Exotic Boozy Pancakes

2 x 500g packs frozen
  tropical fruit
6tbsp rum
50g (2oz) butter
2tbsp golden caster
  sugar

6 ready-made
  pancakes
200ml carton crème
  fraîche
freshly grated nutmeg,
  to serve

1 Put the fruit into a large frying pan. Add the rum, butter and sugar and cook over a low heat for 7–10 minutes or until the fruit has thawed but isn't too soft. Remove the fruit with a slotted spoon, cover and set aside. Bring the juice in the pan to the boil, then cook for 7–10 minutes or until reduced to a syrupy consistency.

2 Meanwhile, heat the pancakes in a microwave on High for 1 minute 50 seconds (based on a 900W oven), or according to the packet instructions. Alternatively, wrap the pancakes in foil and steam over a pan of boiling water for 5 minutes until heated through.

3 Serve each pancake topped with fruit and drizzled with the syrup. Add a generous dollop of crème fraîche, then sprinkle a little nutmeg over the top.

Serves 6
Preparation: 5 minutes
Cooking time: 20 minutes
Per serving: 500 cals; 29g fat; 49g carbohydrate

Lime Fruits

zest and juice of
  4 limes, about 150ml
  (¼ pint)
3tbsp golden caster
  sugar

6 pieces tropical fruit,
  such as papaya,
  melon or mango,
  peeled and sliced

1 Heat the lime juice in a small pan with the sugar. Bring to the boil and allow to bubble for 2–3 minutes or until all the sugar has dissolved.
2 Just before serving, add the lime zest to the warm syrup. Arrange the tropical fruits on serving plates and spoon over the lime syrup. Serve immediately.

Serves 4
Preparation: 6 minutes
Cooking time: 5 minutes
Per serving: 120 cals; 0g fat; 31g carbohydrate

Hot Mango and Banana Salad

2 large oranges
2 firm but ripe
  mangoes, about 700g
  (1½lb) total weight
4 small bananas
25g (1oz) very low-fat
  spread

1tsp light muscovado
  sugar
2tbsp rum
2tbsp lemon or lime
  juice

1 Coarsely grate the zest of 1 orange and squeeze the juice. Peel the remaining orange and slice thickly. Cut the mango across either side of the stone, then cut the flesh into large pieces and peel. Remove any flesh from around the stone and cut all the flesh into bite-sized pieces. Peel and thickly slice the bananas.
2 Melt the low-fat spread in a large non-stick frying pan. Add the sugar, mango and banana and cook for 2–3 minutes until just beginning to soften.
3 Pour in the rum, orange and lemon or lime juices and the orange slices. Bring to the boil, then serve immediately, decorated with the grated orange zest.

Serves 4
Preparation: 10 minutes   Cooking time: 5 minutes
Per serving: 170 cals; 2g fat; 34g carbohydrate

Toffee Bananas

3 firm bananas, peeled
  and cut into chunks
3tbsp plain flour
1½tsp cornflour

1 egg white
oil, to deep-fry
125g (4oz) sugar
2tbsp sesame seeds

1 Dust the bananas with a little flour. Mix the remaining flour with the cornflour and egg white and stir well to form a paste.
2 Half-fill a deep pan with oil and heat to 180°C or until a cube of day-old bread dropped into the oil browns in 30 seconds.
3 Dip the banana chunks in the paste and then fry, a few at a time, in the hot oil until golden. Remove the bananas with a slotted spoon, drain on kitchen paper and keep them warm while you cook the remaining bananas in the same way.

4 To make the sesame caramel, put the sugar and 2tbsp water in a heavy-based pan and heat gently until the sugar dissolves. Bring to the boil, without stirring, and boil until the mixture is straw-coloured. Sprinkle in the sesame seeds and cook briefly until the mixture turns golden. Immediately remove the pan from the heat, add the fried bananas and stir to coat.
5 Have ready a bowl of iced water. Tip the bananas into the water to set the caramel. Remove at once with a slotted spoon and serve.

Serves 4
Preparation: 10 minutes
Cooking time: 20 minutes
Per serving: 320 cals; 9g fat; 58g carbohydrate

13

Hot puddings

382

Top left: Fruit Kebabs with Spiced Pear Dip, page 377; Top right: Mincemeatand Ricotta Tart, page 388; bottom left: Ginger Glazed Pineapple, page 377;bottom right: Barbecued Figs with Honey and Marsala, page 379.

Sticky Plum Tart

125g (4oz) plain flour,
  plus extra to dust
1tsp ground cinnamon
salt
75g (3oz) butter
1 egg yolk

450g (1lb) plums,
  halved, stoned and
  sliced
2tbsp golden caster
  sugar
3tbsp apricot jam or
  redcurrant jelly

1 Sift the flour into a food processor, add the cinnamon, a pinch of salt, the butter and egg yolk and whiz for 30 seconds or until evenly combined. Add 1tbsp chilled water and whiz for 30 seconds. Knead together lightly, then roll out on a lightly floured surface to a 25.5cm (10 inch) diameter circle. Put on a baking sheet and chill for 10–15 minutes.

2 Preheat the oven to 200°C (180°C fan oven) mark 6. Prick the pastry all over with a fork. Bake for 20–25 minutes or until golden brown, then remove from the oven.

3 Arrange the plums over the cooked pastry and sprinkle with the sugar. Put back in the oven and cook for 45–50 minutes or until the plums are tender.

4 Melt the jam or jelly with 2tbsp water, bring to the boil and bubble for 1 minute. Brush or spoon over the warm tart. Serve warm.

Serves 6
Preparation: 5 minutes, plus chilling
Cooking time: 1 hour 5 minutes–1¼ hours
Per serving: 240 cals; 12g fat; 33g carbohydrate

Rhubarb and Apple Cobbler

900g (2lb) rhubarb, cut
  into 2.5cm (1 inch)
  lengths
450g (1lb) Bramley or
  other cooking apples,
  peeled, quartered,
  cored and sliced
135g (4½oz) golden
  caster sugar
200g (7oz) plain flour
1tbsp cornflour
½tsp ground ginger

65g (2½oz) butter,
  diced, plus a knob
grated zest of 1 orange
2tsp baking powder
pinch of salt
125ml (4fl oz)
  buttermilk (or full-fat
  milk plus a squeeze of
  lemon juice)
2tbsp double cream
1tsp demerara sugar

1 Preheat the oven to 220°C (200°C fan oven) mark 7. Put the fruit, 75g (3oz) sugar, 50g (2oz) flour, the cornflour, ginger, knob of butter and orange zest in a 25.5cm (10 inch) shallow ovenproof dish, toss to mix and put to one side.

2 To make the cobbler dough, sift the remaining flour, the baking powder and salt together into a bowl. Rub in the diced butter until the mixture resembles fine breadcrumbs. Stir in the remaining sugar, then add the milk and mix with a knife to a soft dough.

3 Spoon the dough on to the fruit in clumps, making sure it doesn't completely cover it. Mix the cream with the demerara sugar and drizzle over the top.

4 Stand the dish on a baking tray and bake for 10 minutes. Reduce the oven temperature to 190°C (170°C fan oven) mark 5 and bake for 20–30 minutes or until the cobbler is puffed and brown and the fruit is just soft.

5 Remove from the oven and leave the pudding to stand for 10 minutes. Serve with pouring cream or custard.

Serves 6
Preparation: 20 minutes plus standing
Cooking time: 30–40 minutes
Per serving: 370 cals; 13g fat; 63g carbohydrate

Bananas Grilled with Cardamom Butter

2 green cardamom
** pods, split**
50g (2oz) butter
50g (2oz) light

muscovado sugar
4 bananas, unpeeled,
** slit along their length**

1 Beat the seeds of the cardamom pods into the butter and sugar.
2 Preheat the grill. Open out the bananas a little and put on a grill pan. Spoon a little of the flavoured butter into each one. Grill for 3–5 minutes, basting with the butter, until the bananas are soft and beginning to caramelise.
3 Serve the bananas piping hot with a little of the buttery sauce and some vanilla ice cream.

Serves 4
Preparation: 5 minutes
Cooking time: 5 minutes
Per serving: 220 cals; 11g fat; 32g carbohydrate

Rhubarb Crumble

450g (1lb) rhubarb,
** chopped**
2 balls stem ginger in
** syrup, drained and**
** roughly chopped**

125g (4oz) lig
** muscovadc**
75g (3oz) bu
125g (4oz) plain flou

1 Preheat the oven to 180°C (160°C fan oven) mark 4. Put the rhubarb in a 1.1 litre (2 pint) pie dish. Mix in the stem ginger and sprinkle half the sugar over the rhubarb.
2 Put the butter and flour in a food processor, and whiz briefly until it resembles breadcrumbs. Add the remaining sugar and pulse once or twice to mix everything.
3 Spoon the topping over the fruit and bake the crumble for 50 minutes–1 hour or until it is golden brown and bubbling. Serve warm or cool, with cream or custard.

Serves 6
Preparation: 15 minutes
Cooking time: 50 minutes–1 hour
Per serving: 250 cals; 10g fat; 39g carbohydrate

Impress-your-friends Apple Tart

375g pack ready-rolled
** puff pastry**
500g (1lb 2oz) Cox's
** apples**

juice of 1 lemon
golden icing sugar, to
** dust**

1 Preheat the oven to 200°C (180°C fan oven) mark 6. Put the pastry on a 28 x 38cm (11 x15 inch) baking sheet and roll over it lightly with a rolling pin to smooth down the pastry. Score lightly around the edge, to create a 3cm (1¼ inch) border.
2 Core and thinly slice the apples (don't peel them), then toss them in the lemon juice.
3 Carefully arrange the apple slices on top of the pastry, within the border. Turn the edge of the pastry halfway over, so that it reaches the edge of the apples, then press down and use your fingers to crimp the edge. Dust heavily with icing sugar.
4 Bake for 20–25 minutes until the pastry is cooked and the sugar has caramelised. Serve warm, dusted with more icing sugar.

Serves 8
Preparation: 15 minutes
Cooking time: 20–25 minutes
Per serving: 210cals; 11g fat; 25g carbohydrate

Plum and Cardamom Pie

250g (9oz) ready-rolled sweet shortcrust pastry
plain flour, to dust
900g (2lb) mixed yellow and red plums, halved, stoned and quartered
2–3 green cardamom pods, split open, seeds removed and crushed or chopped
50–75g (2–3oz) golden caster sugar, plus extra to dust
beaten egg or milk, to glaze

1 Heat a flat baking sheet in the oven at 220°C (200°C fan oven) mark 7.
2 Roll out the pastry on a lightly floured surface a little thinner into a rough circle about 30cm (12 inches) in diameter. Put it on a floured baking sheet, preferably without a lip.
3 Pile the fruit in the centre of the pastry and sprinkle with the crushed cardamom seeds and sugar (if the plums are tart you'll need all of it, if ripe and sweet use a little less). Fold in the pastry edges and pleat together around the plums.
4 Brush the pastry with beaten egg or milk and sprinkle with sugar. Put on the preheated sheet and bake for 30 minutes or until the pastry is golden brown and the plums just tender. The juices will begin to bubble a little from the pie as it cooks.
5 Remove from the oven and leave the pie to cool for 10 minutes. Carefully loosen the pastry around the edges and cool for another 20 minutes. Transfer very carefully to a serving plate. Sprinkle the pie with a little extra sugar and serve warm with cream or vanilla ice cream.

Serves 6
Preparation: 15 minutes, plus cooling
Cooking time: 30 minutes
Per serving: 280 cals; 12g fat; 44g carbohydrate

American-style Plum Cobbler

900g (2lb) plums, halved and stoned
175g (6oz) golden caster sugar, plus 3tbsp
1tbsp cornflour
250g (9oz) self-raising flour
100g (3½oz) chilled unsalted butter, diced
175ml (6fl oz) buttermilk or whole natural yogurt

1 Preheat the oven to 200°C (180°C fan oven) mark 6. Cut the plums into chunky wedges. Tip into a 25.5 x 18 x 7.5cm (10 x 7 x 3 inch) ovenproof dish and toss together with the 3tbsp sugar and the cornflour.
2 Put the flour into a processor, add the butter and 100g (3½oz) sugar and whiz until the mixture forms fine crumbs. Add the buttermilk or yogurt and whiz for a few seconds until just combined.
3 Scatter clumps of the squidgy dough over the plums, leaving some of the fruit exposed. Sprinkle the cobbler with the remaining sugar and bake for 40 minutes until the fruit is tender and the topping is pale golden.

Serves 6
Preparation: 25 minutes
Cooking time: 40 minutes
Per serving: 467 cals; 14g fat; 48g carbohydrate

Top left: Saucy Hot Lemon Puddings, page 397; top right: Rustic Blackberry and Apple Pie, page 389; bottom left: Rhubarb and Pear Crumble, page 399; bottom right: Warm Ginger and Ricotta Cheesecake, page 394.

Warm Ginger and Ricotta Cheesecake

225g (8oz) digestive
  biscuits
75g (3oz) butter, melted
200g (7oz) full-fat soft
  cheese
225g (8oz) ricotta
  cheese
4tbsp double cream
3 eggs, separated
1tbsp cornflour

1 ball stem ginger in
  syrup, drained and
  finely chopped, plus
  stem ginger syrup
  from the jar
125g (4oz) golden icing
  sugar, sifted
300ml (½ pint) single
  cream
2tsp whisky

1 Preheat the oven to 200°C (180°C fan oven) mark 6. To make the base, put the biscuits into a food processor and whiz to fine crumbs. Add the melted butter and mix until well combined.

2 Line the base of a 20.5cm (8 inch) spring-release cake tin with baking parchment and cover the base with two-thirds of the crumb mixture, then put to one side.

3 For the filling, put the cheeses, double cream, egg yolks, cornflour, ginger and 1tbsp ginger syrup in the cleaned processor bowl and whiz briefly until the mixture is evenly blended and the ginger is roughly chopped through it. Transfer to a large bowl.

4 Whisk the egg whites in a clean grease-free bowl until soft peaks form. Gradually whisk in the sugar, keeping the meringue very stiff and shiny. Fold into the ginger mixture and spoon into the tin. Sprinkle over the remaining biscuit crumbs.

5 Bake the cheesecake for 30 minutes. Cover loosely with foil, reduce the oven temperature to 180°C (160°C fan oven) mark 4 and bake for 45 minutes or until the filling feels just set in the centre. Remove from the oven and leave to cool on a wire rack for 15 minutes; the cheesecake will sink slightly.

6 To make the sauce, put the single cream, 2tsp ginger syrup and the whisky in a pan and heat, but do not boil.

7 Unmould the cheesecake and serve warm with the ginger and whisky sauce.

Serves 6–8
Preparation: 25 minutes
Cooking time: 1¼ hours, plus cooling
Per serving: 760–570 cals; 56–42g fat; 55–41g carbohydrate

See picture, page 392

Bermuda Banana Pudding

40g (1½oz) butter, at
  room temperature,
  plus extra to grease
5tbsp light muscovado
  sugar
6 large bananas – 5
  mashed, 1 sliced

3tbsp plain flour, sifted
3tbsp milk
few drops of vanilla
  extract

1 Preheat the oven to 190°C (170°C fan oven) mark 5. Grease a 16.5cm (6½ inch) diameter shallow cake tin and line the base with non-stick baking parchment. Beat the butter with the sugar until combined. Add the mashed bananas, flour, milk and vanilla extract and mix well. Fold in the sliced banana. Pour the mixture into the tin. Bake for 45–50 minutes or until firm to the touch.

2 Remove from the oven and turn out, then remove the paper. Cut into eight, arrange two wedges on each plate and serve with vanilla ice cream (page 360).

Serves 4
Preparation: 15 minutes, plus cooling
Cooking time: 50 minutes
Per serving: 310 cals; 9g fat; 58g carbohydrate

Baked Egg Custard

butter, to grease
600ml (1 pint) full-fat
  milk
3 large eggs

2tbsp golden caster
  sugar
freshly grated nutmeg,
  to taste

1 Preheat the oven to 170°C (150°C fan oven) mark 3. Grease a 900ml (1½ pint) ovenproof dish. Warm the milk in a pan, but do not boil. Whisk the eggs and sugar together lightly in a bowl, then pour on the hot milk, stirring.

2 Strain the mixture into the prepared dish. Grate the nutmeg on top and bake in the middle of the oven for about 45 minutes until set and firm to the touch. Serve hot or cold.

Serves 4
Preparation: 5 minutes
Cooking time: 45 minutes
Per serving: 210 cals; 13g fat; 15g carbohydrate

Oven-baked Mini Christmas Puddings

150g (5oz) each
  currants, raisins and
  sultanas
150g (5oz) each dates
  and prunes, chopped
100ml (3½fl oz) each
  Grand Marnier and
  Guinness
finely grated zest and
  juice of 1 orange
175g (6oz) butter, plus
  extra to grease
175g (6oz) molasses
  sugar
3 eggs, beaten

75g (3oz) self-raising
  flour, sifted
1tbsp ground mixed
  spice
1 carrot, about 75g
  (3oz), peeled and
  grated
150g (5oz) fresh white
  breadcrumbs
75g (3oz) blanched
  almonds, toasted and
  chopped
50g (2oz) pecans,
  toasted and chopped

1 Put the dried fruit in a large bowl with the alcohol, orange zest and juice and leave to macerate.

2 Grease twelve 150ml (¼ pint) ovenproof cups or individual pudding moulds and line each with a 25.5cm (10 inch) square piece of muslin, or line the bases with baking parchment. (Don't worry if you only have six moulds – you can bake the puds in two batches, and the uncooked mixture will happily sit overnight.)

3 Put the butter and sugar in a large bowl and, using an electric hand mixer, whisk for 5 minutes until pale and fluffy. Beat in the eggs, one at a time, adding a little flour if the mixture looks as if it might curdle. Using a large metal spoon, carefully fold in the remaining flour, the mixed spice, carrot, breadcrumbs, nuts, soaked fruit and alcohol until just combined.

4 Divide the mixture among the cups or moulds. Smooth the surfaces, gather the muslin up and over each pudding, then twist and secure with string.

5 Preheat the oven to 180°C (160°C fan oven) mark 4. Wrap each pudding in foil, put in a roasting tin and pour in enough boiling water to come two-thirds of the way up the cups. Cover the whole tin with foil and bake for 2½ hours. Remove from the oven and cool, then remove the puddings from the cups and wrap in foil. Store in a cool dark place.

6 To serve, preheat the oven to 180°C (160°C fan oven) mark 4. Take the puddings out of their foil wrappers and put the muslin-covered puddings back in their basins. Wrap completely in new foil. Put in a roasting tin and pour in enough boiling water to come two-thirds of the way up their sides. Cover the roasting tin with foil and reheat in the oven for 1 hour. When ready to serve, have an ovenproof glove to hand and a sharp pair of scissors to snip the puds out of their wrappings.

Makes 12 x 150ml (¼ pint) individual puddings
Preparation: 30 minutes   Cooking time: 2½ hours
Per serving: 470 cals; 20g fat; 65g carbohydrate

Hot puddings

Sticky Marmalade Pudding

175g (6oz) butter
175g (6oz) light
  muscovado sugar
about 300g (11oz)
  Seville orange
  marmalade
2 seedless oranges,
  peeled, all pith
  removed and sliced
  thinly into rounds

2 large eggs, beaten
175g (6oz) self-raising
  flour
1½tsp ground ginger
40g (1½oz) stem ginger
  in syrup, drained and
  finely chopped

1 Preheat the oven to 180°C (160°C fan oven) mark 4. Line the base of a round 23cm (9 inch) wide, minimum 5cm (2 inch) deep tin with non-stick baking parchment. Warm 50g (2oz) each of the butter and sugar with half the marmalade. Spoon into the tin and arrange the orange slices over.

2 Beat together the remaining butter and sugar. Gradually beat in the eggs. Sift the flour and ground ginger and fold into the mixture with the remaining marmalade and the stem ginger. Spread over the oranges.

3 Stand the tin on a baking sheet and bake for 1 hour 10 minutes or until just firm to the touch. If necessary, cover with foil.

4 Remove from the oven and loosen around the edges of the tin, then invert the pudding on to an edged serving plate. Serve warm with custard.

Serves 8
Preparation: 20 minutes
Cooking time: 1 hour
Per serving: 370 cals; 20g fat; 45g carbohydrate

Glazed Berry Pudding

butter to grease
1 vanilla pod or 1tsp
  vanilla extract
4 large eggs, separated
50g (2oz) golden caster
  sugar
25g (1oz) plain flour
142ml carton double
  cream
150ml (¼ pint) full-fat
  milk

225g (8oz) icing sugar,
  plus extra to dust
450g (1lb) mixed red
  fruits, frozen compôte
  or conserve
blueberries and
  raspberries, to
  decorate

1 Lightly grease eight 150ml (¼ pint) ramekins and put in the freezer to chill. Split the vanilla pod lengthways and scrape the seeds into the bowl with the egg yolks. Combine the yolks and caster sugar and beat until pale, then stir in the flour.

2 Bring the cream and milk to the boil in a small pan then pour over the yolks, stirring. Return the mixture to the pan and cook over a gentle heat for 2 minutes, stirring all the time, or until thick and smooth. Turn into a clean bowl, add the vanilla extract, if using, cover and cool.

3 Put the egg whites and icing sugar in a large heatproof bowl set over a pan of simmering water and whisk for 10 minutes until thick. Remove from the heat and whisk until cool.

4 Put 2tbsp of the fruits in the base of each ramekin. Fold the meringue into the custard and pile on top of the fruits, then put back in the freezer for at least 7 hours or until firm.

5 Preheat the oven to 220°C (200°C fan oven) mark 7. Remove the ramekins from the freezer, put on a baking sheet and dust thickly with icing sugar. Bake for 20 minutes, decorate with the berries and serve immediately.

Serves 8
Preparation: 20 minutes, plus freezing
Cooking time: 25 minutes
Per serving: 300 cals; 12g fat; 45g carbohydrate

Sweet Carrot Pudding

450g (1lb) carrots,
 peeled and coarsely
 grated
750ml (1¼ pints) full-fat
 milk
150ml (¼ pint) single
 cream
75g (3oz) sugar
1tbsp treacle

3tbsp melted butter
125g (4oz) ground
 almonds
seeds of 6 green
 cardamoms, crushed
25g (1oz) sultanas
chopped pistachios, to
 decorate

1 Put the carrots in a large heavy-based pan. Pour in the milk and cream and bring to the boil, stirring constantly. Reduce the heat and simmer very gently, stirring occasionally to prevent sticking, for at least 2 hours until the milk has evaporated and the mixture is greatly reduced.
2 Stir in the sugar and treacle, then simmer for 30 minutes, stirring occasionally to prevent sticking.

3 Add the melted butter, almonds, cardamom seeds and sultanas. Cook, stirring, for 5–10 minutes until the mixture begins to look oily on the surface. Transfer to a serving dish and decorate with the pistachios. Serve hot or cold.

Serves 4–6
Preparation: 5 minutes
Cooking time: 2¾ hours
Per serving: 630–420 cals; 44–30g fat;
46–31g carbohydrate

Saucy Hot Lemon Puddings

50g (2oz) butter, plus
 extra to grease
125g (4oz) golden
 caster sugar
finely grated zest and
 juice of 2 lemons

2 eggs, separated
50g (2oz) self-raising
 flour
300ml (½ pint) semi-
 skimmed milk

1 Preheat the oven to 190°C (170°C fan oven) mark 5. Lightly grease four 200ml (7fl oz) ovenproof cups. Cream together the butter, sugar and lemon zest in a bowl until pale and fluffy. Beat in the egg yolks, then the flour until combined. Stir in the milk and lemon juice – the mixture will curdle but don't panic. Whisk the egg whites in a clean grease-free bowl until they stand in soft peaks, then fold into the lemon mixture. (The mixture will still look curdled – don't worry.) Divide the mixture among the four cups and stand them in a roasting tin.

2 Pour in enough boiling water to come at least halfway up their sides and bake the puddings for 35–40 minutes or until spongy and light golden. If you prefer softer tops, cover the entire tin with foil. When cooked, the puddings will have separated into a tangy lemon custard layer on the bottom, with light sponge on top.

Serves 4
Preparation: 10 minutes
Cooking time: 35–40 minutes
Per serving: 340 cals; 15g fat; 46g carbohydrate

See picture, page 392

Easy Jam Sponge Pudding

125g (4oz) butter, softened, plus extra to grease
4tbsp raspberry jam
grated zest of ½ orange, plus about 8tbsp juice
50g (2oz) golden caster sugar
1 large egg, lightly beaten
125g (4oz) self-raising flour, sifted

1 Grease the inside of four 175ml (6fl oz) pudding basins with butter. Put 1tbsp jam in the base of each and put to one side. Preheat the oven to 200°C (180°C fan oven) mark 6.
2 Whisk together the butter and orange zest with a small electric whisk until smooth. Whisk in the sugar until thoroughly combined – about 10 minutes – then gradually whisk in the egg. Fold in the flour, then sufficient orange juice to give a soft dropping consistency. Spoon on top of the jam and smooth the surfaces.
3 Grease four discs of foil, measuring about 12.5cm (5 inches) across, and cover the puddings with them, folding under the rim to secure. Put the basins in a large roasting tin. Pour in enough boiling water to come at least halfway up their sides. Cook for 45 minutes or until the puddings are risen, cooked to the centre and golden brown on top. Lift out of the roasting tin, unmould when ready and serve with pouring cream or custard.

Serves 4
Preparation: 20 minutes
Cooking time: 45 minutes
Per serving: 460 cals; 28g fat; 50g carbohydrate

Queen of Puddings

600ml (1 pint) full-fat milk
25g (1oz) butter
grated zest of 1 large lemon
3 large eggs, separated
175g (6oz) golden caster sugar
100g (3½oz) fine fresh breadcrumbs
4tbsp lemon curd

1 Put the milk, butter and lemon zest in a pan and heat gently until the butter melts. Put to one side until lukewarm. Mix the egg yolks with 25g (1oz) sugar in a bowl until thoroughly combined, then blend in the warm milk. Add the breadcrumbs and pour into a 1.1 litre (2 pint) ovenproof dish. Leave to stand for 20 minutes. Preheat the oven to 180°C (160°C fan oven) mark 4.
2 Put the dish in a roasting tin and pour in enough boiling water to come halfway up the side of the dish. Bake for 25–30 minutes or until just set to the centre. Remove from the oven and leave to cool for about 20 minutes. Spread the lemon curd over the top. Reduce the oven temperature to 170°C (150°C fan oven) mark 3.
3 Whisk the egg whites in a clean grease-free bowl until stiff peaks form, then whisk in 3tbsp sugar, 1tbsp at a time, until stiff and glossy. Carefully fold in the rest of the sugar with a large spoon. Spoon the meringue on top of the lemon curd and bake for 10–15 minutes or until golden and crisp. Serve warm or at room temperature.

Serves 6
Preparation: 10 minutes, plus standing and cooling
Cooking time: 50 minutes
Per serving: 330 cals; 12g fat; 48g carbohydrate

Date and Walnut Pudding with Chocolate Sauce

125g (4oz) butter, softened, plus extra to grease	roughly chopped
	50g (2oz) unsalted butter
125g (4oz) golden caster sugar	50g (2oz) light muscovado sugar
3 eggs, beaten	50g (2oz) good-quality plain dark chocolate (with minimum 50% cocoa solids), in pieces
175g (6oz) self-raising flour	
3tbsp milk	
75g (3oz) walnuts, toasted and roughly chopped	
175g (6oz) pitted dates,	100ml (3½fl oz) double cream

1 Half-fill a steamer or large pan with water and put it on to boil. Grease a 1.1 litre (2 pint) pudding basin.
2 Put the 125g (4oz) butter, the caster sugar, eggs, flour and milk in a bowl and beat with an electric beater until smooth. Fold in the nuts and dates.
3 Spoon the mixture into the prepared pudding basin and smooth the surface. Cover with greased and pleated greaseproof paper and foil, and secure under the rim with string.
4 Steam the pudding for 2 hours, checking the water level from time to time and topping up with boiling water as necessary. Lift the pudding out of the pan and leave to rest for 15 minutes.
5 Meanwhile, make the chocolate fudge sauce. Put the unsalted butter, muscovado sugar and chocolate into a pan and heat gently until the chocolate has melted. Add the cream, bring to a simmer and let bubble for 3 minutes until thickened.
6 To serve, unmould the pudding on to a warmed plate. Cut into wedges and serve with the chocolate fudge sauce poured over.

Serves 8
Preparation: 20 minutes, plus standing
Cooking time: 2 hours
Per serving: 550 cals; 33g fat; 59g carbohydrate

Rhubarb and Pear Crumble Pudding

450g (1lb) rhubarb, cut into 2.5cm (1 inch) pieces	75g (3oz) self-raising flour
2 ripe pears, peeled, cored and roughly chopped	2 shortbread fingers
	50g (2oz) whole hazelnuts
75g (3oz) demerara sugar	500g tub Greek-style yogurt
1tsp ground cinnamon	
50g (2oz) chilled butter	

1 Preheat the oven to 180°C (160°C fan oven) mark 4. Put the fruit into a small shallow baking dish, sprinkle over 25g (1oz) sugar and the cinnamon and mix well.
2 To make the crumble, put the butter in a food processor, add the flour and remaining sugar and whiz until it resembles rough breadcrumbs.
3 Break the shortbread fingers into pieces and add to the processor with the hazelnuts. Whiz again for 4–5 seconds until the crumble is blended but still looks rough. Sprinkle the crumble over the fruit, spreading it up to the edges and pressing down with the back of a wooden spoon.
4 Bake for 40–45 minutes or until the topping is golden brown and crisp. Remove from the oven and leave to cool.
5 Divide half the cooled crumble among eight 200ml (7fl oz) serving dishes or glasses. Spoon the yogurt on top, then finish with the remaining crumble. Using a knife or skewer, make a figure of eight to swirl the crumble roughly into the yogurt. Serve warm or chilled.

Serves 8
Preparation: 25 minutes
Cooking time: 40–45 minutes
Per serving: 300 cals; 18g fat; 28g carbohydrate

See picture, page 392

Summer Gratin

3 ripe peaches, halved, stoned and sliced
225g (8oz) wild strawberries or raspberries

3tbsp Kirsch or Eau de Vie de Mirabelle
4 large egg yolks
50g (2oz) sugar

1. Put the peach slices in a bowl with the strawberries or raspberries and 2tbsp Kirsch or Eau de Vie.
2. Put the egg yolks, sugar, remaining Kirsch and 2tbsp water in a heatproof bowl set over a pan of barely simmering water. Whisk for 5–10 minutes or until the mixture leaves a trail and is warm in the centre. Remove from the heat. Preheat the grill.
3. Arrange the fruit in four shallow heatproof dishes and spoon the sauce over. Cook under the grill for 1–2 minutes until light golden. Serve immediately.

Serves 4
Preparation: 15 minutes
Cooking time: 15 minutes
Per serving: 180 cals; 6g fat; 22g carbohydrate

Spiced Cherries in Madeira Syrup

150g (5oz) golden caster sugar
600ml (1 pint) Madeira or sweet sherry
1 vanilla pod
1 basil sprig

zest of 1 lemon, plus a splash of juice
2 x 454g cans pitted cherries, drained
lemon zest, to decorate (optional)

1. Make a syrup by dissolving the sugar in the Madeira or sherry over a low heat. Add the vanilla pod, basil and lemon zest. Bring to the boil, then reduce the heat and simmer until slightly thick – about 5 minutes.
2. Pour into a serving dish, add the cherries and a splash of lemon juice to taste, then chill.
3. Decorate the cherries with lemon zest if you like and serve with a spoonful of crème fraîche, accompanied by shortbread biscuits.

Serves 6
Preparation: 10 minutes, plus chilling
Cooking time: 10 minutes
Per serving: 280 cals; 0g fat; 50g carbohydrate

Almond, Apple and Pineapple Puddings

50g (2oz) chilled butter, diced, plus extra to grease
50g (2oz) plain flour, plus extra to dust
1 apple, cut vertically into six slices
75g (3oz) golden caster sugar, plus extra to dust
1tsp baking powder
pinch of salt
50g (2oz) ground almonds

100g (3½oz) each cooking apple and pineapple, peeled, cored and diced
1 large egg, lightly beaten
¼tsp almond essence
crystalised violets, mint sprigs and crushed cardamom seeds, to decorate

1. Preheat the oven to 180°C (160°C fan oven) mark 4. Grease six 150ml (¼ pint) pudding basin moulds or ramekins, line the bases with greaseproof paper and dust the sides with flour. Using a pastry cutter the same size as the base of the moulds, stamp out circles from the apple slices. Dust the slices with sugar and fry in a hot non-stick frying pan until caramelised on both sides. Place a slice in the base of each mould.
2. Sift the flour, baking powder and salt into a bowl, then add the sugar, almonds and diced butter. Rub in until the mixture resembles fine crumbs. (Alternatively, you can whiz the mixture in a food processor.) Stir in the cooking apple, pineapple, egg and almond essence.
3. Spoon the mixture into the moulds until they're half full. Bake for 35–40 minutes or until golden and firm in the centre. Remove from the oven and leave the puddings in the moulds for 15 minutes, then carefully run a knife inside the mould to loosen the puddings. Turn out and decorate with crystalised violets, mint sprigs and crushed cardamom seeds.

Serves 6
Preparation: 20 minutes
Cooking time: 45 minutes, plus standing
Per serving: 230 cals; 13g fat; 26g carbohydrate

Pear and Cranberry Strudel

75g (3oz) butter, melted
zest and juice of 1
lemon
25g (1oz) golden caster
sugar
1tbsp fresh white
breadcrumbs
1tsp ground cinnamon
125g (4oz) fresh
cranberries

550g (1¼lb) William or
Comice pears, cored
and sliced
50g (2oz) Brazil nuts,
chopped and toasted
7 sheets filo pastry
icing sugar, to dust

1 Preheat the oven to 190°C (170°C fan oven) mark 5.
   Grease a large baking sheet. Mix the lemon zest with
   1tbsp caster sugar, the breadcrumbs and cinnamon
   and put to one side.
2 Put 6 cranberries on one side, then toss the rest with
   the pears, lemon juice and nuts. Mix in the breadcrumb
   mixture.
3 Lay a clean tea-towel on a board and put three sheets
   of filo pastry on it, each overlapping the other by
   12.5cm (5 inches) to make a rectangle measuring
   56 x 48cm (22 x 19 inches). Brush with melted butter,
   then put three more sheets on top and brush again.
4 Spoon the pear mixture along the nearest, longest
   length and roll up. Trim the edges, then carefully lift on
   to the baking sheet so the seam is underneath.
5 Brush the remaining sheet of filo pastry with butter,
   fold in half and cut out six holly leaves. Arrange three
   together on one half of the log and the remaining three
   on the other half and brush with melted butter.
6 Sprinkle the strudel with the remaining caster sugar
   and bake for 40–45 minutes, covering with foil if the
   top browns too quickly.
7 Remove from the oven and arrange the reserved
   cranberries on the holly leaves, then dust the strudel
   heavily with icing sugar. Serve at once with a dollop of
   thick cream.

Serves 8
Preparation: 20 minutes
Cooking time: 40–45 minutes
Per serving: 210 cals; 12g fat; 24g carbohydrate

Mincemeat Streusel

340g pack sweet
   dessert pastry
75g (3oz) self-raising
   flour
finely grated zest of ½
   lemon
50g (2oz) unsalted
   butter, chilled and cut
   into cubes, plus extra
   to grease

50g (2oz) light
   muscovado sugar
25g (1oz) ground
   almonds
350g jar mincemeat

1 Preheat the oven to 180°C (160°C fan oven) mark 4.
   Grease a 33 x 10cm (13 x 4 inch) fluted rectangular tin
   and line the base with greaseproof paper.
2 Roll out the pastry on a lightly floured surface to fit the
   tin, line the tin and prick the pastry with a fork. Line the
   pastry case with baking parchment, fill with baking
   beans and bake for 15 minutes. Remove the
   parchment and beans and bake for a further
   15 minutes, then leave to cool for 5 minutes.
3 To make the streusel topping, put the flour and lemon
   zest in a bowl and rub in the butter, until the mixture
   becomes crumbly. Stir in the sugar and almonds.
4 Spread the mincemeat evenly over the pastry and
   sprinkle the streusel on top. Bake for 15 minutes until
   the topping is golden. Remove from the oven and leave
   to cool for 30 minutes. Remove from the tin, cut into
   slices and serve warm.

Serves 8
Preparation: 15 minutes
Cooking time: 45 minutes
Per serving: 430 cals; 20g fat; 52g carbohydrate

Hot puddings

Chocoholics

The title of this chapter says it all – you know if you're one or not. No half measures. So, you'll be in heaven here with spectacular chocolate cakes, gateaux and roulades; custards, creams and terrines – smooth and rich; and intensely flavoured puddings – lusciously gooey chocolate centres encased in rich chocolate sponge.

Then there are soft, melting meringues enveloped in chocolate – Chocolate-dipped Brown Sugar Meringues, and Chocolate and Hazelnut Meringues, topped with cream, fruit and chocolate curls; not to mention a chocolate version of Baked Alaska and a Chocolate Strawberry Pavlova.

And what goes perfectly with a cup of tea, coffee or, even hot chocolate? Chocolate cookies and brownies – try the White and Dark Chocolate Cookies for a tempting treat.

If you're baking someone a special cake, make them one to remember – the Wicked Chocolate Cake is a rich chocolate and marzipan cake drizzled with chocolate ganache and decorated with sugared almonds. Or, simply The Best Chocolate Cake in the World – rich, delicious and perfect for any occasion.

Easy Chocolate Curls

200g (7oz) good-quality white or dark chocolate

knob of butter

1 Melt the chocolate and butter in a heatproof bowl set over a pan of barely simmering water, stirring until smooth. Pour into a small rectangular container (a 250g margarine tub is ideal) and leave to cool and harden.
2 Before shaping the curls, leave the chocolate at warm room temperature to soften slightly, then turn the chocolate out on to a marble slab or clean surface.
3 Hold the chocolate in a piece of kitchen paper and use a swivelled vegetable peeler to shave off curls along the length of the block.
4 Store the curls, interleaved with greaseproof paper, in an airtight container in a cool place for up to one week.

Preparation: 15 minutes, plus cooling
Cooking time: 10 minutes
Per batch: 1050 cals; 58g fat; 130g carbohydrate

Baked Chocolate and Coffee Custards

284ml carton semi-skimmed milk
142ml carton double cream
200g (7oz) good-quality plain chocolate, semi-sweet such as Bournville, broken into small pieces
4 large egg yolks

1tbsp golden caster sugar
3tbsp very strong cold black coffee
125g (4oz) mascarpone
1tsp icing sugar
grated zest and juice of ½ orange, plus extra zest to decorate (optional)

1 Preheat the oven to 170°C (150°C fan oven) mark 3. Put the milk, cream and chocolate in a heavy-based pan over a very gentle heat until melted. Stir until smooth.
2 Mix the egg yolks, caster sugar and coffee in a bowl, then pour on the warm chocolate milk. Mix briefly, then strain through a sieve into a jug. Pour the mixture into six 150ml (¼ pint) ovenproof custard cups or ramekins.
3 Stand the dishes in a large roasting tin and pour enough boiling water into the tin to come halfway up their sides. Bake for 20–25 minutes or until just set and still a little wobbly in the middle – they'll firm up as they cool. Carefully lift the dishes out of the roasting tin and leave to cool, then stand them on a small tray and chill for at least 3 hours.
4 To make the topping, beat the mascarpone, icing sugar, orange zest and juice together until smooth. Cover and chill for 1–2 hours.
5 To serve, put a spoonful of the mascarpone mixture on top of each custard and decorate with grated orange zest, if using. Serve with thin shortbread biscuits.

Serves 6
Preparation: 15 minutes, plus chilling
Cooking time: 20–25 minutes
Per serving: 460 cals; 36g fat; 31g carbohydrate

See picture, page 409

Chocolate Terrine with Vanilla Bean Sauce

350g (12oz) good-quality plain dark chocolate (with 70% cocoa solids), broken into small pieces
40g (1½oz) cocoa powder
oil, to grease
6 large eggs, beaten, plus 4 large egg yolks
125g (4oz) light muscovado sugar

284ml carton double cream
5tbsp brandy (optional)
568ml carton single cream
1 vanilla pod, split, seeds removed and reserved
75g (3oz) golden caster sugar
½tsp cornflour
cocoa powder, to dust

1 Put the chocolate and cocoa in a heatproof bowl set over a pan of barely simmering water and stir occasionally until melted and glossy. Leave to cool.

2 Preheat the oven to 150°C (130°C fan oven) mark 2. Grease a 900g (2lb) loaf tin and line the base with greaseproof paper. Whisk together the 6 beaten eggs and the muscovado sugar, then whisk the double cream until soft peaks form. Gradually combine the egg mixture, chocolate and cream. Add the brandy, if using. Pour the mixture into the loaf tin and tap on a work surface to level.

3 Stand the loaf tin in a roasting tin and pour enough boiling water into the tin to come halfway up the sides of the loaf tin, then cover with non-stick baking parchment. Bake for 1¾ hours or until just set at the centre. Remove from the oven and leave in tin for 30 minutes, then lift out and chill overnight.

4 To make the sauce, gently heat the single cream and vanilla seeds in a heavy-based pan until the cream just comes to the boil. Put to one side to cool for 15 minutes.

5 Whisk the egg yolks with the caster sugar and cornflour, add a little of the cooled cream and whisk until smooth. Add the remaining cream and stir well. Pour back into the cleaned pan and stir over a medium heat for 5 minutes or until thickened (it should coat the back of a spoon). Strain, cool, cover and chill.

6 Serve the terrine in slices with the vanilla bean sauce poured around, dusted with cocoa powder.

Serves 12
Preparation: 45 minutes, plus cooling and chilling
Cooking time: 1¾ hours
Per serving: 480 cals; 36g fat; 28g carbohydrate

White Chocolate Mousse

100ml (3½fl oz) milk
1 cinnamon stick
250g (9oz) good-quality white chocolate, broken into pieces
284ml carton double cream
3 large egg whites

50g (2oz) good-quality plain dark chocolate (with minimum 50% cocoa solids), in one piece
a little cocoa powder and ground cinnamon, to decorate

1 Put the milk and cinnamon stick in a small pan and warm over a medium heat until the milk is almost boiling. Take the pan off the heat and put to one side.
2 Meanwhile, bring a small pan of water to a gentle simmer. Put the white chocolate in a small heatproof bowl and put it over the pan. Turn the heat off and leave the bowl over the hot water for 15 minutes or until the chocolate has melted. Take the bowl off the pan and leave to cool a little.
3 Strain the warm milk on to the melted chocolate and stir until completely smooth. Leave to cool for 10 minutes.
4 Whip the cream in a bowl until it just begins to hold its shape – it should still be a bit floppy. Whisk the egg whites in a clean grease-free bowl until soft peaks form.
5 Using a large metal spoon, fold the whipped cream into the chocolate mixture, then carefully fold in the egg whites. Spoon the mixture into six 150ml (¼ pint) small bowls or glasses and chill for up to 4 hours or overnight.
6 Pull a vegetable peeler across the edge of the plain chocolate to make rough curls and sprinkle them over the mousse. Dust with cocoa powder and a pinch of cinnamon to serve.

Serves 6
Preparation: 15 minutes, plus chilling
Cooking time: 15 minutes
Per serving: 180 cals; 15g fat; 3g carbohydrate

Cheat's Chocolate Pots

500g carton fresh custard

200g (7oz) good-quality plain dark chocolate (with minimum 50% cocoa solids), broken into pieces

1 Put the custard in a small pan with the chocolate pieces. Heat gently, stirring all the time, until the chocolate has melted.
2 Pour the mixture into four small coffee cups, put on to saucers and serve immediately, or leave the mixture to cool slightly and serve as a chocolate sauce with vanilla ice cream.

Serves 4
Preparation: 5 minutes
Cooking time: 5 minutes
Per serving: 380 cals; 17g fat; 53g carbohydrate

Chocolate Mousse

350g (12oz) good-quality plain chocolate, semi-sweet such as Bournville, broken into pieces

6 tbsp rum, brandy or cold black coffee
6 large eggs, separated pinch of salt

See picture, page 409

Serves 6–8
Preparation: 20 minutes, plus ch[...]
Per serving: 440–330 cals; 24–1[...]
38–28g carbohydrate

1 Put the chocolate and rum, brandy or black coffee in a heatproof bowl set over a pan of barely simmering water. Leave to melt, stirring occasionally. Remove from the heat. Cool for 3–4 minutes, stirring frequently.
2 Beat the egg yolks with 2tbsp water, then beat into the chocolate mixture until evenly blended.
3 Whisk the egg whites with the salt in a clean grease-free bowl until stiff peaks form, then fold into the chocolate mixture.
4 Pour into a 1.4–1.7 litre (2½–3 pint) soufflé dish or divide among six to eight 150ml (¼ pint) ramekins. Chill for at least 4 hours, or overnight, until cot.

Chocolate Pots

2 x 100g bars dark chocolate, roughly broken

500g carton fromage frais

1 Melt the chocolate in a heatproof bowl set over a pan of simmering water, stirring occasionally.
2 Put the fromage frais in a heatproof bowl set over a pan of simmering water and warm for just 4 minutes.
3 Pour the fromage frais into the chocolate and mix. Spoon into four coffee cups and chill for 15 minutes–2 hours before serving.

Serves 4
Preparation: 5 minutes
Cooking time: 5 minutes, plus chilling
Per serving: 390 cals; 28g fat; 19g carbohydrate

Chocolate-dipped Brown Sugar Meringues

3 large egg whites
50g (2oz) golden caster sugar
125g (4oz) light muscovado sugar

200g (7oz) good-quality plain dark chocolate (with minimum 50% cocoa solids)

1 Line three baking sheets with baking parchment and preheat the oven to 130°C (110°C fan oven) mark ½.
2 Whisk the egg whites in a clean grease-free bowl until stiff peaks form. Mix both sugars together, then add to the whites, 1tbsp at a time, and whisk in until the meringue is stiff and shiny.
3 Secure the parchment to each baking sheet with a little meringue, then shape the mixture into quenelles as follows: using two dessertspoons and working quickly, take a scoop of the meringue with one spoon and scrape from one to the other three times to form a smooth oval. Carefully transfer each meringue to the parchment, spacing them well apart.

4 Bake for 1½ hours or until the meringues lift off the baking parchment easily. Remove from the oven now for a gooey centre or leave in a cooling oven for a further 2 hours to dry out completely.
5 Melt the chocolate in a heatproof bowl (deep enough to dip the meringues up to halfway) set over a pan of barely simmering water, stirring occasionally. Dip the meringues to half-coat them in chocolate, then leave to set on parchment. When cool, arrange on a plate and serve with whipped cream.

Makes about 20
Preparation: 30 minutes
Cooking time: 1½–3½ hours, to taste
Per meringue: 90 cals; 3g fat; 16g carbohydrate

Chocolate and Hazelnut Meringues

125g (4oz) hazelnuts, toasted
125g (4oz) golden caster sugar
75g (3oz) good-quality plain dark chocolate (with 70% cocoa solids), in pieces

2 large egg whites
284ml carton double cream
strawberries and redcurrants, to decorate
chocolate curls (page 404, optional)

1 Preheat the oven to 110°C (100°C fan oven) mark ¼. Line two baking sheets with non-stick baking parchment. Put the hazelnuts in a food processor with 3tbsp sugar and whiz to a fine powder. Add the chocolate and pulse until roughly chopped.
2 Whisk the egg whites in a clean grease-free bowl until stiff peaks form. Gradually whisk in the remaining sugar, 1tbsp at a time, until the meringue is stiff and shiny. Fold in the nut mixture.

3 Put spoonfuls of the meringue in rough mounds, about 9cm (3 inches) in diameter, on the baking sheets. Bake for about 45 minutes or until the meringues have dried out just enough to peel off the parchment.
4 Gently push in the base of each meringue to form a deep hollow and return to the oven for 1¼ hours or until crisp and dry. Transfer to a wire rack and leave to cool.
5 Whip the cream until it just holds its shape, then spoon three-quarters on to the meringues. Leave in the fridge to soften for up to 2 hours.
6 To serve, put a meringue on each serving plate and top with the remaining cream, the fruit and chocolate curls, if using. Serve immediately.

Serves 6
Preparation: 25 minutes, plus softening
Cooking time: 2 hours
Per serving: 440 cals; 35g fat; 29g carbohydrate

Top left: Baked Chocolate and Coffee Custards, page 404; top right: Chocolate and Hazelnut Meringues, page 408; bottom left: Nutty Chocolate Truffles, page 412; bottom right: Chocolate Mousse, page 407.

Baked Alaska

50g (2oz) butter, plus extra to grease
200g (7oz) plain chocolate digestive biscuits, finely crushed
600ml (1 pint) good-quality chocolate ice cream
2 chocolate flake bars, roughly chopped

4 large egg whites
225g (8oz) golden caster sugar
50g (2oz) desiccated coconut
cocoa powder, to dust
toasted coconut shavings (optional)

1 Lightly grease a baking sheet. Melt the butter and while it is still hot stir in the biscuits. Using a 6cm (2½ inch) pastry cutter as a template, press the mixture into six circles on the baking sheet and freeze for 30 minutes.

2 Beat the ice cream to soften it slightly and pile into mounds on the biscuit bases. Make a shallow hollow in the centre of each ice cream mound and fill with the chocolate flakes. Return to the freezer for at least 1 hour until firm.

3 Put the egg whites and sugar in a large bowl set over a pan of barely simmering water. Using an electric whisk, beat for 10 minutes or until the mixture is thick and glossy. Fold in the desiccated coconut. Leave to cool for 5 minutes.

4 Cover the ice cream mounds completely with a thick layer of meringue. Return to the freezer for at least 4 hours or overnight.

5 To serve, preheat the oven to 220°C (200°C fan oven) mark 7. Bake the puddings for 5 minutes or until golden. Dust with cocoa powder, top with toasted coconut, if using, and serve immediately.

Serves 6
Preparation: 20 minutes, plus freezing
Cooking time: 5 minutes
Per serving: 630 cals; 30g fat; 84g carbohydrate

Chocolate and Ginger Truffles

142ml carton double cream
125g (4oz) good-quality plain chocolate, roughly chopped

15 ready-to-eat ginger slices

1 Pour the cream into a small pan and bring to the boil. Turn off the heat, add the chocolate and stir to mix. Pour into a bowl, leave to cool, then chill for 2 hours.

2 Put a 1cm (½ inch) nozzle into a piping bag and spoon in the chocolate ganache. Arrange 12 ginger slices on a tray and pipe a blob of ganache on to each. Put to one side. (You can freeze any leftover ganache and use to make more truffles.)

3 Thinly slice the three remaining pieces of ginger and use to decorate the top of each chocolate truffle. Chill overnight. Remove from the fridge 10–15 minutes before serving.

Makes 12
Preparation: 10 minutes, plus chilling
Cooking time: 3 minutes
Per truffle: 120 cals; 9g fat; 12g carbohydrate

Chocolate Peanut Butter Chunks

butter, to grease
400g (14oz) good-
quality white
chocolate, broken
into pieces

400g (14oz) good-
quality plain
chocolate, broken
into pieces
150g (5oz) crunchy
peanut butter

1 Grease a shallow 30.5 x 20.5cm (12 x 8 inch) tin and line with baking parchment.
2 Melt the white chocolate in a heatproof bowl set over a pan of barely simmering water. Stir until smooth, then remove the bowl from the pan. Melt the plain chocolate in the same way and remove from the heat.
3 Add the peanut butter to the white chocolate and stir well until smooth.
4 Drop alternate spoonfuls of each chocolate into the prepared tin, then tap the tin to level the mixture. Drag a skewer through both mixtures to create a marbled effect. Tap the tin again to level the mixture, then chill for 2–3 hours until firm.
5 Turn out on to a board and cut into 10 fingers, then cut each finger into 8 chunks. Pack into boxes or an airtight container, separating the layers with baking parchment. Store in the fridge for up to one month.

Makes 80
Preparation: 30 minutes, plus chilling
Cooking time: 10–15 minutes
Per chunk: 70 cals; 4g fat; 6g carbohydrate

14

Chocoholic

Nutty Chocolate Truffles

100g (3½oz) hazelnuts
200g (7oz) good-quality
plain dark chocolate
(with minimum 50%
cocoa solids), broken
into pieces

25g (1oz) butter
142ml carton double
cream
3tbsp each cocoa
powder and golden
icing sugar

1 Put the hazelnuts in a dry frying pan and heat gently for 3–4 minutes, shaking the pan occasionally, to toast all over. Put 30 whole nuts into a bowl and leave to cool. Whiz the remaining nuts in a processor until finely chopped, then tip into a shallow dish and put to one side.

2 Melt the chocolate in a heatproof bowl set over a pan of barely simmering water, stirring occasionally. Put the butter and cream in a separate pan and heat gently until the butter has melted, then bring just to the boil and remove from the heat. Carefully stir into the chocolate and whisk until cool and thick, then chill for 1–2 hours.

3 Sift the cocoa and icing sugar into separate shallow dishes. Scoop up 1tsp of truffle mix and push a whole hazelnut into the centre. Working quickly, shape into a ball, then roll in the cocoa powder, icing sugar or chopped nuts. Repeat with the remaining mixture. Store in an airtight container in the fridge for up to two weeks.

Makes about 30
Preparation: 15–20 minutes
Cooking time: 12 minutes, plus chilling
Per truffle: 80 cals; 6g fat; 6g carbohydrate

See picture, page 409

14

Chocolate Orange Tart

150g (5oz) plain flour,
plus extra to dust
pinch of salt
75g (3oz) unsalted
butter, chilled and cut
into cubes
25g (1oz) golden icing
sugar, plus extra
to dust
grated zest of 1 orange
2 large egg yolks, plus
2 whole medium eggs

175g (6oz) good-quality
plain dark chocolate
(with minimum 50%
cocoa solids), in
pieces
175ml (6fl oz) double
cream
75g (3oz) light
muscovado sugar
1tbsp Grand Marnier or
Cointreau

1 To make the pastry, put the flour, salt and butter into a processor and pulse until the mixture resembles breadcrumbs. Add the icing sugar and orange zest, pulse again to mix, then add the egg yolks and pulse until the mixture just comes together to form a soft dough.

2 Turn the dough out on to a lightly floured surface and knead gently to form into a ball. Flatten slightly, then wrap in clingfilm and chill for at least 30 minutes.

3 Roll out the pastry on a lightly floured surface, then use to fill a 20.5cm (8 inch) loose-based tart tin. Prick the base all over with a fork, put the tin on a baking sheet and chill for 30 minutes. Preheat the oven to 190°C (170°C fan oven) mark 5.

4 Line the tart with greaseproof paper and fill with baking beans. Bake for 15 minutes, then remove the paper and beans and bake for a further 5–10 minutes until the pastry is dry to the touch. Remove from the oven and put to one side.

5 Reduce the oven temperature to 170°C (150°C fan oven) mark 3. To make the filling, melt the chocolate in a heatproof bowl set over a pan of barely simmering water, stirring occasionally, then cool for 10 minutes.

6 Put the cream, muscovado sugar, whole eggs and liqueur into a bowl and stir, using a wooden spoon to mix thoroughly. Slowly add the chocolate and stir in, then pour the mix into the pastry case and bake for
30 minutes until just set.

7 Serve warm or cold: cut it into slices, dust liberally with icing sugar and serve with crème fraîche.

Serves 8
Preparation: 30 minutes, plus chilling
Cooking time: 1 hour, plus cooling
Per serving: 430 cals; 30g fat; 33g carbohydrate

See picture, page 416

14

Chocoholic

Chocolate Strawberry Pavlova

4 egg whites
225g (8oz) golden
  caster sugar
1tbsp cornflour
2tsp distilled malt
  vinegar
½tsp vanilla extract
450g (1lb) strawberries

284ml carton double
  cream
1tbsp icing sugar, plus
  extra to dust
chocolate-coated
  strawberries and mint
  leaves, to decorate

1 Preheat the oven to 130°C (110°C fan oven) mark ½.
   Draw a 23cm (9 inch) circle on a sheet of non-stick
   baking parchment. Turn the paper over and put on a
   baking sheet. Put the egg whites in a clean grease-
   free bowl and whisk until frothy using an electric whisk.
   Add the caster sugar 1tbsp at a time, whisking
   thoroughly after each addition, until stiff and shiny
   (don't hurry this process or the meringue will be floppy
   and weep). With the machine running slowly, whisk in
   the cornflour, vinegar and vanilla extract.
2 Spread the meringue on the baking parchment, within
   the marked circle, leaving a large dip in the centre.
   Rough up the edges with a palette knife. Bake for
   1¼ hours or until crisp around the edges and soft in the
   centre. Remove from the oven and leave to cool, then
   peel off the lining paper.
3 Hull and halve the strawberries. Lightly whip the cream,
   then whisk in 1tbsp icing sugar. About 1 hour before
   serving, spoon the cream and strawberries into the
   centre of the pavlova. Top with chocolate-coated
   strawberries and mint leaves and dust with icing sugar.

Serves 8
Preparation: 40 minutes
Cooking time: 1¼ hours
Per serving: 330 cals; 19g fat; 42g carbohydrate

Chocolate and Chestnut Torte

50g (2oz) butter
200g (7oz) Bourbon or
  chocolate digestive
  biscuits, very finely
  crushed
225g (8oz) good-quality
  milk chocolate
250g (9oz) mascarpone
75g (3oz) unsweetened
  chestnut purée
4 large eggs, separated

50g (2oz) golden caster
  sugar
142ml carton extra-
  thick double cream
175g (6oz) good-quality
  plain chocolate, plus
  extra to decorate
white chocolate
  truffles, to decorate
cocoa powder, to dust

1 Melt the butter and while it is still hot stir in the biscuits.
   Press the mixture into a 20.5cm (8 inch) spring-release
   cake tin and chill for about 20 minutes or until firm.
2 Meanwhile, melt the milk chocolate in a heatproof bowl
   set over a pan of barely simmering water. Put the
   mascarpone and chestnut purée in a large bowl and
   beat together, then beat in the warm melted chocolate
   thoroughly.
3 Using an electric whisk, beat the egg yolks with the
   sugar until pale and thick, then, using a large metal
   spoon, stir into the chestnut mixture. Next, fold in the
   cream.
4 Whisk the egg whites in a clean grease-free bowl until
   soft peaks form, then, using a large metal spoon, stir
   one large spoonful into the chocolate mixture. Carefully
   fold in the remainder, pour on to the biscuit base and
   freeze overnight.
5 To decorate the torte, cut two strips of non-stick
   baking parchment, each 35.5cm (14 inches) long and
   5cm (2 inches) wide. Melt the plain chocolate in a small
   heatproof bowl set over a pan of barely simmering
   water and spread it evenly along the parchment strips.
6 Take the torte out of the freezer, run a palette knife
   around the outside, then unclip and remove the spring-
   release tin. Carefully wrap the chocolate-covered strips
   (with the chocolate side facing inwards) around the
   torte and return the torte to the freezer for about
   1 hour.
7 Peel away the parchment strips to leave a thin
   chocolate 'collar' around the torte, then put in the
   fridge to thaw overnight. Remove from the fridge,
   arrange the white chocolate truffles on top around the
   edge, then dust generously with cocoa powder and
   grate over some plain chocolate just before serving.

Serves 8–10
Preparation: 1 hour, plus chilling and freezing
Per serving: 780–620 cals; 55–44g fat;
63–50g carbohydrate

Chocolate Cup Cakes

125g (4oz) unsalted
  butter, softened
125g (4oz) light
  muscovado sugar
2 eggs, beaten
15g (½oz) cocoa
  powder, sifted
100g (3½oz) self-
  raising flour, sifted

pinch of baking powder
200g (7oz) good-quality
  plain dark chocolate
  (with 70% cocoa
  solids)
142ml carton double
  cream

1 Preheat the oven to 190°C (170°C fan oven) mark 5. Put the butter, sugar, eggs, cocoa powder, flour and baking powder into the large bowl of a freestanding mixer or in a food processor. Mix slowly to start with and then increase the speed slightly until the mixture is well combined.

2 Roughly chop half the chocolate and fold into the creamed mixture.

3 Line muffin tins with 18 muffin cases. Divide the mixture among them. Lightly flatten the surface with the back of a spoon. Bake for 20 minutes or until risen and cooked. Remove from the oven and cool in the cases.

4 To decorate, break up the remaining chocolate and put with the cream into a heavy-based pan and heat until melted together. Leave to cool for 10 minutes and thicken slightly, then pour over the cooled cakes. Leave to set for 30 minutes before serving.

Makes 18
Preparation: 15 minutes
Cooking time: 20 minutes
Per cake: 300 cals; 15g fat; 40g carbohydrate

See picture, page 416

14

Chocoholic

Chocolate Meringue Roulade

5 large egg whites
175g (6oz) golden caster sugar
1tsp cornflour
4tbsp half-fat crème fraîche, plus extra to serve
125g (4oz) chocolate spread

50g (2oz) cooked vacuum-packed chestnuts, roughly chopped (optional)
icing sugar and cocoa powder, to dust
chocolate curls (page 404), to decorate

1 Preheat the oven to 110°C (90°C fan oven) mark ¼. Line a 20.5 x 30.5cm (8 x 12 inch) Swiss roll tin with non-stick baking parchment.

2 Using an electric whisk, whisk the egg whites in a large grease-free heatproof bowl until frothy, then whisk in the sugar. Stand the bowl over a pan of gently simmering water and whisk at high speed until very thick and shiny, about 4–5 minutes. Take off the heat and whisk in the cornflour.

3 Spoon the mixture into the prepared tin and level the surface, then bake for 1 hour or until just firm on top. Remove from the oven and leave to cool for 1 hour; don't worry if the meringue weeps a little.

4 Beat the crème fraîche into the chocolate spread. Fold in the chopped chestnuts, if using.

5 Turn the meringue out on to a sheet of baking parchment dusted with icing sugar and carefully peel off the lining parchment. Make a shallow cut in the meringue, 2.5cm (1 inch) in from the edge of a short end. Spread the chocolate mixture over the meringue and roll it up, from the cut end.

6 Dust with icing sugar and cocoa and decorate with chocolate curls. Serve with half-fat crème fraîche.

Serves 6–8
Preparation: 30 minutes, plus cooling
Cooking time: 1 hour
Per serving: 370–280 cals; 14–10g fat; 59–44g carbohydrate

Black Forest Roulade

125g (4oz) good-quality plain dark chocolate (with 70% cocoa solids), in pieces
4 large eggs, separated
125g (4oz) golden caster sugar, plus extra to dust
142ml carton whipping cream

1tsp icing sugar, plus extra to dust
75ml (3fl oz) Greek-style yogurt
2 x 425g cans morello cherries, drained, pitted and halved
cocoa powder, to dust

1 Preheat the oven to 180°C (160°C fan oven) mark 4. Line a 33 x 23cm (13 x 9 inch) Swiss roll tin with non-stick baking parchment.

2 Melt the chocolate in a heatproof bowl set over a pan of barely simmering water. Stir until smooth, then leave to cool. Whisk the egg yolks and caster sugar together in a large bowl until thick and creamy. Whisk in the melted chocolate.

3 Whisk the egg whites in a clean grease-free bowl until stiff and shiny. Lightly fold into the chocolate mixture. Pour into the prepared tin and smooth the surface, then bake for 20 minutes or until firm to the touch.

4 Turn the roulade out on to a sheet of greaseproof paper dusted with icing sugar and carefully peel off the lining parchment. Cover with a damp cloth and leave to cool for 30 minutes.

5 For the filling, lightly whip the cream with the icing sugar, then fold in the yogurt. Spread the filling over the cold roulade and scatter the cherries on top. Roll up from one of the narrow ends, using the greaseproof paper to help. Chill for 30 minutes.

6 Slice the roulade and serve, dusted with cocoa powder and icing sugar.

Serves 10
Preparation: 35 minutes, plus cooling
Cooking time: 20 minutes
Per serving: 260 cals; 14g fat; 30g carbohydrate

Top left: White and Dark Chocolate Cookies, page 419; top right: The Ultimate Brownie, page 419; bottom left: Chocolate Cup Cakes, page 415; bottom right: Chocolate Orange Tart, page 413.

Gooey Chocolate Soufflés

125g (4oz) golden
  caster sugar
50g (2oz) cocoa
  powder
9 egg whites, at room
  temperature
pinch of cream of
  tartar

15g (½oz) good-quality
  plain dark chocolate
  (with 60–70% cocoa
  solids), coarsely
  grated or finely
  chopped
2tsp dark rum
1tsp vanilla extract

1 Preheat the oven to 180°C (160°C fan oven) mark 4. Sift 100g (3½oz) sugar with the cocoa powder and put to one side.

2 Put the egg whites and the cream of tartar in a clean grease-free bowl and, using an electric whisk, beat until foamy. Continue whisking at high speed, gradually adding the remaining sugar 1tbsp at a time, until the meringue holds stiff peaks.

3 Using a large metal spoon, carefully fold the sugar and cocoa mixture into the meringue with the chocolate, rum and vanilla extract. The mixture should be evenly combined but still stiff.

4 Spoon the mixture into eight 175ml (6fl oz) ovenproof tea or coffee cups. Stand the cups in a large roasting tin and pour enough boiling water into the tin to come at least halfway up their sides. Bake for 12–15 minutes or until the soufflés are puffed and set round the edges but still soft in the centre. Serve at once.

Serves 8
Preparation: 10 minutes
Cooking time: 12–15 minutes
Per serving: 110 cals; 2g fat; 18g carbohydrate

Chocolate, Prune and Orange Soufflés

butter, to grease
5tbsp golden caster
  sugar
175g (6oz) pitted,
  ready-to-eat prunes
2tbsp vegetable oil
5tbsp unsweetened
  orange juice

50g (2oz) good-quality
  plain chocolate,
  chopped into small
  pieces
grated zest of 1 orange
5 egg whites
¼tsp cream of tartar
pinch of salt
icing sugar, to dust

1 Preheat the oven to 180°C (160°C fan oven) mark 4. Lightly grease eight 150ml (¼ pint) ramekins and sprinkle with 1tbsp caster sugar.

2 Put the prunes, oil and orange juice in a blender and whiz for 2–3 minutes to form a purée. Transfer to a large bowl and stir in the chocolate, 2tbsp of the remaining caster sugar and the orange zest.

3 Put the egg whites, cream of tartar and salt in a clean grease-free bowl and whisk until stiff but not dry. Add the remaining 2tbsp caster sugar and continue to whisk until the mixture is very stiff and shiny.

4 Using a large metal spoon, stir a quarter of the egg whites into the prune mixture, then gently fold in the remainder.

5 Spoon the mixture into the ramekins. Stand them in a large roasting tin and pour enough boiling water into the tin to come halfway up their sides. Bake for 15–20 minutes or until the soufflés are just set. Remove from the oven, dust with icing sugar and serve immediately.

Makes 8
Preparation: 20 minutes
Cooking time: 15–20 minutes
Per serving: 150 cals; 5g fat; 26g carbohydrate

Top left: Banana and Chocolate Bread Pudding, page 421; top right: Celebration Chocolate Cake, page 431; bottom left: White Chocolate and Red Fruit Trifle, page 426; bottom right: Gooey Chocolate Souffés, page 424.

Baking

What better smell than the enticing aroma coming out of your kitchen of home-baked bread, a moist, fragrant cake, or a big tray of cookies? Small bakes, cakes, sweet and savoury breads, tray bakes, biscuits and sponges are all here – easy to make and just the thing with a cup of tea or when friends pop round.

Whip up a tray of Caramelised Hazelnut Shortbread, some Macaroons, or Sultana and Pecan Cookies just before friends arrive and fill the house with the tempting smell of baking.

Enjoy the simple pleasure of a slice of home-baked Quick Zucchini, Lemon and Parmesan Bread spread with Sun-dried Tomato Butter – a fantastic combination. Someone having a celebration? Try the wonderful Marshmallow Meringue Cake or the Walnut and Coffee Layer Cake.

Finally, Christmas Cake. The Classic or Light and Easy, filled with fruit and nuts, drenched in alcohol and finished with smooth white icing are truly festive favourites. And don't forget the Freeze-ahead Mince Pies, with banana, marmalade and whisky. Scrumptious.

Lemon and Saffron Cake

175g (6oz) unsalted
 butter, softened, plus
 extra to grease
grated zest of
 1½ lemons, plus
 225ml (8fl oz) lemon
 juice
625g (1lb 7oz) golden
 caster sugar

5 large eggs, separated
3tbsp ground almonds
275g (10oz) self-raising
 flour, sifted
large pinch of saffron
 (optional)
lemon slices and rose
 petals, to decorate
 (optional)

1 Preheat the oven to 170°C (150°C fan oven) mark 3. Grease a 23cm (9 inch) spring-release cake tin and line the base with greaseproof paper. Beat together the butter, lemon zest and 275g (10oz) caster sugar in a large mixing bowl until thoroughly combined, then mix in 75ml (3fl oz) lemon juice, 1tbsp at a time. Beat in the egg yolks and ground almonds, then fold in the flour.

2 Whisk the egg whites in a large clean grease-free bowl until soft peaks form. Using a large metal spoon, stir a quarter of the egg whites into the butter mixture, then gently fold in the remainder with 2tbsp cold water.

3 Pour the mixture into the prepared cake tin and smooth the top. Bake for 50–60 minutes or until a skewer inserted in the centre comes out clean. Remove from the oven and leave the cake in the tin to cool for 30 minutes.

4 Meanwhile, make the syrup. Put the remaining lemon juice and caster sugar, the saffron and 300ml (½ pint) water in a heavy-based pan. Dissolve the sugar over a low heat, then bring to the boil. Put to one side until the cake is cool.

5 Leaving the cake in the tin, put the tin on a baking tray with a lip. Drizzle the lemon syrup over the cake and leave to soak in for 30 minutes.

6 Unmould the cake, slice and, if you like, decorate with lemon slices and rose petals. Serve with crème fraîche or mascarpone.

Serves 8–10
Preparation: 30 minutes, plus cooling and soaking
Cooking time: 1 hour
Per serving: 670–540 cals; 26–21g fat;
 108–87g carbohydrate

Lemon Syrup Cake

250g pack unsalted
 butter, softened, plus
 extra to grease
5 unwaxed lemons,
 plus juice of 2 lemons
525g (1lb 3oz) golden
 caster sugar
5 eggs, beaten
175g (6oz) self-raising
 flour, sifted

75g (3oz) semolina
100g (3½oz) ground
 almonds, sifted
150ml (¼ pint) brandy
3tbsp runny honey
50g (2oz) blanched
 almonds

1 Grease a 23cm (9 inch) spring-release cake tin and line the base with greaseproof paper.

2 Put 3 lemons in a pan, cover with cold water and bring to the boil. Boil for 45 minutes or until tender. Lift out of the pan and cool. When cold, cut in half, remove the pips and roughly chop the flesh. Put in a food processor and whiz for 2 minutes to a purée.

3 Preheat the oven to 180°C (160°C fan oven) mark 4. Cream the butter and 225g (8oz) sugar with an electric whisk until light and fluffy. Gradually add the eggs, stirring in a little flour if the mixture looks as if it may curdle.

4 Using a large metal spoon, fold in the remaining flour, the semolina, ground almonds and lemon purée. Spoon into the prepared cake tin and bake for 40–50 minutes or until a skewer inserted comes out clean. Remove from the oven and leave the cake in the tin to cool for 20 minutes.

5 Meanwhile, make the syrup. Cut each of the remaining 2 lemons into 12 wedges. Put the remaining sugar, the brandy, lemon juice and honey in a pan. Add 150ml (¼ pint) water and heat gently to dissolve the sugar. Increase the heat and boil for 3 minutes. Add the lemon wedges and cook for 5 minutes or until soft. Add the blanched almonds to the pan.

6 Put the cake on a serving plate, pierce it several times with a skewer and spoon the lemon pieces and almonds on top. Pour the syrup over and serve with yogurt.

Cuts into 16 slices
Preparation: 25 minutes, plus cooling
Cooking time: 1 hour 50 minutes
Per slice: 420 cals; 20g fat; 52g carbohydrate
See picture, page 438

Raspberry and Peach Cake

200g (7oz) unsalted
 butter, melted, plus
 extra to grease
250g (9oz) self-raising
 flour, sifted
100g (3½oz) golden
 caster sugar
4 eggs, beaten
small punnet, about
 125g (4oz),
 raspberries

2 large almost-ripe
 peaches or
 nectarines, halved,
 stoned and sliced
4tbsp apricot jam
juice of ½ lemon

1 Preheat the oven to 190°C (170°C fan oven) mark 5. Grease a 20.5cm (8 inch) spring-release cake tin and line the base with baking parchment.
2 Put the flour and sugar into a large bowl. Make a well in the centre, add the melted butter and the eggs and mix well.
3 Spread half the mixture over the base of the cake tin and add half the raspberries and sliced peaches or nectarines. Spoon on the remaining cake mixture, smooth over, then add the remaining raspberries and peaches, pressing them down into the mixture slightly.
4 Bake for 1–1¼ hours or until risen and golden and a skewer inserted into the centre comes out clean. Remove from the oven and leave in the tin to cool for 10 minutes.
5 Warm the jam and the lemon juice together and brush over the top of the cake to glaze.

Serves 8
Preparation: 15 minutes plus cooling
Cooking time: 1–1¼ hours
Per serving: 410 cals; 24g fat; 45g carbohydrate

See picture, page 438

Orange and Almond Cake

butter, to grease
60g (2oz) fine
 breadcrumbs, plus
 extra to line the tin
juice of 3 oranges, plus
 grated zest of
 1 orange
125g (4oz) ground
 almonds

1tbsp orange-flower
 water (if available)
4 eggs, separated
125g (4oz) golden
 caster sugar
½tsp salt
150ml (¼ pint)
 whipping cream

1 Preheat the oven to 180°C (160°C fan oven) mark 4. Grease a square cake tin, line with baking parchment and grease again, then sprinkle with breadcrumbs. Mix the breadcrumbs, orange juice and zest, then add the almonds and the orange-flower water, if using.
2 Beat the egg yolks with the sugar and salt until almost white. Add to the first mixture. Beat the egg whites in a clean grease-free bowl until stiff peaks form, then fold in. Pour into the prepared cake tin and bake for about 40 minutes.
3 Remove from the oven and leave in the tin until cold. When cold, turn the cake out and cover the top with whipped cream. For a special occasion, sprinkle the cream-smothered cake with silver balls and surround it with a silver ribbon to decorate.

Serves 10
Preparation: 20 minutes plus cooling
Cooking time: 40 minutes
Per serving: 180 cals; 9g fat; 18g carbohydrate

Marshmallow Meringue Cake

225g (8oz) golden
   caster sugar
125g (4oz) light
   muscovado sugar
6 large eggs, separated
1tsp cornflour
½tsp vinegar
50g (2oz) flaked
   almonds, toasted
   (optional)
450ml (¾ pint) full-fat
   milk
1tsp vanilla extract
200g (7oz) small white
   marshmallows

284ml carton double
   cream, lightly
   whipped
125g (4oz) good-quality
   plain chocolate, semi-
   sweet such as
   Bournville,
   roughly chopped
4 bananas, about 450g
   (1lb)
chocolate shavings
   and icing sugar, to
   dust

1 Preheat the oven to 130°C (110°C fan oven) mark ½. Line two baking sheets with non-stick baking parchment. Using a felt-tip pen, mark out two 23cm (9 inch) diameter circles on the baking parchment, then turn the paper over.

2 To make the meringue, sift the caster and muscovado sugars together. Whisk the egg whites in a clean grease-free bowl until they're stiff and dry. Whisk in the sugars, 1tbsp at a time, until the mixture is glossy and very stiff – about 5 minutes; then whisk in the cornflour and vinegar.

3 Spoon just over half the meringue on to one of the baking sheets in a garland shape and sprinkle with half the almonds, if using. Spread the remaining mixture evenly over the other circle to cover it completely. Sprinkle with the remaining almonds and bake for 2–2½ hours, then turn off the oven and leave the meringues inside to cool for 30 minutes.

4 To make the ice cream, bring the milk to scalding point in a small pan, add the vanilla extract, then pour over the egg yolks, whisking. Pour back into the clean pan and cook over a low heat, stirring until the custard coats the back of a spoon. Place the marshmallows in a bowl, pour the strained warm custard over them and stir gently until they've almost melted.

5 Cool quickly, then cover and chill for 30 minutes. Fold the cream into the custard. Pour into a freezerproof container and freeze for 3–4 hours or until just firm. (Alternatively, if you have an ice cream machine, churn the custard until just firm to give a smoother texture.) Stir in the chocolate and freeze the ice cream until you're ready to assemble the cake.

6 About 30 minutes before serving, remove the ice cream from the freezer to soften. Place the meringue circle on a serving plate. Slice the bananas and scatter evenly over the base, reserving a few to stir into the softened ice cream.

7 Using a spoon or ice cream scoop, spoon the ice cream mixture over the bananas and place the meringue garland on top, pressing down gently. Decorate with chocolate shavings and a dusting of icing sugar then serve immediately.

Serves 10–12
Preparation: 45 minutes, plus chilling, freezing and softening
Cooking time: 2½ hours, plus cooling
Per serving: 570–470 cals; 27–22g fat; 76–64g carbohydrate

See picture, page 438

15

Baking

Walnut and Coffee Layer Cake

300g (10oz) unsalted butter at room temperature, plus extra to grease
250g (9oz) walnuts, plus extra to decorate
100g (3½oz) plain flour
9 large eggs

250g (9oz) golden caster sugar
3tbsp instant coffee granules
450g (1lb) golden icing sugar, sifted
gold almond dragées, to decorate (optional)

1 Preheat the oven to 170°C (150°C fan oven) mark 3. Grease a 23cm (9 inch) spring-release cake tin and line the base with non-stick baking parchment. Whiz the walnuts in a food processor until roughly chopped. Add the flour and whiz to a fine powder. Put to one side.

2 Separate the eggs, then put the yolks in the bowl of a food mixer and 5 egg whites in a large mixing bowl. (Freeze the remaining whites for use later.) Add the caster sugar to the yolks and beat until the mixture is pale and very thick.

3 Using a metal spoon, fold the walnut and flour powder into the yolk mixture. Whisk the egg whites in a clean grease-free bowl until soft peaks form. Add one-third of the egg white to the yolk mixture, then carefully fold in the rest. Pour the mixture into the prepared tin.

4 Bake for 55–60 minutes or until a skewer inserted in the centre for 30 seconds comes out clean. Remove from the oven and leave in the tin to cool for 15 minutes, then turn out on to a cooling rack.

5 To make the filling, dissolve the coffee in 3tbsp boiling water and put to one side. Put the butter in a bowl and beat until very soft and creamy. Gradually beat in 300g (10oz) icing sugar and 4tsp of the dissolved coffee (reserve the rest) until well combined and fluffy.

6 Cut the cake horizontally into three layers. Put the bottom layer on a serving plate and spread half the filling over it. Gently press the second layer into position and spread with the remaining filling. Lift the top of the cake into position and press down gently. The cake can be frozen at this stage.

7 For the icing, put the remaining icing sugar into a bowl, add ½–1tsp of the reserved coffee and 2–3tbsp boiling water and combine thoroughly. Pour the icing on to the cake, then, using a round-bladed palette knife, quickly spread in an even layer to the edge. Scatter the extra walnuts and the gold dragées, if using, around the edge. Allow the icing to set (about 2 hours) before serving. The cake will keep well for about 5 days.

Serves 12
Preparation: 1 hour, plus cooling and setting
Cooking time: 55–60 minutes
Per serving: 670 cals; 41g fat; 69g carbohydrate

15

Carrot Cake

250ml (8fl oz) sunflower oil, plus extra to grease
225g (8oz) light muscovado sugar
3 large eggs
225g (8oz) self-raising flour
large pinch of salt
½tsp each ground mixed spice, ground nutmeg and ground cinnamon
250g (9oz) carrots, peeled and coarsely grated
50g (2oz) butter, preferably unsalted, at room temperature
225g pack Philadelphia cream cheese
25g (1oz) golden icing sugar
½tsp vanilla extract
8 pecan halves, roughly chopped

1 Preheat the oven to 180°C (160°C fan oven) mark 4. Grease two 18cm (7 inch) sandwich tins and line the bases with greaseproof paper.
2 Using a hand-hold electric whisk, whisk the oil and muscovado sugar together to combine, then whisk in the eggs, one at a time.
3 Sift the flour, salt and spices together over the mixture, then gently fold in, using a large metal spoon. Tip the carrots into the bowl and fold in.
4 Divide the cake mixture between the prepared tins and bake for 30–40 minutes or until golden and a skewer inserted into the centre comes out clean. Remove from the oven and leave in the tins for 10 minutes, then turn out on to a wire rack to cool.
5 To make the frosting, beat the butter and cream cheese together in a bowl until light and fluffy. Sift in the icing sugar, add the vanilla extract and beat well until smooth.
6 Spread one third of the frosting over one cake and sandwich together with the other cake. Spread the remaining frosting on top and sprinkle with the pecans. Store the cake in an airtight container and eat within 2 days. Alternatively, the cake will keep for up to 1 week in an airtight tin if it is stored before the frosting is applied.

Cuts into 12 slices
Preparation: 15 minutes
Cooking time: 40 minutes, plus cooling
Per slice: 450 cals; 32g fat; 38g carbohydrate

Sticky Ginger Ring

100g (3½oz) butter, cut into cubes, plus extra to grease
100g (3½oz) dark muscovado sugar
3tbsp black treacle
100ml (3½fl oz) full-fat milk
2tbsp brandy
1 large egg, beaten
150g (5oz) plain flour
2tsp each ground ginger and ground cinnamon
1tsp bicarbonate of soda
75g (3oz) ready-to-eat pitted prunes, coarsely chopped
225g (8oz) golden icing sugar, sifted
2 balls stem ginger in syrup, drained and cut into thin strips

1 Preheat the oven to 150°C (130°C fan oven) mark 2. Using your hands, generously grease a 600ml (1 pint) capacity, 22cm (8½ inch) round ring mould with butter. (If you don't have a ring mould, cook the mixture in a 450g (1lb) loaf tin for 1 hour 5 minutes–1 hour 10 minutes, or use a 16cm (6½ inch) square, 4cm (1½ inch) deep, tin and bake for 55 minutes.)
2 Put the butter, sugar and treacle in a pan and heat gently until melted, stirring all the time. Add the milk and brandy and, when cool, beat in the egg.
3 Sift the flour, spices and bicarbonate of soda into a large mixing bowl, make a well in the centre, pour in the treacle mixture and stir together until all the flour has been combined. It should have a soft dropping consistency. Stir in the prunes.
4 Pour the mixture into the prepared mould and bake for 1 hour, or until the cake is firm to the touch and a skewer inserted in the centre comes out clean. Remove from the oven and leave in the tin to cool for 10 minutes, then loosen the sides of the cake and turn out on to a wire rack. At this stage you can wrap the cake in greaseproof paper and keep in an airtight container for 1 week.
5 To make the icing, mix the icing sugar with about 2tbsp hot water to create a coating consistency. Pour over the cake, allowing it to drizzle down the sides, then decorate with the stem ginger. Leave to set.

Serves 8
Preparation: 15 minutes
Cooking time: 1 hour
Per serving: 420 cals; 13g fat; 75g carbohydrate

Top left: Sticky Ginger Ring, page 439; top right: Lemon Syrup Cake, page 434; bottom left: Raspberry and Peach Cake, page 435; bottom right: Marshmallow Meringue Cake, page 436.

Coffee Genoese Sponge

50g (2oz) butter, plus extra to grease
4 large eggs
125g (4oz) golden caster sugar
125g (4oz) plain flour
2tbsp instant espresso granules
250g tub mascarpone
125g (4oz) golden icing sugar, sifted, plus extra to dust

1 Preheat the oven to 190°C (170°C fan oven) mark 5. Grease two 18cm (7 inch) sandwich tins and line the bases with non-stick baking parchment.
2 Put the butter in a bowl and melt in the microwave on High for 30 seconds (based on a 900W oven).
3 Put the eggs and caster sugar into the bowl of a freestanding electric mixer and whisk until pale and creamy. Lift the whisk – the mixture should be thick enough to leave a trail. Using a large metal spoon, fold half the flour into the mixture.
4 Dissolve 1tbsp espresso granules in 2tsp boiling water, mix into the butter and pour half around the edge of mixture. Add the remaining flour, then the rest of the coffee and butter. Gradually fold in.
5 Divide the mixture between the prepared tins and bake for 25 minutes until risen, firm to the touch and shrinking away from the sides of the tin. Remove from the oven and upturn on to wire racks and cool.
6 Dissolve the remaining espresso granules in 1tbsp boiling water, then mix with the mascarpone and icing sugar and use to sandwich the cake together. Dust with icing sugar.

Serves 8
Preparation: 15 minutes
Cooking time: 25 minutes, plus cooling
Per serving: 410 cals; 23g fat; 46g carbohydrate

Sour Cherry Cakes

175g (6oz) butter, at room temperature
175g (6oz) golden caster sugar
3 eggs
175g (6oz) self-raising flour, sifted
pinch of baking powder
75g pack dried sour cherries
2tbsp milk
225g (8oz) golden icing sugar, sifted
3tbsp lemon juice, strained

1 Preheat the oven to 190°C (170°C fan oven) mark 5. Line a muffin tin with 12 muffin cases.
2 Put the butter, sugar, eggs, flour and baking powder in the large bowl of a freestanding electric mixer or in a food processor. Mix slowly to start with, then increase the speed slightly until the mixture is well combined.
3 Reserve 12 dried sour cherries, then fold in the remainder and mix everything together.
4 Spoon the mixture into the cases and bake for 15–20 minutes, until pale golden, risen and springy to the touch. Remove from the oven and cool on a wire rack.
5 To make the icing, put the icing sugar in a bowl and mix with the lemon juice to make a smooth dropping consistency. Spoon the icing on to the cakes and decorate each with a reserved sour cherry. Leave to set before serving.

Makes 12
Preparation: 30 minutes
Cooking time: 15–20 minutes
Per cake: 330 cals; 14g fat; 50g carbohydrate

See picture, page 445

Lemon and Coconut Sponge

250g (9oz) unsalted
  butter, softened, plus
  extra to grease
500g (1lb 2oz) golden
  caster sugar
6 eggs
375g (13oz) self-raising
  flour, sifted

1tsp vanilla extract
142ml carton soured
  cream
zest of 2 lemons, plus
  juice of 2½ lemons
150g (4½oz)
  sweetened,
  tenderised coconut

1 Preheat the oven to 180°C (160°C fan oven) mark 4.
   Grease a deep 20.5cm (8 inch) cake tin and line with
   greaseproof paper.
2 Cream the butter and 375g (13oz) sugar in a large bowl
   until light and fluffy. Add the eggs one at a time and
   beat in. If the mixture looks likely to curdle, add 1tbsp
   flour.
3 Add the remaining flour, the vanilla extract, soured
   cream, lemon zest, juice of 2 lemons and 100g (3½oz)
   coconut, then fold together. Pour into the prepared tin
   and bake for 1¼ hours until well risen, golden and a
   skewer inserted into the centre comes out clean.
   Remove the cake from the oven.
4 To make the topping, put the remaining sugar in a pan
   and add the juice of ½ lemon. Heat gently to dissolve
   the sugar, then bring to the boil and simmer for 1–2
   minutes to make a syrup. Pierce the top of the cake all
   over with a thin skewer. Pour the syrup over, allowing
   it to sink into the cake and drip down the sides, then
   sprinkle with the remaining coconut.

Serves 12
Preparation: 20 minutes
Cooking time: 1 hour 20 minutes
Per serving: 560 cals; 30g fat; 71g carbohydrate

Buttercream

75g (3oz) unsalted
  butter, softened
175g (6oz) icing sugar,
  sifted

few drops of vanilla
  extract
1–2tbsp milk or water

1 Put the butter into a bowl and beat with a wooden
   spoon until it is light and fluffy.
2 Gradually stir in the icing sugar, vanilla extract and milk
   or water. Beat well until light and smooth.

Makes 250g (9oz)
Preparation: 5 minutes
Per 25g (1oz): 130 cals; 6g fat; 18g carbohydrate

Note: This quantity is sufficient to cover the top of a
20.5cm (8 inch) cake. To make enough to cover the
top and sides, increase the quantities by one-third.

Variations
Orange, lime or lemon buttercream: Replace the
vanilla extract with a little finely grated orange, lime
or lemon zest. Add 1–2 tbsp juice from the fruit
instead of the milk, beating well to avoid curdling the
mixture. If the mixture is to be piped, omit the zest.
Chocolate buttercream: Blend 1tbsp cocoa powder
with 2tbsp boiling water and cool before adding to
the mixture.
Coffee buttercream: Replace the vanilla extract with
2tsp instant coffee granules dissolved in 1tbsp
boiling water; cool before adding to the mixture.

Victoria Jam Sandwich with Mascarpone

175g (6oz) butter, at
  room temperature,
  plus extra to grease
175g (6oz) golden
  caster sugar
3 eggs, beaten
175g (6oz) self-raising
  flour, sifted

150g (5oz) mascarpone
1tsp milk (optional)
1tsp icing sugar
  (optional), plus extra
  to dust
4tbsp raspberry
  conserve

1 Preheat the oven to 180°C (160°C fan oven) mark 4.
   Grease two 18cm (7 inch) sandwich cake tins and line
   the bases with greaseproof paper.
2 Put the butter and caster sugar into a large bowl and
   cream together with a hand-held electric beater (or a
   freestanding electric mixer) until light and fluffy.
3 Gradually beat in the eggs until the mixture is smooth,
   then, using a large metal spoon or spatula, gently fold
   in the flour.
4 Divide the mixture between the prepared tins and
   gently level the surface with a palette knife. Bake for
   about 25 minutes until golden, firm to the touch and
   beginning to shrink away from the sides of the tin.
5 Remove from the oven and leave the cakes in the tins
   to cool for 5 minutes, then turn out each layer on to a
   wire rack and leave to cool completely.
6 To make the filling, beat the mascarpone to loosen,
   adding the milk if it is too thick to spread. Sweeten with
   icing sugar, if you like.
7 Spread the mascarpone on top of one cake layer, then
   cover with the raspberry conserve. Put the other layer
   on top and lightly press the two together. Using a fine
   sieve, dust the top liberally with icing sugar.

Cuts into 6–8 slices
Preparation: 20 minutes
Cooking time: 25 minutes, plus cooling
Per slice: 610–460 cals; 39–30g fat;
61–46g carbohydrate

Variations
Basic Victoria sandwich: Omit the mascarpone and
simply sandwich the cake layers together with
raspberry or strawberry conserve. Dredge the top
with caster sugar.
Chocolate sandwich cake: Replace 3tbsp flour
with cocoa powder. Sandwich the cakes with vanilla
or chocolate buttercream (page 441).
Coffee sandwich cake: Blend 2tsp instant coffee
granules with 1tbsp boiling water. Cool and add to
the creamed mixture with the eggs. Sandwich the
cakes with vanilla or coffee buttercream (page 441).
Citrus sandwich cake: Add the finely grated zest of
1 orange, lime or lemon to the mixture. Sandwich the
cakes together with orange, lime or lemon
buttercream (page 441).

See picture, page 445

15

Baking

Classic Christmas Cake

150g (5oz) each organic currants, organic sultanas and organic raisins
100g (3½oz) natural glacé cherries, halved
50g (2oz) preserved stem ginger in syrup, drained and chopped
grated zest and juice of 1 unwaxed lemon, plus juice of ½ lemon
1tsp vanilla extract
75ml (2½fl oz) each ginger wine and Cognac, plus extra Cognac to drizzle
175g (6oz) butter, at room temperature, plus extra to grease
175g (6oz) dark muscovado sugar
2 eggs, beaten
175g (6oz) self-raising flour
1tsp ground mixed spice
½tsp each ground cinnamon and ground ginger
50g (2oz) mixed nuts, such as almonds, walnuts and brazils, roughly chopped
50g (2oz) carrots, peeled and coarsely grated
700g (1½lb) almond paste (page 444)
800g (1¾lb) royal icing (overleaf)
green and red food colourings
edible glitter flakes (optional)

1 Put the dried fruit, glacé cherries, stem ginger, lemon zest and juice and the vanilla extract into a bowl. Pour the ginger wine and Cognac over, stir, then cover and leave to macerate in a cool place for 1–5 days.

2 Preheat the oven to 170°C (150°C fan oven) mark 3. Grease a 20.5cm (8 inch) round, 7.5cm (3 inch) deep cake tin and line with baking parchment. Wrap a double layer of brown paper, 2.5cm (1 inch) deeper than the tin, around the outside of the tin and secure with string. This will prevent the outside of the cake from overcooking.

3 Cream the butter and sugar together in a large bowl, using a freestanding mixer if you have one, for 5 minutes until light and fluffy. Add the eggs, one at a time, mixing well between each addition. If the mixture looks like curdling, add 2tbsp flour with the second egg.

4 Sift the remaining flour and spices together, then fold half into the creamed mixture.

5 Put half the soaked fruit mixture into a food processor with some of the soaking liquid and whiz to a purée. Fold this into the cake mixture together with the remaining soaked fruit and liquor, the nuts, carrots and the remaining flour.

6 Turn the mixture into the prepared cake tin and spread evenly, then make a dip in the middle. Bake for 2 hours or until a skewer inserted into the centre for 30 seconds comes out clean. Remove from the oven and leave the cake in the tin to cool for 20 minutes, then turn out on to a wire rack and drizzle with 2tsp Cognac. Leave to cool completely.

7 Wrap the cake in greaseproof paper and foil and store in an airtight tin for up to 1 month.

8 About 5 days before Christmas, unwrap the cake and put it on a 25.5cm (10 inch) board. Cut off a quarter of the almond paste and wrap in clingfilm. Use the rest of the almond paste to cover the top and sides of the cake, adding the trimmings to the wrapped portion. Leave the cake to dry for a day or two before applying the royal icing.

9 Spread half the royal icing over the top and sides of the cake with a palette knife. Either pipe the rest of the icing in wavy lines on top of the cake or apply with the palette knife and flick up to create peaks, resembling snow.

Cuts into 16 slices
Preparation: 45 minutes, plus macerating
Cooking time: 2 hours, plus cooling
Per slice: 240 cals; 12g fat; 30g carbohydrate

Light and Easy Christmas Cake

175g (6oz) butter, softened, plus extra to grease
375g (13oz) raisins
150ml (¼ pint) dark rum
175g (6oz) golden caster sugar, plus extra for the physalis
3 eggs, beaten
150g (5oz) ground almonds

175g (6oz) self-raising flour
zest of 1 small orange
3tbsp apricot jam
500g pack fondant icing
a little icing sugar and edible gold lustre dust
6 physalis (cape gooseberries), unwashed

1 Preheat the oven to 170°C (150°C fan oven) mark 3. Grease a 20.5cm (8 inch) loose-based cake tin and line with greaseproof paper. Soak the raisins in a bowl with the rum and put to one side.
2 Put 175g (6oz) butter into a bowl. Using an electric hand whisk, beat in the caster sugar, one large spoonful at a time, until light and fluffy. Beat in the eggs, a little at a time, then add the almonds and mix well. Stir in the soaked raisins. If the mixture looks curdled, leave for 5 minutes to allow the almonds to swell, then stir again.
3 Using a large metal spoon, fold in the flour and orange zest. Spoon the mixture into the prepared tin and smooth the top. Bake for 50 minutes–1 hour or until a metal skewer inserted into the centre comes out clean. Remove from the oven and leave the cake in the tin to cool for 10 minutes, then turn out on to a wire rack to cool completely.
4 Carefully turn the cake upside down, put on a serving plate and remove the greaseproof paper.
5 To decorate the cake, heat the jam in a pan for 2–3 minutes, sieve into a bowl, then brush over the top and sides of the cake. Roll out the icing to a 35.5cm (14 inch) circle, lift it on to the cake and smooth over the top and sides. Cut away any extra icing.
6 Before serving, sift 2tbsp icing sugar into a bowl and mix in a knifepoint of gold lustre, then tip into a fine sieve or tea strainer and dust over the top of the cake.
7 Pull the leaves back from the physalis to reveal the fruit. Put the caster sugar in a bowl and dip in the physalis – the sugar will cling to the sticky surface. Arrange the fruit on top of the cake. Finish by tying a gold ribbon around the cake.

Makes 1 x 20.5cm (8 inch) cake, cuts into 12 slices
Preparation: 20 minutes
Cooking time: 50 minutes–1 hour
Per serving: 550 cals; 20g fat; 85g carbohydrate

Almond Paste

225g (8oz) ground almonds
125g (4oz) golden caster sugar
125g (4oz) golden icing sugar

1 large egg (see note)
1tsp lemon juice
1tsp sherry
1–2 drops of vanilla extract

1 Put the almonds, caster sugar and icing sugar into a bowl and mix. In a separate bowl, whisk the egg with the remaining ingredients and add to the dry mixture.
2 Stir well to mix, pounding gently to release some of the oil from the almonds. Knead with your hands until smooth. Cover until ready to use.

Makes 450g (1lb)
Preparation: 10 minutes
Per 25g (1oz): 130 cals; 7g fat; 15g carbohydrate

Note: If you wish to avoid using raw egg to bind the almond paste, mix the other liquid ingredients with a little water instead.

Royal Icing

2 large egg whites, or 1 tbsp egg albumen powder

2tsp liquid glycerine (optional)
450g (1lb) icing sugar, sifted

1 If using the egg whites and the glycerine, put them in a bowl and stir just enough to break up the egg whites. If using albumen powder, mix according to the instructions on the packet.
2 Add a little icing sugar and mix gently with a wooden spoon to incorporate as little air as possible.
3 Add a little more icing sugar as the mixture becomes lighter. Continue to add the icing sugar, stirring gently but thoroughly until the mixture is stiff and stands in soft peaks. For coating it should form soft peaks; for piping it should be a little stiffer.

Makes 450g (1lb)
Preparation: 20 minutes
Per 25g (1oz): 100 cals; 0g fat; 26g carbohydrate

Top left: Victoria Sandwich with Mascarpone, page 442; top right: Wholemeal Banana Muffins, page 450; bottom left: Sour Cherry Cakes, page 440; bottom right: Kugelhopf, page 447.

Lemon Angel Cakes

vegetable cooking
  spray, to grease
50g (2oz) plain flour
1tbsp cornflour
100g (3½oz) golden
  caster sugar
5 large egg whites
¼tsp salt

½tsp cream of tartar
½tsp each vanilla
  extract and rosewater
seeds from 3 large
  cardamom pods,
  finely crushed
grated zest of 1 lemon

1 Preheat the oven to 170°C (150°C fan oven) mark 3. Grease an 18cm (7 inch) square cake tin and line the base with non-stick baking parchment. Sift the flour, cornflour and 50g (2oz) sugar into a bowl and put to one side.

2 Whisk the egg whites in a clean grease-free bowl with the salt, cream of tartar, vanilla extract, rosewater and 1tbsp cold water until stiff peaks form. Gradually whisk in the remaining sugar and continue to whisk until stiff and glossy. Sift the flour mixture over the egg whites and carefully fold in the cardamom seeds and lemon zest. Spoon into the prepared tin and level the surface.

3 Bake for 35 minutes or until firm to the touch and the cake has shrunk from the sides of the tin. Remove from the oven and loosen round the sides with a palette knife, then flip the tin upside down on to a cooling rack and leave the cake in the tin to cool.

4 Remove the cake from the tin and cut into 9 squares, then halve to make 18 triangles. Serve plain or with fromage frais, berries and pineapple, dusted with icing sugar.

Makes 18 triangles
Preparation: 20 minutes, plus cooling
Cooking time: 35 minutes
Per triangle: 40 cals; trace fat; 9g carbohydrate

Pastel Meringues

4 large egg whites
250g (9oz) icing sugar,
  sifted

1tsp vanilla extract
red food colouring

1 Preheat the oven to 130°C (110°C fan oven) mark ½. Line three baking trays with baking parchment.

2 Put the egg whites in a clean grease-free bowl of a freestanding mixer and whisk until stiff. Add the sugar 1tbsp at a time, whisking well between additions for a stiff, shiny meringue. The mixture shouldn't move around in the bowl. Whisk in the vanilla extract.

3 Divide the mixture into two. Add 1–2 drops of red food colouring, one drop at a time, to one bowl to make a pale pink and add 2–3 drops to the other bowl for a darker pink. Mix each well.

4 For oval shapes, take two dessertspoons. Take a spoonful of mixture and use the other spoon to scrape the meringue away from you on to the parchment. For hearts, fit a piping bag with a 1cm (½ inch) plain nozzle and pipe heart shapes on to the parchment.

5 Bake for 1 hour, turn off the heat and leave in the oven for 1–1 ½ hours to dry out. Remove from the oven and cool on a wire rack. Store in an airtight container for up to 2 weeks.

Serves 10
Preparation: 30 minutes, plus drying out
Cooking time: 1 hour
Per serving: 100 cals; 0g fat; 26g carbohydrate

Top left: Carrot Tray Bake, page 461; top right: Dainty Cup Cakes, page 450; bottom left: Vanilla and White Chocolate Cup Cakes, page 451; bottom right: Figgy Fruit Slice, page 458.

Carrot Tray Bake

100g (3½oz) butter, chopped, plus extra to grease
125g (4oz) carrots, peeled and grated
100g (3½oz) each cultanas and chopped dried dates
50g (2oz) tenderised coconut
1tsp ground cinnamon
½tsp freshly grated nutmeg
330g bottle maple syrup
150ml (¼ pint) apple juice

zest and juice of 2 oranges, plus pared zest from ½–1 orange
225g (8oz) wholemeal self-raising flour, sifted
2tsp bicarbonate of soda
125g (4oz) walnut pieces
200g (7oz) cream cheese
200ml carton crème fraîche
2tbsp icing sugar
1tsp vanilla extract

1 Preheat the oven to 190°C (170°C fan oven) mark 5. Grease a 23 x 23cm (9 x 9 inch) cake tin and line with greaseproof paper.
2 Put the butter, carrots, sultanas, dates, coconut, spices, maple syrup, apple juice and the orange zest and juice of 2 oranges in a large pan. Cover and bring to the boil, then cook for 5 minutes. Tip into a bowl and leave to cool.
3 Put the flour, bicarbonate of soda and walnuts in a large bowl and stir together. Add the cooled carrot mixture and stir well.
4 Spoon the mixture into the prepared tin and bake for 45 minutes–1 hour until firm. Remove from the oven and leave in the tin for 10 minutes, then turn out on to a wire rack and leave to cool.
5 To make the topping, finely slice the orange zest from the remaining orange. Put the cream cheese, crème fraîche, sugar and vanilla extract in a bowl and stir with a spatula. Spread over the cake and top with the zest.

Serves 15   Preparation: 30 minutes
Cooking time: about 1 hour
Per serving: 370 cals; 24g fat; 38g carbohydrate

See picture, page 453

Chocolate and Pistachio Biscotti

300g (11oz) plain flour
75g (3oz) cocoa powder
1tsp baking powder
150g (5oz) plain chocolate chips
150g (5oz) shelled pistachio nuts

1tsp salt
75g (3oz) unsalted butter, softened
225g (8oz) granulated sugar
2 large eggs, beaten
1tbsp icing sugar

1 Preheat the oven to 180°C (160°C fan oven) mark 4. Line a large baking sheet with non-stick baking parchment.
2 Mix the flour with the cocoa powder, baking powder, chocolate chips, pistachios and salt.
3 Using an electric whisk, beat together the butter and sugar until light and fluffy. Gradually whisk in the eggs.
4 Stir the dry ingredients into the mixture until it forms a stiff dough. With floured hands, shape the dough into two slightly flattened logs, each about 30.5 x 5cm (12 x 2 inches). Sprinkle with icing sugar. Put the logs on the baking sheet and bake for 40–45 minutes or until they are slightly firm to the touch.
5 Remove from the oven and cool the logs on the baking sheet for 10 minutes, then cut diagonally into 2cm (¾ inch) thick slices. Arrange them, cut side down, on the baking sheet and bake again for 15 minutes or until crisp. Cool on a wire rack. Keep the biscotti in an airtight container for up to 1 week or freeze them for up to 1 month.

Makes 30 biscuits
Preparation: 15 minutes
Cooking time: 1 hour 10 minutes
Per biscuit: 160 cals; 7g fat; 20g carbohydrate

Top left: Orange Tuile Biscuits, page 462; top right: Macaroons, page 462; bottom left: Chocolate and Pistachio Biscotti, page 461; bottom right: Spiced Start Biscuits, page 463.

Walnut Bread

50g (2oz) butter, softened, plus extra to grease
500g (1lb 2oz) strong white flour with kibbled grains of rye and wheat, sifted, plus extra to dust
7g pack fast-action dried yeast
2tsp salt
2tbsp malt extract
3 garlic cloves, peeled and crushed
100g pack walnut pieces
1tbsp milk

1   Lightly grease a 20.5cm (8 inch) spring-release tin. Put the flour, yeast and salt in the bowl of a freestanding mixer with dough hook attachment. Add 300ml (½ pint) lukewarm water and 1tbsp malt extract, then mix to a pliable dough. Increase the speed and machine-knead for 5 minutes.

2   Turn out the dough on a lightly dusted surface and roll into a rectangle measuring about 40.5 x 20cm (16 x 11 inches). Mix the butter with the garlic and spread over the dough. Scatter the walnuts over and, starting at the long edge, roll up into a sausage. Cut into eight slices and put into the prepared tin. Cover with lightly oiled clingfilm and leave to rise in a warm place for 45 minutes or until doubled in size.

3   Preheat the oven to 220°C (200°C fan oven) mark 7 and put a baking sheet in to heat. Remove the clingfilm from the dough, cover the dough with foil, put on the hot baking sheet and bake for 20 minutes.

4   Reduce the oven temperature to 200°C (180°C fan oven) mark 6 and bake for 40 minutes. Remove from the oven and leave in the tin to cool. Freeze for up to 1 month.

5   To cook from frozen, cover, put on a hot baking sheet and bake at 220°C (200°C fan oven) mark 7, for 45 minutes. Mix the milk with the remaining malt extract and brush the glaze over the bread. Bake, uncovered, for 5 minutes or until golden brown. Leave in the tin to cool slightly, then turn out and serve warm.

Serves 8
Preparation: 20 minutes, plus rising and freezing
Cooking time: 1 hour 50 minutes
Per serving: 330 cals; 12g fat; 48g carbohydrate

Top left: Sweet Cherry Bread, page 472; top right: Sweet Mocha Bread, page 471; bottom left: Cranberry Biscuits, page 465; bottom right: Lime Drizzle Loaf, page 475.

Sauces and salsas

A really good savoury sauce will brighten up a simple bowl of pasta, anoint a plainly grilled chop, or complement a perfectly cooked whole fish. Pour some thick, chunky Fresh Tomato Sauce, with garlic, oregano and basil, over cooked penne or other pasta shapes, crumble some cheese on top and put under the grill until it's bubbling. Simple, but guaranteed to cheer anyone up.

Pesto, too, is made in minutes and can be done in advance and kept in the fridge. The Roast Nut and Herb Pesto, with parsley, almonds and garlic, is great with grilled vegetables.

For pan-fries, a Creamy Mushroom and Wine Sauce is ready in the time it takes to cook the meat and its smooth richness works so well with steaks and chicken. Having a barbecue? Try the home-made mayonnaises and dressings. Caper and Lemon Dressing, with its kick of chilli and garlic, is fantastic with fish cakes or grilled salmon, while Smoky Pepper Mayo is great for dunking fat, sticky sausages in.

If you're sharing a big bowl of creamy vanilla ice cream, pour over some Strawberry or Passion-fruit Sauce for a fruity combination, or try the Heavenly Fudge Sauce for pure indulgence.

Rich Tomato Sauce

50g (2oz) butter
1 onion, peeled and
  finely chopped
2 garlic cloves, peeled
  and finely chopped
2 x 400g cans plum
  tomatoes with
  their juice

3tbsp sun-dried tomato
  paste
2 oregano sprigs, or
  1tsp dried
salt and pepper

1 Melt the butter in a pan, add the onion and garlic and cook gently for about 10 minutes until softened.
2 Add the tomatoes with the tomato paste and oregano and cook, uncovered, over a low heat for 25–30 minutes, stirring occasionally, until the sauce is thick and pulpy.
3 Discard the oregano and season to taste.

Serves 4–6
Preparation: 10 minutes
Cooking time: about 40 minutes
Per serving: 150–100 cals; 11–7g fat;
11–7g carbohydrate

Tomato and Basil Sauce

1tbsp extra-virgin olive
  oil
3 garlic cloves, peeled
  and crushed
500g carton creamed
  tomatoes or passata

1 bay leaf and 1 thyme
  sprig
salt and pepper
golden caster sugar
3tbsp chopped basil

1 Heat the oil in a pan, add the garlic and fry for 30 seconds only – cook it very briefly; if it browns it will taste bitter.
2 Immediately add the tomatoes or passata, bay leaf and thyme. Season to taste and add a large pinch of sugar. Bring to the boil, then reduce the heat and simmer, uncovered, for 5–10 minutes.
3 Remove the bay leaf and thyme, add the basil and use immediately. This is good with pasta, or cooked meats such as lamb, pork or chicken.

Serves 4
Preparation: 5 minutes
Cooking time: 15 minutes
Per serving: 60 cals; 3g fat; 6g carbohydrate

Sauces and salsas

Creamy Mushroom and Wine Sauce

2tbsp oil
2 shallots or 1 onion,
peeled and
finely diced
175g (6oz) button or
cup mushrooms,
sliced
150g (5oz) mixed wild
mushrooms, sliced

2 garlic cloves, peeled
and crushed
150ml (¼ pint) white
wine
200ml (7fl oz) crème
fraîche
salt and pepper
2tsp chopped thyme

1 Heat the oil in a pan, add the shallots and cook gently for 10 minutes. Add all the mushrooms and garlic and cook over a high heat for 4–5 minutes until tender and all the moisture has been driven off. Pour in the wine, bring to the boil and let bubble until reduced by half.
2 Add the crème fraîche, 100ml (3½fl oz) water and seasoning. Bring to the boil and bubble for 5 minutes or until the liquid is slightly thickened and syrupy.
3 Add the thyme, adjust the seasoning a immediately. This sauce is great with pan-frie chicken.

Serves 6
Preparation: 10 minutes
Cooking time: 20 minutes
Per serving: 190 cals; 18g fat; 3g carbohydrate

Curried Coconut Sauce

2tbsp extra-virgin olive
oil
175g (6oz) onions,
peeled and
finely chopped
2 garlic cloves, peeled
and crushed

2.5cm (1 inch) piece
fresh root ginger,
peeled and grated
3–4tbsp mild curry
paste
3tbsp coconut milk
powder
salt

Serves 6
Preparation: 5 minutes
Cooking time: 20 minutes
Per serving: 80 cals; 7g fat; 3g carbohydrate

1 Heat the oil in a pan, add the onions with 1tbsp water and cook gently for 10 minutes or until softened and golden brown.
2 Add the garlic, ginger and curry paste and cook for 1–2 minutes.
3 Mix the coconut milk powder with 450ml (¾ pint) warm water, stir into the curried mixture and bring to the boil. Let it bubble for 5–10 minutes. Season with salt to taste. This curried sauce is particularly good with fish and shellfish.

Wild Mushroom Sauce

25g (1oz) butter
2 shallots, blanched in
   boiling water, drained,
   peeled and finely
   chopped
100g (3½oz) button
   mushrooms, sliced
100g (3½oz) wild
   mushrooms, sliced

50ml (2fl oz) brandy
200ml (7fl oz) red wine
2tsp plain flour
600ml (1 pint) hot
   chicken stock
salt and pepper

1 Melt the butter in a large frying pan, add the shallots and
   fry for 1 minute. Add all the mushrooms and cook for
   2 minutes, then pour in the brandy. Bring to the boil
   and bubble to reduce by half. Add the wine, return to
   the boil and reduce until syrupy.
2 Stir in the flour, mix until smooth, then add the stock.
   Bring to the boil and bubble for 15–20 minutes until
   syrupy. Season. Cover and refrigerate for up to two
   days; bring slowly to the boil to use. Good with steaks.

Serves 8
Preparation: 10 minutes
Cooking time: 30 minutes
Per serving: 60 cals; 3g fat; 2g carbohydrate

Shallot and Mushroom Sauce

400g (14oz) shallots,
   blanched in boiling
   water, drained and
   peeled
1tbsp olive oil
300ml (½ pint) red wine
225g (8oz) button
   mushrooms,
   quartered
1 celery stalk, cut in
   half

4 thyme sprigs
40g (1½oz) butter
350g (12oz) shallots,
   blanched in boiling
   water, drained and
   peeled
1tsp golden caster
   sugar
15g (½oz) plain flour

1 To make the sauce, finely chop 2 shallots. Heat the
   olive oil in a pan and cook the chopped shallots until
   golden brown. Add the wine, bring to the boil and
   bubble until reduced to about 2tbsp.
2 Add the mushrooms and cook for 3–4 minutes. Add
   600ml (1 pint) water, the celery and thyme, bring to the
   boil, then reduce the heat and simmer for 20 minutes.
3 Meanwhile, heat 25g (1oz) butter in a frying pan and add
   the remaining whole shallots and the sugar. Cover and
   cook over a low heat for 20–25 minutes.

4 Remove the thyme and celery from the sauce and pour
   over the shallots. Bring to the boil and bubble,
   uncovered, until reduced by half. To thicken the sauce,
   soften the remaining butter and combine with the flour,
   then whisk into the sauce. Simmer for 1–2 minutes,
   then season and serve. A good sauce for pan-fried
   steak or chicken.

Serves 4–6
Preparation: 10 minutes
Cooking time: 1 hour 20 minutes
Per serving: 170–110 cals; 12–8g fat;
12–8g carbohydrate

Onion Sauce

125g (4oz) unsalted butter
5 onions, peeled and sliced
1.1 litres (2 pints) semi-skimmed milk
2 cloves

125g (4oz) plain flour
½tsp freshly grated nutmeg
142ml carton double cream
salt and pepper

1 Put 50g (2oz) butter in a pan and melt over a low heat. Add the onions and cook for 25 minutes until soft but not coloured. Stir to make sure they don't stick. Take off the heat and mash.
2 Meanwhile, pour the milk into a pan and add the cloves. Bring to the boil, then turn off the heat and leave to infuse.
3 Melt the remaining butter in a pan. Add the flour and nutmeg and stir with a wooden spoon for 2–3 minutes until the mixture browns.

4 Add one-third of the milk, stirring all the time to remove any lumps. As the sauce starts to thicken, stir in the remaining milk, leaving the cloves behind in the pan. Bring to the boil, then reduce the heat and simmer for 1 minute.
5 Stir in the cream, then add the cooked mashed onions. Season and continue to cook over a low heat for 30 minutes, stirring every now and then. Spoon into a warm bowl and serve with roast goose.

Serves 8
Preparation: 10 minutes
Cooking time: 55 minutes
Per serving: 360 cals; 24g fat; 29g carbohydrate

See picture, page 487

Caramelised Onion Sauce

scant 60g (2½oz) butter
250g (9oz) onions, peeled and finely sliced
4tsp golden caster sugar
4tsp balsamic vinegar

200ml (7fl oz) white wine
450ml (¾ pint) fresh chicken or vegetable stock
salt and pepper
20g (¾oz) plain flour

1 Melt 40g (1½oz) butter in a pan, add the onions and cook gently for 5–10 minutes or until soft.
2 Add the sugar and vinegar, bring to the boil and bubble until almost all the liquid has evaporated and the onions are dark brown.
3 Add the wine and bring to the boil, then bubble to reduce by half. Add the stock, bring to the boil and bubble for 5 minutes; season to taste.

4 To thicken the sauce, soften the remaining butter and combine with the flour. Whisk into the bubbling sauce, a little at a time, and simmer for 3–4 minutes. Check the seasoning and serve, or cover and chill for up to 24 hours, then reheat the sauce in a pan. This goes well with roast pork.

Serves 4–6
Preparation: 10 minutes
Cooking time: 45–50 minutes
Per serving: 190–120 cals; 12–8g fat; 14–9g carbohydrate

Sweet Onion and Mustard Sauce

75g (3oz) butter
350g (12oz) onions, peeled and finely sliced
200ml (7fl oz) hot

brown stock, such as beef or chicken
1tbsp Dijon mustard
1tsp sugar
salt and pepper

1   Melt the butter in a heavy-based pan, add the onions, cover and cook over a low heat for 20–25 minutes. Cook, uncovered, for a further 5 minutes or until all the liquid has evaporated and the onions have turned golden brown.
2   Add the hot stock, mustard and sugar and season well. Bubble for about 10 minutes or until reduced and syrupy. This sauce goes well with bubble and squeak.

Serves 4–6
Preparation: 5 minutes
Cooking time: 40 minutes
Per serving: 180–120 cals; 15–10g fat;
8–5g carbohydrate

Mustard and Caper Sauce

2 hard-boiled eggs
2tsp smooth Dijon mustard
2tbsp white wine vinegar

8tbsp olive oil
2tbsp chopped capers
1tbsp chopped shallot
pinch of sugar
salt and pepper

1   Mash the egg yolks with the mustard. Add the vinegar and slowly whisk in the olive oil.
2   Add the capers, shallot and a pinch of sugar. Season well and serve with grilled fish, beef, pork or sausages.

Serves 4–6
Preparation: 15 minutes
Per serving: 280–190 cals; 29–19g fat;
1–1g carbohydrate

Parsley Sauce

300ml (½ pint) full-fat milk
15g (½oz) each butter and plain flour

2tbsp chopped flat-leafed parsley
salt and pepper

1   Put the milk, butter and flour in a pan. Heat gently, whisking all the time, and bring to the boil. Simmer for 3–5 minutes, then add the parsley and season well. Use at once – it goes well with roasted cod.

Serves 4–6
Preparation: 5 minutes
Cooking time: 3–5 minutes
Per serving: 90–60 cals; 6–4g fat;
7–4g carbohydrate

Red Onion and Thyme Confit

3tbsp olive oil
450g (1lb) red onions,
  peeled and
  finely chopped
1tsp chopped thyme
200ml (7fl oz) dry white
  wine

3tbsp wine vinegar
2tbsp dark muscovado
  sugar
salt and pepper

1   Heat the olive oil in a small pan, then add the onions and
   thyme. Cook, stirring, for 10 minutes or until the onions
   are soft.
2   Add the wine, vinegar and sugar to the pan. Bring
   to the boil, then reduce the heat and simmer gently
   for 40 minutes or until the onions are very soft and
   almost all the liquid has evaporated. Season well and
   serve warm.

Serves 4
Preparation: 15 minutes
Cooking time: 55 minutes
Per 1tbsp: 20 cals; 1g fat; 2g carbohydrate

Hot Harissa Paste

25g (1oz) dried red
  chillies
1 garlic clove, peeled
  and chopped
1 tsp caraway seeds

1 tsp cumin seeds
1 tsp coriander seeds
pinch of salt
olive oil

1   Soak the chillies in hot water for 1 hour. Drain well, then
   put in a pestle and mortar or electric mill with the garlic,
   spices and salt and grind to a paste.
2   Put into a small jar, cover with olive oil and seal. Harissa
   will keep in the fridge for up to 2 months. The oil can
   be used in salad dressings.

Serves 4
Preparation: 10 minutes, plus standing
Per serving 15 cals; 3g fat; 0g carbohydrate

Apple Sauce

2 large Bramley
  cooking apples,
  peeled, cored and
  roughly chopped
juice of 1 orange and
  1 lemon

50g (2oz) light
  muscovado sugar
25g (1oz) butter
good pinch of freshly
  grated nutmeg
salt and pepper

1   Put the apples in a pan and add the orange and lemon
   juice and 125ml (4fl oz) water. Cook gently for 5–10
   minutes until the apples are soft.
2   Take off the heat and mash the apples, then add the
   sugar, butter and grated nutmeg. Season, then return
   to the hob and bring to the boil. Reduce the heat and
   simmer for 1 minute. Traditionally served with roast
   pork, but also great with goose.

Serves 8
Preparation: 5 minutes
Cooking time: 6–11 minutes
Per serving: 70 cals; 3g fat; 13g carbohydrates

See picture, page 487

Cranberry, Honey and Ginger Sauce

zest of 1 and juice of
2 large oranges
350g (12oz) fresh or
thawed frozen
cranberries
4tbsp runny honey

150ml (¼ pint) port or
red wine
2.5cm (1 inch) piece
fresh root ginger,
peeled and finely
grated

1 Put all the ingredients into a pan and bring to the boil,
then reduce the heat and simmer gently, uncovered, for
about 25 minutes.
2 Using a slotted spoon, remove about half the
cranberries and put them into a blender. Whiz until
smooth, then return the purée to the pan and mix in well.
3 Taste the sauce and add extra honey if necessary.
Cool, put into an airtight container and freeze for up
to one month.

Serves 8
Preparation: 10 minutes
Cooking time: 25–30 minutes
Per serving: 60 calories, 0g fat, 11g carbohydrate

Cranberry and Red Onion Marmalade

2tbsp olive oil
500g (1lb 2oz) red
onions, peeled and
sliced
juice of 1 orange
1tbsp pickling spice

150g (5oz) dark
muscovado sugar
150ml (¼ pint) ruby port
450g (1lb) fresh
cranberries

1 Heat the olive oil in a pan and fry the onions gently for
5 minutes. Add the orange juice, spice, sugar and port
and simmer gently for 40 minutes.
2 Add the cranberries and cook over a medium heat for
20 minutes. Cool and chill for up to two days. Serve at
room temperature.

Serves 12
Preparation: 10 minutes, plus chilling
Cooking time: 1 hour 5 minutes
Per serving: 110 cals; 2g fat; 20g carbohydrate

Cranberry Sauce

350g (12oz) cranberries
125g (4oz) golden
caster sugar
grated rind and juice of
1 orange

1–2tbsp port
8 juniper berries,
crushed

1 Put all the ingredients in a pan, bring to the boil,
then reduce the heat and simmer until the cranberries
pop and the sauce thickens. Serve at Christmas with
the turkey.

Serves 8
Preparation: 5 minutes
Cooking time: 5 minutes
Per serving: 70 cals; 0g fat; 18g carbohydrate

*Top left: Cranberry Sauce, page 486; top right: Onion Sauce,
page 483; bottom left: Apple Sauce, page 485; bottom right:
Special Bread Sauce, page 478.*

Preserves

Stuck for ideas for an unusual present? Why not give a jar of Spiced Clementines and Kumquats in Brandy, or Spiced Pickled Peaches? Tart up the jar with a fancy label and some raffia and it will look very special indeed.

The same goes for chutnies – friends will love your homemade Mango and Ginger; Pumpkin, Apricot and Almond; or Spiced Pepper, and they're so easy to make.

Pickles are great served with cold meats, Ploughman's, salads, fish and chips, black pudding you name it. Summer Pickle is packed with vegetables, mushrooms and tomatoes and is perfect for serving when you're having a barbecue. While Pickled Onions and Pickled Red Cabbage are great Christmas favourites.

And talking of Christmas, the Almond Whisky Mincemeat; Spicy Carrot; or Mixed Fruit and Nut mincemeats will really get your mince pies talked about. Packed with fruit, spices, nuts and alcohol, they can be made ahead and kept for months.

Jam – rich and dark, light and lemony, or sweet and sharp, smeared on to buttery toast or crumbly scones, it's what teatime is all about. And don't forget the marmalade – try Ginger and Grapefruit Jelly, with the citrus tang of grapefruit and the spicy zing of fresh and preserved ginger.

Get preserving!

Blackberry and Apple Jam

900g (2lb) Bramley or other cooking apples, peeled, cored and diced
juice of 1 large lemon
900g (2lb) blackberries
1.2kg (2¾lb) granulated sugar
5tbsp crème de mûre (blackberry liqueur)
15g (½oz) butter

1 Put the apples and 300ml (½ pint) water into a preserving pan and bring to the boil. Reduce the heat and cook gently for 10–12 minutes or until soft.
2 Add the lemon juice and blackberries and return to the boil, then reduce the heat and simmer for 12–15 minutes or until the blackberries begin to break up.
3 Add the sugar to the pan and heat slowly until it has dissolved, stirring occasionally. Increase the heat and cook at a rolling boil for 10–12 minutes. Add the liqueur and test for a set.
4 Once setting point is reached, stir in the butter and leave to settle. Take off the heat, remove the scum with a slotted spoon and leave to stand for 15 minutes, then pot and cover and label the jars.

Makes 2.7kg (6lb)
Preparation: 10 minutes, plus standing
Cooking time: 50 minutes
Per 1tbsp serving: 30 cals; trace fat; 9g carbohydrate

Strawberry Jam

900g (2lb) strawberries, hulled
1kg (2¼lb) sugar with pectin
juice of ½ lemon

1 Put the strawberries in a preserving pan with the sugar and lemon juice. Heat gently until the sugar has dissolved, stirring frequently.
2 Bring to the boil and boil steadily for about 4 minutes or until setting point is reached.
3 Take off the heat, remove any scum with a slotted spoon and leave to stand for 15–20 minutes.
4 Stir the jam gently, then pot and cover and label the jars.

Makes 1.8kg (4lb)
Preparation: 10 minutes, plus standing
Cooking time: 10 minutes
Per 1tbsp serving: 60 cals; 0g fat; 15g carbohydrate

Blackcurrant Jam

900g (2lb) blackcurrants
1.4kg (3lb) sugar

1 If you have time, gently prick each currant and place in a bowl with the sugar. Cover and leave overnight.
2 Transfer the fruit and sugar to a pan, bring slowly to the boil and boil for 3 minutes or until setting point is reached.
3 Remove the pan from the heat and leave for about 30 minutes, until a skin begins to form. Stir gently to distribute the fruit, then pot and cover and label the jars.

Makes 2.3kg (5lb)
Preparation: 10 minutes, plus standing
Cooking time: 10 minutes
Per 1tbsp serving: 65 cals; 0g fat; 17g carbohydrate

Top left: Piccalilli, page 509; top right: Strawberry and Redcurrant Jam, page 514; bottom left: Seville Orange Marmalade, page 517; bottom right: Mixed Dill Pickle page 508.

Cooking to impress

There comes a time when you really want to throw a good bash. It might be casual or you might want to make it extra special, but either way you'll want to impress.

Catering for crowds needn't be daunting – keep it simple, get organised and don't panic! The Entertaining Menu for 10 has a simple but tasty starter that can be assembled ahead of time, then an amazing chilled chicken, prawn and rice dish, followed by fruit salads and a delicious cake that will be truly memorable.

And that goes for the Winter Menu for 20, too. With two sides of roasted salmon as its centrepiece, the menu also includes easy bites and salads with a grand finale of a luscious black cherry and mascarpone gateau.

The thought of cooking a full Christmas lunch can send some cooks running for the gin, but the Perfect Christmas Lunch for 8 will be just that – perfect. The turkey is the star of the show, but its co-stars all play their part, from the Crisp and Crunchy Roast Potatoes, to the Sweet-glazed Chipolatas and Brussels Sprouts with Hazelnut Butter. And then – the grand finale: a fabulous Christmas pudding, flamed in brandy and served with Boozy Cream and Muscovado Butter. Impressive, indeed.

Brunch Menu

SERVES 8

Soft-boiled Eggs with Rosemary and Garlic Fingers

American Pancakes with Secret Muscovado Bacon

Sweet Spiced Oranges

American Pancakes

175g (6oz) self-raising flour, sifted
2tsp baking powder
1 pinch of salt
142ml carton soured cream
3 large eggs, beaten
75g (3oz) unsalted butter

1 Put the flour in a large bowl. Stir in the baking powder and salt and make a well in the centre.
2 Whisk the soured cream, 100ml (3½fl oz) cold water and the eggs together in a jug. Gradually whisk this mixture into the flour until you have a smooth, slightly thick batter.
3 Put a large solid non-stick frying pan over a medium heat. Add 1tsp butter and heat until it shimmers. Spoon half a ladle of batter into the middle of the pan to make a thickish pancake.
4 After about 1 minute bubbles will appear on the surface of the pancake, at which point it's ready to be turned. Flip it over and cook for 45 seconds on the other side – it should puff up like a little soufflé. Lift the pancake on to a warm plate and continue with the remaining batter mixture and butter.
5 Serve the pancakes with the muscovado bacon (opposite) and a drizzle of maple syrup, or with Greek-style yogurt and honey.

Serves 8
Preparation: 10 minutes
Cooking time: 15 minutes
Per serving: 210 cals; 14g fat; 17g carbohydrate

Soft-boiled Eggs with Rosemary and Garlic Fingers

8 large eggs
2 rosemary and garlic
  focaccia, each cut
  into 8 slices
butter

1 Bring a large pan of water to the boil. Prick the bottom of each egg with a pin. Once the water is boiling, lower in the eggs. Cook for 4 minutes for soft and runny or 6 minutes for medium-boiled.
2 Meanwhile, toast the focaccia slices, then spread with butter. Serve with the eggs.

Serves 8
Preparation: 5 minutes
Cooking time: 10 minutes
Per serving: 400 cals; 24g fat; 33g carbohydrate

Secret Muscovado Bacon Recipe

vegetable oil   **4tbsp light muscovado**
700g (1½lb) smoked   **sugar**
  back bacon rashers

1 Preheat the grill. Lightly oil a baking sheet and put the bacon in a single layer on top – you may need to do two batches.
2 Sprinkle the bacon with sugar and grill until crisp.

Serves 8
Preparation: 5 minutes
Cooking time: 20 minutes
Per serving: 330 cals; 26g fat; 5g carbohydrate

Sweet Spiced Oranges

3 cloves   **300ml (½ pint) distilled**
1 cinnamon stick   **malt vinegar**
small piece fresh root **6 large navel oranges,**
  ginger, peeled and   **thinly sliced**
  bruised   **150ml (¼ pint) maple**
225g (8oz) golden   **syrup**
  caster sugar

1 Put the spices, sugar and vinegar in a large pan with 600ml (1 pint) cold water. Heat gently until the sugar has completely dissolved, then bring to the boil and bubble for 10 minutes to make a thin syrup.
2 Put the orange slices in the pan, reduce the heat and simmer for 5 minutes until tender but not broken down. Lift out the oranges and pack into a sterilised jar.
3 Boil the syrup until reduced by half, then stir in the maple syrup and pour over the oranges to cover. Seal and cool. Keep in a cool place for up to two months.

Serves 8
Preparation: 10 minutes
Cooking time: 25 minutes
Per serving: 210 cals; trace fat; 55g carbohydrate

Friday-night Menu

SERVES 8

Smoked Haddock Fish Pie

Green Bean and Pea Salad

Caramelised Pineapple

Smoked Haddock Fish Pie

1.8kg (4lb) large floury potatoes, preferably Maris Piper or Desirée, peeled and roughly chopped
salt and pepper
3 medium-sized undyed smoked haddock or cod fillets, about 1.1kg (2½lb), cut into 5 x 5cm (2 x 2 inch) pieces

2 x 20g packs flat-leafed parsley, or 1 medium bunch, roughly chopped
2 fat garlic cloves, peeled and crushed
about 175g (6oz) unsalted butter
olive oil, to fry
1tbsp Dijon mustard
500ml carton full-fat crème fraîche

1 Put the potatoes into a large pan of lightly salted water and bring to the boil, then reduce the heat and simmer for about 20 minutes until very tender.
2 Meanwhile, put the fish into a bowl, add the parsley and garlic and toss gently to coat.
3 Heat 40g (1½oz) butter in a large frying pan with a drizzle of olive oil until it starts to foam. Put half the fish pieces into the pan and fry over a very high heat for about 1 minute until they form a golden crust on the underside. Turn over and fry on the other side until the fish is opaque – just 2–3 minutes or it will overcook.
4 Take the pan off the heat and add half the mustard and half the crème fraîche to the fish. Leave it to melt in the heat of the pan (without stirring, to prevent the fish from breaking up), then spoon the mixture into a large ovenproof serving dish.
5 Wipe out the pan and repeat steps 3 and 4 with another 40g (1½oz) butter and the remaining fish, mustard and crème fraîche. The fish mixture will look quite liquid at this stage, but that's fine.
6 Preheat the grill. Drain the potatoes, tip them back into the pan and return to the heat for 1–2 minutes to dry. Mash with the remaining butter, plenty of pepper and 6tbsp of the fish cooking liquid. Beat the potatoes, taste for seasoning, then spoon the mash over the fish.
7 Pop the dish under the grill for a few minutes until the potato is golden, then serve immediately.

Serves 8
Preparation: 30 minutes
Cooking time: 30 minutes
Per serving: 670 cals; 46g fat; 37g carbohydrate

Green Bean and Pea Salad

3 slices ready-made
  garlic bread
200g (7oz) fine French
  beans
salt
190g pack shelled peas
2 x 120g bags salad
  leaves
6tbsp extra-virgin olive
  oil
1tbsp white wine
  vinegar
1tbsp wholegrain
  mustard
½ small garlic clove,
  peeled and crushed
pinch of golden caster
  sugar
mint sprigs, to garnish

1 Preheat the grill. Toast the garlic bread on both sides
   under a hot grill until golden and crisp. Leave to cool,
   then put into a food processor or blender and whiz to
   make rough breadcrumbs.
2 Cook the French beans in boiling salted water for
   5 minutes, then add the peas. Bring back to the boil and
   bubble for 2 minutes until the beans are just tender.
   Drain the vegetables well, then drop into a bowl of iced
   water to cool immediately and keep their fresh green
   colour; drain well again.
3 Put the vegetables into a large bowl, then put the salad
   leaves on top. Cover with clingfilm and chill.
4 To make the dressing, whisk together the remaining
   ingredients in a bowl, then toss with the salad leaves,
   vegetables and breadcrumbs. Garnish with mint sprigs
   and serve.

Serves 8
Preparation: 25 minutes
Cooking time: 10 minutes
Per serving: 140 cals; 10g fat; 10g carbohydrate

Caramelised Pineapple

1 large, ripe pineapple
4 passion fruit
juice of 1 orange
4tbsp light muscovado
  sugar

1 Using a sharp knife, cut the top and tail off the
   pineapple. Stand the fruit on a board and cut away all
   the peel, slicing from top to bottom. Slice the flesh into
   12 rounds, then cut each in half.
2 Preheat the grill. Halve the passion fruit and spoon the
   juice and seeds into a sieve resting over a bowl. Stir well
   to extract the juice. Discard the seeds, then add the
   orange juice to the bowl.
3 Lay half the pineapple slices in a single layer on a
   baking sheet, then sprinkle with half the sugar and half
   the fruit juice. Grill for about 2–3 minutes until the sugar
   begins to bubble and caramelise, then spoon the
   pineapple and juices into a dish. Grill the rest of the
   pineapple with the remaining sugar and juice.
4 Put three pieces of pineapple on each serving plate
   with some of the cooking juices. Delicious served with
   a scoop or two of mango sorbet.

Serves 8
Preparation: 20 minutes
Cooking time: 10 minutes
Per serving: 120 cals; 0g fat; 31g carbohydrate

Saturday Dinner

SERVES 8

Prawn and Guacamole Cocktail

Sticky Honey and Ginger Chicken

Mango and Red Pepper Relish

Coconut Rice

Apricot and Coconut Tart

Prawn and Guacamole Cocktail

400g (14oz) cooked, peeled king prawns
150ml (¼ pint) salad dressing, such as Roasted Red Pepper Dressing (page 000)
2 ripe avocados, peeled, stoned and sliced
16 cherry tomatoes, quartered
4 little gem lettuces, halved and shredded
2 x 300g tubs fresh guacamole dip
2 limes, cut into wedges
black pepper

1 Put the prawns and 6tbsp dressing in a bowl, stir, then cover. Put the avocado and tomatoes in a separate small bowl, stir in the remaining dressing, then cover. Chill both bowls in the fridge for 2 hours.
2 To serve, put the lettuce leaves in the base of eight dishes. Spoon the avocado and tomatoes on top, then the prawns and a dollop of guacamole. Finish with a lime wedge and a grinding of black pepper.

Serves 8
Preparation: 20 minutes, plus marinating
Per serving: 460 cals; 42g fat; 9g carbohydrate

Sticky Honey and Ginger Chicken

2tsp ground turmeric
250g (9oz) runny honey
10cm (4 inch) piece
   fresh root ginger,
   peeled and finely
   grated
2 fat garlic cloves,
   peeled and crushed

grated zest and juice of
   2 large limes
175g (6oz) sweet Thai
   chilli dipping sauce
8 chicken breasts, skin
   on
600ml (1 pint) white
   wine

1 To make the marinade, put the turmeric, honey, ginger, garlic, lime zest and juice and chilli sauce into a bowl, then whisk to combine. Make several deep slashes through the skin and flesh of each chicken breast, then add them to the bowl and stir to coat in the mixture. Cover with clingfilm and leave in the fridge overnight.

2 Preheat the oven to 220°C (200°C fan oven) mark 7. Lift the chicken breasts from the marinade and put them, skin side up, in a roasting tin just large enough to hold them in a single layer (any larger and the marinade will burn). Spoon over 4tbsp of the marinade and roast for 30–35 minutes until the chicken is golden and cooked through. Keep warm.

3 Put the remaining marinade into a pan with the wine and bring to the boil. Bubble for 10–12 minutes until reduced by half and syrupy. Serve the chicken with the sauce and Mango and Red Pepper Relish (below).

Serves 8
Preparation: 15 minutes, plus marinating
Cooking time: 40–50 minutes
Per serving: 400 cals; 18g fat; 25g carbohydrate

Mango and Red Pepper Relish

2 ripe mangoes, peeled
   and chopped
125g (4oz) roasted red
   peppers from a jar,
   halved, deseeded and
   sliced
2 small red onions,
   peeled and finely
   sliced

4tbsp sweet Thai chilli
   dipping sauce
grated zest of 2 limes,
   plus the juice of
   3 limes
20g pack of coriander

1 Put the mango in a bowl with the red peppers and onions. Add the dipping sauce, lime zest and juice, toss together, cover and chill until needed.

2 Just before serving, roughly chop the coriander leaves, add to the relish and mix well.

Serves 8
Preparation: 10 minutes
Per serving: 50 cals; trace fat; 11g carbohydrate

Coconut Rice

25g (1oz) butter
450g (1lb) long-grain
   rice, rinsed and
   drained

1tsp salt
50g (2oz) creamed
   coconut

1 Melt the butter in a large pan, add the rice and stir to coat all the rice in butter. Add 1.1 litres (2 pints) cold water and the salt. Cover the pan and bring to the boil, then reduce the heat and simmer for 20–25 minutes (or as stated on the packet) until all the water has been absorbed.

2 Once cooked, remove the pan from the heat and add the creamed coconut. Cover the pan with a clean tea-towel and replace the lid to allow the coconut to melt and the rice to absorb any steam. Fluff up with a fork before serving.

Serves 8
Preparation: 5 minutes
Cooking time: 20–25 minutes
Per serving: 270 cals; 7g fat; 45g carbohydrate

Apricot and Coconut Tart

375g pack Saxby's
  dessert pastry
flour, to dust
125g (4oz) butter,
  softened
125g (4oz) golden
  caster sugar
2 eggs
75g (3oz) ground
  almonds
25g (1oz) desiccated
  coconut, plus extra to
  sprinkle

zest and juice of
  ½ small orange
400g can apricot
  halves in juice,
  drained
1tbsp golden icing
  sugar, to glaze, plus
  a little to dust

1 Preheat the oven to 190°C (170°C fan oven) mark 5 and put a heavy flat baking sheet in to preheat. Roll the pastry out on a lightly floured surface and use to line a 23cm (9 inch) fluted flan tin. Prick the base of the pastry with a fork, then line with greaseproof paper and fill with baking beans.

2 Put the pastry case on the baking sheet and bake for 15 minutes. Remove the baking beans and cook for 10 minutes until dry and pale golden. Leave the baking sheet in the oven and put the pastry case aside to cool.

3 Using an electric whisk, beat together the butter and caster sugar until light and creamy, then gradually beat in the eggs. Using a wooden spoon, stir in the ground almonds, coconut and orange zest.

4 Spoon the filling into the pastry case, then top with the apricots, skin side up. Put the tart back on the baking sheet and bake for 40–45 minutes until golden (cover with foil if the top gets too dark). The filling won't be totally set but will firm up as it cools.

5 Mix the icing sugar and orange juice in a bowl to a thin icing. Remove the tart from the oven and spoon the icing evenly over the tart, then sprinkle with coconut. Return to the oven for 5–10 minutes to glaze the top. To serve, dust with icing sugar and a little coconut.

Serves 8
Preparation: 35 minutes
Cooking time: 1 hour 10 minutes–1 hour 20 minutes
Per serving: 530 cals; 35g fat; 51g carbohydrate

Easter Menu

SERVES 8

Stuffed Leg of Lamb

Redcurrant and Red Wine Sauce

Sweet Roasted Carrots

Purple Sprouting Broccoli with Pine Nuts

Minted Sugarsnaps

Saffron-baked Potatoes

Chocolate Truffle Torte

Stuffed Leg of Lamb

25g (1oz) butter
75ml (3fl oz) olive oil
1 small red onion, peeled and finely chopped
450g (1lb) chestnut mushrooms, finely chopped
1tbsp chopped oregano
½ x 20g pack thyme, leaves stripped, plus extra sprigs to garnish

20g pack flat-leafed parsley, finely chopped
salt and pepper
1 leg of new-season lamb, about 2.7kg (6lb), knucklebone removed but end bone left in
2 medium garlic bulbs

1 First make the stuffing. Melt the butter in a frying pan with 2tbsp olive oil. Add the onion and fry gently for 10–15 minutes until soft and golden. Add the mushrooms and cook over a brisk heat for 15–20 minutes – the juices will evaporate and the mixture become dryish, but continue to cook, stirring all the time, until the mushrooms begin to turn golden brown at the edges. Add the herbs and cook for 1 minute. Remove from the heat, season and leave to cool.

2 Preheat the oven to 190°C (170°C fan oven) mark 5. Open out the lamb and spread the mushroom stuffing over the meat. Reshape the lamb and sew securely with string. Weigh the lamb and calculate the cooking time. Allow 25 minutes per 450g (1lb) for lamb with just a tinge of pink – for this leg it should be about 2½–3 hours.

3 Put the lamb in a roasting tin and season. Transfer to the oven and baste occasionally to keep the meat succulent. Halfway through the cooking time, put a few thyme sprigs on top.

4 About 1 hour before the end of the cooking time, rub the whole garlic bulbs with a little oil and put them in the oven alongside the lamb for 45 minutes–1 hour until very soft. Remove from the oven and keep them warm until ready to serve.

5 To tell if the lamb is cooked to your liking, insert a skewer into the centre, remove it, then press the flat of the skewer against the meat: the pinker the juice that runs out, the rarer the meat. When it's sufficiently cooked, remove the lamb to a carving board and cover with a tent of foil to keep warm while you make the Redcurrant and Red Wine Sauce (page 000).

6 To serve, carve the lamb and garnish with the roasted garlic, broken into cloves. Drizzle with a little of the sauce and hand the rest round in a jug.

Serves 8
Preparation: 40 minutes
Cooking time: 3 hours–3 hours 40 minutes, plus resting
Per serving: 400 cals; 23g fat; 2g carbohydrate

Redcurrant and Red Wine Sauce

600ml (1 pint) fruity red wine
6tbsp redcurrant jelly
3tbsp Worcestershire sauce
juice of 1 lemon and 1 orange
roasting juices from the lamb
2tbsp plain flour
2tsp English mustard powder

1 Pour the wine into a small pan and add the redcurrant jelly, Worcestershire sauce and lemon and orange juice. Heat very gently until the jelly melts.
2 Spoon off the fat from the tin the lamb was roasted in until 2tbsp remains. Put the tin over a low heat and stir in the flour and mustard powder to make a smooth paste.
3 Increase the heat and pour in the wine mixture a little at a time. Mix with a wooden spoon after each addition, scraping up any crusty bits. Once all the wine is in, swap the spoon for a whisk and whisk until the sauce is smooth. Reduce the heat and bubble gently for 10 minutes, then pour into a warm jug.

Serves 8
Preparation: 10 minutes
Cooking time: 25 minutes
Per serving: 120 cals; 4g fat; 12g carbohydrate

Sweet Roasted Carrots

900g (2lb) whole new baby carrots, trimmed
4tbsp fat and roasting juices from the lamb
salt and pepper

1 After the lamb has been in the oven for 2 hours, put the carrots in a roasting tin. Spoon over the fat and roasting juices from the lamb and toss to coat. Season well, then roast for 45 minutes–1 hour.
2 Remove from the oven and transfer to a serving dish.

Serves 8
Preparation: 10 minutes
Cooking time: 45 minutes–1 hour
Per serving: 60 cals; 4g fat; 7g carbohydrate

Purple Sprouting Broccoli with Pine Nuts

50g (2oz) pine nuts
1.1kg (2½lb) purple sprouting broccoli
50g (2oz) raisins
small knob of butter

1 Put the pine nuts in a frying pan and dry-fry them for 2–3 minutes until golden. Put to one side.
2 Bring a large pan of water to the boil. Trim the ends off the broccoli and chop any large stems in two. Add to the water and cook for 5–6 minutes. Add the raisins and cook for another 2–3 minutes until the broccoli is tender.
3 Drain the broccoli and raisins, then toss with the pine nuts and the butter. Serve immediately.

Serves 8
Preparation: 5 minutes
Cooking time: about 10 minutes
Per serving: 110 cals; 7g fat; 8g carbohydrate

Saffron-baked Potatoes

generous pinch of
  saffron strands
600ml (1 pint) hot
  vegetable stock
50g (2oz) butter,
  melted, plus extra to
  grease

12 medium-sized
  baking potatoes,
  preferably Desirée,
  peeled
salt and pepper
leaves from ½ x 20g
  pack thyme

1 Preheat the oven to 190°C (170°C fan oven) mark 5. Put the saffron strands in a small bowl, add 2tbsp hot stock and leave to soak for 10 minutes, then stir into the remaining stock.

2 Meanwhile, grease a deep ovenproof dish. Cut the potatoes into thin slices and arrange them in the dish in layers, sprinkling each layer with thyme and seasoning well.

3 Spoon the melted butter over the potatoes, then pour the hot saffron stock over the top. Transfer to the oven and cook uncovered for 1–1¼ hours, basting occasionally, until the liquid is completely absorbed and the potatoes are crisp and golden brown. Season, then serve immediately.

Serves 8
Preparation: 30 minutes
Cooking time: 1–1¼ hours
Per serving: 270 cals; 6g fat; 52g carbohydrate

Minted Sugarsnaps

500g (1lb 2oz)
  sugarsnap peas
2 mint sprigs

15g (½oz) butter
salt and pepper

1 Bring a large pan of water to the boil, then add the peas and one mint sprig. Bring back to the boil, then reduce the heat and simmer for 3–4 minutes. Drain well and return to the warm pan.

2 Add the butter and seasoning, then toss to coat. Tip the peas into a warm serving bowl and garnish with the remaining mint sprig.

Serves 8
Preparation: 2 minutes
Cooking time: about 10 minutes
Per serving: 40 cals; 2g fat; 3g carbohydrate

flavourless oil, such as
   safflower, to oil
3 large eggs, plus
   3 large egg yolks
150g (5oz) golden
   caster sugar
25g (1oz) plain flour
1tbsp cocoa powder,
   plus extra to dust
3tbsp Tia Maria
300g (11oz) good-
   quality plain dark
   chocolate (with
   minimum 50% cocoa
   solids), broken into
   chunks

200g (7oz) good-quality
   plain chocolate, semi-
   sweet such as
   Bournville, broken
   into chunks
568ml carton double
   cream
1tbsp instant espresso
   coffee
chocolate mini eggs
   and cocoa-dusted
   almonds, to decorate

1 Preheat the oven to 180°C (160°C fan oven) mark 4. Oil a 20.5cm (8 inch) loose-based cake tin and line the base with non-stick baking parchment.

2 To make the cake base, put the whole eggs into the bowl of a food mixer, add 75g (3oz) sugar, then mix on high speed until doubled in volume and very thick. (Or beat, using a hand-held electric whisk, in a large heatproof bowl set over a pan of simmering water until thick, then remove from the heat and whisk until cool.)

3 Sift the flour and cocoa powder together over the mixture and fold in carefully. Don't overfold, as you'll knock out the air and create a flat cake.

4 Pour the cake mixture into the prepared tin and bake for 25–30 minutes until well risen and shrinking away from the sides of the tin. Remove from the oven and leave the cake base in the tin for 10 minutes, then turn out and put on a wire rack, keeping the parchment on. Drizzle with the Tia Maria and put to one side to cool.

5 Remove the parchment and put the paper upside down in the cake tin. Brush with oil and return the cake base to the tin, turning it upside down and pressing firmly to fit.

6 Next, make the truffle mixture. Put all the chocolate in a heatproof bowl with half the cream and the espresso coffee, then set over a pan of simmering water. Once the chocolate has melted, stir gently to combine. Leave to cool.

7 Whip the remaining cream in a large bowl until soft peaks form. In another bowl, beat together the egg yolks and remaining sugar, using an electric whisk, until pale and fluffy. Whisk this mixture into the cooled chocolate, then fold gently into the whipped cream. Immediately pour over the cake base in the tin, then chill for at least 3 hours, or preferably overnight, until the truffle mixture has set firm.

8 To serve, run a warm knife around the edge of the torte and carefully remove from the tin. Dust with cocoa and decorate with mini eggs and cocoa-dusted almonds. Cut into slices to serve. The torte will keep in the fridge for up to five days.

Serves 10
Preparation: 40 minutes, plus chilling
Cooking time: 30–35 minutes
Per serving: 690 cals; 52g fat; 45g carbohydrate

18

Entertaining Menu

SERVES 10

Easiest Ever Canapés

Spicy Chicken and Prawn Rice with Crisp Fried
Shallots and Coconut Mayonnaise (see page 492)

Poached Peaches in Strawberry Syrup

Fresh Mango and Pineapple Salad

Orange and White Chocolate Cake

Easiest Ever Canapés

**200g (7oz) smoked
  salmon slices
100g (3½oz) full-fat
  soft cheese or
  goat's cheese
1tbsp dill-flavoured
  mustard or creamed
  horseradish
200g pack prosciutto
  (lightly smoked,
  Italian dry-cured ham)**

**about 2tbsp smooth
  fruity chutney, such
  as mango
1 large courgette
about 2tbsp hummus
20g pack chives, finely
  chopped
1 roasted red pepper,
  finely chopped
black pepper**

1 Lay the salmon slices out on a sheet of greaseproof paper. Spread thinly with a little soft cheese or goat's cheese, then very thinly with mustard or horseradish. Roll up into bite-sized rolls.
2 Lay the prosciutto on a board. Spread thinly with the cheese, then with chutney and roll up into bite-sized rolls.
3 Pare the courgette into wafer-thin strips with a vegetable peeler. Lay them on a board, spread with the cheese and hummus, then roll up.

4 Stand the rolls on end on a flat plate or greaseproof-lined baking sheet (trim bases if necessary). Cover with clingfilm and chill.
5 About 2 hours before serving, top each roll with a little cheese. Dip the salmon rolls into the chopped chives, the prosciutto rolls into the red pepper, and the courgette rolls into a little coarsely ground black pepper. Chill until ready to serve.

Serves 10
Preparation: 20 minutes
Per serving: 140 cals; 9g fat; 3g carbohydrate

Spicy Chicken and Prawn Rice with Crisp-fried Shallots

4 small skinless boneless chicken breasts, cut into bite-sized pieces
150ml (¼ pint) olive oil
2tsp ground turmeric
salt
450g (1lb) long-grain rice, washed
425g (15oz) shallots, blanched in boiling water, drained, peeled
4 garlic cloves, peeled and crushed
10cm (4 inch) piece fresh root ginger, peeled and finely grated
2tbsp garam masala
100g (3½oz) shelled pistachio nuts
150ml carton natural yogurt
150ml (¼ pint) chicken stock
200ml (7fl oz) vegetable oil
450g (1lb) cooked, peeled tiger prawns
6tbsp mild lime pickle
juice of 2 limes, about 6tbsp
6tbsp runny honey
2 x 20g packs basil, roughly torn
small bunch of flat-leafed parsley, roughly chopped
20g pack coriander, roughly chopped

1 Put the chicken in a bowl and stir in 2tbsp olive oil and the turmeric.
2 Put 1.7 litres (3 pints) cold water into a large pan, bring to the boil and add a good pinch of salt. Add the rice a little at a time so the water stays boiling. Stir once, then boil for 8 minutes and drain well.
3 In another large pan heat 2tbsp olive oil. Slice 225g (8oz) shallots thinly into rounds and add to the pan. Fry for 10 minutes or until soft and golden. Add the garlic and ginger and fry for 3–4 minutes, then remove the shallot mixture from the pan. Fry the chicken in batches for 10 minutes or until golden brown. Return all the chicken and the shallot mixture to the pan.
4 Stir in the garam masala and cook for 1–2 minutes, then add the nuts, yogurt and stock and stir over the heat for 1 minute.
5 Spoon the rice on to the chicken, then cover the pan with foil and a tight-fitting lid. Reduce the heat and cook gently for 10 minutes. Remove from the heat and let the rice rest (still covered) for 5 minutes. Uncover and leave to cool. Transfer to a bowl, cover and chill.
6 To make the crisp-fried shallots, heat the vegetable oil in a small pan. Finely slice the remaining shallots, add a spoonful to the pan and deep-fry until golden. Remove with a slotted spoon and drain on kitchen paper. Repeat until all the shallots are cooked.
7 Mix the prawns with the lime pickle, lime juice, honey and remaining olive oil.
8 When ready to serve, stir the herbs and the prawn mixture into the rice. Garnish with the crisp-fried shallots and serve with Coconut Mayonnaise (see page 000).

Serves 10
Preparation: 25 minutes
Cooking time: 55 minutes, plus resting
Per serving: 600 cals; 32g fat; 52g carbohydrate

Cooking to impress

Poached Peaches in Strawberry Syrup

75cl dry white wine
175g (6oz) golden
   caster sugar
2.5cm (1 inch) piece
   fresh root ginger,
   peeled and sliced

450g (1lb) strawberries,
   hulled
8 ripe, firm peaches
lemon juice, to taste

1 Put the wine, sugar and ginger in a large pan. Thinly slice 125g (4oz) strawberries and add them to the pan. Bring to the boil, stirring to dissolve the sugar.
2 Add the peaches to the pan and cover with a piece of greaseproof paper and a lid. Bring the liquid back to the boil, then reduce the heat and simmer the fruit for 5 minutes or until tender. Take off the heat and leave in the pan to cool.
3 Take the cooled peaches out of the pan with a slotted spoon and ease off the skins. Cut in half, discard the stones, and put in a large serving bowl. Halve the remaining strawberries and add to the bowl.
4 Bring the poaching liquid to the boil and bubble for 20–25 minutes or until well reduced and syrupy. Add a squeeze of lemon juice to taste. Allow the syrup to cool, then strain through a sieve over the fruit. Cover with clingfilm and chill overnight.

Serves 10
Preparation: 10 minutes
Cooking time: 35–40 minutes, plus chilling
Per serving: 140 cals; 0g fat; 29g carbohydrate

Fresh Mango and Pineapple Salad

¼ large red chilli,
   deseeded and finely
   chopped
2 garlic cloves, peeled
   and crushed
2.5cm (1 inch) piece
   fresh root ginger,
   peeled and finely
   grated
juice of 3 large limes,
   about 9tbsp
125ml (4fl oz) olive oil
3tbsp light muscovado
   sugar
leaves from 20g pack
   coriander
leaves from 2 x 20g
   packs mint
1 ripe, firm mango,
   peeled, stoned and
   cut into fine slices

½ ripe pineapple,
   peeled, cored and cut
   into fine shards
200g (7oz) small pak
   choi
225g bag baby spinach
   leaves, or a mixture of
   spinach, watercress
   and rocket
leaves from 20g pack
   flat-leafed parsley
1tbsp salted peanuts,
   toasted under the grill
   and finely chopped
1 bunch of spring
   onions, finely
   shredded

1 First, make the dressing. Put the chilli, garlic, ginger, lime juice, olive oil and sugar into a food processor or blender and whiz for 10 seconds to combine. Add the coriander and half the mint and whiz together for 5 seconds to chop roughly.
2 Put the mango and pineapple in a large bowl and pour over half the dressing. Put the remainder in a bowl and reserve for the Coconut Mayonnaise (page 000). Cover both with clingfilm and chill for at least 2 hours or up to 24 hours.
3 Chop the green pak choi leaves off the top of the stalks and roughly chop the white fleshy part. Add all of it to the bowl of marinated fruit with the spinach, parsley and remaining mint. Sprinkle with the peanuts and spring onions and serve immediately.

Serves 10
Preparation: 25 minutes, plus chilling
Per serving: 190 cals; 12g fat; 20g carbohydrate

Orange and White Chocolate Cake

oil
6 large eggs, separated
250g (9oz) golden
caster sugar
150g (5oz) each self-
raising flour and
ground almonds
grated zest of 2 and
juice of 3 large
oranges
100g (3½oz) golden
granulated sugar

250ml (8fl oz) sweet
white wine
225g (8oz) good-quality
white chocolate,
chopped
568ml carton double
cream
350g (12oz)
strawberries, hulled
and thinly sliced

1 Preheat the oven to 180°C (160°C fan oven) mark 4. Oil a deep 23cm (9 inch) round cake tin and line the base with greaseproof paper.

2 Put the egg whites in a clean grease-free bowl and whisk until soft peaks form. Gradually beat in 50g (2oz) caster sugar and whisk until the mixture stands in stiff peaks and looks glossy.

3 Put the egg yolks and remaining caster sugar in another bowl. Whisk until soft and moussey, then carefully stir in the flour to make a paste.

4 Using a clean metal spoon, add a third of the egg white to the paste and fold in carefully. Put the remaining egg white, ground almonds and orange zest in the bowl and fold in, taking care not to knock too much volume out of the egg whites. You should end up with a smooth batter.

5 Spoon into the prepared tin and bake for 35 minutes or until a skewer inserted in the centre comes out clean. Remove from the oven and cool in the tin for 10 minutes, then turn out on to a wire rack to cool completely.

6 To make the syrup, put the granulated sugar, wine and orange juice in a pan and stir over a gentle heat until the sugar has dissolved. Bring to the boil and bubble for 5 minutes or until syrupy. Cool and put to one side.

7 To make the ganache, put the chocolate in a heatproof bowl with half the cream and set over a pan of simmering water. Leave until the chocolate has melted, then stir. (Don't stir the chocolate until it has completely melted.) Cool until beginning to thicken, then beat with a wooden spoon until cold and thick. Put the remaining cream into a bowl and whip lightly. Beat a large spoon of the whipped cream into the chocolate cream to loosen it, then fold in the remainder. Cover and chill for 2 hours.

8 Cut the cake in half horizontally, pierce all over with a skewer and put it, cut sides up, on an edged tray or baking sheet. Spoon the syrup over. Leave to soak in.

9 Spread a quarter of the ganache over the base cake and scatter with 225g (8oz) strawberries. Cover with the top half of the cake and press down lightly. Using a palette knife, smooth the remaining ganache over the top and sides of the cake. Cover loosely and chill for up to 4 hours. Decorate with the remaining strawberries and serve.

Serves 14
Preparation: 35 minutes
Cooking time: 35–40 minutes, plus chilling
Per serving: 530 cals; 34g fat; 48g carbohydrate

The Perfect Christmas Lunch

SERVES 8

Smoked Salmon with Prawn and Avocado Salsa

Bacon-roasted Turkey
with Chestnut, Shallot and Orange Stuffing

Crisp and Crunchy Roast Potatoes

Brussels Sprouts with Hazelnut Butter

Roast Roots with Garlic and Pepper

Spiced Red Cabbage

Sweet-glazed Chipolatas

Cranberry, Honey and Ginger Sauce (page 000)

Special Bread Sauce (page 000)

The Ultimate Christmas Pudding
with Boozy Cream and Muscovado Butter

Smoked Salmon with Prawn and Avocado Salsa

2 large ripe but firm avocados, peeled, stoned and roughly chopped
350g (12oz) cooked, peeled king prawns
6 small spring onions, finely sliced
3tbsp chopped coriander
zest and juice of 3 limes, plus extra wedges to garnish
8tbsp olive oil
salt and pepper
225g (8oz) smoked salmon slices

1 To make the salsa, put the avocados into a large bowl, then add the prawns, spring onions, coriander, lime zest and juice and olive oil. Mix well, season, cover and chill until ready to serve with the salmon.
2 Divide the salmon among eight serving plates and top each with some salsa. Garnish each with a lime wedge and serve.

Serves 8
Preparation: 15 minutes
Per serving: 290 cals; 23g fat; 1g carbohydrate

Bacon-roasted Turkey

5.4–6.3kg (12–14lb)
  turkey with giblets
  removed to make
  stock
Chestnut, Shallot and
  Orange Stuffing,
  (opposite)
125g (4oz) butter,
  softened, plus extra
  to grease

salt and pepper
3 rosemary sprigs
300g (11oz) rindless
  smoked streaky
  bacon rashers

1 Take the turkey out of the fridge 30 minutes before stuffing to take the chill off. Preheat the oven to 220°C (200°C fan oven) mark 7.

2 Put the turkey on a board, breast side down. Use your hands to push some of the stuffing into the neck end of the turkey, easing it up between the flesh and the skin towards the breast. Don't pack it in too tightly as it will expand on cooking.

3 Shape the protruding stuffing into a neat round, then tuck the neck skin under the bird and secure with a skewer. Weigh the bird and calculate the cooking time if outside the range given for this recipe (see below).

4 Put any leftover stuffing into a greased ovenproof dish. Cover with buttered foil.

5 Put one or two large sheets of strong foil across a large roasting tin. Put the turkey in the middle and spread the butter all over it. Season with a little salt and plenty of pepper and pop two rosemary sprigs inside the cavity. Overlap the bacon rashers across the turkey breast, snip over the remaining rosemary and tie the legs together with string.

6 Bring the edges of the foil together and make into a pleat along the length of the breastbone, but well above it to make a 'tent' with plenty of air space above the breast.

7 Put the turkey on a low shelf in the main oven and roast for about 30 minutes. Reduce the oven temperature to 170°C (150°C fan oven) mark 3 and cook for a further 3½ hours.

8 Fold back the foil from the top and sides of the turkey and push the bacon slices off the breast to allow the skin to brown. Increase the oven temperature to 200°C (180°C fan oven) mark 6 and cook the turkey for 30–40 minutes, basting it with the juices twice during this time.

9 When the bird is cooked, transfer it to a warm carving platter – you'll need help at this stage, so you can tip the bird upright and let the cooking juices run back into the roasting tin.

10 Cover the turkey with foil and leave to rest for 30–40 minutes before carving, while you make the gravy and finish the vegetables.

Serves 8 (with leftovers)
Preparation: 15 minutes
Cooking time: about 4 hours 40 minutes
Per 125g (4oz) meat: 250 cals; 10g fat;
0g carbohydrate

Is your turkey a different size?
3.5–4.9kg (8–11lb) Cook for 30 minutes at 220°C (200°C fan oven) mark 7, then for 2½–3 hours at 170°C (150°C fan oven) mark 3.
Finally, cook for 30 minutes uncovered at 200°C (180°C fan oven) mark 6.
6.8–9kg (15–20lb) Cook for 50 minutes at 220°C (200°C fan oven) mark 7.
Reduce the temperature to 170°C (150°C fan oven) mark 3 and cook for 4–5 hours.
Finally, cook for 30 minutes uncovered at 200°C (180°C fan oven) mark 6.

Cooking to impress

Chestnut, Shallot and Orange Stuffing

50g (2oz) butter
6 shallots, blanched in boiling water, drained and roughly chopped
4 celery sticks, roughly chopped
1 rosemary sprig, snipped
1tbsp chopped flat-leafed parsley
175g (6oz) firm white bread, cut into rough dice

2 cooking apples, about 225g (8oz), peeled, cored and chopped
125g (4oz) cooked, peeled chestnuts, roughly chopped
zest of 1 large orange
salt and pepper
450g (1lb) good-quality coarse pork sausagemeat

1 Melt the butter in a large frying pan and gently fry the shallots, celery and rosemary for 10–12 minutes until the vegetables are golden and softened. Tip into a large bowl (there's no need to wash the pan). Add the parsley, bread, apples, chestnuts and orange zest to the bowl. Season and mix well.

2 Divide the sausagemeat into walnut-sized pieces. Fry in batches in the pan until golden and cooked through. Add to the bowl with the stuffing mix and stir. Cool, then use to stuff the turkey (opposite). Put any leftover stuffing into a greased ovenproof dish, cover with foil and cook with the chipolatas (page 000).

Makes enough to stuff a 5.4–6.3kg (12–14lb) turkey
Preparation: 15 minutes
Cooking time: 20–25 minutes
Per serving: 100 cals; 6g fat; 9g carbohydrate

Crisp and Crunchy Roast Potatoes

1.8kg (4lb) potatoes, preferably King Edward, cut into two bite-sized pieces
salt

2tsp paprika
2–3 tbsp goose or white vegetable fat

1 Put the potatoes in a pan of lightly salted water, bring to the boil and boil for 7 minutes, then drain well in a colander. Add the paprika to the colander, then cover and shake the potatoes roughly, so they become fluffy around the edges.

2 Melt the fat in a large roasting tin on the hob. When it sizzles, add the potatoes and tilt the tin to coat, taking care because the fat will splutter.

3 Roast the potatoes above the turkey at 170°C (150°C fan oven) mark 3 for about 30 minutes. Then roast at 200°C (180°C fan oven) mark 6 for a further 40 minutes. Move the potatoes only once or twice during cooking, otherwise the edges won't crisp and brown. Season with a little salt before serving.

Serves 8
Preparation: 20 minutes
Cooking time: 1 hour 10 minutes
Per serving: 250 cals; 10g fat; 39g carbohydrate

Brussels Sprouts with Hazelnut Butter

50g (2oz) butter, at
  room temperature
100g (3½oz) blanched
  hazelnuts, toasted
  and roughly chopped
freshly grated nutmeg
salt and pepper
1.4kg (3lb) Brussels
  sprouts

lemon juice
cooked bacon from
  turkey (page 000), or
  300g (11oz) rindless
  smoked streaky
  bacon rashers

1 Put the butter into a bowl and beat to soften. Add the hazelnuts and nutmeg and season. Mix well. Wrap in greaseproof paper and foil and chill until needed.
2 Cook the sprouts in boiling salted water for 7–10 minutes or until tender but with a slight bite. Drain well then toss in the hazelnut butter. Add a squeeze of lemon juice, crumble the bacon from the turkey over and tip into a serving dish. Alternatively, grill the uncooked bacon until crisp and crumble over the sprouts.

Serves 8
Preparation: 5 minutes
Cooking time: 10 minutes
Per serving: 190 cals; 15g fat; 8g carbohydrate

Roast Roots with Garlic and Pepper

1.4kg (3lb) mixed
  carrots and parsnips,
  peeled and cut into
  5cm (2 inch) wedges
3 fat garlic cloves,
  peeled and cut in half

1tsp black
  peppercorns, crushed
4tbsp olive oil
chopped flat-leafed
  parsley, to garnish

1 Preheat the oven to 200°C (180°C fan oven) mark 6. Put the carrots and parsnips into a large pan of boiling water and cook for 10 minutes. Drain, put back into the pan and add the garlic, pepper and olive oil. Toss for 2–3 minutes.
2 Roast the vegetables for 1 hour. Transfer to a serving dish, garnish with parsley and serve.

Serves 8
Preparation: 15 minutes
Cooking time: 1 hour 25 minutes
Per serving: 130 cals; 6g fat; 16g carbohydrate

Spiced Red Cabbage

25g (1oz) butter
3 red onions, peeled
  and finely chopped
900g (2lb) red cabbage,
  shredded
2 Bramley cooking
  apples, peeled, cored
  and chopped

4tbsp each redcurrant
  jelly (or light
  muscovado sugar if
  you prefer) and
  red wine vinegar
1 each cinnamon stick
  and clove
2 thyme sprigs
salt and pepper

1 Preheat the oven to 170°C (150°C fan oven) mark 3. Melt the butter in a large flameproof casserole, then fry the onions for 7–10 minutes until beginning to soften.
2 Stir in the remaining ingredients. Season the mixture well, then cover the casserole and cook in the oven for 2 hours, stirring once or twice during cooking.
3 Remove from the oven, tip the cabbage into a serving dish and discard the thyme, cinnamon stick and cloves.

Serves 8
Preparation: 20 minutes
Cooking time: 2 hours 10 minutes
Per serving: 100 cals; 3g fat; 17g carbohydrate

Sweet-glazed Chipolatas

450g (1lb) chipolata
  sausages
3tbsp home-made
  Cranberry, Honey and
  Ginger Sauce (page
  000)

1tbsp olive oil
rosemary sprigs, to
  garnish (optional)

1 Put the sausages into a plastic container and add the sauce and olive oil. Toss together, then cover and chill until ready to cook.
2 Preheat the oven to 200°C (180°C fan oven) mark 6. Spread the chipolatas out on a baking sheet and cook for 30–40 minutes. Remove from the oven and arrange the chipolatas around the turkey. Garnish with rosemary sprigs, if you like.

Serves 8
Preparation: 5 minutes
Cooking time: 30–40 minutes
Per serving: 230 cals; 20g fat; 6g carbohydrate

The Ultimate Christmas Pudding

200g (7oz) each
  currants, sultanas
  and raisins
75g (3oz) candied peel,
  finely chopped
1 small apple, peeled,
  cored and grated
1tsp each ground
  cinnamon, cloves and
  freshly grated nutmeg
¼tsp mixed spice
1tbsp each brandy and
  rum

125ml (4fl oz) beer
175g (6oz)
  breadcrumbs
175g (6oz) suet
100g (3½oz) each
  sifted flour and light
  muscovado sugar
2 eggs, beaten
butter, to grease
25ml (1fl oz) brandy, to
  flame

1 Put the currants, sultanas, raisins, candied peel, apple, ground cinnamon, cloves, nutmeg and mixed spice into a large bowl. Pour in the brandy, rum and beer. Stir everything together, then cover and leave to soak in a cool place for at least 1 hour – preferably overnight.

2 Add the breadcrumbs, suet, flour, sugar and beaten eggs to the bowl and mix really well.

3 Grease a 1 litre (1¾ pint) pudding basin and line with a 60cm (24 inch) square piece of muslin. Spoon the mixture into the basin and flatten the surface. Gather the muslin over the top of the mixture, then secure with string. Tie a piece of string around the basin just under the rim and knot. Don't cut the string, but bring the ends over the top of the bowl and secure to the string on the other side to make a handle. Trim the muslin.

4 To cook the pudding, put the basin on an upturned, heatproof plate in a deep pan. Fill the pan with water to come halfway up the side of the basin. Bring to a simmer. Cover the pan with a tight-fitting lid and steam for 6 hours. Top up the water level as necessary with boiling water – probably every hour. Remove the bowl from the pan. Cool the pudding in the bowl, then lift it out of the bowl, in its muslin. Wrap in clingfilm and a double layer of tin foil. Keep in a cool, dark place until Christmas.

5 To serve, steam the pudding for 2½ hours, checking the water level every 40 minutes and topping up, if necessary, with boiling water. Unmould the pudding on to a serving plate, garnish with a holly sprig and take to the table. Warm the brandy in a small pan until hot, pour into a small ladle, light with a match and pour over the pudding. The flames will disappear almost immediately and the pudding is then ready to serve.

Serves 12
Preparation: 30 minutes, plus soaking
Cooking time: 6 hours, plus reheating
Per serving: 387 cals; 14g fat; 62g carbohydrate

Boozy Cream

125g (4oz) chopped
  dried fruit, such as
  figs or prunes
125ml (4fl oz) crème de
  cacao or
  Grand Marnier
568ml carton double
  cream

100ml (3½fl oz) brandy
pinch of freshly grated
  nutmeg
about 1tbsp golden
  icing sugar

1 Put the fruit in a bowl, add the crème de cacao or Grand Marnier and soak for 10 minutes.

2 Lightly whip the cream in a large bowl until thickened. Fold in the brandy, nutmeg, fruit and juices and a little icing sugar to taste. Transfer to a serving bowl and chill until ready to serve.

Serves 8
Preparation: 15 minutes
Per serving: 400 cals; 36g fat; 12g carbohydrate

Muscovado Butter

250g (9oz) unsalted
  butter, softened
225g (8oz) light
  muscovado sugar

8tbsp Grand Marnier or
  Cointreau

1 Put the butter into a large bowl and add the sugar. Using an electric hand whisk, cream together until smooth and pale.

2 Add the Grand Marnier or Cointreau, a little at a time, and continue to whisk for about 5 minutes until thick and mousse-like. Transfer to a serving bowl and chill until needed.

Serves 8
Preparation: 10 minutes
Per serving: 380 cals; 26g fat; 34g carbohydrate

Buttery Potatoes and Celeriac

175g (6oz) unsalted butter
900g (2lb) potatoes, peeled and very thinly sliced (slices not washed)

1 celeriac head, about 700g (1½lb), peeled and thinly sliced
salt and pepper
freshly grated nutmeg

1 Preheat the oven to 190°C (170°C fan oven) mark 5. Melt the butter in a heavy-based pan.

2 Line the base of a 25cm (10 inch) loose-based cake tin with baking parchment and brush with a little melted butter. Layer up the potato and celeriac slices, slightly overlapping, seasoning each layer well with salt, pepper and nutmeg. Finish by drizzling with butter and seasoning generously again.

3 Cover with baking parchment, then put a 23cm (9 inch) cake tin filled with baking beans on top to compact the cake, making it easier to slice. Bake for 1 hour 10 minutes or until the potatoes are tender. Remove from the oven, cool, cover and chill overnight.

4 To heat up, invert the tin on to a heatproof serving plate and warm in the oven at 190°C (170°C fan oven) mark 5 for 10 minutes, then brown under a preheated grill for 5–10 minutes. Serve sliced into wedges.

Serves 8
Preparation: 30 minutes
Cooking time: 1 hour 10 minutes
Per serving: 250 cals; 19g fat; 19g carbohydrate

Braised Shallots and Chestnuts with Pancetta and Sage

130g pack cubed pancetta
1tbsp goose fat or olive oil
500g (1lb 2oz) shallots, blanched in boiling water, drained and peeled
1tbsp golden caster sugar
150ml (¼ pint) red wine
2tbsp red wine vinegar

a few thyme sprigs
4 sage leaves, shredded, plus a few extra leaves to garnish
300ml (½ pint) hot giblet or chicken stock
salt and pepper
400g (14oz) whole cooked chestnuts

1 Dry-fry the pancetta for 5 minutes until cooked and golden, then put to one side.

2 Add the goose fat or olive oil to the pan and gently fry the shallots for 10 minutes or until golden.

3 Add the sugar to the pan and stir to dissolve, then heat for 1–2 minutes until it begins to caramelise. Add the wine and vinegar, scraping the base of the pan to dissolve any rich sticky bits, and gently simmer until the liquid has reduced slightly.

4 Add the thyme, shredded sage and hot stock, then season and cook for 20 minutes.

5 Add the chestnuts and cook for 10 minutes until there's just enough liquid left to glaze. Transfer to a serving dish and serve.

Serves 8
Preparation: 10 minutes
Cooking time: 50 minutes
Per serving: 200 cals; 10g fat; 25g carbohydrate

Braised Red Cabbage

½ medium red
cabbage, about 500g
(1lb 2oz), shredded
1 red onion, peeled and
finely chopped
1 Bramley apple,
peeled, cored and
chopped
25g (1oz) light
muscovado sugar

1 cinnamon stick
pinch of ground cloves
¼tsp freshly grated
nutmeg
2tbsp each red wine
vinegar and red wine
juice of 1 orange
salt and pepper

1 Put all the ingredients into a large pan and stir to mix well.
2 Put the pan, covered, over a low heat and cook gently for about 1½ hours, stirring the cabbage from time to time to prevent it from burning on the bottom.
3 When the cabbage is tender, remove the pan from the heat and discard the cinnamon stick. Serve at once, or cool, put into a bowl, cover and chill the cabbage overnight.
4 To reheat, put the cabbage into a pan, add 2tbsp cold water and cover with a tight-fitting lid. Bring to the boil, then reduce the heat and simmer for 25 minutes.

Serves 8
Preparation: 10 minutes
Cooking time: 1½ hours
Per serving: 40 cals; trace fat; 10g carbohydrate

Grand Marnier Oranges and Passion Fruit

8 large sweet oranges
6 passion fruit
150g (5oz) golden
caster sugar

6tbsp Grand Marnier

1 Use a vegetable peeler to pare strips of peel from two oranges. Cut the strips into needle-fine shreds, then put into a heavy-based pan.
2 Cut the top and bottom off each orange, then use a sharp knife to remove all the skin and pith, then discard. Slice the fruit into rounds, saving the juice, then put the fruit into a bowl. Add the juice to the pan.
3 Cut each passion fruit in half, scooping the juice and seeds of three into the pan. Push the seeds and pulp of the remaining fruit through a sieve held over the pan, so the juice drips through; discard the seeds.
4 Add the sugar to the pan, set it over a medium heat and leave to dissolve completely. Increase the heat and, swirling the pan occasionally, allow the sugar to caramelise gently – it should take about 10 minutes to become syrupy.
5 Remove the pan from the heat and add the Grand Marnier to the syrup – it may splutter as you do this, so protect your hands with a cloth. Cool the syrup, then pour it over the oranges. Cover and chill for up to two days before serving.

Serves 8
Preparation: 30 minutes
Cooking time: 10 minutes
Per serving: 160 cals; 0g fat; 36g carbohydrate

Boxing Day Menu

SERVES 10

Honey and Mustard Glazed Ham

Carrot, Peanut and Coriander Salad

Avocado, Clementine and Chicory Salad

Cannellini Bean and Sunblush Tomato Salad

Apricot and Peach Trifle

Honey and Mustard Glazed Ham

4kg (9lb) ham, bone in
1 onion, peeled and
  quartered
1 carrot, peeled and
  chopped into three
1 celery stick, chopped

1 sprig each parsley,
  rosemary and thyme
1 bay leaf
handful of cloves
4tbsp runny honey
4tbsp Dijon mustard

1 Put the ham into a pan. Add the vegetables and herbs. Cover with water and bring to the boil. Reduce the heat and simmer, half-covered, for 2¼ hours.
2 Transfer the ham to a roasting tin. Preheat the oven to 220°C (200°C fan oven) mark 7. Using a sharp knife, remove and discard the skin to leave a thin layer of fat.
3 Score the fat lightly in a diamond pattern and stud each diamond with a clove. Put the honey into a bowl, add the mustard and mix well. Brush the mixture all over the exposed fat. Roast the ham for 15 minutes until golden.

Serves 10 with plenty for leftovers
Preparation: 15 minutes
Cooking time: 2½ hours
Per 150g (5oz): 180 cals; 8g fat; 0g carbohydrate

Carrot, Peanut and Coriander Salad

900g (2lb) carrots,
  peeled and grated or
  shredded
100g (3½oz) unsalted
  peanuts, toasted and
  roughly chopped
100g (3½oz) sultanas

2 x 20g packs
  coriander, chopped
7tbsp olive oil
3tbsp white wine
  vinegar
1tbsp runny honey
salt and pepper

1 Put the carrots, peanuts, sultanas and coriander into a large bowl and mix well.
2 To make the dressing, put the olive oil, vinegar and honey into a small bowl and season well to taste. Whisk everything together.
3 Pour the dressing over the salad and toss well. Leave at room temperature for 30 minutes for the flavours to mingle.

Serves 10
Preparation: 10 minutes, plus marinating
Per serving: 200 cals; 14g fat; 14g carbohydrate

Avocado, Clementine and Chicory Salad

juice of 1 orange
8tbsp olive oil
20g pack dill, finely
 chopped
salt and pepper
6 chicory heads, leaves
 separated
4 ripe avocados,
 peeled, stoned and
 sliced

6 clementines or
 satsumas, peeled and
 thinly sliced into
 rounds
50g (2oz) pine nuts,
 toasted

1 To make the dressing, put the orange juice into a bowl and add the olive oil and dill. Season and whisk everything together.
2 Divide the chicory among two platters and arrange the avocados and clementines or satsumas on top. Just before serving, sprinkle over the pine nuts and spoon the dressing on top.

Serves 10
Preparation: 10 minutes
Per serving: 280 cals; 27g fat; 7g carbohydrate

Cannellini Bean and Sunblush Tomato Salad

1 small red onion,
 peeled and very finely
 sliced
3tbsp red wine vinegar
handful each chopped
 mint and flat-leafed
 parsley
4 x 400g cans
 cannellini beans, well
 drained and rinsed

6tbsp extra-virgin olive
 oil
6 celery sticks, finely
 sliced
100g (3½oz) sunblush
 tomatoes, snipped
 in half

1 Put the onion into a small bowl, add the vinegar and toss. Leave to marinate for 30 minutes – this stage is important as it takes the astringency out of the onion.
2 Add the remaining ingredients and toss everything together.

Serves 10
Preparation: 5 minutes, plus marinating
Per serving: 130 cals; 8g fat; 11g carbohydrate

Apricot and Peach Trifle

2 x packs trifle
 sponges, each
 containing eight
 sponges, or 1 x 440g
 ready-made Madeira
 cake
6tbsp apricot jam
4tbsp sherry
4 x 415g cans apricots
 in natural fruit juice,
 drained

2 x 415g cans peaches
 in natural fruit juice,
 drained
568ml carton double
 cream
500g carton fresh
 custard
250g tub mascarpone
50g (2oz) pecan nuts,
 toasted

1 Cut the trifle sponges in half horizontally and spread one half with the apricot jam. Cover with the other half to make mini sandwiches. If using cake, cut into slices first, then sandwich together in pairs with jam. Use to line a large glass serving bowl. Drizzle over the sherry, then add the apricots.
2 Put the peaches into a food processor or blender and whiz to a purée. Pour over the apricots in an even layer.
3 Put the cream into a large bowl and whisk until soft peaks form. Chill. Put the whisk to one side – you needn't rinse it.
4 Put the custard and mascarpone into a large bowl and whisk together briefly to mix well. Pour over the fruit in an even layer.
5 Spoon the whipped cream over the custard mix and scatter the top with pecan nuts.

Serves 10
Preparation: 20 minutes
Per serving: 830 cals; 51g fat; 90g carbohydrate

Winter Menu

SERVES 20

Mozzarella Nibbles

Tangy Chicken Bites

Roasted Salmon

Winter Leaf Salad

Roasted Root Vegetable Salad

Classic Coleslaw

Cheese and Onion tart

Cheat's Gateau

Boozy Oranges with Orange Cream

Mozzarella Nibbles

85g pack Parma ham
2 x 125g tubs bocconcini (mini mozzarella balls), drained
397g jar pitted black and green olives, drained and halved
125g (4oz) each roast artichokes and peppers, cut into small pieces
bunch of basil leaves

1 Wrap a little Parma ham around each mozzarella ball.
2 Push a halved olive on to a cocktail stick, then add a piece each of artichoke and pepper, a basil leaf, then the Parma and mozzarella ball. Repeat to make 30 nibbles. Serve immediately or cover and chill for up to 1 hour.

Makes 30
Preparation: 15 minutes
Per nibble: 40 cals; 3g fat; trace carbohydrate

Tangy Chicken Bites

2 x 50g pack mini croustades
about 275g (10oz) fruity chutney
2 roast chicken breasts, skinned and torn into small pieces
275ml (9fl oz) crème fraîche
thyme sprigs

1 Spread out the croustades on a board and spoon about ½tsp chutney into each one.
2 Top with a few shreds of chicken, a small blob of crème fraîche and a few thyme leaves. Serve immediately.

Makes 48
Preparation: 10 minutes
Per bite: 50 cals; 3g fat; 4g carbohydrate

Roasted Salmon

2 lemons, sliced plus the juice of ½ lemon
2 salmon sides, filleted, each 1.4kg (3lb), skin on, boned and trimmed
salt and pepper
2tbsp dry white wine
500ml carton crème fraîche
500g carton natural yogurt
2tbsp horseradish sauce
3tbsp chopped tarragon
4tbsp capers, roughly chopped, plus extra to garnish
¼ cucumber, deseeded and diced, plus extra to garnish
2 large bunches of watercress, to serve
lemon and cucumber slices, to garnish

1 Preheat the oven to 190°C (170°C fan oven) mark 5. Take two big pieces of foil, each large enough to wrap a salmon side, and put a piece of greaseproof paper on top of each.

2 Divide the lemon slices among each piece of greaseproof and lay each salmon side on top, skin side up. Season well, then pour over the lemon juice and wine.

3 Score the skin at 4cm (1½ inch) intervals across the width of each salmon fillet, keeping the side in one piece, to mark 10 portions.

4 Scrunch the foil around each salmon, keeping it loose so the fish doesn't stick. Put on to two separate racks in the oven and cook for 45 minutes until the flesh is just opaque.

5 Unwrap the foil and cook for 20 minutes until the skin crisps up and the fish is cooked. To check, ease a knife into one of the slashes in the skin. Remove the fish from the oven and cool quickly in a cold place. Re-wrap and chill.

6 To make the dressing, put the crème fraîche, yogurt, horseradish sauce, tarragon, capers and diced cucumber in a large bowl. Season and mix well, then cover and chill.

7 To serve, cut through the slashes in each salmon side to make 10 portions. Put on a bed of watercress and garnish with the lemon and cucumber slices. Serve with the dressing, garnished with capers and diced cucumber.

Serves 20
Preparation: 15 minutes
Cooking time: 1 hour 5 minutes
Per serving: 370 cals; 27g fat; 3g carbohydrate

Winter Leaf Salad

3tbsp each white wine vinegar and walnut oil
6tbsp olive oil
salt and pepper
100g (3½oz) lamb's lettuce
2 heads radicchio
4 heads red chicory
200g (7oz) walnuts, toasted and roughly chopped

1 Put the vinegar, walnut and olive oils in a screw-topped jar, season and shake well to mix.

2 Tear all the salad leaves into bite-sized pieces and put in a large bowl. Add the walnuts and toss to mix.

3 To serve, shake the dressing again, then pour over the salad and toss well. Divide among two large bowls.

Serves 20
Preparation: 20 minutes
Per serving: 110 cals; 11g fat; 1g carbohydrate

Cooking to impress

Roasted Root Vegetable Salad

4 butternut squash,
  halved, deseeded and
  cubed
6 large carrots, peeled
  and cut into chunks
10 thyme sprigs
6tbsp olive oil
salt and pepper
8 red onions, peeled
  and cut into wedges

4tbsp balsamic vinegar
4 x 410g cans
  chickpeas, drained
  and rinsed
100g (3½oz) pine nuts,
  toasted
4 x 100g bags wild
  rocket

1 Preheat the oven to 190°C (170°C fan oven) mark 5. Divide the squash and carrots among two large deep roasting tins. Scatter over the thyme and drizzle each with 2tbsp olive oil, then season and roast for 20 minutes.

2 Remove the tins from the oven, give them a good shake to make sure the vegetables aren't sticking, then divide the onions among the tins. Drizzle 1tbsp oil over each and toss to coat. Continue to roast for 20 minutes or until all the vegetables are tender.

3 Remove the roasted vegetables from the oven and discard any twiggy bits of thyme. Drizzle 2tbsp vinegar over each tin, stir in and put to one side to cool.

4 To serve, put the chickpeas into a large bowl. Add the cooled vegetables, pine nuts and rocket (reserving some for a garnish). Toss everything together. Divide among two large serving dishes and garnish each with a little rocket.

Serves 20
Preparation: 20 minutes
Cooking time: 40 minutes
Per serving: 170 cals; 8g fat; 19g carbohydrate

Classic Coleslaw

5tbsp red wine vinegar
250ml (8fl oz) olive oil
2tbsp Dijon mustard
salt and pepper
1 small red and 1 small
  white cabbage, each
  shredded

4 carrots, peeled and
  grated
75g (3oz) flat-leafed
  parsley, finely
  chopped

1 First, make the dressing. Pour the vinegar into a large screw-topped jar. Add the olive oil and mustard and season well. Screw on the lid and shake well.

2 Put the cabbage and carrots into a large bowl. Toss together so the vegetables are well mixed, then add the parsley.

3 Shake the dressing again, pour over the cabbage mixture and toss well to coat. Divide the coleslaw among two large bowls to serve.

Serves 20
Preparation: 20 minutes
Per serving: 140 cals; 10g fat; 8g carbohydrate

Cheese and Onion Tart

40g (1½oz) unsalted
  butter
4 red onions, peeled
  and thinly sliced
2tbsp golden caster
  sugar
1tbsp sherry vinegar
juice of ¼ lemon

375g pack ready-rolled
  puff pastry
2tbsp milk, to glaze
200g (7oz) soft goat's
  cheese,
  roughly crumbled
basil leaves, to garnish

1 Melt the butter in a pan. Add the onions and sugar, then cover and cook over a low heat for 20 minutes, stirring occasionally, or until softened. Stir in the vinegar and lemon juice and cook, uncovered, for 5–10 minutes. Take off the heat and cool.

2 Preheat the oven to 180°C (160°C fan oven) mark 4. Put the pastry on a non-stick baking sheet and roll out to measure 28 x 38cm (11 x 15 inches). Score around the edge leaving a 2.5cm (1 inch) border, then brush the edge with milk. Bake for 15–20 minutes until golden. Remove from the oven and leave to cool.

3 Use a palette knife to push down the middle square of pastry. Spread the onion mixture evenly over the central square, then scatter over the cheese. Return to oven for 10 minutes until the cheese is golden and the tart is warm. Scatter the basil leaves on top, then cut the tart into pieces and serve.

Serves 10
Preparation: 15 minutes
Cooking time: 50 minutes–1 hour
Per serving: 290 cals; 20g fat; 24g carbohydrate

Cheat's Gateau

500g tub mascarpone
1tbsp golden icing
  sugar, sifted, plus
  extra to dust
2 x 425g cans pitted
  black cherries in
  syrup, drained

1kg box of panettone
50g (2oz) good-quality
  plain dark chocolate
  (with minimum 50%
  cocoa solids), broken
  into pieces

1 Put the mascarpone in a bowl, add the sugar and mix well. Gently stir in the cherries.

2 Slice the panettone horizontally through the middle into three slices. Using a palette knife, spread half the mascarpone mixture over the base of the panettone, then spread the rest on to the middle layer. Carefully sandwich the cake together.

3 Melt the chocolate in a small heatproof bowl set over a pan of simmering water. Dust the panettone with icing sugar. Drizzle the melted chocolate on top.

Serves 20
Preparation: 10 minutes
Cooking time: 3 minutes
Per serving: 300 cals; 19g fat; 32g carbohydrate

Boozy Oranges with Orange Cream

8 large juicy oranges
6tbsp Cointreau
  (optional)
568ml carton double
  cream

1tbsp golden icing
  sugar, sifted

1 Grate the zest from 2 oranges, put in a small bowl and put to one side.

2 Put the oranges on a board and use a sharp knife to cut the top and bottom off each. Next, cut off all the peel and white pith. Cut the flesh into rounds, pouring any juice into a large serving bowl. Put the slices in the bowl, add 3tbsp Cointreau, if using, and put to one side.

3 Whip the cream in a bowl until just thick, then stir in the remaining Cointreau, almost all the orange zest and the sugar. Scatter over the remaining zest and serve with the oranges.

Serves 20
Preparation: 15 minutes
Per serving: 160 cals; 14g fat; 7g carbohydrate

Acidulated water Water to which lemon juice or vinegar has been added in which fruit or vegetables, such as pears or Jerusalem artichokes, are immersed to prevent discolouration.

Al dente Italian term commonly used to describe food, especially pasta and vegetables, which are cooked until tender but still firm to the bite.

Antipasto Italian selection of cold meats, fish, salads etc., served as a starter.

Au gratin Describes a dish that has been coated with sauce, sprinkled with breadcrumbs or cheese and browned under the grill or in the oven. Low-sided gratin dishes are used.

Bain-marie Literally, a water bath, used to keep foods, such as delicate custards and sauces, at a constant low temperature during cooking. On the hob a double saucepan or bowl over a pan of simmering water is used; for oven cooking, the baking dish(es) is placed in a roasting tin containing enough hot water to come halfway up the sides.

Baking blind Pre-baking a pastry case before filling. The pastry case is lined with greaseproof paper and weighted down with dried beans or ceramic baking beans.

Baking powder A raising agent consisting of an acid, usually cream of tartar and an alkali, such as bicarbonate of soda, which react to produce carbon dioxide. This expands during baking and makes cakes and breads rise.

Bard To cover the breast of game birds or poultry, or lean meat with fat to prevent the meat from drying out during roasting.

Baste To spoon the juices and melted fat over meat, poultry, game or vegetables during roasting to keep them moist. The term is also used to describe spooning over a marinade.

Beat To incorporate air into an ingredient or mixture by agitating it vigorously with a spoon, fork, whisk or electric mixer. The technique is also used to soften ingredients.

Béchamel Classic French white sauce, used as the basis for other sauces and savoury dishes.

Beurre manié Equal parts of flour and butter kneaded together to make a paste. Used to thicken soups, stews and casseroles. It is whisked into the hot liquid a little at a time at the end of cooking.

Bind To mix beaten egg or other liquid into a dry mixture to hold it together.

Blanch To immerse food briefly in fast-boiling water to loosen skins, such as peaches or tomatoes, or to remove bitterness, or to destroy enzymes and preserve the colour, flavour and texture of vegetables (especially prior to freezing).

Bone To remove the bones from meat, poultry, game or fish, so that it can be stuffed or simply rolled before cooking.

Bottle To preserve fruit, jams, pickles or other preserves in sterile glass jars.

Bouquet garni Small bunch of herbs – usually a mixture of parsley stems, thyme and a bay leaf – tied in muslin and used to flavour stocks, soups and stews.

Braise To cook meat, poultry, game or vegetables slowly in a small amount of liquid in a pan or casserole with a tight-fitting lid. The food is usually first browned in oil or fat.

Brochette Food cooked on a skewer or spit.

Brûlée A French term, literally meaning 'burnt' used to refer to a dish with a crisp coating of caramelised sugar.

Butterfly To split a food, such as a large prawn or poussin, almost in half and open out flat, so that it will cook more quickly.

Calorie Strictly a kilocalorie, this is used in dietetics to measure the energy value of foods.

Canapé Small appetiser, served with drinks.

Candying Method of preserving fruit or peel by impregnating with sugar.

Caramelise To heat sugar or sugar syrup slowly until it is brown in colour; ie forms a caramel.

Carbonade Rich stew or braise of meat, which includes beer.

Casserole A dish with a tight-fitting lid used for slow-cooking meat, poultry and vegetables, now used to describe food cooked in this way.

Charcuterie French term for cooked pork products, including hams, sausages and terrines.

Chill To cool food in the fridge.

Chine To sever the rib bones from the backbone, close to the spine. This is done to meat joints, such as loin of pork or lamb, to make them easier to carve into chops after cooking.

Clarify To remove sediment or impurities from a liquid. Stock is clarified by heating with egg white, while butter is clarified by melting and skimming. Butter that has been clarified will withstand a higher frying temperature.

To clarify butter heat until melted and all bubbling stops. Take off the heat and let stand until the sediment has sunk to the bottom, then gently pour off the fat, straining it through muslin.

Compote Mixture of fresh or dried fruit stewed in sugar syrup. Served hot or cold.

Concassé Diced fresh ingredient, used as a garnish. The term is most often applied to skinned, deseeded tomatoes.

Coulis A smooth fruit or vegetable purée, thinned if necessary to a pouring consistency.

Court bouillon Aromatic cooking liquid containing wine, vinegar or lemon juice, used for poaching delicate fish, poultry or vegetables.

Consistency Term used to describe the texture of a mixture, eg firm, dropping or soft.

Cream To beat together fat and sugar until the mixture is pale and fluffy, and resembles whipped cream in texture and colour. The method is used in cakes and puddings which contain a high proportion of fat and require the incorporation of a lot of air.

Crêpe French term for a pancake.

Crimp To decorate the edge of a pie, tart or shortbread by pinching it at regular intervals to give a fluted effect.

Croquette Seasoned mixture of cooked potato and fish, meat, poultry or vegetables shaped into a small roll, coated with egg and breadcrumbs and shallow-fried.

Croûte Circle or other shaped piece of fried bread, typically used as a base for serving small game birds.

Croûtons Small pieces of fried or toasted bread, served with soups and salads.

Crudités Raw vegetables, usually cut into slices or sticks, typically served with a dipping sauce as an appetiser.

Crystallise To preserve fruit in sugar syrup.

Curdle To cause sauces or creamed mixtures to separate once the egg is added, usually by overheating or over-beating.

Cure To preserve fish, meat or poultry by smoking, drying or salting.

Daube Braising meat and vegetables with stock, often with wine and herbs added.

Deglaze To heat stock, wine or other liquid with the cooking juices left in the pan after roasting or sautéeing, scraping and stirring vigorously to dissolve the sediment on the bottom of the pan.

Dégorge To draw out moisture from a food, eg salting aubergines to remove bitter juices.

Dice To cut food into small cubes.

Draw To remove the entrails from poultry or game.

Dredge To sprinkle food generously with flour, sugar, icing sugar etc.

Dress To pluck, draw and truss poultry or game. The term is also used to describe tossing a salad in vinaigrette or other dressing.

Dry To preserve food, such as fruit, pasta and pulses by dehydration.

Dust To sprinkle lightly with flour, cornflour, icing sugar etc.

Emulsion A mixture of two liquids, which do not dissolve into one another, such as oil and vinegar. Vigorous shaking or heating will emulsify them, as for a vinaigrette.

En croûte Term used to describe food that is wrapped in pastry before cooking.

En papillote Term used to describe food that is baked in a greaseproof paper or baking parchment parcel and served from the paper.

Enzyme Organic substance in food that causes chemical changes. Enzymes are a complex group. Their action is usually halted during cooking.

Escalope Thin slice of meat, such as pork, veal or turkey, from the top of the leg, usually pan-fried.

Extract Concentrated flavouring, which is used in small quantities, eg yeast extract, vanilla extract.

Ferment Chemical change deliberately or accidentally brought about by fermenting agents, such as yeast or bacteria. Fermentation is utilised for making bread, yogurt, beer and wine.

Fillet Term used to describe boned breasts of birds, boned sides of fish, and the undercut of a loin of beef, lamb, pork or veal.

Flake To separate food, such as cooked fish, into natural pieces.

Flambé Flavouring a dish with alcohol, usually brandy or rum, which is then ignited so that the actual alcohol content is burned off.

Folding in Method of combining a whisked or creamed mixture with other ingredients by cutting and folding so that it retains its lightness. A large metal spoon or plastic-bladed spatula is used.

Frosting To coat leaves and flowers with a fine layer of sugar to use as a decoration. Also an American term for icing cakes.

19

Glossary

Fry To cook food in hot fat or oil. There are various methods: shallow-frying in a little fat in a shallow pan; deep-frying where the food is totally immersed in oil; dry-frying in which fatty foods are cooked in a non-stick pan without extra fat; *see also* Stir-frying.

Galette Cooked savoury or sweet mixture shaped into a round.

Garnish A decoration, usually edible, such as parsley or lemon, which is used to enhance the appearance of a savoury dish.

Glaze A glossy coating given to sweet and savoury dishes to improve their appearance and sometimes flavour. Ingredients for glazes include beaten egg, egg white, milk and syrup.

Gluten A protein constituent of grains, such as wheat and rye, which develops when the flour is mixed with water to give the dough elasticity.

Grate To shred hard food, such as cheese and carrots, with a grater or food processor attachment.

Griddle A flat, heavy, metal plate used on the hob for cooking scones or for searing savoury ingredients.

Grind To reduce foods such as coffee beans, nuts and whole spices to small particles using a food mill, pestle and mortar, electric grinder or food processor.

Gut To clean out the entrails from fish.

Hang To suspend meat or game in a cool, dry place for a number of days to tenderise the flesh and develop flavour.

Hull To remove the stalk and calyx from soft fruits, such as strawberries.

Infuse To immerse flavourings, such as aromatic vegetables, herbs, spices and vanilla, in a liquid to impart flavour. Usually the infused liquid is brought to the boil, then left to stand for a while.

Julienne Fine 'matchstick' strips of vegetables or citrus zest, sometimes used as a garnish.

Knead To work dough by pummelling with the heel of the hand.

Knock back To knead a yeast dough for a second time after rising, to ensure an even texture.

Lard To insert small strips of fat or streaky bacon into the flesh of game birds and dry meat before cooking. A special larding needle is used.

Liaison A thickening or binding agent based on a combination of ingredients, such as flour and water, or oil and egg.

Macerate To soften and flavour raw or dried foods by soaking in a liquid, eg soaking fruit in alcohol.

Mandolin A flat wooden or metal frame with adjustable cutting blades for slicing vegetables.

Marinate To soak raw meat, poultry or game – usually in a mixture of oil, wine, vinegar and flavourings – to soften and impart flavour. The mixture, which is known as a marinade, may also be used to baste the food during cooking.

Medallion Small round piece of meat, usually beef or veal.

Mince To cut food into very fine pieces, using a mincer, food processor or knife.

Mocha Term which has come to mean a blend of chocolate and coffee.

Parboil To boil a vegetable or other food for part of its cooking time before finishing it by another method.

Pare To finely peel the skin or zest from vegetables or fruit.

Pâte The French word for pastry, familiar in pâte sucrée, a sweet flan pastry.

Pâté A savoury mixture of finely chopped or minced meat, fish and/or vegetables, usually served as a starter with bread or toast.

Patty tin Tray of cup-shaped moulds for cooking small cakes and deep tartlets. Also called a bun tin.

Pectin A naturally occurring substance found in most varieties of fruit and some vegetables, which is necessary for setting jams and jellies. Commercial pectin and sugar with pectin are also available for preserve-making.

Pickle To preserve meat or vegetables in brine or vinegar.

Pith The bitter white skin under the thin zest of citrus fruit.

Pluck To remove the feathers from poultry and game birds.

Poach To cook food gently in liquid at simmering point; the surface should be just trembling.

Pot roast To cook meat in a covered pan with some fat and a little liquid.

Prove To leave bread dough to rise (usually for a second time) after shaping.

Purée To pound, sieve or liquidise vegetables, fish or fruit to a smooth pulp. Purées often form the basis for soups and sauces.

Reduce To fast-boil stock or other liquid in an uncovered pan to evaporate water and concentrate the flavour.

Refresh To cool hot vegetables very quickly by plunging into ice-cold water or holding under cold running water in order to stop the cooking process and preserve the colour.

Render To melt fat slowly to a liquid, either by heating meat trimmings, or to release the fat from fatty meat, such as duck or goose, during roasting.

Glossary

Rennet An animal-derived enzyme used to coagulate milk in cheese-making. A vegetarian alternative is available.

Roast To cook meat by dry heat in the oven.

Roulade Soufflé or sponge mixture rolled around a savoury or sweet filling.

Roux A mixture of equal quantities of butter (or other fat) and flour cooked together to form the basis of many sauces.

Rub-in Method of incorporating fat into flour by rubbing between the fingertips, used when a short texture is required. Used for pastry, cakes, scones and biscuits.

Salsa Piquant sauce made from chopped fresh vegetables and sometimes fruit.

Sauté To cook food in a small quantity of fat over a high heat, shaking the pan constantly – usually in a sauté pan (a frying pan with straight sides and a wide base).

Scald To pour boiling water over food to clean it, or loosen skin, eg tomatoes. Also used to describe heating milk to just below boiling point.

Score To cut parallel lines in the surface of food, such as fish (or the fat layer on meat), to improve its appearance or help it cook more quickly.

Sear To brown meat quickly in a little hot fat before grilling or roasting.

Seasoned flour Flour mixed with a little salt and pepper, used for dusting meat, fish etc., before frying.

Shred To grate cheese or slice vegetables into very fine pieces or strips.

Sieve To press food through a perforated sieve to obtain a smooth texture.

Sift To shake dry ingredients through a sieve to remove lumps.

Simmer To keep a liquid just below boiling point.

Skim To remove froth, scum or fat from the surface of stock, gravy, stews, jam etc. Use either a skimmer, a spoon or kitchen paper.

Smoke To cure meat, poultry and fish by exposure to wood smoke.

Souse To pickle food, especially fish, in vinegar flavoured with spices.

Steam To cook food in steam, usually in a steamer over rapidly boiling water.

Steep To immerse food in warm or cold liquid to soften it, and sometimes to draw out strong flavours.

Sterilise To destroy bacteria in foods by heating.

Stew To cook food, such as tougher cuts of meat, in flavoured liquid which is kept at simmering point.

Stir-fry To cook small even-sized pieces of food rapidly in a little fat, tossing constantly over a high heat, usually in a wok.

Suet Hard fat of animal origin used in pastry and steamed puddings. A vegetarian alternative is readily available.

Sugar syrup A concentrated solution of sugar in water used to poach fruit and make sorbets, granitas, fruit juices etc.

Sweat To cook chopped or sliced vegetables in a little fat without liquid in a covered pan over a low heat to soften.

Tepid The term used to describe temperature at approximately blood heat, ie 37°C (98.7°F).

Thermometer, Sugar/Fat Used for accurately checking the temperature of boiling sugar syrups, and fat for deep-frying respectively. Dual purpose thermometers are obtainable.

Truss To tie or skewer poultry or game into shape prior to roasting.

Unleavened Flat bread, such as pitta, made without a raising agent.

Vanilla sugar Sugar in which a vanilla pod has been stored to impart its flavour.

Whipping (whisking) Beating air rapidly into a mixture either with a manual or electric whisk. Whipping usually refers to cream.

Zest The thin coloured outer layer of citrus fruit, which can be removed in fine strips with a zester.

Index

Index

19

Index

559

19

Index

Index

Index

19

Index

576